Santa Fe Recipe

A Cookbook of Recipes from Favorite Local Restaurants

by
Joan Stromquist and Carl Stromquist

 Tierra Publications

Tierra Publications
2801 Rodeo Road
Suite B-612
Santa Fe, New Mexico 87505
(505) 983-6300

Additional copies may be obtained by contacting Tierra Publications. For your convenience, order forms are included in the back of the book.

Cover design by James Finnell
Chama Graphics
Santa Fe, New Mexico

Photographs by Mark Nohl
Santa Fe, New Mexico

First Printing: July 1989
Second Printing: December 1989
Third Printing: April 1991

Library of Congress Catalog Card Number:
89-51056

ISBN: 0-9622807-0-4

Printed in the United States of America

Acknowledgements

This cookbook is dedicated to the chefs and restaurant owners of Santa Fe who so generously took time from their busy schedules to provide us with these recipes. Needless to say, without their cooperation, this book would not have been possible.

We also give our warm thanks to Mark Nohl for his contribution of the wonderful photographs of New Mexico, along with his creative input.

To James Finnell we offer our appreciation for his creation of the book's striking cover. He successfully captured the feeling of Santa Fe's magical charm.

For their help in editing and proof reading, we thank Bob Godwin and Sonya Moore. Also, we are grateful to Suzanne Vilmain for her initial design suggestions.

Joan Stromquist
Carl Stromquist
Santa Fe, New Mexico

Photography

The photographs used in this book are the work of award winning Mark Nohl, a native of Santa Fe. Mark has been with the New Mexico Tourism and Travel Division as staff photographer since 1973, promoting the state through his beautiful photographs of its scenic wonders. Over this time he has compiled a film library of thousands of color slides.

Readers of *New Mexico Magazine* are familiar with Mark's work, as he is one of its most frequent contributors. He displays his photographs in galleries and art shows across the nation. His work also has appeared in numerous magazines, both in the United States and Europe.

Cover Art

The talented James Finnell of Chama Graphics is both a free-lance illustrator and a fine artist. With 25 years of experience, he has worked on many national accounts, such as Continental Airlines, Nissan, Parker Brothers, and Mattel.

Jim's favorite subject matter for painting is locomotives, and he is well-known among the nation's train buffs. Recently his interest in portraying mechanical subjects has expanded to include exotic cars, and his reputation is growing in this area as well.

Special Note

For those of you who do not have access to many of the Southwestern ingredients mentioned in these recipes, we have arranged with the Chile Shop in Santa Fe to supply these items through their mail order service. Please see page 300 for their address.

Table of Contents

vi

Food Categories

Soups

Salads

Salad Dressings

Santa Fe Recipe

Downtown Street Sign, Santa Fe, New Mexico

The Bishop's Lodge

Known as an oasis of Southwestern hospitality, The Bishop's Lodge is a full service resort ranch located in the beautiful Sangre de Cristo mountains. The luxurious dining is only one of its many alluring amenities!

Recipes

Cold Watermelon Soup

Southwestern Carpaccio of Beef

Pecan Watercress Salad with Pears and Bleu Cheese

Scallops and Asparagus á la Toledo

Vaquero Beef Roast

Codfish Andalouse

Artichoke and Spinach Casserole

Santa Cruz Rancher Potatoes

Piña Colada Mousse

Executive Chef Richard Pointer was born in Austria, and received his extensive experience in various European countries. *"This cold soup is a very regional European recipe, popular from southern Germany to northern Italy. People eat it in the afternoon, between lunch and dinner, to tide them over."*

Cold Watermelon Soup

3	pounds watermelon meat, seeded
2	tablespoons sugar
4	ounces mineral water
8	ounces sweet white wine *(riesling or liebfraumilch)*
½	teaspoon lemon juice
1	cantaloupe, peeled and finely diced
1	slice honeydew melon, peeled and finely diced

Place the watermelon in a food processor or blender. Blend it on low speed for 3 minutes, or until the melon has reached a puréed consistency, but is not foamy.

Pour the melon in a medium mixing bowl. Add the sugar, mineral water, and wine. Blend them together.

Add the lemon juice and stir it in.

Cover and store the mixture in the refrigerator until it is cold.

Serve in a soup bowl.

Garnish with the diced cantaloupe and honeydew.

serves 4

Southwestern Carpaccio of Beef

8 ounces beef tenderloin fillet, fat and skin removed, sliced paper thin
1½ teaspoons red chile powder
1½ tablespoons hot water
½ jalapeño pepper, seeded and finely diced
3 tablespoons mayonnaise
1 tablespoon Parmesan cheese, grated
1 teaspoon cilantro, finely chopped
2 pieces white bread, toasted, crust removed, and cut into triangles

Place the slices of beef on a sheet of butcher paper. Place another sheet of paper over the top. Slightly press the flat together.

Place the flat in the freezer and let it sit for 15 minutes.

In a small bowl place the chile powder and the hot water. Let it sit for 5 minutes, or until the chile powder is dissolved.

Add the jalapeño and mayonnaise. Mix everything together.

Spread the sauce on the bottom of a cold plate.

Neatly arrange the beef slices in an overlapping pattern around the plate. The sauce should be at both the center and the edge of the plate.

Carefully sprinkle the Parmesan, cilantro, and capers over the top.

Serve with the toast.

serves 4

"The Southwestern Carpaccio of Beef is a take-off of steak tartare, a very popular dish on the east coast. We have added the jalapeño and chile to give the mayonnaise a Southwestern flavor."

"Your butcher should have a professional slicing machine, and he can cut the beef into paper thin slices for you. If the meat is frozen then it is much easier to slice."

"This dish can be served as an appetizer. Or, if you increase the portions of beef per person, it makes a delightful entrée."

Pecan Watercress Salad with Pears and Bleu Cheese

2	bunches watercress, washed, dried, and stems removed
2	ripe Bosc pears, cored and julienned
½	cup bleu cheese, crumbled
⅛	cup pecan nuts, chopped
¼	cup balsamic vinegar
⅔	cup good olive oil
1	dash white pepper
1	teaspoon sugar
⅓	teaspoon salt

Arrange the watercress in a circle in the center of a large plate.

Fan out the julienned pears around the edges.

Sprinkle the salad with the bleu cheese and pecans.

In a small bowl place the vinegar, olive oil, white pepper, sugar, and salt. Whisk everything together until the dressing is well blended.

Dribble the dressing over the salad.

serves 4

"This salad is a favorite with our customers. The idea came from someone who had hired us to do a large banquet. Many times people will give us their own recipes, and request that we prepare them for large dinner parties they are hosting. We get a lot of interesting ideas that way! This recipe in particular has proved to be very popular."

"The pears are those small brown ones that are very sweet, sometimes called salad pears."

"The vinaigrette has basic proportions that should be just right for the average person. But if it's too sweet or sour, it can be adjusted to the individual taste."

"The dressing should not be mixed so vigorously that it becomes foamy. Just mix it well, but keep it clear."

Scallops and Asparagus á la Toledo

1	pound medium scallops
	flour (as needed)
2	tablespoons butter
½	cup dry Spanish sherry
½	teaspoon saffron
1	cup heavy cream
½	lemon, squeezed
⅓	teaspoon salt
1	bunch pencil asparagus (18 to 24), washed, with tough stems cut off
½	teaspoon salt
1	teaspoon butter

Dip the scallops in the flour and lightly coat them.

In a medium saucepan place the butter and melt it on medium. Add the scallops and sauté them for 2 to 3 minutes, or until they are ⅔ done (white on the outside but dark in the middle). Remove the scallops from the saucepan. Place them on paper towels to drain off the butter.

Add the sherry to the sauce pan. Deglaze the pan by cooking over medium heat until the bottom residue dissolves.

Add the saffron and reduce the mixture by 20%. Add the cream and reduce the mixture by 40%.

Add the scallops and cook them for 2 minutes, or until they are done. Remove the saucepan from the heat. Remove the scallops with a slotted spoon and place them in a medium bowl.

Add the lemon juice and the ⅓ teaspoon of salt to the sauce. Strain the sauce through a sieve and return it to the saucepan. Return the scallops to the sauce. Keep the mixture warm over low heat.

In another medium saucepan add the asparagus, the ½ teaspoon salt, and the butter. Cover the asparagus with water, and boil them with a lid on until they are tender. Remove the cooked asparagus and drain off the water.

On a large platter arrange the asparagus in a sun ray pattern, leaving a circle in the center. Neatly arrange the scallops in the center circle. Cover with the sauce.

serves 4

"This is a traditional continental dish that I brought with me over from Europe. We used to make it in French restaurants, and it was always a very popular entrée."

"Take care to cook the ingredients correctly. The scallops should not be underdone, nor overdone. The sauce should be nicely reduced. And the asparagus should be crisp in the middle – not overcooked."

"When I worked in Monte Carlo I was fortunate enough to prepare a gala banquet for the Prince and Princess of Monaco. It was a big celebration of the fiftieth anniversary of the existence of the principality. I remember Princess Grace as being very beautiful, and very well decorated!"

Vaquero Beef Roast

2	ounces bacon, cut in ¼" squares
1	carrot, peeled and diced
1	parsnip, peeled and diced
1	yellow onion, diced
3	pounds beef chuck roast with skin, fat, and bones removed
3	tablespoons flour
3	tablespoons tomato paste
1½	tablespoons tequila
1	quart beef bouillon
2	cups Spanish red wine
1	tablespoon peppercorns
3	bay leaves
⅓	teaspoon margarita salt
1	green bell pepper, seeded and cut into rings
1	red bell pepper, seeded and cut into rings

"This is an adaptation of the old Yankee pot roast, with the addition of some Southwestern flavors."

In a large, heavy saucepan sauté the bacon squares on medium heat for 2 minutes.

Add the carrot, parsnip, and onion. Sauté them for 2 minutes.

Remove the bacon and vegetables, and place them in a small bowl. Leave the heated bacon grease in the saucepan.

Dip the roast into the flour so that it is completely coated.

Brown the roast on all sides in the bacon grease. Leave the roast in the saucepan.

Return the vegetables and bacon to the saucepan.

Add the tomato paste, tequila, beef bouillon, wine, peppercorns, bay leaves, and salt.

Bring the sauce to a rolling boil *(skim off any foam that appears)*. Cover, and simmer the meat on medium low heat for 1¾ hours, or until it is tender.

When the roast is done, slice the meat. Place the slices on a platter and pour the sauce over them. Garnish with the green and red bell pepper rings.

serves 4

"The key to the success of this recipe is to cook the beef until it is really tender. You should be able to pull the meat apart with two forks. If this doesn't happen, then you must cook it longer. Otherwise the sauce won't be properly absorbed."

Codfish Andalouse

2	cups water
1	cup white Chardonnay wine
½	teaspoon salt
⅓	teaspoon white pepper
1	shallot, diced
2	sprigs parsley
2½	pounds fresh cod fillets, cut into 4 pieces
3	tablespoons butter, softened
1	tablespoon butter
1	red bell pepper, julienned
1	yellow onion, sliced, with rings separated
1	tomato, julienned
2	mushrooms, thinly sliced
2	tablespoons bread crumbs

In a large, heavy saucepan place the water, wine, salt, white pepper, shallots, and parsley. Cook everything over medium heat for 3 minutes.

Add the cod. Partially cover the saucepan with a lid, leaving ⅓ open. Cook the cod on medium heat for 10 minutes, or until it is done (it should be bright white throughout).

Remove the fish from the broth and place it on a buttered baking sheet. Keep the fish warm on the lowest heat in the oven.

Reduce the broth by 20%. Strain the broth through a fine sieve and return it to the saucepan.

Remove the broth from the heat. Mix in the 3 tablespoons of soft butter. Cover and keep warm.

In a large, heavy skillet melt the 1 tablespoon of butter. Add the red pepper, onion, tomato, and mushrooms. Sauté them for 2 minutes.

Preheat the oven to 375°. Spread the vegetables over the cod on the baking sheet. Sprinkle the bread crumbs on top. Bake the cod and vegetables in the center of the oven for 8 minutes.

Place the fish and vegetables on a serving plate. Pour the sauce over the top.

serves 4

"Fresh cod needs a little bit of work. It doesn't really have a lot of taste, so it's a good idea to prepare a flavorful butter, or a good, concentrated sauce to go with it. Once you do that, it's really a wonderful fish! It's also up and coming in popularity, especially because it's so reasonably priced."

"I brought this recipe with me from my time in Atlanta, Georgia. It's a nice substitution for a whole artichoke, which can be somewhat time consuming and messy to eat. It makes a very good and healthy side dish, and was always popular in the South."

"Our food is basically American cooking, with a good touch of the Southwest, and maybe about forty percent Continental. A good combination!"

Artichoke and Spinach Casserole

2	tablespoons olive oil
2	cloves garlic
1	12-ounce can of artichoke hearts, drained and chopped
8	cups fresh spinach, washed, stems removed, and chopped
1	dash white pepper
1	dash nutmeg
2	ounces Gruyère cheese, finely grated
3	tablespoons mayonnaise
2	eggs

Place the oil in a large saucepan and heat on medium until it is hot.

Add the garlic and sauté it for 1 minute.

Add the artichoke hearts and sauté them for 1 minute.

Add the spinach and sauté it for 1 minute.

Remove the pan from the heat. Add the white pepper, nutmeg, and Gruyère cheese. Stir everything together.

In a small bowl place the mayonnaise and the eggs. Whip them together and then fold them into the lukewarm spinach mixture.

Preheat the oven to 375°.

Pour the mixture into a buttered casserole dish and bake on the middle shelf for 25 minutes, or until it is done.

serves 4

Santa Cruz Rancher Potatoes

3   **medium baking potatoes, washed**
⅓   **teaspoon margarita salt**
4   **strips bacon, diced**
1   **red bell pepper, julienned**
½   **teaspoon whole comino seeds** *(or ½ teaspoon cumin)*
¼   **cup Monterey Jack cheese, grated**
2   **scallions, thinly sliced**

In a small saucepan place the potatoes and salt and boil them until they are just done.

Cut the potatoes into cubes *(approximately 16 cubes per potato)*.

In a large saucepan place the bacon and sauté it on medium heat.

Add the bell pepper, comino seeds, and boiled potato cubes. Sauté until the potatoes are golden brown.

Preheat the oven to 375°.

Place the potatoes in a small baking dish. Sprinkle the cheese over the top.

Heat the potatoes in the oven for 3 minutes, or until the cheese is melted.

Sprinkle the scallions over the top.

serves 4

"This is a side dish that we serve at our mountain top cook-outs, along with steaks and a salad bar. Guests ride their horses to this outdoor cooking site, about a mile from the lodge. We have outdoor tables and grills..... it's good food, and good fun!"

"The main thing with this recipe is to thoroughly cook the potatoes. Don't anticipate that they will continue to cook after you remove them from the high heat. Potatoes only cook at a very high temperature, and once it is lowered, they stop cooking. So, be careful, or you may end up with hard potatoes!"

Piña Colada Mousse

1	**pound vanilla ice cream**
2	**egg yolks**
1½	**ounces rum**
3	**tablespoons piña colada mix** *(don't shake!)*
4	**maraschino cherries**
4	**pineapple rings**

In a medium bowl place the ice cream and let it sit at room temperature until it is soft.

Beat the softened ice cream until it has reached a creamy consistency.

Add the egg yolks. Beat at a high speed for 3 minutes.

Add the rum and the thick part of the piña colada mix. Beat them for 30 seconds.

Pour the mixture into attractive glasses. Place them in the refrigerator for 20 minutes, or until they are chilled.

Garnish each with a maraschino cherry in the middle of a pineapple ring.

serves 4

"The Piña Colada Mousse is a very common item in our banquet dessert selection. It's a nice, cool, summer dish.....very light, and easy to digest. Plus, it's easy to make, and people love it."

"Our restaurant services families that come to stay at the lodge for up to two weeks. We have a cuisine that appeals to both adults and children, and we aren't really interested in keeping up with the most innovative or modern trends. Rather, we try to offer a very solid and tasty food line that most people will like."

Mission Church, Laguna Pueblo, New Mexico

Celebrations

Celebrations! It's the perfect answer if you are in the mood for good times, good cooking, and good company. This jewel of a restaurant serves delicious, generous portions of food with a friendly southern hospitality.....so that every customer leaves feeling warm and satisfied.

Recipes

Louisiana Boiled Shrimp
Party Marinade

Celebrations Gumbo

Fettucini with
Asparagus and Scallops

Spicy Louisiana Ribs
Savory Barbecue Sauce

Curry Chicken
in Baked Acorn Squash

Picadillo

Spicy Sautéed Shrimp
Cheese Grits

Sweetheart Fudge Pie
Strawberry-Apple Pie

Southern bred owner, Sylvia Johnson, claims, *"This is one of the most outstanding appetizers you will ever serve. You can't beat this recipe..... it's just delicious."*

Louisiana Boiled Shrimp in Party Marinade

Louisiana Boiled Shrimp

4	cups water
3	bay leaves
4	cloves garlic
3	onions, peeled
3	celery stalks, crushed
1	lemon, juiced
1	teaspoon salt
2½	pounds small shrimp
4	onions, sliced
1	box bay leaves
	Party Marinade *(recipe on next page)*

In a large, heavy pot place the water, the 3 bay leaves, garlic, onions, celery stalks, lemon juice, and salt. Bring to a boil and then simmer for 20 minutes.

Add the shrimp and simmer them for 10 to 12 minutes, or until they are cooked.

Remove the shrimp and let them cool. Peel and devein the shrimp.

In a large bowl make alternating layers of the shrimp, sliced onions, and the box of bay leaves.

Cover the shrimp layers with the Party Marinade.

Cover the bowl and refrigerate for at least 24 hours.

serves 10-12

Party Marinade

1¼	cups salad oil
¾	cup vinegar, warmed
1½	teaspoons salt
1½	teaspoons celery seed
2½	tablespoons capers and juice
1	dash tabasco
¼	cup Worcestershire sauce
1	tablespoon yellow mustard

In a medium bowl place all of the ingredients and whisk them together.

"I got this recipe from friends in southern Louisiana. Baton Rouge is a real party town.....and this is real party food!"

"The shrimp is just permeated with the taste of the bay leaves, onion, and garlic. And you can eat the onions after you are done with the marinade."

"Try to use Gulf Shrimp because they are very firm. I like to use a small to medium size shrimp..... they are tastier, and anything much bigger is a struggle to deal with when it's on a cocktail pick!"

Celebrations Gumbo

5	pounds onions, chopped
2½	pounds bell pepper, seeded, washed, and chopped
4	stalks celery, chopped
4	cups fresh okra, chopped
4	cups crushed tomatoes
6	pounds cooked chicken, shredded
3	pounds Polish sausage, chopped, sautéed, and drained
2	pounds white fish fillets
5	pounds small shrimp, peeled
4	tablespoons garlic powder
2	tablespoons dried oregano
2	tablespoons dried basil
4	tablespoons dry mustard
2	tablespoons chicken base
2	tablespoons clam base
2	pounds lard
4	cups flour
8	cups cooked white rice
½	cup fresh parsley, minced

In a heavy, 10 quart pot place the onions, peppers, celery, okra, and tomatoes.

Cover the vegetables with water and simmer them for 2 hours.

Add the rest of the ingredients, except for the lard, flour, rice, and parsley. Simmer everything for 1 hour.

In a large, heavy skillet place the lard and melt it.

Add the flour and whisk it vigorously over low heat for 20 minutes, or until it is a dark brown in color.

Very carefully and slowly add the roux to the hot fish broth (it will smoke and bubble furiously). Stir, until it calms down.

Place the gumbo in individual serving bowls. Put a large dollop of rice in the center. Sprinkle with the parsley.

serves 10-12

"This gumbo recipe has taken me years to perfect. A south Louisiana offshore oil man helped me to develop it, and it is so authentic that it's incredible. I have never had anyone taste this gumbo who didn't say it's the best they've ever had!"

"It's a very dangerous process when you pour the hot roux into the hot liquid.....it bubbles and it can just erupt all over the stove! So, be very, very careful, and STIR!"

"A strong arm is required to make this recipe.....you can't be frail. I used to whisk the roux for 55 minutes, and that really was a chore."

Fettucini with Asparagus and Scallops

36	5" long asparagus spears
6	tablespoons butter
8	cloves garlic, finely minced
1½	pounds scallops
3	cups heavy cream
2	pounds egg fettucini, cooked al dente
⅓	cup fresh basil, finely chopped
¼	cup fresh parsley, finely chopped
	salt *(to taste)*
	pepper *(to taste)*
1	cup Parmesan cheese, freshly grated

In a medium saucepan cook the asparagus spears until they are just tender. Rinse them in cold water and drain them thoroughly.

In a large, heavy skillet place the butter and melt it.

Add the garlic and sauté it for 2 minutes, or until it is soft.

Add the scallops and gently stir them for 3 to 4 minutes, or until they are done.

Add the cream, fettucini, basil, parsley, salt, and pepper. Stir everything together and simmer for 3 minutes.

Add the Parmesan cheese and stir it in.

Place the fettucini on individual serving plates. Garnish with 6 asparagus spears and serve immediately.

serves 6

"The great way to hold this recipe until you are ready to serve it is to cook the pasta, drain it, and then immediately put it in ice water. Then you drain it again, add a good grade of virgin olive oil, and mix it into the cold pasta. When you are ready to serve the dish, lower it into simmering water to reheat it, drain it, and then pour your sauce on."

"I like to make this recipe when asparagus is in season. Make sure that you use a very good, dried, imported fettucini."

Spicy Louisiana Ribs
with Savory Barbecue Sauce

Spicy Louisiana Ribs

2	gallons water
2	teaspoons salt
2	teaspoons pepper
½	cup cayenne pepper
½	cup tabasco
5	onions, chopped
8	pounds beef ribs
	Savory Barbecue Sauce *(recipe follows)*

In a large, heavy saucepan place the water, salt, pepper, cayenne pepper, tabasco, and onions. Bring the ingredients to a boil and reduce to a simmer.

Add the ribs and simmer them for 10 to 15 minutes, or until they are done. Turn off the heat and let the ribs stay in the water for 10 minutes more.

Preheat the oven to 350°. Coat the ribs thoroughly with the Savory Barbecue Sauce and place them in a baking pan. Bake the ribs for 30 to 40 minutes, or until they get crispy. The ribs may also be charbroiled.

serves 4

Savory Barbecue Sauce

1	cup prepared chile sauce
½	cup prepared steak sauce
1	tablespoon dry mustard
4	tablespoons horseradish
2	tablespoons molasses
2	tablespoons red wine vinegar
2	tablespoons jalapeño pepper, minced
2	tablespoons garlic juice
2	tablespoons tamarind paste, dissolved in hot water
2	tablespoons tabasco *(or to taste)*
3½	cups catsup

In a medium bowl whisk everything together. Refrigerate up to one week. Bring to room temperature before serving.

"The par-boiling of the meat is the secret of barbecuing. Actually, it's a very closely guarded secret, and I probably shouldn't be giving it out! But the meat comes out so much more tender this way, and the seasoning is nice and strong."

"If you are barbecuing the ribs you can tell if the coals are hot enough by holding your hands four inches over them. If your hands burn, then the coals are ready to cook the ribs. I like the fire to char the ribs, and I serve this dish strictly with a potato salad and a Caesar salad."

"You know, I was told one time that if I ever gave out any recipes like this, that I should always withhold at least one ingredient. That way no one could ever fix it exactly like mine. But don't you worry, I haven't done that!"

Curry Chicken in Baked Acorn Squash

4	large acorn squash, cut in half lengthwise, and hollowed
2	sticks butter
2	medium onions, chopped
8	cloves garlic, minced
2	stalks celery, diced
4	tablespoons flour
4	cups milk
3	tablespoons curry powder
½	teaspoon nutmeg
1	cup carrots, finely grated
1½	cups currants
4	cups chicken breasts, cooked and shredded
½	cup fresh cilantro, finely chopped
	salt *(to taste)*
	pepper *(to taste)*
4	tablespoons dark brown sugar

Cut off the ends of the squash so that they will sit upright on a plate. In a baking pan place the squash halves, faces down. Pour ½" of water into the pan.

Preheat the oven to 375°. Bake the squash for 45 minutes to 1 hour, or until they are tender. Remove the squash from the oven and let them cool to room temperature.

In a medium saucepan melt 1¼ sticks of the butter. Add the onions, garlic, and celery. Sauté them for 3 to 4 minutes. Whisk in the flour and cook for 1 minute. Add the milk, curry powder, and nutmeg, while whisking constantly. Cook until the mixture begins to thicken.

Add the carrots, currants, and chicken. Simmer for 15 to 20 minutes. Stir frequently. Add the cilantro, salt and pepper.

In a small saucepan melt the remaining ¾ stick of butter. Mix in the brown sugar.

In a baking pan place the squash halves, face side up. Drizzle the brown sugar mixture over the faces. Preheat the oven to 350°. Place the squash in the oven and reheat them.

Place one squash half on each plate. Fill in the center with the curried chicken mixture.

serves 8

"If you are a curry fan then you will love this dish. You can use either currants or raisins. I don't see that much difference, so if you are on a budget, raisins are definitely the way to go."

"To me, this is a recipe I would use in the fall of the year, because of the acorn squash. I'm seasonally oriented because of my background. In the south, our cuisine revolves around what is fresh in the garden."

"In Louisiana we had a huge vegetable garden with a tractor and everything. Everyone grows their own vegetables there because the growing season is nine months out of the year. To be able to serve a huge, snow white cauliflower, or to go outside and pick the okra right off the trees, or to have luscious, red tomatoes.....why would you buy a nasty tomato in the wintertime from the store?"

Picadillo

⅓	cup olive oil
10	cloves garlic, minced
3	large yellow onions, minced
3	green bell peppers, seeded, washed, and cut into ½" cubes
3	pounds ground beef
3	cups tomato sauce
⅓	cup tomato paste
3	cups green chiles, diced
8	tablespoons cumin
2	cups pitted green olives, drained and sliced
1	bottle beer
8	cups cooked white rice

In a large, heavy saucepan place the olive oil and heat on medium until it is hot. Add the garlic, onions, and green peppers. Sauté them until they are soft.

Add the ground beef and cook it for 8 to 10 minutes, or until all of the pink color is gone. Strain out the grease.

Add the tomato sauce, tomato paste, green chiles, cumin, olives, and beer. Mix the ingredients together.

Simmer the stew for ½ hour, stirring frequently.

Serve over the white rice, in individual bowls.

serves 8

"This is a great recipe for red meat lovers, and it's just the tastiest thing! The green olives are so unusual and they give it a really different flavor. Also, it's very economical."

"I have found that a lot of stews, soups, and casseroles do really well with a bottle of beer used as part of the liquid."

"Our restaurant is very eclectic.....the food is Southwestern, northern New Mexican, and a lot of southern Louisiana."

"We definitely cater to the locals. Half the people who come here for breakfast or lunch will come for five days a week. They come to get their power food! The locals are the bread and butter of our business.....and they are my personal friends as well."

Spicy Sautéed Shrimp
with Cheese Grits

Spicy Sautéed Shrimp

2	tablespoons vegetable oil
6	slices bacon, diced
½	cup all purpose flour
1	pound medium shrimp, peeled and deveined
½	cup mushrooms, sliced
2	cloves garlic, crushed
3	scallions, cut into ½" diagonal slices
1	tablespoon fresh lemon juice
½	teaspoon hot red pepper sauce
½	teaspoon salt
½	teaspoon freshly ground black pepper
	Cheese Grits *(recipe on next page)*

In a large, heavy skillet place the vegetable oil and heat it over low heat. Add the bacon and sauté it for 4 to 5 minutes, or until it begins to get crisp. Remove the skillet from the heat.

In a large plastic bag place the flour. Add the shrimp, a few at a time, and shake them until they are well coated with the flour.

Place the skillet with the oil and the bacon back on the burner, and raise the heat to medium.

Add the shrimp, and sauté them for 2 minutes.

Add the mushrooms and garlic. Sauté them for 2 to 3 minutes, or until the shrimp are just pink and tender.

Add the scallions, lemon juice, hot red pepper sauce, salt, and pepper. Sauté for 1 minute.

Serve with the Cheese Grits.

serves 4

"This is a nice and spicy dish that I got from a close friend of mine in Louisiana. It's a very southern recipe, especially because of the grits."

"The cooking in southern Louisiana is very sophisticated, as far as I'm concerned, even though it is very rural and country. Southern cooking is a mixture of French, Spanish, American, and, of course, whatever one has to cook with that is fresh that day."

Cheese Grits

1	cup quick *(not instant)* **grits**
4	cups water
¾	cup cheddar cheese, grated
¼	cup Parmesan cheese, freshly grated
¼	cup butter
½	teaspoon salt
¼	cup hot red pepper sauce
⅛	teaspoon white pepper
1	dash cayenne pepper
¼	cup cheddar cheese, grated

In a medium saucepan place the grits and the water. Cook them according to the package directions, and remove from the heat.

Add the ¾ cup of cheddar cheese, the Parmesan cheese, butter, salt, hot red pepper sauce, white pepper, and cayenne pepper. Stir and blend the ingredients together well.

Sprinkle the ¼ cup of cheddar cheese over the top.

Serve immediately.

Serves 4

"Be sure to use the quick grits, not the instant grits. Quick grits are the hull of the rice."

"The bounty in Louisiana is incredible! You have all of the seafood you could ever want, and of course the growing season is for most of the year."

"What sets apart the cooking in southern Louisiana is probably the fact that the people are so interested in seasoning. They use tons of cayenne, black pepper, garlic, fresh oregano, thyme, cumin, and, of course, tabasco sauce, which is produced in Avery Island."

Sweetheart Fudge Pie

½ cup butter, softened
¾ cup brown sugar, firmly packed
3 eggs
12 ounces semisweet chocolate chips, melted in a double boiler
2 teaspoons instant coffee powder
1 teaspoon rum extract
½ cup all purpose flour
1 cup walnuts, coarsely chopped
1 9" unbaked pastry shell
1 cup whipping cream, whipped
Maraschino cherries, with stems

In a medium bowl place the butter, and cream it.

Gradually add, and beat in, the brown sugar. Beat at a medium speed until it is fluffy.

Add the eggs one at a time, while beating constantly.

Add the melted chocolate, coffee powder, and rum extract. Mix the ingredients together well.

Add the flour and walnuts and stir them in.

Place the pastry shell in a buttered pie tin. Pour the mixture into the pie shell.

Preheat the oven to 375°. Bake the pie for 25 minutes. Cool it on a wire rack, and then chill.

Before serving, artistically place the whipped cream on top of the pie. Garnish it with the maraschino cherries.

serves 6

"Chocoholics will love this pie.....everyone will love this pie! In a word, I would fast for three days to have just one slice, it's that rich and delicious!"

"There are no tricks to making this pie.....there is nothing exotic about it, just plain ol' chocolate chips."

Strawberry-Apple Pie

2	9" pie rounds
5	Granny Smith apples, peeled, cored, and sliced
2	pints fresh strawberries, stems removed, rinsed and cut into halves
5	tablespoons cornstarch
2	cups sugar
1	egg yolk
1	tablespoon cold water

Preheat the oven to 450°.

Line a buttered pie tin with one 9" pie round.

In a large bowl place the apples, strawberries, cornstarch, and sugar. Mix them together well.

Place the mixture in the pie tin.

Place the remaining 9" pie round on top. Crimp the edges together. Make a decorative pattern around the rim with a fork or your fingers.

Pierce the top crust into a decorative pattern with a small knife or fork *(to make steam vents)*.

In a small bowl place the egg yolk and cold water, and mix them together.

Using a pastry brush gently brush the egg and water mixture on top of the crust.

Place the pie on a cookie sheet, and then put it into the middle of the oven. Reduce the heat to 350°.

Bake for 1 to 1½ hours, or until the juices are bubbling. If the crust begins to get too brown, lay a piece of foil over the top.

serves 6

"This pie tastes like rhubarb, which is so hard to get, and it is so delicious! The flaky pie shell is so good with the wonderful tart flavor of the fruit. The color is beautiful, too."

"This recipe is the simplest thing in the world to make. You can buy the ready made pie crust from the refrigerator section in your grocery store."

"Our restaurant is just a precious little place. We try to have it pristine clean, with flowers everywhere. Everyone tells us that they feel a good, vibrant energy here. And, I definitely don't want anyone to leave the table hungry!"

Adobe Wall Detail in Spring, Santa Fe, New Mexico

Commes Chez Vous

Commes Chez Vous means *"as in your own home"* and, indeed, with its casual elegance and friendly service, you are made to feel pampered, yet right at home. This gourmet restaurant combines the pleasing feeling of Mediterranean airiness with an intimate French coziness.

Recipes

Herring with Apple and Cream Sauce

Marinated Chicken Breast Red Chile Vinaigrette Green Peppercorn Mustard

Sopa de Lima

Duck Salad Orange Vinaigrette

Sautéed Shrimp Chile Coconut Milk Sauce

Veau Sambre Meuse

Ganache Tart

Chef Ron Losey, the creative force behind this lively cuisine says, *"This recipe has been with the restaurant a long time because of its popularity. The apples give it a sweetness that goes well with the tartness of the lemon, and the chives lend it a nice bite. This sauce blends well with the herring. It's very good!"*

Herring with Apple and Cream Sauce

2	apples *(Granny Smith)*, peeled, cored, and finely diced
½	onion, minced
1½	cups heavy cream
1	tablespoon fresh chives, minced
1	tablespoon fresh lemon juice
1	pound herring, marinated in wine and strained
1	bunch bibb lettuce, washed, dried, and leaves separated
1	tomato, thinly sliced
18	black olives

In a medium bowl place the apples, onion, cream, chives, and lemon juice. Mix them together.

Add the herring and mix it in.

Cover, refrigerate, and marinate overnight.

On individual plates place several pieces of the lettuce leaves. Put the herring on top. Garnish with the tomato slices and the olives.

serves 6

Marinated Chicken Breast
with Red Chile Vinaigrette
and Green Peppercorn Mustard

Marinated Chicken Breast

3   **chicken breasts, boned and halved**
     Red Chile Vinaigrette *(recipe follows)*
½   **red bell pepper, seeded, washed, and julienned**
½   **green bell pepper, seeded, washed and julienned**
     Green Peppercorn Mustard *(recipe on next page)*

In a medium bowl place the chicken breasts. Cover them with the Red Chile Vinaigrette.

Cover the bowl tightly with a saran wrap and refrigerate overnight.

Preheat the oven to 350°. Place the chicken in a pan and bake it for 45 minutes, or until it is just done, but still juicy.

Cut each chicken breast into strips. Fan them out onto individual serving plates.

Place a different colored bell pepper strip in between each chicken strip. Pour a line of the Green Peppercorn Mustard across the middle of the chicken.

serves 6

"I love this recipe.....it's really a fun one, and it is my consummate party appetizer dish. If you have time, it's nice to cut the peppers into squares (onions, too), and skewer them with the chicken. I like the vegetables to be raw, so that they are really crunchy, but some people may prefer to lightly sauté them first."

Red Chile Vinaigrette

3   **tablespoons red chile powder** *(New Mexican)*
½   **teaspoon ground cloves**
½   **teaspoon ground cumin**
½   **teaspoon oregano**
½   **teaspoon salt**
¼   **teaspoon pepper**
1½   **cups red wine vinegar**
1   **cup olive oil**

In a food processor place all of the ingredients *(except for the olive oil)* and blend them together.

Slowly dribble in the oil while the food processor is running.

"For the chile powder you can use whatever degree of heat you want, depending on how hot you want the dish to be. Try to get a pure chile powder, one that has not been mixed with other ingredients. I look for a dark red color, which has a richer, smokier flavor."

"The fact that the chicken is marinated overnight gives it a nice, rich tang. The combination of red chile and mustard is really excellent. And the tomato taste is just a hint, but gives it a slight citrus, tart flavor."

"What I like to do is to get different cookbooks and experiment with a variety of cuisines from around the world. A lot of times I will take ingredients from a certain place, and then maybe prepare it with a French technique. It's fun to play around, and I like to have fun!"

Green Peppercorn Mustard

½	**bunch cilantro, chopped**
2	**tablespoons green peppercorns**
2	**scallions, chopped**
1	**cup tomato juice**
1½	**cups Dijon mustard**
	salt *(to taste)*
	pepper *(to taste)*

In a blender place the cilantro, green peppercorns, scallions, and a small amount of the tomato juice. Blend the ingredients together.

In a medium bowl place the blended mixture, the rest of the tomato juice, the mustard, salt, and pepper. Mix everything together well.

Cover the bowl and refrigerate overnight.

Sopa de Lima

1	large chicken
½	bunch cilantro, chopped
10	black peppercorns
2	cloves garlic, minced
6	quarts water
2	sticks butter
1	red bell pepper, minced
1	yellow bell pepper, minced
1	onion, minced
2	ears corn, husked, with the kernels cut off
½	zucchini, minced
¾	cup flour
3	limes
	salt *(to taste)*
	pepper *(to taste)*

In a large, heavy pot place the chicken, cilantro, peppercorns, garlic, and water. Simmer the chicken for 2 hours.

Remove the chicken from the pot and skin it. Remove the meat and chop it into small pieces.

Strain the stock through a sieve and reserve it.

In a large, heavy pot place the butter and melt it over medium heat.

Add the chopped chicken, bell peppers, onion, corn, and zucchini. Sauté them for 2 to 3 minutes.

Add the flour and stir constantly for 2 minutes.

Slowly add the reserved stock while stirring constantly, until a smooth consistency is achieved. If more liquid is needed add some water.

Cut 2 of the limes in half. Squeeze the juice into the soup and then add the limes.

Add the salt and pepper to taste.

Continue to simmer the soup until the vegetables are done and the flavors have blended. Remove the limes.

Thinly slice the remaining lime and serve one slice in each bowl of soup.

serves 6

"Sopa de Lima is a traditional Mexican soup. The only ingredients that are essential for it to be traditional are the chicken, cilantro, black peppercorns, garlic, limes, and wine. You can add tomatoes, potatoes, carrots, or any number of different things. I like the corn because it's a nice combination with the chiles, lime, and chicken. I also like to add some more minced garlic to the strained broth. But then, I'm a real garlic lover!"

"Don't leave the limes in the soup too long. Maybe you should remove them after half an hour. However, in Mexico the people will use a very bitter type of lime because they like the taste. But me, I like the tartness more than the bitter."

Duck Salad
with Orange Vinaigrette

Duck Salad

1	**duck**
5	**slices bacon, cooked, drained, and crumbled**
2	**tablespoons carrots, grated**
1	**cup pecans, chopped**
	Orange Vinaigrette (recipe follows)
2	**bunches spinach, washed, dried, with stems removed and torn**
1	**head butter lettuce, washed, dried, and torn**
½	**red onion, thinly sliced**

Preheat the oven to 400°. Place the duck in a roasting pan and bake it for 2 hours, or until it is just slightly pink, but still juicy.

Remove the duck from the oven and let it cool. Skin, bone, and chop the duck into bite size pieces.

In a medium bowl place the duck, bacon, carrots, and pecans. Mix everything together. Drizzle on the Orange Vinaigrette to taste, and toss the ingredients well.

In a medium bowl place the spinach and lettuce and toss them together. Arrange the salad on individual plates. Place the duck mixture on top. Garnish with the onion slices.

serves 6

Orange Vinaigrette

1	**cup dry sherry**
½	**cup balsamic vinegar**
1	**tablespoon Grand Marnier**
1	**orange, juiced**
2	**teaspoons thyme**
½	**teaspoon salt**
¼	**teaspoon pepper**
¾	**cup olive oil**

In a food processor place all of the ingredients except for the olive oil, and blend them together. Slowly dribble in the oil while the food processor is still running.

"One day I had some duck I needed to use up, so I devised this recipe. I thought to myself, 'Well, the classic thing to do with duck is a Duck á la Orange', which gave me the idea for the orange juice. Then I got the idea for the sherry. And, pecans and bacon struck me as a good idea.....so it just kind of evolved. And it came out great!"

"Check the duck after an hour and a half to see how it's doing. It should come out pink and juicy."

"I like to use the big pieces of the lettuce underneath, and tear the spinach on top of it. This makes a more attractive presentation."

"If you have time to do it, you can mix the sherry, Grand Marnier, and vinegar, and then let it sit for two or three days, so you are actually making your own sherry vinegar."

Sautéed Shrimp
with Chile Coconut Milk Sauce

Sautéed Shrimp

1   tablespoon olive oil
30   medium shrimp, shelled and deveined
       Chile Coconut Milk Sauce *(recipe follows)*
3   cups cooked white rice

In a large pot place the olive oil and heat it on medium until it is hot. Add the shrimp and sauté them for 2 to 3 minutes, or until they begin to turn pink.

Add the Chile Coconut Milk Sauce to the shrimp and cook until the sauce thickens slightly.

Serve the shrimp and sauce over the hot rice.

serves 6

Chile Coconut Milk Sauce

2   tablespoons vegetable oil
1   large onion, minced
3   Anaheim chiles, minced
½   teaspoon garlic, minced
3   anchovy fillets, minced
⅔   teaspoon lime zest *(the green part of the skin grated off)*
⅔   teaspoon fresh ginger, minced
½   teaspoon salt
¼   teaspoon pepper
1   teaspoon curry paste
1   teaspoon tamarind paste
1½   tablespoons brown sugar
3   cups coconut milk
2   cups fish stock or clam juice

(continued on next page)

"When I first made this dish our bartender said she had eaten the same thing when she was in Indonesia. It's a spicy recipe, which I like."

"We Americans tend to think that chiles are somewhat exotic, but actually they are very common all over the world, especially where there are hot climates. Eating a hot and spicy dish in a hot climate will actually help to cool you off by regulating your body temperature."

"When you are using spice powders or pastes, you should always cook them for a little while in hot oil. This will bring out the flavors. If you can't find the curry or tamarind paste, you can make your own by mixing the powder with a bland oil.....not olive oil!"

"I can read a recipe and immediately know if it will be something I'll like or not. I also can tell right off what I want to do with it."

In a medium saucepan place the oil and heat it until it is hot. Add the onion and chile, and sauté them until the onions are translucent.

Add the garlic, anchovy fillets, lime zest, and ginger. Toss them constantly for 1 minute.

Add the salt, pepper, curry paste, tamarind paste, and brown sugar. Stir everything for 1 minute.

Add the coconut milk and fish stock. Heat the sauce slowly to a simmer.

Veau Sambre Meuse

2	pounds veal loin or butt, cut into 18 slices, and pounded until thin
	salt *(as needed)*
	pepper *(as needed)*
½	cup flour, or as needed
1	tablespoon olive oil
12	large mushrooms, diced
1	teaspoon shallots, minced
12	sun-dried tomatoes, diced
1	tablespoon fresh tarragon, minced
½	cup dry vermouth
½	cup dry white wine
1	cup veal stock *(see page 71)*
1	cup heavy cream
1	tablespoon olive oil

Sprinkle the veal with the salt and pepper.

Dredge the veal in the flour, and shake off the excess. Set the veal aside.

In a large skillet place the 1 tablespoon of olive oil and heat it on medium until it is hot. Add the mushrooms and shallots. Sauté them for 2 to 3 minutes.

Add the tomatoes, tarragon, vermouth, wine, stock, and cream. Simmer the sauce until it is reduced by half.

In another large skillet place the other tablespoon of olive oil and heat it until it is hot. Quickly sear the veal slices on one side.

Turn the slices over and add the sauce. Cook for 2 minutes, or until the sauce thickens.

serves 6

"This is a classic French recipe that I've changed a little. I added the vermouth and substituted sun-dried tomatoes for regular tomatoes, which gives it a heartier flavor."

"Pound your veal fairly thin, but not to a paper-thin consistency. Otherwise it will dry out, and veal is very touchy that way. Sauté the one side very quickly, just so that it browns. Then turn it over and add the sauce. You can make the sauce as thick as you want, by further reducing."

Ganache Tart

2   cups pecans
¾   cup sugar
4   tablespoons butter, melted
16   ounces semisweet chocolate
2   cups cream
1   egg yolk

In a food processor place the pecans, sugar, and butter. Pulverize the mixture. Press the mixture into a 10" tart pan.

Preheat the oven to 375°. Bake the crust for 10 minutes, or until it is golden brown.

In a double boiler place the chocolate and melt it.

In another double boiler place the cream and heat it until it is scalding hot. Beat the egg yolk into the chocolate. Beat in the hot cream.

Pour the mixture into the shell.

Chill the tart for 2 hours in the refrigerator.

serves 6

"There's only one word to describe this dessert.....decadent!"

"You don't need to butter the pie pan because there's enough butter in the crust to melt through. The combination of the chocolate, pecans, and butter is very sensuous."

"I believe that eating should be an adventure..... it should be fun and exciting. When I go to a restaurant I always like to try something I haven't had before – something different. And I carry this philosophy over into my cooking, by constantly experimenting with different flavors. To me, the taste of the food is the most important thing. You might say I'm more taste oriented than visually oriented. Although, I believe that the food should look good, too."

Pecos National Monument, Pecos, New Mexico

e.k. mas

e.k. mas?.....The clever name of this delightful restaurant is a phonetic spelling of the Spanish idiom, *"¿Y, qué mas?"*. Or, to translate loosely, *"And, what more could you want?"* And, with these delicious dishes, what more could *anyone* want?

Recipes

Peanut Soup

*Shrimp Dim Sum
Oriental Dipping Sauce*

*Belgian Endive-Chevre Salad
Dijon Dressing*

*Roast Duckling
Savory Apple Chutney*

*Spanakopita
Tzatziki*

*Grilled Tuna
Curried Caper Sauce*

*Chocolate-Hazelnut
Mousse Cake*

Chef and part-owner, Robert Goodfriend, recalls, *"When I lived in Michigan, the* Detroit News *did an article on peanuts. They asked me to create a recipe that they could use in the write-up. After several nights of thinking about it, I came up with this one. The response has been great! It's a nice, rich soup, but without the cream."*

Peanut Soup

¼   cup butter
3   tablespoons flour
2   quarts chicken stock
2   cups smooth peanut butter *(no sugar)*
2   cloves garlic, crushed
¼   teaspoon cayenne pepper
      salt *(to taste)*
      pepper *(to taste)*
1   carrot, julienned
1   small red bell pepper, julienned
1   small yellow bell pepper, julienned

In a medium saucepan place the butter and heat it on medium until it is melted. Add the flour and stir it for 5 minutes, or until the roux is light brown in color.

Add the chicken stock and boil it for 2 minutes, stirring constantly. Reduce the heat to low.

Stir in the peanut butter with a wire whisk.

Add the garlic, cayenne pepper, salt, and pepper.

Lightly steam the red and yellow bell peppers.

Garnish the soup with the carrot, and the red and yellow peppers.

serves 6

Shrimp Dim Sum
with Oriental Dipping Sauce

Shrimp Dim Sum

8	ounces medium shrimp, peeled and deveined
1½	cups Napa cabbage, finely chopped
4	scallions, minced
½	teaspoon garlic, minced
½	teaspoon cornstarch
1	tablespoon soy sauce
1	tablespoon dry sherry
1	pinch five spice powder
1	teaspoon coarse red chile seeds *(or several dashes of cayenne pepper)*
12	egg roll wraps
	Oriental Dipping Sauce *(recipe on next page)*

Run the shrimp through a meat grinder, or coarsely chop them in a food processor. Place them in a medium bowl.

Add the remainder of the ingredients and mix them together thoroughly by hand.

Cut each egg roll wrap into a 3" circle *(you can use a cookie cutter)*.

Moisten the edges with water and place approximately 1 tablespoon of the filling into the centers.

Fold the egg rolls in half and crimp the edges shut.

Place the egg rolls in an oiled steamer with the crimped edges standing up. Steam them for 5 minutes, or until they are thoroughly heated.

Serve with the Oriental Dipping Sauce.

serves 6

"These dim sum are really great! You can serve them for appetizers or for an entire lunch. The recipe is such that you can plug in anything you want.....lobster, scallops, pork.....and they always will come out delicious. Another plus is that they are steamed, and not deep-fried."

"A lot of the recipes that we offer at e.k. mas are variations on things that my two partners and I personally miss from our favorite restaurants in Detroit."

Oriental Dipping Sauce

½   cup soy sauce
½   cup water
¼   cup dry sherry
1   teaspoon sugar
1   teaspoon rice wine vinegar
1   tablespoon minced scallion
½   teaspoon minced garlic

In a small bowl place all of the ingredients and mix them together well. Cover, and store in the refrigerator for 1 hour.

Belgian Endive-Chevre Salad
with Dijon Dressing

Belgian Endive-Chevre Salad

4	heads Belgian endive lettuce
	Dijon Dressing *(recipe on next page)*
½	cup poppy seeds
1	stick Montrachet cheese, cut into six ¾" slices
½	cup pine nuts, lightly toasted
1	red bell pepper, seeded, washed, and thinly sliced
1	leek, washed and cut into thin match sticks

Separate the leaves of the endive. Trim off the ends if they are tough. Thoroughly wash and dry the lettuce and place it in a large mixing bowl. Toss the endive with ½ of the Dijon Dressing.

Arrange the endive leaves in a star pattern on 6 salad plates.

Preheat the oven to 350°.

Roll the slices of cheese in the poppy seeds. Place them on an oiled baking sheet.

Bake the cheese slices for 3 minutes, or until they are soft.

Remove the cheese slices with a metal spatula and place them in the center of the endive leaves.

Sprinkle on the toasted pine nuts. Scatter on the red bell peppers and leeks.

Drizzle the remainder of the Dijon Dressing over the salad.

serves 6

"Don't let the cheese get too gooey in the oven or you'll never be able to get it off the baking sheet with a spatula. After you place the cheese in the middle of the endive, the internal heat allows it to ooze out onto the plate. It looks really beautiful! Then you have your juliennes for some color, and a slightly chaotic look."

"I like a little bit of chaos in every plate. It kind of reminds me of the restaurant business!"

Dijon Dressing

1	teaspoon Dijon mustard
¼	cup balsamic vinegar
1	cup good olive oil
½	teaspoon salt
1	pinch white pepper
¼	teaspoon finely minced garlic

Place the mustard in a small bowl.

While whisking continuously, add a tiny amount of vinegar, and then a tiny amount of olive oil, alternately, until the full amounts are blended.

Add the salt, pepper, and garlic. Whisk them together.

"Balsamic vinegar is a red wine vinegar aged in oak. It should not be difficult to find. Otherwise, any good red wine vinegar will do."

"I have a very personal and intimate viewpoint on man's relationship with food. You've got to respect the food. Be gentle and caring. Don't be brutal!"

Roast Duckling
with Savory Apple Chutney

Roast Duckling

3   **Long Island ducks, 5 pounds each**
     salt (as needed)
     pepper (as needed)
     basil (as needed)
     thyme (as needed)
     Savory Apple Chutney (recipe on next page)

Wash the ducks thoroughly and pat them dry.

Open the wings and cut them off at the second joint. Remove the fat surrounding the body cavity. Remove the giblet sack and neck.

Prick the ducks well with a fork or knife. Season them with the salt, pepper, basil, and thyme.

Place the wings and necks on a baking pan. Place the seasoned ducks on top of the wings and necks, breast side up.

Preheat the oven to 325°. Bake the ducks for 3 hours.

Remove the ducks from the oven and let them stand for 1 hour.

Cut each duck in half, down the middle. Bone the ducks by removing the rib bones, and any of the bones that you care to take out.

Preheat the oven to 375°.

Put the boned (or semi-boned) ducks back onto the baking pan. Bake them in the oven for 10 minutes and then remove them.

Place the ducks under a preheated broiler to make the skin crisp.

Serve with Savory Apple Chutney.

serves 6

"The duck should be crisp, succulent, and not overcooked. Making this duck is a great way to impress your guests. You can show them that you really know what you are doing in the kitchen!"

"This recipe might sound complicated, but it's really a very simple, American dish. It's incredibly good! In fact, we've had people from Beijing, China eat this duck and they say it's the best they've ever had."

"Be careful not to burn the skin. However, it can be slightly charred. That way you can be sure that all of the fat has burned away, and it's nice and crisp."

"I recommend serving the duck with yams, either baked or sautéed in butter."

Savory Apple Chutney

1   **tablespoon oil**
1½   **cups onion, thinly sliced**
¾   **cup crystallized ginger, julienned**
1   **cup raisins**
1   **cup brown sugar**
⅓   **cup red wine vinegar**
⅛   **cup Worcestershire sauce**
3   **tablespoons curry powder**
5   **green, tart apples, peeled, cored, and thinly sliced**

In a large skillet place the oil and heat it on medium until it is hot. Add the onions and sauté them for 2 to 3 minutes, or until they wilt.

Add the ginger and the raisins and sauté them for 2 minutes.

In a small mixing bowl place the brown sugar, vinegar, Worcestershire sauce, and curry. Mix them together.

Add the mixture to the sauté pan and boil it for 1 minute.

Add the apples and continue to boil, until the chutney thickens.

Cover tightly, refrigerate, and store for at least 24 hours to allow the flavors to marry.

Reheat before serving.

"People love this chutney. The flavors are robust, and it tastes much richer than it actually is. Try to let it sit for as long as possible.....maybe up to a week. By then, the flavors are incredible."

"If the crystallized ginger pieces are hardened, steam them for a few minutes and they will soften up."

Spanakopita with Tzatziki

Spanakopita

5	cups spinach, chopped and cooked
½	cup ricotta cheese, firmly packed
¾	cup feta cheese, firmly packed
½	teaspoon garlic, minced
½	teaspoon black pepper
1	egg, lightly beaten
¼	cup scallions, minced
⅓	cup fresh dill, finely chopped
¼	pound butter, melted
12	sheets fresh phyllo dough
	Tzatziki *(recipe on next page)*

In a large bowl place all of the ingredients *(except for the melted butter, phyllo dough, and Tzatziki)* and mix them together.

On a large cutting board place one of the rectangular slices of the phyllo dough. The long side should face you.

Dip a pastry brush into the melted butter. Sprinkle a few drops of the butter over the phyllo sheet and then spread them around with the brush. Work quickly!

Place a new sheet of phyllo dough directly on top of the buttered sheet. Butter the new sheet in the same manner. Repeat this process until 4 phyllo sheets are buttered and stacked on top of each other.

Cut the stacked, buttered, phyllo sheets exactly in half, across the width. Divide the spinach mixture into 6 equal portions. On one of the halves of the phyllo stacks place one portion of the spinach mixture. It should be in a 2" strip, 1" from the end closest to you, and 1½" from each side.

Fold the buttered sides over the mixture, lengthwise. Tamp the sides down, except where the spinach mixture is *(otherwise it will ooze out)*.

Carefully roll the phyllo forward, starting with the end containing the spinach mixture. Do not roll it too tightly. The finished roll should be approximately 2" wide by 4" long.

Repeat this process on the other half of the phyllo sheets. Two spanakopitas are now made.

(continued on next page)

"Please don't be intimidated by the seeming complexity of this recipe. It really is not that difficult, and is more than worth the effort. The second time around, it will be a snap!"

"It is difficult to verbally explain how to assemble the spanakopita rolls without having pictures to visually show you how. So, read the instructions over several times before you begin, just to be sure that you understand them."

"You must work very fast to prevent the phyllo dough from drying out. Some people like to cover the phyllo with a kitchen towel that has been saturated with water and then thoroughly wrung out."

"Be sure not to wrap the phyllo too tight. The filling expands in the oven, and it may pop the rolls open."

"When working with phyllo, you must have the light touch. I have found this experience to be a great lesson in humility!"

"This sauce is great as a dip. It is also excellent served with Greek olives, thinly sliced cheese, and a good, dark bread."

"If you don't want to take the trouble to hand chop the cucumber, you can put it in a food processor or blender. Use the on/off button for just a second at a time, making sure that the cucumber comes out with a coarse, rather than a puréed, texture."

Repeat the entire process twice more, using 4 phyllo sheets each time, so that a total of 6 spanakopita rolls are made.

Preheat the oven to 425°.

Lightly oil a baking sheet *(do not use butter)*.

Lightly butter the spanakopita rolls on the sides and tops, using the pastry brush and the remainder of the melted butter.

Place the buttered spanakopita rolls on the oiled baking tray. Bake for them 15 to 20 minutes, or until they are golden brown.

Serve with the Tzatziki.

serves 6

Tzatziki

2	**cups plain yogurt**
2	**cucumbers, peeled, seeded, and finely minced**
½	**teaspoon salt**
¼	**teaspoon garlic, minced**
1	**tablespoon mint, chopped**

Place the yogurt in a cheesecloth. Place it in a strainer for at least 2 hours, until the excess liquid drains out.

Place the strained yogurt in a medium mixing bowl.

Place the minced cucumbers in a strainer and mix in the salt.

Let the cucumbers sit for 20 minutes, or until the moisture drains out.

Add the strained cucumbers to the yogurt. Add the garlic and mint. Mix everything together.

Cover and refrigerate for several hours before serving.

42

Grilled Tuna
with Curried Caper Sauce

Grilled Tuna

6	**8-ounce tuna steaks**
	salt *(to taste)*
	pepper *(to taste)*
3	**cloves garlic, finely minced**
	Curried Caper Sauce *(recipe follows)*

Season both sides of the tuna with the salt, pepper, and garlic.

Grill the tuna until it is rare. The tuna should be cool and red in the center.

Serve with the Curried Caper Sauce.

serves 6

Curried Caper Sauce

6	**ounces white wine**
1½	**cups heavy whipping cream**
2	**tablespoons fresh lemon juice**
1	**teaspoon garlic, minced**
1	**teaspoon shallots, minced**
2	**tablespoons curry powder**
3	**tablespoons capers**
1½	**sticks butter**
	salt *(to taste)*
	white pepper *(to taste)*

In a medium saucepan place the wine, cream, lemon juice, garlic, shallots, curry, and capers. Bring the sauce to a boil and reduce it by ½.

Add the butter and cook it over high heat, stirring constantly, until the sauce becomes thick. Season it with the salt and pepper.

Remove the pan from the stove. Continue to stir for one minute more.

"Our food is simple and basic, but with great flavors.....the kind of food I love to eat!"

"The cooks at e.k. mas prepare all of their dishes on one six-burner stove with only one oven. We have to be perfectly organized in order to co-ordinate everything with such a small kitchen. If we could do it over, we certainly would have looked for a larger space."

Chocolate-Hazelnut Mousse Cake

1 **pound bittersweet chocolate**
1 **pound butter**
16 **eggs, room temperature, separated**
2 **ounces Frangelico liquor**
   fresh berries
   whipped cream

In a double boiler place the chocolate and butter and heat them until they are melted.

Add the egg yolks and briskly whip the mixture for 1 minute over the heat.

Remove the pan from the burner and whisk the ingredients for 1 minute more.

In a medium bowl place the egg whites and beat them until they form soft peaks *(firm but not stiff, with the tops of the peaks slightly drooping)*.

Fold the egg whites into the chocolate mixture.

Add the Frangelico and mix it in.

Preheat the oven to 300°.

Pour the mixture into a 10" buttered and floured cake pan.

Bake for approximately 40 minutes. The mousse cake should be wiggly in the center *(3" diameter)* when the pan is jiggled. The center also should be slightly springy to the touch. After 20 minutes check it every 5 to 7 minutes, or until the desired consistency is reached.

Remove the mousse cake from the oven and let it sit for at least 3 hours at room temperature. Do not refrigerate.

Slice and serve with fresh berries and whipped cream.

serves 6

"It is hard to explain exactly how long the mousse cake should cook. I go by my intuition and experience."

"The time depends on a number of factors, such as the size of your oven, the way it heats, and the altitude you are cooking at. If the cake is slightly gooey in the center when you remove it, that is good. It will continue to cook slightly until it is cooled to room temperature. Even if it's gooey when you serve it, there's no problem because all you are doing is serving a cake with some mousse in the middle!"

"Instead of baking it as a cake, the mousse may be served cold. Ladle the mousse into glasses and refrigerate them for at least 5 hours."

"If you want to reduce this recipe, it's simple. The ratio is one egg to one ounce of chocolate to one ounce of butter."

Springer House – Winter Adobe Detail, Santa Fe, New Mexico

El Farol

Distinguished as the first *tapas* restaurant in Santa Fe, the historic El Farol offers a fascinating array of tasty and exotic appetizers, sometimes called *little bites from Spain*. Mix and match to your heart's content.....even the most eclectic of tastes can be satisfied!

Recipes

Quinoa Salad

Clams á la Madrilena

Ceviche

Tortilla Española
Romesco Sauce

Grilled Salmon
Aioli
Sun-Dried Tomato Pesto

Rabbit in White Wine Sauce

A favorite of chef Ned Laventall, the Quinoa Salad is nutritious and flavorful. This recipe is a variation of the traditional bulgur tabouli, and has a delicious nutty flavor.

Quinoa Salad

2½	tablespoons olive oil
1	cup quinoa grain
1	bay leaf
1½	cups water
1	teaspoon salt
1	medium carrot, grated
3	scallions, sliced
1	lemon, juiced
½	bunch cilantro, finely chopped
1	jalapeño pepper, finely diced

In a large, heavy saucepan place the olive oil and heat it on medium until it is hot. Add the quinoa and the bay leaf and stir them until the quinoa is lightly toasted.

Add the water and allow it to come to a boil.

Cover and simmer on low heat for 20 minutes, or until the quinoa is soft, fluffy, and dry.

Remove the quinoa from the heat. Cool and chill it.

In a large bowl place the quinoa and the remainder of the ingredients. Toss them together thoroughly.

serves 6-8

Clams á la Madrilena

12	medium clams *(live in shells)*, rinsed
½	cup white wine
2	tablespoons olive oil
1	small onion, diced
1	green chile, roasted, peeled, seeded, and diced
3	stalks celery, diced
1	red bell pepper, seeded, washed, and diced
2	white potatoes, peeled and diced
1	bunch scallions, thinly sliced
1	clove garlic, finely chopped
1	tablespoon flour
4	cups clam juice
1	bunch Italian parsley, finely minced
	salt *(to taste)*
	white pepper *(to taste)*

In a medium saucepan place the clams and the white wine. Cover the pan and steam the clams until the shells are wide open.

Remove the pan from the heat and cool to room temperature. Keep the pan covered.

In a large saucepan place the olive oil and heat it on medium. Add the onions, chile, celery, red pepper, potatoes, and scallions. Sauté them for 3 to 4 minutes, or until the onions are transparent.

Add the garlic and sauté it for 2 minutes.

Add the flour and cook it for 5 minutes, stirring frequently.

Remove the clams from the liquid and cut them out of the shells. Strain the liquid through a fine sieve and add it to the sautéed vegetables.

Add the four cups of clam juice, bring to a boil, and then simmer, stirring occasionally.

(continued on next page)

"Red chowder, white chowder.....why not green chowder?"

"This soup is a kind of olive oil based roux (rather than butter based), and the fresh Italian parsley is the key to its unique color and taste. Feel free to experiment with other ingredients, but remember that the ratio of oil to flour is the critical element."

Chop the clams coarsely and add them to the broth.

Add the parsley.

Stir and simmer until the potatoes are just cooked. Season with the salt and pepper.

serves 6-8

"Our food is not subtle in taste.....the flavors are full and robust. And it must look gorgeous!"

Ceviche

2   **pounds fresh scallops**
1   **bunch scallions, thinly sliced**
1   **large jalapeño pepper, thinly sliced**
1   **bunch cilantro, finely chopped**
6   **limes, juiced**

Trim the tough strips from each scallop. If the scallops are very large, cut them into quarters.

In a medium bowl place all of the ingredients and marinate them in the refrigerator for 2 hours.

serves 6-8

"This recipe is so simple, and yet the taste is wonderfully complex."

Tortilla Española
with Romesco Sauce

Tortilla Española

6   tablespoons olive oil
10 medium, white potatoes, peeled and cut into ¼"
    slices
1   medium onion, peeled, halved, and thinly sliced
6   large eggs, beaten
¼   teaspoon salt
    Romesco Sauce *(recipe on next page)*

Preheat the oven to 350°. In a small roasting pan place the olive oil and the potatoes. Cover the pan. Bake the potatoes for 20 minutes.

Carefully uncover the pan. Add the onions and spread them around evenly. Don't stir the potatoes.

Recover the pan and bake the potatoes for another 10 minutes, or until they are just done.

Remove the pan from the oven and let the potatoes cool to room temperature.

In a large bowl place the eggs and beat them. Fold in the potatoes and onions. Add the salt and carefully stir it in.

In a seasoned cast iron *(or teflon)* 8" skillet place 2 teaspoons of the olive oil *(from the roasting pan)*. Heat it on high until it is hot. Carefully add the potato and egg mixture. Cook it for 1 minute while gently shaking the pan.

Lower the heat to the lowest possible temperature and cook the tortilla for 15 minutes, or until it is firm.

Place a plate on top of the skillet and turn it over so that the tortilla is on the plate.

Return the tortilla to the skillet and cook the other side for 8 to 10 minutes, or until it is nicely browned.

Serve with the Romesco Sauce.

serves 6

"This is the traditional omelette from Spain. But the Romesco Sauce really adds a wonderfully unique flavor."

"At El Farol the layout of the tapas is very colorful. It's fun to order a lot of different dishes and then have everybody in your party share them."

Romesco Sauce

2	chile pequin pods
2	cloves garlic
1	tablespoon sliced almonds, toasted
⅓	cup olive oil
¼	teaspoon vinegar
¼	teaspoon salt
1	large can *(17½ ounce)* pimientos

(Caution: Do not breathe the fumes from the roasting chile pods!!)

In a small, dry skillet place the chile pods and toss them around on medium heat until they start to blacken.

In a food processor or blender place the garlic, almonds, and chile pods. Coarsely chop them.

Add the olive oil, vinegar, salt, and pimientos. Purée them to an almost smooth consistency.

"Chile pequin pods are those little dark red peppers in plastic bags, found in the Mexican food section. Treat them with respect! And when you roast them – be sure that you don't breath the fumes!"

Grilled Salmon with Aioli and Sun-Dried Tomato Pesto

Grilled Salmon

8	3-ounce salmon fillets, boneless
16	Calamata olives, pitted
1	lemon, cut into 8 wedges
	Aioli *(recipe follows)*
	Sun–Dried Tomato Pesto *(recipe follows)*

Grill the salmon fillets for 2 minutes on each side, or until they are just done.

Place two salmon fillets on individual serving plates. Garnish them with the olives and lemon wedges.

Serve them with side dishes of the Aioli and the Sun-Dried Tomato Pesto.

serves 4

Aioli

1	small egg
1	clove garlic
2	tablespoons olive oil
2	teaspoons fresh lemon juice
½	teaspoon salt

In a food processor place the egg and the garlic, and blend them together. Gradually add the olive oil, while constantly blending. Add the lemon juice and salt, and blend them in.

Sun-Dried Tomato Pesto

1½	tablespoons sun-dried tomatoes
1	clove garlic
5	leaves fresh basil
1½	tablespoons olive oil

(continued on next page)

"I love the taste of sun-dried tomatoes. The water that they soak in is the base for some of my sauces. I am always looking for more uses for these tomatoes."

"If the Aioli does not have the proper consistency (like mayonnaise), then you should make it with one egg yolk instead of using the whole egg."

"A tapas restaurant has a unique format in that so many different kinds of food are offered. The customers can create their own special combination of whatever intrigues them. It's hard to get bored here."

Re-constitute the sun-dried tomatoes in boiling water. Strain *(save the water for soups or sauces)*, cool, and chill thoroughly.

In a food processor or blender place the garlic and chop it. Add the sun-dried tomatoes and basil and blend them together.

Gradually add the olive oil, while blending constantly, to achieve a pesto consistency.

Rabbit in White Wine Sauce

1	tablespoon olive oil
1	3 pound rabbit, cut in 8 pieces, with fat, sinew, and most bones removed
	white flour *(as needed)*
1	small onion, diced
1	stalk celery, diced
2	cloves garlic, minced
4	tomatoes, cut in chunks
⅓	bunch fresh oregano, chopped
1	cup Spanish white wine
2	cups beef stock
10	Calamata olives, seeded and halved

In a large skillet place the olive oil and heat it on high. Dredge the rabbit pieces lightly in the flour. Place the rabbit pieces in the hot oil and lightly brown them on both sides. Remove the rabbit and drain it on paper towels.

Add the onion, celery, and garlic to the remaining oil. Sauté them for 3 minutes, or until the onions are transparent.

Add the tomatoes and oregano, and cook them for 3 to 5 minutes, or until the tomatoes are soft. Add the wine and cook for 2 minutes, or until the liquid is reduced by ½.

Add the beef stock and olives. Bring the sauce to a boil. Add the rabbit and simmer everything for ½ hour, or until the rabbit is tender.

serves 6-8

"You can buy a whole rabbit from your butcher and either have him cut it up, or you can do it yourself. Sometimes you can find one already sectioned from the grocery store. At El Farol we always buy the rabbits whole and cut them ourselves. But then, we do everything from scratch."

"Calamata olives are those strong tasting Greek black olives found in the gourmet section of your grocery store."

"This dish should be served with baked yams that have cooled, and then been sliced."

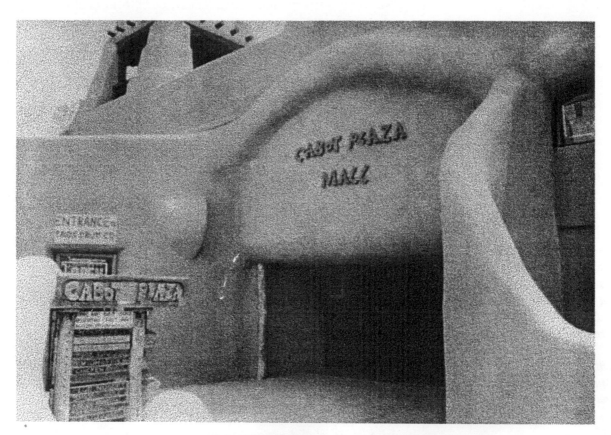

Cabot Plaza Mall, Taos, New Mexico

Ernie's

Located in a beautifully restored Victorian adobe home, Ernie's serves excellent food with a strong European influence. From the intimate, well appointed dining rooms to the lively chatter of the pet parrot in the entry, Ernie's guarantees you a pleasant dining experience.

Owner/chef Ernie Bolleter is a native of Switzerland, where small lake fish are a standard in most restaurants. He says, *"This recipe is a classic from Lake Geneva, and, it's delicious!"*

Fillet de Perch "Hotel d'Angleterre"

2	**pounds small, lake perch fillets** *(if larger, cut them into 1 ounce strips)*
16	**ounces light beer**
½	**cup flour** *(or as needed)*
2	**cups oil** *(or as needed)*
2	**sticks unsalted butter**
¼	**cup fresh parsley, chopped**
1	**lemon, wedged**

In a medium bowl place the perch fillets and the beer. Soak them for 1 hour, and drain them well.

Thoroughly coat the fish fillets in the flour.

In a small skillet place the oil and heat it until it is very hot *(almost smoking)*.

Fry the fillets *(3 or 4 at a time)* for 3 minutes, or until they are golden brown.

In a large skillet place the butter and melt it on medium until it is foamy.

Add the fish fillets and swirl them around until they are well coated.

Place the fish fillets on a serving platter. Dribble the remaining butter over them.

Sprinkle the parsley on top. Serve with the lemon wedges.

serves 4

54

Oysters Boulevard
with Hollandaise Sauce

Oysters Boulevard

1	tablespoon butter
½	cup celery, finely chopped
½	cup red onions, finely chopped
½	cup scallions, finely chopped
½	cup mushrooms, finely chopped
½	cup fresh salad shrimp, finely chopped
1	tablespoon flour
1	cup dry white wine
3	dashes tabasco sauce
3	dashes Angostora bitters
24	oysters, washed and opened on the half shell
2	cups Hollandaise Sauce *(recipe on next page)*
½	cup heavy cream, whipped

In a medium skillet place the butter and heat it on medium until it is melted. Add the celery, onions, scallions, mushrooms, and shrimp. Sauté them for 2 to 3 minutes, or until the vegetables are slightly softened.

Add the flour and stir it in for 1 minute.

Add the white wine and stir it for 2 to 3 minutes. Add the tabasco and bitters.

Place the oysters on a baking sheet. Place a small amount of the sauce on top of each oyster.

Preheat the oven to 500°. Bake the oysters for 5 minutes in the center of the oven.

In a medium bowl place the Hollandaise Sauce and the whipped cream, and carefully fold them together. Spoon a small amount on top of each oyster.

Broil the oysters for 2 minutes, until they are lightly browned.

serves 4-6

"I picked up this recipe up from a chef friend of mine who was trained in Cajun cooking. It's a delicious appetizer.....very rich. Even someone who isn't too fond of oysters will like it."

"This recipe is somewhat complicated, although it's not difficult to make. I usually prepare these oysters on special occasions.....because they are special!"

Hollandaise Sauce

3	egg yolks
2	tablespoons water
8	ounces clarified **butter, warmed** *(not hot)*
¼	**lemon, juiced**
1	**dash salt**
1	**dash cayenne pepper**

Heat a double boiler to medium. Add the egg yolks and water, and whisk them constantly for 3 to 4 minutes, or until the mixture is creamy and airy.

Remove the mixture from the heat. Very slowly, while whisking constantly, add the warm, clarified butter.

Add the lemon juice, salt, and cayenne pepper, and whisk them in.

"Actually, this is a simplified version of a classic Hollandaise, which is much more complicated to make. If you are serving the sauce with something very delicate, like white asparagus, which doesn't have much taste on its own, then you can tell the difference, and the classic version tastes much better. But, with these oysters the simpler version is fine."

"When you are beating the egg yolks and water, be sure to beat around the edges of the pot.....you don't want to get scrambled eggs!"

Jalapeño Chowder

1	whole chicken
2	quarts water
1	teaspoon salt
2	bay leaves
1	teaspoon peppercorns

(Note: Save the ends and stems from the following vegetables.)

6	stalks celery, diced
3	tomatoes, peeled, seeded, and diced
1	bunch scallions, sliced
2	jalapeño peppers, seeded and chopped
1	medium onion, chopped
3	green bell peppers, seeded, washed, and diced
½	cup bacon grease
¾	cup flour
2	small zucchinis, diced
2	avocados, quartered and sliced
1	cup whole corn
	blue corn tortilla chips

In a large, heavy soup pot place the chicken, water, and salt. Bring the water to a boil and then reduce it to a simmer. Skim the foam off the top.

Add the bay leaves, peppercorns, and the stems and ends of the vegetables. Cook for 1 hour, or until the chicken is done.

Remove the chicken from the pot and let it cool. Skin and bone the chicken. Cut it into small chunks. Strain the chicken broth through a sieve and pour it back in the pot.

In a large skillet place the bacon grease and heat it on medium until it is hot. Add the flour and stir it until it is lightly browned. Add the roux to the broth.

Add the celery, tomatoes, scallions, jalapeño, onion, and bell peppers to the broth. Cook for 30 minutes, or until the vegetables are barely done.

Add the chicken, zucchini, avocados, and corn. Cook them for 5 minutes. Correct the seasoning if necessary.

Garnish with the blue corn tortilla chips.

serves 8

"This soup is my invention. It's something I make when I need to use up leftover chicken stock. I have made this soup many times, and it always comes out different because I put leftover items in it. But, I think that this recipe is very close to the basic one."

"The flavor is fairly hot, but not too spicy. The jalapeños give it a nice bite. Be sure to remove the seeds. Otherwise you will burn your lips, unless you are used to the hotness."

"You can have this as a whole meal, it's so filling. Just serve it with a good bread or some corn tortillas."

Consommé Navidad

1   **quart beef consommé** *(recipe on next page)*
1   **firm avocado, diced**
6   **green chiles, peeled, seeded, and diced**
2   **tomatoes, peeled, seeded, and diced**
1   **cup whole corn, drained**
½   **cup black olives, diced**
½   **cup fresh chives, chopped**
3   **corn tortillas, cut into small strips**
1   **cup vegetable oil**

In a large saucepan place the beef consommé and heat it on medium until it is hot *(do not boil)*.

Add the rest of the ingredients *(except for the tortillas and oil)* and simmer them for 10 minutes, or until they are well heated.

In a large, heavy skillet place the oil and heat it on high until it is very hot. Quickly fry the tortilla strips until they are crisp and golden. Drain them on paper towels.

Serve the soup in individual bowls. Garnish with the tortilla strips.

serves 6

"I took a basic consommé and added the corn, chiles, tomatoes, olives, chives, and tortilla chips.....so it has a definite Southwestern flavor."

"This is something I make only on Christmas day, so it is a very special dish to me."

"This recipe should be simple for anyone to make, after the basic consommé is made. Be careful that you do not boil the consommé. If you must reheat it, do so in a double boiler, if possible."

Beef Consommé

1	pound lean ground beef
2	medium stalks celery, minced
1	medium carrot, minced
1	medium leek, minced
1	medium onion, minced
2	egg whites, lightly beaten
1	cup cold water
4	peppercorns
1	bay leaf
2	quarts beef bouillon *(recipe on next page)*, **warmed**
2	ounces cognac
1	pinch nutmeg
1	pinch cayenne pepper

In a large saucepan place the ground beef, celery, carrots, leek, onion, egg whites, water, peppercorns, and the bay leaf. Mix everything together well.

Add the warmed bouillon and mix it in.

Heat the mixture until it barely comes to a boil, or until a foam appears on the top.

Immediately reduce the heat to low, and simmer the broth for 2 hours.

Very carefully push the foam down with a wide spoon so that the clear liquid rises. Gently spoon out the clear liquid and strain it through a cloth.

Let it sit for 5 minutes and then skim off any fat.

Add the cognac, nutmeg, and cayenne pepper. Carefully stir them in.

"The tricky thing with making consommé is that it should never come to a rolling boil. Also, when you strain it, don't disturb the foam. If you make a mistake and the consommé gets some foam in it, it will taste just as good, but it will look cloudy.....it won't look as pretty. The idea is that the consommé should be completely clear. You should be able to see everything that is in it, all the way to the bottom, just like a clear Swiss mountain lake."

Beef Bouillon

2	pounds beef bones, washed and cut into small pieces
3	quarts water
½	leek, washed and coarsely chopped
1	medium onion with skin on
2	cloves garlic
5	peppercorns
3	cabbage leaves
1	medium carrot
1	bay leaf
1	tablespoon salt

In a large, heavy soup pot place the bones and the water, and bring them to a boil. Skim off the foam.

Add the remainder of the ingredients and simmer for 2 to 3 hours. Strain the broth through a cheesecloth.

Veal and Shrimp Thermidor

"This recipe was created when I had some veal and shrimp left over. It's a hot, spicy dish, but the Marsala gives it a nice, sweet flavor. It's important to use the brand I've suggested. I've tried a lot of other kinds and this is the only one that tastes right."

2	tablespoons butter
24	ounces veal fillet, sliced into ⅛" pieces
24	medium shrimp, peeled and deveined
½	teaspoon salt
2	teaspoons paprika
½	teaspoon cayenne pepper
1	tablespoon flour
½	cup dry Florio Marsala *(no substitution)*
1½	cups heavy cream
3	cups cooked white rice

In a large skillet place the butter and heat it on medium until it melts. Add the veal and sauté it for 1 to 2 minutes. Add the shrimp and sauté it for 1 minute.

Add the salt, paprika, and cayenne pepper. Stir everything together. Add the flour and sauté for 1 minute.

"You serve the sauce over the veal and shrimp, on top of the rice. It's delicious!"

Add the Marsala and reduce the sauce by ⅓. Add the cream and simmer until the sauce has the consistency of heavy cream. Serve over the rice.

serves 4

Stuffed Flank Steak

6	ounces veal, ground
6	ounces pork, ground
6	ounces fat back, ground and unsalted
¼	cup white wine
1	teaspoon salt
1	teaspoon white pepper
½	teaspoon nutmeg
1	tablespoon scallions, chopped
1	tablespoon black olives, chopped
1	tablespoon mushrooms, chopped
2	slices ham, diced
2	pounds thick flank steak
1	tablespoon flour (or, as needed)
2	tablespoons vegetable oil
1	small carrot, chopped
1	small celery stalk, chopped
½	small onion, chopped
2	cloves garlic, chopped
1	sprig fresh rosemary
1	tablespoon tomato paste
1	tablespoon flour
¾	cup white wine
3	cups beef stock

In a food processor place the veal, pork, fat back, ¼ cup of white wine, salt, white pepper, and nutmeg. Blend them together until they are pasty smooth. Add a few drops of ice cold water if the mixture is too thick.

Place the blended mixture in a bowl. Add the scallions, black olives, mushrooms, and ham. Work them in with a wooden spoon.

Place the mixture in a pastry bag with no tip.

Carefully cut a large pocket into the flank steak, horizontally, using a long, thin knife.

Place the filled pastry bag deep into the pocket of the flank steak. Squeeze the stuffing into the steak. Close the hole on the side of the steak by sewing it, or by weaving a small brochette stick through it. Pat the top of the stuffed steak to evenly spread out the stuffing.

(continued on the next page)

"Usually stuffed flank steaks are rolled, and the stuffing tends to ooze out. So, I came up with the idea of making a pocket. To cut the pocket is the hardest part of the recipe, but once that's done, it's easy! If you go to a good butcher, he can probably cut it for you. If you cut the pocket yourself and make a mistake and poke the knife through somewhere, don't worry! When you sear the meat it should seal up."

"This dish looks really pretty when you slice it. The center of the steak has a lot of different colored things in it, and it looks like a pâté."

"Cooking this is simple. It's almost like cooking a pot roast. It tastes wonderful!"

Coat both sides of the stuffed steak with the 1 tablespoon of the flour. Use more flour if necessary.

In a roasting pan place the oil and heat it on medium until it is very hot. Brown the steak for 2 minutes on each side.

Reduce the heat to medium and add the carrots, celery, onion, garlic, and rosemary. Sauté them for 2 to 3 minutes.

Add the tomato paste and the 1 tablespoon of flour. Stir them in.

Add the ¾ cup of white wine and deglaze the pan, until the bits on the bottom are loosened.

Add the beef stock. Cover the pan with a piece of foil that is punched with holes.

Preheat the oven to 350°. Braise the stuffed steak for 1 to 1½ hours, or until the meat falls off easily when stuck with a fork. Remove the meat from the pan when it is done.

Place the sauce and vegetables in a blender and purée them together.

Place the puréed mixture in a small saucepan and reduce it over medium heat until it is the consistency of heavy cream.

At an angle, slice the beef into ½" wide pieces. Keep the pieces intact.

Pour just a little sauce over the top.

Serve the rest of the sauce on the side.

serves 6-8

Stuffed Romaine Lettuce

2	gallons water
2	tablespoons salt
1	whole head romaine lettuce intact, washed
6	slices bacon, diced
½	medium onion, diced
½	teaspoon vegetable salt seasoning
1	cup chicken stock, heated
1	tablespoon butter, melted

In a large saucepan place the water and the salt. Bring it to a boil.

Add the head of romaine lettuce and boil it until the ribs are tender, but not mushy.

Remove the cooked lettuce and immediately place it in ice water. Drain it well, and then carefully squeeze out any excess liquid with your hands.

In a small skillet place the bacon, and fry it over medium heat. Drain off most of the grease. Add the onions and sauté them until they are tender.

Place the cooked lettuce head on a cutting board. Beat it with the side of a large, wide French knife, until it is well flattened. Cut off the core at the bottom, and flatten it some more.

Slice upwards into the ribs of the lettuce head, from the bottom towards the top. Cut across the bottom of the lettuce head just enough to make it straight.

From the top to the bottom, fold over ⅓ of the lettuce head.

Place the bacon and onion mixture in the center of the lettuce head. Sprinkle on the vegetable salt seasoning.

Fold the lettuce head in half from the top towards the bottom, over the bacon and onion mixture. Slice it into 6 pieces.

Place the stuffed lettuce in a small baking dish. Pour the heated chicken stock over it. Dribble on the melted butter. Cover the pan with foil.

Preheat the oven to 350°. Bake it for 15 minutes.

serves 6

"One of the places I worked at in Switzerland on Lake Geneva served this dish. The instructions are complicated because it's hard to explain without visually showing how, but it's really very simple. If you could see someone make it on a TV show, then it would look really easy!"

"People can never figure out what is in this dish. They usually think that it's spinach, because the idea of a cooked romaine just doesn't occur to them. They are always surprised when they find out. The flavor in the lettuce is really good, and the bacon and onion give it an excellent flavor."

"You want to cook the romaine until it is just done. If it is overcooked it will look terrible and the recipe won't come out right."

Fresh Peach with Almond Cream

2½ cups milk, heated
1 teaspoon vanilla
4 egg yolks
½ cup flour
1¼ cups sugar
1 cup sugar
2 cups sliced almonds, toasted
1 pint whipping cream
¾ cup simple syrup *(½ cup sugar dissolved in ½ cup water)*
3 ripe peaches, blanched, peeled, halved, and pitted

In a medium saucepan place the milk and vanilla, and heat them on medium.

In a medium bowl place the egg yolks, flour, and the 1¼ cups of sugar. Mix them together. Add the hot milk, while whisking rapidly to prevent lumping.

Pour the mixture back into the saucepan that contained the hot milk. Place it over a medium heat and stir constantly until the custard is thick and creamy. Set it aside to cool.

In a small saucepan place the 1 cup of sugar and heat it slowly until the sugar melts and turns a golden brown.

In a shallow baking pan place the almond slices. Pour the caramelized sugar over the almonds. Let it harden.

Break up the hardened caramel almond and place it in the center of a terry cloth towel. Bring the ends together and twist them. Beat the caramel almond with a wooden mallet until it is finely crushed.

Add all but ½ cup of the crushed candy to the custard mixture and mix it in.

In a medium bowl place the whipping cream and beat it until soft peaks form. Fold half of the whipped cream into the custard mixture.

In a small bowl place the simple syrup mixture. Add the peaches and let them soak for 30 minutes.

Place some of the caramel custard mixture into the bottom of 6 champagne glasses. Place the peach halves, upside down, over the custard. Garnish with the rest of the whipped cream and the candy.

serves 6

"The peaches that you use must be nice and ripe, preferably ones that are locally grown. A canned peach would be better than a bad fresh one. This recipe will work with fresh pears, also, which are usually available all year round."

"The only reason for putting the peaches in the sugar water is to keep them fresh until you are ready to serve them."

"This is a very rich, delicious dessert! It tastes yummy!"

Old Torreone, Lincoln, New Mexico

The Evergreen

Nestled in the Sangre de Cristos below the Santa Fe ski area, The Evergreen offers a spectacular mountain setting, along with excellent food. The ambiance is an appealing contrast between the rustic and the elegant.....and the food is first class all the way!

Executive Chef Bob Godwin says, *"This is my adaptation of a traditional Spanish salad.....not that it's a classic recipe, but all of the ingredients are Spanish in origin. You can use an Italian olive oil, but I prefer to maintain the integrity of the dish by using the Spanish, which has a stronger flavor."*

Spanish Roasted Bell Pepper Salad

1	green bell pepper
1	red bell pepper
1	yellow bell pepper
1	clove garlic, minced
⅓	cup Spanish cold-pressed virgin olive oil
2	tablespoons balsamic vinegar
¼	teaspoon salt
¼	teaspoon white pepper
2	heads bibb lettuce, washed, dried, and leaves separated
1	large tomato, peeled and wedged
½	cup cooked garbanzo beans
1	dozen Manzanilla olives

Preheat the oven to 450°. Place the peppers on a baking tray and, turning on all sides, roast them until they are uniformly blistered. Immediately place the peppers in ice water. Leave them there until they are chilled.

Peel and seed the peppers. Cut them into thin strips.

In a medium glass bowl place the garlic, olive oil, vinegar, salt, and pepper and whisk them together. Add the peppers to the dressing. Cover, and refrigerate them for 2 hours.

Place the whole lettuce leaves onto chilled salad plates.

Strain the marinated peppers and place them on top of the lettuce *(save the liquid dressing)*.

Artfully arrange the tomato, garbanzo beans, and olives on top of the lettuce. Dribble the remaining dressing over the salad.

serves 4

Steamed Oysters
with Southwestern Sauce

Steamed Oysters

24	whole oysters, in their shells, well scrubbed
½	cup fresh lime juice
¼	cup fresh lemon juice
2	tablespoons olive oil
½	cup water
2	cloves garlic, minced
1	small onion, diced
1	mild green chile *(Anaheim)*, diced
2	tablespoons cilantro, chopped
⅛	teaspoon salt
¼	teaspoon white pepper
1	lime, wedged
	Southwestern Sauce *(recipe on next page)*

In a large, heavy pot, place all of the ingredients *(except for the wedged lime and the Southwestern Sauce)*. Mix them together.

Cover and simmer them for 5 to 10 minutes, depending on the desired doneness of the oysters.

Carefully open the oysters with an oyster knife or a dull paring knife.

Place the oysters on a plate, in their half-shells, and garnish them with the lime wedges. Serve with the Southwestern Sauce.

serves 4

"I have always loved ceviche, which is normally raw fish marinated in lime, cilantro, and onions. The acid in the citrus actually cooks the fish. In this recipe the oysters are steamed in a mixture of ceviche ingredients, and the flavor is very light and wonderful."

"The green chiles are usually Anaheim peppers.....about six inches long, green, and mild. Do not confuse them with the smaller hot jalapeño or serrano peppers."

"Be sure to give the oysters a good scrubbing with a vegetable brush, and rinse them well under cold, running water. Because you are cooking the whole oysters with the shells on, you don't want any sand or debris to get in the liquid."

"If you are apprehensive about opening the shells with an oyster knife (this can be difficult), don't worry! The steaming will cause the shells to loosen up, and you should find the shucking to be quite easy."

Southwestern Sauce

1	small onion, coarsely chopped
4	cloves garlic, coarsely chopped
2	medium shallots, coarsely chopped
3	ounces chipotle peppers
½	cup water
3	cups bottled chile sauce
3	tablespoons cilantro, chopped
¼	cup fresh lime juice
1	teaspoon cumin
1	teaspoon chile powder

In a food processor place the onion, garlic, shallots, chipotle peppers, and water. Blend everything together.

Place the blended mixture in a medium bowl and add the remaining ingredients.

Mix well, cover, and refrigerate the sauce overnight.

"The most important ingredient in the sauce is the chipotle peppers, which actually are smoked jalapeño peppers. They are usually packed with Adobo sauce, which is very flavorful, and also smokey in taste. Sold in six to seven ounce cans, they should not be hard to find. These chipotle peppers are what give the sauce its Southwestern flavor."

Cream of Wild Mushroom and Piñon Soup

1	tablespoon peanut oil
1	pound fresh wild mushrooms, cleaned and chopped

(save a few caps for the garnish)

½	small onion, chopped
2	cloves garlic, diced
⅓	cup dry white wine
1	bay leaf
1	sprig thyme
1	quart water
4	tablespoons butter
3	tablespoons flour
½	cup piñon nuts, toasted and puréed
2	cups light cream
½	cup Madeira wine
1	tablespoon butter (optional)
1	tablespoon parsley, finely chopped

In a large, heavy pot place the oil and heat it on medium until it is hot. Add the mushrooms, onion, and garlic. Sauté them for several minutes.

Add the white wine, bay leaf, and thyme. Simmer until the liquid is nearly evaporated. Add the water and simmer for 30 minutes.

Strain the mushrooms from the broth and place them in a blender. Purée them until they are smooth.

Return the puréed mushroom mixture to the broth and bring it to a boil. Reduce the heat to medium.

In a small saucepan place the 4 tablespoons of butter and melt it over a medium heat. Add the flour and cook it for 3 to 4 minutes, stirring constantly. Do not let the roux brown.

Add the roux to the broth and stir it constantly for 3 to 4 minutes.

Add the piñon nuts and the light cream. Simmer the soup for 10 minutes. Add the Madeira.

Garnish with the mushroom caps, the 1 tablespoon of butter, and the parsley.

serves 4

"For my own personal cooking, I gather fresh mushrooms from the wild whenever possible. However, this is definitely not recommended for the average person. The morel is the most flavorful and prized mushroom in the Rocky Mountains. But they don't grow every year.....only when the conditions are perfect. However, when they do grow, they grow in great abundance."

"If you can't find one of the more exotic brands of wild mushrooms in your grocery store, it's fine to substitute a button or medium mushroom. But, the flavor from the wild mushrooms is so amazing that it's really worth the effort to try to seek them out."

"We get a lot of compliments on this soup. Try to find a nice, light cream, in between whipping cream and half-and-half (in terms of butterfat content). Otherwise, a good quality half-and-half can be used."

Marinated Chile Chicken with Pine Nut Cilantro Butter

"I developed this recipe because we needed another chicken dish with a Southwestern flavor. It's light and healthy. The butter can be eliminated, but it really adds a nice flavor. This dish is very popular on our menu."

Marinated Chile Chicken

4	8-ounce chicken breasts, boned
½	cup Spanish cold-pressed extra virgin olive oil
½	cup dry white wine
4	cloves garlic, minced
1	shallot, minced
2	tablespoons cilantro, finely diced
1	teaspoon cumin
1	teaspoon chile powder
1	teaspoon achiote or ancho chile powder
1	dash salt
1	dash pepper
	Pine Nut Cilantro Butter *(recipe follows)*

Flatten the chicken breasts with a tenderizing hammer.

Place the remaining ingredients in a blender *(except for the Pine Nut Cilantro Butter)* and purée them. Place the chicken in a glass bowl and coat the pieces with the blended mixture. Cover, and refrigerate the chicken for 4 to 6 hours.

Drain the marinade from the chicken breasts and pat them dry. Broil or grill the chicken until it is done, turning once. Do not overcook. Serve the chicken with a dollop of the Pine Nut Cilantro Butter.

serves 4

"The main idea of a marinade is to cook or tenderize the chicken (or meat). However, in this recipe, the chicken breast is already tender because it has been pounded. This is why it is marinated for only four to six hours, instead of eight to thirty-six hours, which would be common for other meats. If you over-marinate the chicken, it will get mushy."

Pine Nut Cilantro Butter

1	stick butter, warmed to room temperature
2	tablespoons heavy cream
2	tablespoons dry white wine
¼	cup pine nuts, toasted and minced
3	cloves garlic, minced
2	tablespoons cilantro, finely diced
1	pinch salt
1	pinch pepper

In a medium bowl place all of the ingredients. Cream everything together until the butter is smooth.

Roasted Rack of Lamb
with Mint Coriander Glaze

Roasted Rack of Lamb

2	**half lamb racks** *(chine removed by butcher)*
1	**pinch salt**
1	**pinch pepper**
2	**tablespoons peanut oil**
1	**tablespoon garlic oil**
1	**teaspoon thyme**
	Mint Coriander Glaze *(recipe follows)*

Season the racks of lamb with the salt and the pepper.

In a large, heavy skillet place the peanut oil and heat it on medium until it is hot. Lightly brown the lamb on both sides.

Rub the lamb with the garlic oil and the thyme. Place the lamb on a rack in a roasting pan.

Broil the lamb on the middle rack of the oven for 20 minutes, or until the desired doneness is reached.

Carve the lamb at the table. Pour the Mint Coriander Glaze over the top.

serves 4

Mint Coriander Glaze

2	**tablespoons whole coriander, crushed**
2	**tablespoons fresh mint, chopped**
1	**shallot, minced**
1	**tablespoon honey**
½	**cup dry white wine**
¾	**cup veal stock** *(recipe on next page)*
	salt *(to taste)*
	pepper *(to taste)*

In a small saucepan place the coriander, mint, shallots, honey, and wine. Simmer the mixture until it has reduced to 1 tablespoon of liquid.

Add the veal stock. Simmer until the sauce is slightly thick. Add salt and pepper to taste.

"I much prefer a domestic lamb, such as one from Colorado or New Mexico, as opposed to a New Zealand lamb. They are larger, moister, more tender, and not quite so strong in taste."

"In this recipe the manner of cooking the lamb is classic. If the chine is removed, it's a breeze to carve at the table, which adds a very nice touch."

"You can crush the coriander by smashing it with the back of a cooking pot, like I do. Or you can run it through a mill or food processor."

"The veal stock is essential to the great taste of this sauce. It is well worth the trouble to make it from scratch. For the fresh mint, you can use either spearmint or peppermint."

"If you would like to have a stronger and richer stock, then let it simmer longer, until it is again reduced by one half."

"The water that you use must be cold so that it releases the flavors from the veal bones. Be sure that you don't ever boil the stock. Otherwise it will come out cloudy."

One handy tip is that you can freeze the veal stock in an ice cube tray. That way you can use small amounts as you need them."

"The exciting thing about American chefs is their willingness to appreciate the past. But, at the same time they are combining these old traditions with totally new trends in the United States. I definitely respect the classical style of cooking, but I also believe in the value of experimentation. I am always trying to create new and different recipes, especially those that are healthy, but, at the same time, are full of flavor."

Classic Veal Stock

3	pounds veal shank
3	pounds knuckles and bones
2	teaspoons salt
	cold water *(as needed)*
¼	cup flour
1	large sprig fresh thyme
2	bay leaves
4	sprigs parsley
3	garlic cloves, skins left on and chopped
3	stalks celery, coarsely chopped
2	medium carrots, coarsely chopped
2	medium onions, coarsely chopped
4	tomatoes, coarsely chopped
2	leeks, coarsely chopped
4	shallots, coarsely chopped

Preheat the oven to 450°.

Sprinkle the veal shank, knuckles, and bones with the salt. Place them in a pan and bake them for 45 minutes to 1 hour, or until they are evenly browned *(turn them twice)*.

Remove the bones and place them in a large stock pot.

Place the baking pan with the drippings on the stove and heat it on medium. Add the flour and stir it in to make a roux. Put the pan with the roux back into the oven for 5 minutes. Remove it and cool to room temperature.

Fill the stock pot with cold water so that it is 3" from the top. Bring it to a boil. Skim the foam off the top.

Place the thyme, bay leaves, parsley, and cloves in a piece of cheesecloth. Tie it up to make a Bouquet Garni.

Add the Bouquet Garni, roux, and vegetables to the stock pot. Simmer *(do not boil!)* for 4 to 6 hours, or until the water is reduced by ½. Strain it through a cheesecloth. Let it cool, and then refrigerate or freeze it.

Grand Marnier Pecan Crêpes Flambé

Crêpe Batter

¾   **cup flour, sifted**
¼   **teaspoon salt**
1   **tablespoon powdered sugar**
2   **eggs**
2   **egg yolks**
1   **cup milk** (minus 2 tablespoons)
4   **tablespoons butter, melted**
2   **tablespoons Grand Marnier**
3   **tablespoons butter, melted**
     Crêpe Filling (recipe on next page)
     Grand Marnier Pecan Sauce (recipe on next page)

In a medium bowl place the flour, salt, and powdered sugar. Mix them together.

Add the whole eggs and the egg yolks. Slowly mix the ingredients with a wire whisk until they are just blended. Do not over mix.

Slowly add the milk, the 4 tablespoons of melted butter, and the Grand Marnier. Let the mixture stand for 15 minutes at room temperature before making the crêpes.

Heat a French crêpe pan (or an 8" teflon omelette pan) on low heat for 2 minutes. Raise the heat to medium.

Pour part of the 3 tablespoons of the melted butter in the pan. Swish the butter around so that the pan is well coated, and then pour it back out.

Tilt the pan and pour in 2 tablespoons of the batter, or just enough to coat the bottom and ¼" of the sides. Spread the batter around evenly.

Place the pan back on the burner and cook the crêpe until it is golden brown. Using a rubber spatula, turn the crêpe over, and brown the other side for approximately 20 seconds.

Slide the crêpe onto a plate. Repeat this process until all the crêpes are made. Stack the crêpes on top of each other. The batter should make 24 crêpes.

(continued on the next page)

"Don't be afraid to try this dish. Once you get the hang of it, it's a piece of cake! And then you will have the skill in your repertoire forever, which is great, because there are hundreds of different ways to use crêpes.....as appetizers, main dishes, and desserts. Also, this recipe makes twenty-four crêpes, but you really only need twelve crêpes to serve four people, so there is plenty of extra batter to practice with."

"The crêpes freeze nicely, and should keep for at least a month. Cover them with saran wrap and then wrap them in foil."

Spread the crêpe filling on each of the 12 crêpes *(freeze the remaining 12 crêpes)*. Fold the crêpes in half. Fold them in half again, so that they are ¼ of their original size.

Add the crêpes to the Grand Marnier Pecan Sauce. Coat, and heat them. Add a splash or two more of the Grand Marnier.

Light the sauce with a flame.

Using a large spoon, place the crêpes on a platter, and pour the sauce over the top.

serves 4

Crêpe Filling

⅓ pound butter
¼ cup powdered sugar
2 tablespoons Grand Marnier

In a small bowl place the butter and whip it until it is creamy.

Add the powdered sugar and the Grand Marnier.

Whip the filling until it is frothy.

Grand Marnier Pecan Sauce

4 tablespoons butter, melted
½ cup pecans, chopped
3 tablespoons brown sugar
⅓ cup Grand Marnier

In a large frying pan place all of the ingredients. Simmer them over medium heat for 4 to 5 minutes, or until the mixture is barely thickened.

"One nice thing about this recipe is that you can do it all in advance. So, if you are having a special dinner party, you can spend your time enjoying the company of your guests instead of having to work in the kitchen the whole time. Just have the crêpes and sauce ready to go (store the prepared crêpes in the refrigerator), and then, when you are ready for dessert, heat up the sauce, light a flame to it, and voilà!"

"When you are putting a flame to the sauce you should be careful. The Grand Marnier is only eighty percent alcohol, so there won't be a big explosion, but you should watch out!"

Oldest House in the U.S.A., Santa Fe, New Mexico

Francisco's

The romance and charm of the Hotel St. Francis remind one of a casual, European elegance. Its restaurant, Francisco's, has a reputation for consistent excellence, and offers an outstanding, if somewhat eclectic, Italian cuisine.

European trained
Executive Chef Rod Clark
claims that he could eat
dozens and dozens of
these mussels, they are so
good. The main thing is
to be sure that the
mussels are very fresh.

Steamed Mussels

½   teaspoon fresh basil, finely chopped
½   teaspoon fresh thyme, finely chopped
½   teaspoon fresh oregano, finely chopped
½   teaspoon fresh rosemary, finely chopped
1   teaspoon fresh shallots, finely chopped
½   cup Chardonnay wine
½   cup clam juice
12   mussels, rinsed, with beards removed
¼   cup unsalted butter, warmed to room temperature
4   pieces toasted garlic bread

In a large saucepan place all of the ingredients *(except for the mussels, butter, and bread)* and bring them to a boil.

Add the mussels and steam them for 3 to 4 minutes, or until the shells open. Remove the mussels from the saucepan and place them in a warm bowl.

Over medium heat reduce the broth by ½. Add the butter and stir it until it melts. Pour the sauce over the mussels.

Serve the mussels with the garlic bread.

serves 4

Minestrone

½   cup olive oil
½   cup garlic, minced
4   potatoes, diced
2   onions, diced
2   carrots, diced
½   medium head cabbage, diced
2   stalks celery, diced
½   head romaine lettuce, washed and chopped
2   cups spinach, washed, stems removed, and
    chopped
2   cups tomatoes, diced
½   cup fresh parsley, chopped
½   cup fresh oregano, chopped
1   cup fresh basil, chopped
1   cup cooked garbanzo beans, chopped
1   cup lima beans, cooked
1   cup ditalini *(short tubular pasta)*, uncooked
3   bay leaves
1   tablespoon black pepper
3   quarts chicken stock

In a large, heavy soup pot place the olive oil and heat it until it is hot.

Add the garlic, potatoes, onions, carrots, cabbage, celery, romaine, spinach, and tomatoes.

Cover the pot and shake it constantly for 5 minutes over medium heat.

Add the remainder of the ingredients. Simmer for 1 hour, or until they are done.

Refrigerate overnight. Reheat before serving.

serves 8

"Children usually like this soup because it has so many different things in it.....they really get a kick out of it. This is a good way for mothers to get their kids to eat vegetables."

"Minestrone means 'soup', but basically it is known as an Italian vegetable soup."

"If you have cooled the soup then you should let it simmer for fifteen minutes before serving. This is a good idea to do for any soup or stock that you reheat."

Tomato and Red Onion Salad with Spinach Basil Dressing

Tomato and Red Onion Salad

1   head bibb lettuce, washed and dried
2   beefsteak tomatoes, cut into ¼" slices
1   red onion, thinly sliced
1   jar marinated artichoke hearts, drained
8   strips anchovies
    Spinach Basil Dressing *(recipe follows)*

On individual salad plates place several leaves of the bibb lettuce.

Artfully arrange *(in this order)* the tomatoes, red onions, artichoke hearts, and anchovies.

Dribble the Spinach Basil Dressing over the top.

serves 4

Spinach Basil Dressing

1   cup fresh basil, ground
1   cup spinach, ground
1   cup olive oil
½   cup balsamic vinegar
    black pepper, freshly ground *(to taste)*

In a medium bowl place all of the ingredients and mix them together well.

"Be sure to use top quality anchovies. Try to go to an Italian market and buy the best that they have. Most people don't like anchovies, but that's because they've never had a good one. Also, you need top quality vine ripened tomatoes for this recipe."

"The dressing is like a simple basil pesto. The balsamic vinegar adds a lot of flavor, of course, and you can spend as much money on it as you want. I recently read that one bottle went for $3,000 at an auction!"

"Fresh ground pepper and tomatoes have an affinity for each other."

"You can use a lot of decorative imagination when you make this salad. There are a lot of colors to work with.....the red of the tomatoes, the green of the lettuce, the purple of the red onions, and the black of the pepper. This is a nice dish for entertaining because you can make it well in advance and it looks very attractive."

Cioppino

¼   cup olive oil
2   stalks celery, finely chopped
1½   large onions, finely chopped
3   tablespoons garlic, finely chopped
2   carrots, finely chopped
1   pound mushrooms, sliced
6   Roma tomatoes, blanched, peeled, and diced
3   cups tomato purée
2   cups red wine
1   cup Marsala wine
4   cups fish stock
1   bay leaf
2   whole cloves
1½   pounds crab legs
12   mussels
12   cherrystone clams
½   pound swordfish, cut into chunks
½   pound red snapper, cut into chunks
1   pound sea scallops
12   medium shrimp, peeled and deveined
1   teaspoon salt
1   teaspoon black pepper
1   teaspoon fresh oregano, chopped
1   teaspoon fresh thyme, chopped
3   tablespoons fresh basil, chopped
3   tablespoons parsley, chopped

In a very large, heavy soup pot place the olive oil and heat it on medium until it is hot. Add the celery, onions, garlic, carrots, and mushrooms.

Cover the pot with a lid and shake it over the heat for 5 minutes.

Add the Roma tomatoes, tomato purée, red wine, Marsala, fish stock, bay leaf, and cloves. Simmer everything slowly for 1½ hours.

Add the seafood, salt, and pepper. Return the soup to a simmer. Cook it for 10 minutes.

Add the oregano, thyme, basil, and parsley.

serves 8

"Cioppino is a fisherman's stew from San Francisco, not Italy. It's a conglomeration of different things, and twenty different people will make it twenty different ways."

"The most important thing is not to overcook the seafood. If you do, it will break up into little pieces and lose its identity. Then you will have a fish mush!"

Broiled Rosemary Lamb Steak

"I wanted to have a lamb dish other than lamb chops, which are outrageously expensive, as everyone knows. My cooks and I came up with this recipe."

"The reason why we go through the elaborate process of marinating it, pre-roasting it, slicing it, and re-marinating it, is to get it very tender by the time it hits the charbroiler."

"This lamb has a great flavor. Anybody who likes meat will like this recipe, even people who aren't too wild about lamb."

2	carrots, coarsely chopped
3	stalks celery, coarsely chopped
1	small onion, coarsely chopped
¼	cup garlic, minced
2	bunches fresh rosemary, chopped
¼	cup fresh basil, chopped
¼	cup fresh oregano, chopped
¼	cup fresh parsley, chopped
1	tablespoon salt
¼	cup sugar
4	cups olive oil
2	cups red wine vinegar
1	6 pound leg of lamb, boned, rolled, and tied

In a large glass or stainless steel bowl place all of the ingredients *(except for the lamb)* and mix them together.

Add the leg of lamb to the marinade. Cover, and refrigerate it for 3 days.

Remove the lamb and pat it dry.

Preheat the oven to 400°.

Place the lamb in a roasting pan and cook it for 45 minutes. Let it cool.

Slice the lamb into steaks.

Place the lamb steaks back into the marinade. Cover and refrigerate them overnight.

Charbroil the steaks to the desired doneness.

serves 6-8

Timaballo Eggplant Casserole

2	eggplants, cut into ¼" slices
1	tablespoon salt
2	red bell peppers
2	green bell peppers
2	yellow bell peppers
1	tablespoon olive oil
1	tablespoon butter
½	pound mushrooms, sliced
¾	cup vegetable oil *(or as needed)*
1½	cups flour
½	teaspoon salt
¼	teaspoon pepper
4	eggs, lightly beaten
	Marinara Sauce *(recipe on next page)*
½	pound Fontina cheese, thinly sliced

Place the eggplant slices in a colander and sprinkle them with the 1 tablespoon of salt. Let them sit for 1½ hours or until the liquid has drained out.

Remove the eggplant slices and gently squeeze them dry with a terry cloth towel.

Lightly coat the skins of the bell peppers with the olive oil. Place them on an open flame and roast them until they are black all over.

In a large bowl place the roasted bell peppers. Cover the top tightly with saran wrap, and let them sit until they are cool. Peel and seed the peppers. Cut them into julienned strips.

In a medium skillet place the butter and melt it over a medium heat. Add the mushrooms and sauté them for 5 minutes, or until they are tender. Set them aside.

In a large, heavy skillet place the vegetable oil and heat it until it is very hot.

Dredge the eggplant slices in the flour mixed with the salt and pepper. Dip them in the beaten eggs, and fry them on both sides until they are tender and golden brown.

(continued on next page)

"We needed a vegetarian item for our menu, and so I experimented with a variety of things that we already had cut, chopped, and prepared in our kitchen.....and I came up with this. It's like an eggplant Parmesan, but not as rich, and the roasted peppers really make it different."

"To roast the peppers you must do it over an open flame. If you don't have a gas stove then use a barbecue. If you don't have a barbecue then go to a friend's house and borrow his!"

"Put the peppers directly on the fire. In our kitchen we put the grate as close to the flame as possible. Then we turn the flame up to high, and squirt olive oil all over the peppers with a squirter. Just cook them until they are black."

"One thing.....be sure that the oil is very hot when you sauté the eggplant. Otherwise it will soak up too much of the oil."

In a buttered casserole dish make layers *(in this order)* of the Marinara Sauce, ½ of the eggplant slices, the sautéed mushrooms, the julienned bell peppers, the Marinara Sauce, the other ½ of the eggplant slices, the Marinara Sauce, and the Fontina cheese.

Preheat the oven to 350°. Bake the casserole for 40 minutes, or until the cheese is bubbly and brown.

serves 6

Marinara Sauce

1	cup olive oil
1	medium onion, minced
1	cup mushrooms, minced
1	cup celery, minced
1	cup carrots, minced
1	cup leeks, minced
4	cups tomatoes, diced
2	cups tomato purée
3	cups water
½	cup garlic, minced
2	tablespoons fresh thyme, finely chopped
2	tablespoons fresh oregano, finely chopped
2	tablespoons fresh basil, finely chopped
2	bay leaves
½	cup parsley, minced
2	tablespoons sugar
2	tablespoons salt
1	teaspoon black pepper
1	cup dry red wine

In a large, heavy saucepan place the oil and heat it on medium until it is very hot. Add the onion, mushrooms, celery, carrots, and leeks. Cover the pot with a lid and shake it over the heat for 5 minutes.

Add the diced tomatoes, tomato purée, and water. Bring the sauce to a boil and then simmer it for 1 hour.

Add the remainder of the ingredients and simmer the sauce for 45 minutes. Let the sauce cool. Cover the pot and refrigerate the sauce overnight.

"I think that a good Marinara should have a lot of vegetables in it, minced very fine, so you don't have to cook it for very long. I'm not a believer in cooking a Marinara sauce for long hours, because I think that the nutrients are lost and the color isn't as nice."

"The sauce should be fairly thick. You can add more water if necessary. You can use chicken stock if you prefer, but I like to use plain water so that it is a pure vegetarian dish."

Three Nut Chocolate Rum Tart with Almond Butter Crust

Three Nut Chocolate Rum Tart

3	eggs
½	cup sugar
1	pinch salt
1	cup dark corn syrup
½	cup Myers rum
¼	cup butter, melted
1	9" pie round Almond Butter Crust *(recipe on next page)*
1	cup bittersweet chocolate, chopped into small bits
½	cup pecans, chopped
½	cup piñons *(or pine nuts)*, chopped
½	cup almonds, chopped

In a medium bowl place the eggs, sugar, salt, corn syrup, rum, and butter. Beat them together until the ingredients are well mixed.

Place the raw Almond Butter Crust in a 9" pie shell.

Sprinkle the chocolate bits over the bottom of the pie shell. Sprinkle the pecans, piñons, and almonds over the chocolate bits.

Pour the egg mixture into the pie shell.

Preheat the oven to 375°.

Bake the tart for 45 minutes to 1 hour, or until it is done.

serves 6

"I think that this is the easiest thing in the world to make, but I don't know how many times people have messed it up, and I can't figure out why! It's very similar to a pecan pie, which people mess up, too. Maybe it's because they don't use enough eggs.....I don't know."

"You can use any kind of dark rum, but Myers has the best flavor in rums that are affordable."

"Use the best bittersweet chocolate you can find. To get the chocolate into small bits you can wrap it up in a towel and hit it with a hammer, or back over it with your car. One time I had to break up two hundred pounds of chocolate, so we put it into plastic bags, and then put those in gunny sacks, and backed over them with a truck. It worked great!"

Almond Butter Crust

1	tablespoon vanilla
½	teaspoon salt
4	cups sifted pastry flour
1½	cups blanched, peeled almonds, ground to a meal
1½	pounds unsalted butter, softened
3	eggs

In a medium bowl place the vanilla, salt, flour, and almonds. Mix the ingredients together.

Add the butter and eggs and work them in until the entire mixture forms a ball.

Cover the dough and let it sit overnight.

Roll out the dough on a well floured cutting board.

Extra dough may be frozen.

"This recipe should make enough for two or three pie shells. It's a very rich dough and can be used for cookies, or any pastry. There is a lot of butter in it, so the dough should be sticky. When you are working the dough you should add a little more flour, and this is where one's personal skill comes in.....it takes practice to get it right."

Oldest Church in the U.S.A., Santa Fe, New Mexico

Fresca

Fresca means *"fresh"*, and that is the perfect word to describe this delightful restaurant. Fresh in its use of ingredients, and fresh in its style of cooking, this restaurant is earning a growing reputation for serving a cuisine that is both innovative and tasty.

Owner Susie Palazzo enthusiastically praises the talent of her chef, Juan Contreras, and credits him for the delicious recipes offered here.

Brie Vinaigrette

¼   cup olive oil
1   pound French Brie, cut into 8 pieces, and brought to room temperature
4   eggs, beaten
1   cup bread crumbs
2   cups olive oil
1   cup balsamic vinegar
3   teaspoons fresh parsley, chopped fine
2   shallots, chopped fine
¼   teaspoon fresh ground black pepper

In a large, heavy skillet place the ¼ cup of olive oil and heat it on medium until it is hot.

Dip the Brie into the eggs, and then the bread crumbs. Do this several times, until a thick crust is formed.

Fry the Brie on both sides until it is a golden brown.

In a small bowl whisk together the vinegar, the 2 cups of olive oil, parsley, shallots, and pepper.

Pour some of the vinaigrette in small individual serving bowls. Place two pieces of the fried Brie on top.

serves 4

Eggplant Capponata

1	eggplant, peeled and cut into ¼" slices
¼	cup vegetable oil
½	green bell pepper, seeded, washed, and julienned
½	red bell pepper, seeded, washed, and julienned
½	yellow bell pepper, seeded, washed, and julienned
¼	medium onion, thinly sliced
12	Greek black olives
2	teaspoons capers
3	teaspoons olive oil
¼	cup balsamic vinegar
¼	teaspoon salt
¼	teaspoon pepper, freshly ground

Brush both sides of the eggplant slices with the vegetable oil.

Preheat the oven to 400°.

Place the eggplant slices on a cookie sheet. Bake them for 10 minutes, or until they are lightly browned and tender.

Cut the roasted eggplant into 1" triangles.

In a medium bowl place the eggplant, bell peppers, onion, olives, and capers.

In a small bowl place the olive oil, vinegar, salt, and pepper and whisk them together.

Add the dressing to the eggplant mixture and toss everything together well.

Let the ingredients marinate for several hours.

serves 6

Juan says, *"This is a classic Italian recipe that we altered somewhat..... particularly by using the balsamic vinegar, which has a really nice, sweet flavor."*

"This dish is nice and light, but very tasty. You are able to distinguish the individual flavors of all the ingredients. It makes a good appetizer, or you can serve it as a vegetable side dish. It's especially nice to serve in the summertime."

Pizza Veracruz

1	tablespoon olive oil
7	cloves garlic, chopped
¼	cup parsley, chopped
6	cups crushed tomatoes, fresh or canned
¼	cup water
4	teaspoons oregano
1	teaspoon salt
1	teaspoon pepper
6	8" pizza crusts
¼	cup squid, cleaned and cut into rings
½	pound medium shrimp, shelled and deveined
1	green onion, thinly sliced
3	cups Monterey Jack cheese, grated
1	medium tomato, diced
6	tablespoons cheddar cheese, grated
1	pinch oregano

In a large pot place the olive oil and heat it on medium until it is hot. Add the garlic and parsley and sauté them for 2 minutes.

Add the tomatoes and water, and stir them in.

Add the oregano, salt, and pepper, and stir them in. Cook over low heat for 4 minutes.

Place the pizza crusts on 2 oiled baking sheets.

Spread the sauce over the crusts.

In this order, evenly add the squid, shrimp, green onion, Jack cheese, and tomato. Sprinkle the top with the cheddar cheese and the oregano.

Preheat the oven to 500°. Bake the pizzas for 5 minutes, or until the fish is done and the cheese is bubbly.

serves 6

"Susie, the owner, came up with the idea for this recipe, and we worked out the exact proportions and the presentation. People love it, and it has proved to be one of our most popular dishes. In fact, even people who don't like squid will eat this pizza and think it's good."

"This pizza doesn't have a strong seafood flavor. The squid is mild, and we use a Black Tiger Shrimp, which is probably the best shrimp you can find anywhere. They turn a nice pink color and look good on the pizza. The green onions and fresh tomatoes go well with the seafood."

"If one cup of sauce per pizza seems like too much, use a little less."

Shrimp á la Mangione

3	cups rice
6	cups water
6	cloves garlic, chopped
2	tablespoons fresh ginger, peeled and chopped
2	teaspoons fresh parsley, chopped
¼	cup honey
¼	cup sesame oil
½	cup vegetable oil
1	pound large shrimp, peeled and deveined
1	lemon, cut into wedges

Cook the rice in the 6 cups of water.

In a food processor place the garlic, ginger, and parsley, and mince them.

Transfer the mixture to a small saucepan.

Add the honey and sesame oil, and mix everything together well. Cook the sauce for 1 minute, or until it is heated.

In a large, heavy, skillet place the vegetable oil and heat it until it is hot. Add the shrimp and sauté them until they are done *(pink and firm clear through)*.

Place the hot, cooked rice on a platter. Spread the shrimp over the top.

Pour the heated sauce over the shrimp and rice.

serves 4

"This is an Indian recipe that we adapted. We made it more Italian by adding the cilantro and honey. The original dish called for bacon, which we eliminated, but if it sounds good to you, go ahead and add some (just brown it first)."

"Our customers love this dish. It's very easy to make, and has a very interesting flavor."

"Just make sure that you don't let the garlic get brown. Keep it white when you sauté it.....it's much better that way."

Chicken Breast with Goat Cheese and Adobo Sauce

Chicken Breast with Goat Cheese

6	chicken breasts, skinned and boned
¾	cup goat cheese
¼	cup whipping cream
¼	teaspoon salt
¼	teaspoon white or black pepper, freshly ground
	Adobo Sauce *(recipe follows)*

Broil the chicken breasts until they are done.

In a small pot place the goat cheese and the whipping cream.

Heat on low while stirring constantly, until the cheese is melted. Add the salt and pepper.

Spread the Adobo Sauce over a serving platter. Place the chicken breasts on top of the sauce. Pour the cheese sauce over the top of the chicken.

serves 6

Adobo Sauce

1	tablespoon oil
6	ancho chiles, finely chopped
1	teaspoon thyme
4	cloves garlic, finely chopped
2	cups chicken stock
2	teaspoons cornstarch, mixed with 3 teaspoons of cold water
2	teaspoons rice vinegar
¼	teaspoon salt
¼	teaspoon pepper

In a medium saucepan place the oil. Heat it on medium until it is hot. Add the chiles, thyme, and garlic, and sauté them for 2 minutes. Add the chicken stock and bring it to a boil.

Add the cornstarch and water mixture to the chicken stock and stir for 2 to 3 minutes, until the sauce thickens. Stir in the vinegar, salt, and pepper.

"I love goat cheese! I grew up in old Mexico and used to visit my grandmother who had a farm in the center of the country. She had goats and that's where I got my taste for it."

"Basically, this is a recipe from Mexico, although we have changed it somewhat. We took a classic adobo sauce and added some thyme and rice vinegar, which give it a slightly sweet flavor. You can still taste the chile, but it's not so hot that you have to worry about burning your mouth. So, when you eat it, you can relax and just enjoy it!"

Coho Salmon with Thai Green Sauce

Coho Salmon

6   **8-ounce Coho salmon fillets**
      Thai Green Sauce *(recipe follows)*
2   **tablespoons fresh cilantro, chopped**

Preheat the oven to 400°.

Place the salmon fillets on an oiled cookie sheet and bake them for approximately 8 minutes, or until they are done. *(Turn the salmon once after 4 minutes.)*

Pour the Thai Green Sauce over the top.

Sprinkle the cilantro on top of the sauce.

serves 6

Thai Green Sauce

1½   **tablespoons butter**
½   **teaspoon cinnamon**
½   **teaspoon cumin**
2   **cloves garlic, minced**
2   **Anaheim chiles, finely diced**
¼   **medium onion, diced**
1   **cup whipping cream**
      salt *(to taste)*
      pepper *(to taste)*

In a small saucepan place the butter and heat it on medium until it is melted.

Add the cinnamon, cumin, garlic, chiles, and onion. Sauté them for 1 minute.

Reduce the heat to low and add the cream, salt, and pepper. Stir and cook the sauce until the cream lightly bubbles.

"We like to read a lot of recipes and then try them out. But usually they don't work to our satisfaction, so we experiment and play around with them. In this case we had to cut down on the cumin, because it is a very strong spice and it was overpowering the other ingredients. Also, we substituted a milder chile, the Anaheim. When you sauté chiles they get hotter! The Anaheim, when sautéed, is very nice.....not too hot."

"We work with all kinds of fish and make lots of different sauces for them. In this recipe the sauce goes perfectly with the salmon!"

"Keep a close eye on the salmon when you bake it. I don't like it overdone, although some people prefer it that way. Personally, I would check it every few minutes."

Linzer Torte

1	**cup sugar**
3	**tablespoons fresh ginger, peeled and chopped**
¾	**cup almonds, shelled and chopped**
¾	**cup piñon nuts**
1½	**cups sifted flour**
½	**cup butter, melted**
2	**teaspoons cinnamon**
2	**eggs**
½	**lime, juiced**
4	**cups raspberry preserves**

In a food processor place the sugar, ginger, nuts, and flour. Mix everything together.

Add the melted butter, cinnamon, eggs, and lime juice to the food processor. Blend everything together well.

Pat the dough into a buttered, 10" pie pan. Have the dough go up the sides of the pan.

Using a pastry tube, carefully place the raspberry preserves in a crisscross pattern on top of the dough.

Preheat the oven to 350°.

Bake the torte for 35 minutes, until it is nicely browned.

serves 6

"By adding piñon nuts and substituting fresh ginger for ground cloves, we altered a rather classic recipe. You can use any kinds of preserves that you want."

"At Fresca we offer a lot of tapas (appetizers) as well as main dishes. We try to make foods from all over the world.....a little bit of everything."

"Everyone at the restaurant really works together, and we all participate in the creation of new recipes. We are always trying new things out on each other. This way we can keep our customers interested, because we offer new dishes all the time."

Adobe House on Canyon Road, Santa Fe, New Mexico

Garfield Grill

Interesting, gourmet, homemade cooking is a good description of the cuisine offered at the Garfield Grill. From a menu that changes weekly, customers can enjoy healthy, delicious meals that are prepared with the freshest ingredients possible.

Recipes

Grapefruit, Spinach,
and Bleu Cheese Salad

Smoked Trout in
Cornmeal Crêpes
Broiled Tomato Salsa

Pork Tenderloin with
Mustard Greens

Pork Glace

Mexican Drunken Shrimp

Shrimp Fumet

Sautéed Chicken with
Artichoke Hearts and
Marsala Cream Sauce

Fresh Ginger Cheesecake

Cindy Turner and her husband, Jim, do all of the cooking and recipe creating for this very popular restaurant. Cindy says, *"You MUST use a Texas ruby red grapefruit.....otherwise, don't make this dish!"*

Grapefruit, Spinach, and Bleu Cheese Salad

1	bunch spinach, washed, stems removed, and cut into ¾" wide strips
4	Texas ruby red grapefruit, peeled and sectioned, with membranes removed
3	ounces Danish bleu cheese, crumbled
½	cup walnut oil
¼	cup raspberry vinegar

On individual salad plates place the spinach.

Artfully arrange the grapefruit slices on top.

Sprinkle on the bleu cheese.

In a small bowl place the oil and vinegar and mix them together.

Drizzle the dressing over the salad.

serves 4

Smoked Trout in Cornmeal Crêpes with Broiled Tomato Salsa

Smoked Trout

2	cups water
1	cup brown sugar
½	cup rock salt
½	cup kosher salt
2	8-ounce boneless trout
	mesquite chips, soaked in water
4	cornmeal crêpes *(recipe follows)*
	Broiled Tomato Salsa *(recipe on next page)*

In a medium bowl place the water, brown sugar, rock salt, and kosher salt. Mix them together. Add the fish and let them soak in the brine for 6 hours.

Remove the fish, rinse them thoroughly, and dry them.

Smoke the fish in a smoker with the soaked mesquite chips for at least 1 hour, or until they are done but not dried out. The fish also may be cooked in a covered barbecue. Place the soaked mesquite chips on top of the coals so that they smoke. Do not place the fish directly over the coals. Replenish the mesquite chips as needed.

Break up the smoked trout into bite size pieces and place them in the center of each warm cornmeal crêpe.

Fold the crêpes over and cover them with the Broiled Tomato Salsa.

serves 4

Cornmeal Crêpes

¼	cup yellow cornmeal
2	tablespoons flour, sifted
2	medium eggs
½	cup milk
2	tablespoons butter, melted
1	pinch salt
1	tablespoon vegetable oil

(continued on next page)

"If you don't want to deal with smoking your own trout, it is always possible to find smoked trout in the grocery store. In fact, you can use any smoked fish, if you want. If you do smoke it yourself, the trout should be done, but still slightly moist. If you are using a barbecue, make sure that your coals are good and hot. And make sure that your chips keep smoking. Keep adding more chips as they burn up."

"Our customers love this dish. In fact, one woman told me it was the best thing she ever put into her mouth. Now that's a real compliment!"

"This is a variation on any crêpe recipe. The cornmeal adds a nice Southwestern flavor."

In a medium bowl place the cornmeal and the flour. Mix them together.

Add the eggs and mix them in.

Slowly add the milk and mix it in.

Add the butter and salt, and mix them in.

Let the batter sit for 30 minutes.

In a seasoned crêpe pan place the oil and heat it on low until the pan is warm.

Pour out the oil and wipe the pan with a paper towel, so that there is a light film of oil left.

Pour in 2 tablespoons of the batter and roll it around so that it coats the bottom of the pan.

Cook the crêpes for 1 minute over low heat and then turn them over. Cook them for 45 seconds and then place them on individual serving plates. Wipe the pan with the oiled paper towel if necessary.

serves 4

Broiled Tomato Salsa

3   large, ripe tomatoes, stems removed
1   small onion, quartered
1   clove garlic
2   serrano chiles, seeded
¼   teaspoon salt
1½ tablespoons vegetable oil

Preheat the oven to broil.

Place the tomatoes in a baking pan. Broil them for 15 minutes, or until they are brownish black and the juice begins to caramelize.

In a food processor place the broiled tomatoes, onion, garlic, chiles, and salt. Blend them together.

In a large skillet place the oil and heat it to medium. Add the salsa and cook it for 3 minutes while stirring constantly.

"If you are as unlucky as I am, the first crêpes won't come out right, so you need some extra batter for practice. It always takes me two or three to get going!"

"The broiling of the tomatoes gives the salsa a nice, dark, intense flavor. After the tomatoes are broiled be sure to scrape out all of the juices and anything that is stuck to the pan, and add it to the salsa."

"You can leave in the seeds of the chile if you want, but the salsa will be much hotter. I would advise using rubber gloves when handling the hot chiles. Be careful not to rub your eyes!"

Pork Tenderloin with Mustard Greens

½   **cup olive oil**
1   **red onion, thinly sliced**
2   **tablespoons fresh sage, chopped**
2   **pounds lean pork tenderloin, trimmed, cut into 12 pieces, and flattened slightly**
    salt (to taste)
    pepper (to taste)
¼   **cup Pork Glace** (recipe on next page)
1   **cup water**
1   **large bunch mustard greens, washed, dried, and chopped**

In a small bowl place the olive oil, red onion slices, and sage. Let them marinate for at least 2 hours.

Season the pork with the salt and pepper.

Grill (or sauté in olive oil) the pork until the desired doneness is achieved. Set the pork aside and keep it warm.

In a medium saucepan place the Pork Glace and the water. Add the mustard greens and simmer them for 1 to 2 minutes, or until they are wilted.

In a small skillet place 1 tablespoon of the olive oil marinade and heat it until it is hot. Add the onions and sauté them for 2 to 3 minutes over medium heat, or until they are tender.

Place the wilted mustard greens on a serving platter. Cover them with the pork slices, and then top with the onions.

Pour some of the remaining pork stock over the top.

serves 4

"I view this recipe as a southern dish. Basically I just combined ingredients that I thought would go well together. It makes a nice, summer meat dish because we serve the pork warm, not hot. In the hot months of the year I like to offer cold and warm dishes, as well as hot food."

"The mustard greens have a pretty spicy taste. Dandelion greens also work well, and we will use them when they are available."

"When we flatten the pork we do it between two pieces of saran wrap. The pork should be about one quarter inch thick when you are done."

Pork Glace

5	**pounds pork bones**
3	**onions, quartered**
4	**carrots**
2	**stalks celery**
1	**bunch parsley**
3	**bay leaves**
2	**teaspoons thyme**
	water

In a large, heavy saucepan place all of the ingredients and cover them with water.

Bring the ingredients to a boil and then simmer for 8 hours.

Strain the stock and pour it into a bowl.

Cover and refrigerate the stock until the fat congeals on the top. Scrape off the fat.

In a medium saucepan place the stock and cook it until it is reduced to 1 cup.

"We use a lot of meat and fish stocks in our recipes, which we make ourselves in the restaurant. We like the intensity of flavor that the glace gives."

"If you want to make a Chicken Glace you can use the same recipe. Just substitute one large stewing chicken for the pork bones."

Mexican Drunken Shrimp

2	**pounds medium shrimp, peeled and deveined** *(save the shells)*
12	**ounces Mexican beer**
8	**slices bacon**
1	**large onion, chopped**
2	**tablespoons butter**
2	**cloves garlic, minced**
2	**jalapeño peppers, minced**
	salt *(to taste)*
	pepper *(to taste)*
2	**cups Shrimp Fumet** *(recipe on next page)*
2	**cups cooked white rice**

In a medium bowl place the shrimp and the beer. Let them soak for 30 minutes. Drain the shrimp.

In a large skillet fry the bacon and then drain it on paper towels. Let the bacon cool, and then crumble it. Save one tablespoon of the bacon grease.

Heat the bacon grease on medium until it is hot. Add the onions and sauté them for 2 minutes. Drain the fat from the onions.

In a large skillet place the butter, onions, garlic, and chile peppers. Sauté the ingredients for 1 minute on medium.

Add the shrimp, salt, and pepper. Sauté them for 2 to 3 minutes, or until the shrimp is just cooked.

Add the Shrimp Fumet and cook for 2 minutes.

Add the fried bacon and serve immediately over white rice.

serves 4

"This recipe was inspired by a similar dish that we ate in Mexico. We enjoyed it very much and so after we returned home we tried to recreate it, and this is what we came up with."

"We grow our own fresh herbs here, right behind the restaurant. We also try to grow some of our own vegetables. Otherwise we make an effort to buy the vegetables directly from local farmers."

Shrimp Fumet

shrimp shells *(left over from the Mexican Drunken Shrimp, recipe on preceding page)*
½ **small onion, quartered**
2 **carrots, quartered**
1 **bay leaf**
¼ **bunch parsley**
1 **cup white wine**
3 **cups water**

In a medium saucepan place all of the ingredients. Cook them over medium heat for 30 minutes.

Strain the broth and let it cool.

Sautéed Chicken with Artichoke Hearts and Marsala Cream Sauce

4	tablespoons butter
1¼	pounds chicken breasts, skinned, boned, and cut into 1" cubes
16	large mushrooms, quartered
1	box frozen artichoke hearts, cooked and chopped
12	plum tomatoes, peeled, seeded, and chopped
3	tablespoons dry Marsala
2	cups heavy cream
2	tablespoons Chicken Glace (use the Pork Glace recipe on page 97, except substitute a large stewing chicken for the pork bones)
	salt (to taste)
	pepper (to taste)
1	teaspoon fresh tarragon leaves

In a large, heavy skillet place the butter and melt it over a medium heat. Add the chicken and sauté it for 2 minutes, or until it is almost done.

Add the mushrooms and sauté them for 2 minutes.

Add the artichoke hearts, tomatoes, Marsala, cream, Chicken Glace, salt, and pepper. Cook until the sauce thickens slightly.

Garnish with the fresh tarragon.

serves 4

"This is a combination of ingredients that go together very well. It's a nice, simple recipe that always gets rave reviews."

"Don't cook the sauce for too long. If it gets too thick then add a little water.... it should be the consistency of a heavy cream."

Fresh Ginger Cheesecake

½   **cup graham cracker crumbs, crushed**
1   **tablespoon sugar**
1   **tablespoon butter, melted**
¼   **teaspoon ground ginger**
6   **ounces cream cheese, softened**
½   **cup sugar**
2   **egg yolks**
½   **cup sour cream**
2   **tablespoons flour**
1   **teaspoon ginger extract**
½   **teaspoon vanilla**
2   **tablespoons fresh ginger, grated**
1   **pinch salt**
2   **egg whites, beaten until stiff**
24   **fresh strawberries, stemmed and halved**

In a medium bowl place the graham cracker crumbs, sugar, butter, and ground ginger. Mix them together.

Press the mixture into the bottom of a buttered 7" springform pan.

Preheat the oven to 375° and bake the crust for 10 minutes. Let it cool.

In a medium bowl place the cream cheese and sugar, and beat them together.

Add the egg yolks and beat them in.

Add the sour cream, flour, ginger extract, vanilla, fresh ginger, and salt. Beat the ingredients together.

Fold the beaten egg whites into the cream cheese mixture.

Pour the mixture into the prepared crust.

Preheat the oven to 325° and bake the cheesecake for 1 hour. Turn the heat off and let it remain in the oven for 40 minutes.

Cool the cheesecake to room temperature and then refrigerate it until it is chilled.

Garnish with the fresh strawberries.

serves 4

"This is a wonderful recipe that I've worked with quite a bit, changing things around each time. Like so many other people these days I've gotten into using fresh ginger a lot."

"The cheesecake is good because it is not as heavy as some are.....it has a nice light, airy quality to it. And, you definitely get the bite of the ginger."

"Sometimes people are a little apprehensive about eating a cheesecake with ginger in it, but always, if they can be coaxed into trying it, they really like it."

Church Wall Detail, Lincoln, New Mexico

Grant Corner Inn

An exquisite jewel nestled in downtown Santa Fe, the Grant Corner Inn is a charming bed and breakfast Colonial manor home. Serving only breakfast and brunch, the attention to detail is reflected both in the beautifully appointed rooms and in the luscious, homemade meals.

Recipes

Raspberry Fizz

Grant Corner Inn
Orange Frappé

Frittata Burina

Crab Brunch Squares
Red Pepper Cream Sauce

Cheese Chorizo Strata
Pat's Chunky Salsa

Green Chile Crêpes

Cheesy Bulgarian Potatoes
and Sausage

Sautéed Cinnamon Bananas

Super Carrot Coffee Cake

The "Innkeepers in Residence" are owners Louise Stewart and her husband, Pat (as well as daughter "Bumpy"). Louise also has written her own recipe book, *The Grant Corner Inn Breakfast & Brunch Cookbook.* (See page 300.)

Raspberry Fizz

½   cup fresh or frozen raspberries
½   cup apricot nectar, chilled
5   ice cubes
1   tablespoon powdered sugar
½   teaspoon lemon juice, freshly squeezed
¼   cup club soda, chilled
2   lime slices

In a blender place the raspberries, apricot nectar, and ice. Blend on high until the mixture is smooth.

Add the powdered sugar and the lemon juice. Blend for 30 seconds.

Stir in the club soda.

Pour the drink into frosted, stemmed goblets. Garnish with a slice of lime.

serves 2

Grant Corner Inn Orange Frappé

4	cups orange juice, freshly squeezed
1	lemon, juiced
1	large banana, chopped
6	strawberries
¼	cup whipping cream
6	ice cubes
12	leaves fresh mint

Place all of the ingredients *(except for the mint)* in a blender and purée them.

Pour the mixture into iced goblets. Garnish with mint leaves.

serves 6

"At Grant Corner Inn we serve a frappé each day, and it's always a different flavor.....cranberry, apple, banana, pear, apricot, peach, plum, kiwi – whatever! This is the perfect way to use up whatever fruits are a little bit overdone."

"Always refrigerate your stemmed goblets. My feeling is, for the frappé to be right, it must be icy, icy cold.....so much so that you get a headache!"

"My sister, Helen, used to make one of these every single morning when we were growing up in the fifties. She was extremely interested in health foods and yoga at the young age of twelve, long before it became fashionable. She would put wheat germ and a lot of strange stuff into them. So, that's how I got into making these blended drinks, which are one of our best known trademarks."

Frittata Burina

½	15-ounce can artichoke hearts or bottoms, quartered and drained
¼	cup good olive oil
1	clove garlic, minced
1	tablespoon red wine vinegar
2	ounces salami, thinly sliced and julienned
½	cup black olives, pitted
½	cup fresh or frozen peas
1½	cup Mozzarella cheese, grated
6	eggs, lightly beaten

In a small bowl place the artichoke hearts, olive oil, garlic, and vinegar. Marinate the artichoke hearts for ½ hour at room temperature.

Remove the artichoke hearts and pour the marinade into a medium skillet.

Heat the marinade to medium and add the salami. Sauté it for 1 minute and then turn off the heat.

Add the artichokes, olives, and peas, and stir them in. Spread the mixture to evenly cover the bottom of the pan.

Sprinkle ½ of the Mozzarella cheese over the top. Pour the eggs over the mixture.

Cover the skillet with a lid. Cook the frittata over a medium-low heat until the eggs are almost set.

Sprinkle the remaining cheese over the top. Cover the skillet with the lid and cook for 3 minutes.

Turn the frittata out onto a plate and cut it into 4 pieces.

serves 4

"This is one of my own inventions.....I just put in all of my favorite little foods. It sort of reminds me of an Italian antipasto salad that you are making into a brunch dish with eggs."

"You want to make certain that the artichoke hearts are really drained well. You should squeeze them dry with some paper towels."

"This dish would be good with a sauce or some sour cream, flavored with fresh herbs. But, the frittata has such a complicated flavor that the sauce should be simple."

Crab Brunch Squares
with Red Pepper Cream Sauce

Crab Brunch Squares

4	eggs
2⅔	cups milk
¾	teaspoon Dijon mustard
6	ounces Brie, rind removed and cut into ¼" cubes
½	cup black olives, sliced
1	small onion, finely chopped
1	teaspoon Worcestershire sauce
3½	cups cooked rice
1	pound crab meat
	Red Pepper Cream Sauce *(recipe on next page)*
	paprika
2	tablespoons fresh chives, chopped

In a large bowl place the eggs, milk, and mustard. Beat the ingredients together.

Add the Brie, olives, onion, Worcestershire Sauce, rice, and crab. Stir the ingredients together.

Pour the mixture into a greased 9" by 13" baking pan.

Preheat the oven to 325°.

Bake for 40 to 45 minutes, or until a knife inserted into the center comes out clean.

Cut into squares and serve with the Red Pepper Cream Sauce.

Sprinkle with the paprika and garnish with the chives.

serves 10

"I created this recipe, but I can't remember exactly how it evolved. To be perfectly honest (and I probably shouldn't admit this in a cookbook) I don't care much for shellfish. However, I knew I was in the great minority here, and that we needed some good recipes. So, this is one of the results, and we get rave reviews on it."

"The rice and egg batter makes this nice and light and fluffy. You can also prepare it ahead of time, which is handy if you are serving it for a brunch or something."

"I love this sauce! It's so easy to make, and it's terrific on omelettes and frittatas."

"When I wrote my cookbook I wanted it to be a personal statement of what my family and I are all about. We got so many requests from our guests for recipes that we served at breakfast, that we were constantly xeroxing copies of our little index cards. So, I thought, 'Gee, wouldn't it be easier just to put all of these into a book?' So, now when someone asks for a recipe we just whip it out and say, 'Here it is, in our cookbook!'"

Red Pepper Cream Sauce

4	tablespoons unsalted butter
1	large ripe red pepper, seeded and diced
¼	cup thinly sliced green onion
¼	cup all-purpose flour
¼	teaspoon salt
¼	teaspoon white pepper
1¾	cups milk
3	teaspoons fresh lemon juice
2	tablespoons fresh chives, chopped

In a medium saucepan place the butter and melt it over medium heat. Add the red pepper and green onion, and sauté them for 2 minutes.

Add the flour and sauté it for 3 minutes on low heat.

Blend in the salt and white pepper.

Gradually whisk in the milk and lemon juice. Cook for 1 minute.

Pour the sauce into a blender and purée it for 2 minutes, or until the peppers and onions are blended.

Cheese Chorizo Strata
with Pat's Chunky Salsa

Cheese Chorizo Strata

¼   **pound chorizo sausage, cooked and drained**
¼   **cup mild green chiles, chopped**
¼   **fresh jalapeño pepper, minced**
¼   **pound Monterey Jack cheese, cut into ¼" cubes**
3   **cups French bread cubes**
4   **eggs**
¾   **teaspoon cumin**
½   **teaspoon salt**
½   **teaspoon pepper**
2⅔   **cups milk**
½   **stick butter, melted**
     Pat's Chunky Salsa *(recipe on next page)*

In a well greased casserole dish place the sausage and spread it evenly over the bottom.

Add *(in this order)* the chiles, jalapeños, cheese, and bread cubes.

In a medium bowl place the eggs and whisk them together. Add the cumin, salt, pepper and milk. Whisk everything together.

Drizzle the melted butter over the casserole mixture.

Pour the milk mixture into the casserole dish.

Cover, and refrigerate overnight.

Preheat the oven to 300°.

Place the casserole dish in a pan of hot water and bake it for 1½ hours, or until it is puffed and set.

Serve with Pat's Chunky Salsa.

serves 4

"Stratas are really easy to do, and they can also be made ahead of time. We make them by adding all different kinds of things.....mushrooms, chiles, or whatever else sounds good. You can use tortillas instead of bread cubes, which really taste wonderful!"

"Be sure not to overcook this, or it will come out rubbery. Bake it until the egg is just done and then serve it immediately. Put a dollop of sour cream on top if you feel like it."

Pat's Chunky Salsa

2	large firm tomatoes, coarsely chopped
⅔	cup green chiles, roasted, peeled, and chopped
½	cup tomato sauce
1	small onion, finely chopped
3	tablespoons cilantro, finely chopped
2	tablespoons parsley, finely chopped
2	teaspoons red wine vinegar
1	teaspoon fresh lemon juice
1	small hot dried chile, crushed

In a medium porcelain or glass mixing bowl place all of the ingredients. Mix them together.

Let the salsa stand for 2 hours at room temperature.

"Pat has been making his chunky salsa for many, many years – ever since we first met, and everyone has always loved it. He uses a lot of fresh cilantro, and sometimes he sneaks in different things that I don't know about. But this recipe is pretty much the usual way he makes it."

"You can use fresh jalapeños to give it a real zap. Be sure that your lemon juice is fresh. The canned tomato sauce gives it a slight soupiness and you may not want to use all of it. I recommend putting everything together first, to see how the consistency is. Then add the tomato sauce if you think it needs it."

Green Chile Crêpes

½ pound lean ground beef
½ medium onion, coarsely chopped
¼ cup celery, diced
1 clove garlic, minced
1 tomato, diced
1 cup chicken broth
½ pound mild green chiles, roasted, peeled, and chopped
1 tablespoon cornstarch, dissolved in ¼ cup cold water
2 tablespoons cilantro, finely chopped
1 teaspoon basil
1 teaspoon oregano
½ teaspoon salt
½ teaspoon pepper
12 eggs, scrambled
6 crêpes *(see page 72 or 94)*
½ cup Monterey Jack cheese, grated
½ cup Colby cheese, grated
6 cilantro sprigs

In a medium skillet place the ground beef and sauté it until it is cooked.

Add the onion, celery, garlic, and tomato. Cook for 10 minutes while stirring constantly.

Add the broth and the chiles. Bring the mixture to a boil.

Add the cornstarch mixture and stir until the sauce thickens.

Add the spices and cook for 15 minutes.

Divide the scrambled eggs and roll them into the crêpes. Place each filled crêpe on an oven-proof plate.

Cover the crêpes with the green chile and sprinkle on the cheese.

Broil them in the oven until the cheese melts.

Garnish with the cilantro sprigs.

serves 6

"We put beef in our green chile, but it can be eliminated if you wish, and the chile will still be good."

"I personally like to add some cheese inside the crêpe, so that it is really cheesy. I also like to serve it with sour cream on the side."

"Pat created this recipe. He's kind of our Southwestern expert."

Cheesy Bulgarian Potatoes and Sausage

3   **cups cottage cheese**
2   **sticks butter, melted**
1½   **teaspoons salt**
1   **teaspoon pepper**
½   **onion, diced**
6   **large Idaho potatoes, peeled and thinly sliced**
1   **pound hot breakfast sausage, cooked, crumbled, and drained**
4   **eggs**
2   **cups sour cream**
1   **tablespoon fresh chives, chopped**

In a medium bowl place the cottage cheese, butter, salt, pepper, and onion. Stir everything together.

In a well-greased 9" by 13" baking dish make layers of potato slices, sausage, and the cottage cheese mixture, ending with a cottage cheese layer.

Preheat the oven to 375°. Bake for 30 minutes.

In a small bowl place the eggs, sour cream, and chives. Beat them together.

Spread the mixture over the top of the baked casserole.

Bake for another 35 to 45 minutes, or until the topping is puffed and golden brown, and the potatoes are tender.

serves 8

"You can leave out the sausage if you want, or serve it on the side. We always try to be sensitive to the needs of the vegetarians, so most of our recipes taste equally as good with or without the meat."

"People love this dish. I love this dish! I always take home the leftovers."

"These potatoes are so easy to make, and they are wonderful reheated. Just don't over-bake them."

Sautéed Cinnamon Bananas

1   lemon, juiced
2   tablespoons milk
4   ripe, firm bananas, peeled and sliced lengthwise
1   cup corn flake *(or other cereal)* crumbs
2   teaspoons cinnamon
2   teaspoons sugar
3   tablespoons butter, or as needed
½   orange, peeled and sliced
1   kiwi, peeled and sliced

In a low, wide bowl place the lemon juice and the milk and mix them together. Place the sliced bananas in the mixture and thoroughly coat them.

In a plastic bag place the corn flake crumbs, cinnamon, and sugar. Mix them together.

Shake the bananas in the corn flake mixture, one by one.

Place the coated bananas on a large plate and refrigerate them for 15 minutes.

In a large skillet melt the butter over medium-high heat. Sauté the bananas on both sides, until they are golden brown and crispy.

Serve 2 banana slices on individual serving plates. Garnish with the orange and kiwi slices.

serves 4

"The bananas should be somewhat firm......not too ripe. Cook them, and then immediately get them to the table."

"Sautéed bananas are one of my favorite things. I'm always inspired to create recipes with my most favorite ingredients, except, of course, in the dreaded shellfish area."

Super Carrot Coffee Cake

3	cups carrots, grated
1	tablespoon fresh lemon juice
3	cups all purpose flour
1½	cups sugar
2	teaspoons baking powder
2	teaspoons baking soda
1	teaspoon salt
2	teaspoons cinnamon
½	teaspoon cloves
½	teaspoon nutmeg
½	teaspoon allspice
1½	cups vegetable oil
5	eggs
2	teaspoons vanilla
1	cup coconut
1	cup walnuts, chopped
1	cup raisins
1	15-ounce can crushed pineapple, drained
1	tablespoon powdered sugar, sifted

In a small bowl place the carrots and the lemon juice. Toss them together.

In a large bowl sift the flour with the sugar, baking powder, baking soda, salt, and spices.

Beat in the oil. Stir in the carrots. Beat in the eggs and the vanilla. Stir in the coconut, walnuts, raisins, and pineapple.

Pour the mixture into a greased 10" by 14" baking pan.

Preheat the oven to 350°. Bake for 1¼ hours, or until a toothpick inserted into the center comes out clean.

Cool for 25 minutes. Dust with the powdered sugar.

serves 8

"This takes a long time to cook, so you need to be very patient."

"You can ice it and make it into a really spectacular carrot cake dessert. I would recommend using a sour cream frosting. But it's also delicious without anything, and it's wonderful for breakfast."

"This is one of the best carrot cakes I've ever had in my life. The pineapple and coconut really make that special difference."

Museum of Fine Arts, Santa Fe, New Mexico

Guadalupe Cafe

Serving good homemade food in large portions with fresh ingredients, the Guadalupe Cafe is a big favorite with the locals and tourists alike. It offers an innovative and authentic New Mexican cuisine, as well as hearty breads, soups, and desserts.....all made on the premises.

"This is our most popular soup," says owner Isabelle Koomoa. *"If you don't have fresh jalapeños then use the canned variety."*

Jalapeño Cheese Soup

6   **cups chicken broth** *(not salted bouillon)*
8   **stalks celery** *(including the leaves)***, diced**
2   **cups onion, diced**
¾   **teaspoon garlic salt**
¼   **teaspoon white pepper**
2   **pounds Velveeta cheese, cubed**
1   **cup diced jalapeño peppers**
    sour cream

In a large saucepan place the chicken broth, celery, onions, garlic salt, and white pepper. Cook over high heat for 10 minutes, or until the mixture reduces and thickens slightly.

In a blender or food processor place the broth and the cheese. Purée them together until the mixture is smooth.

Return the puréed mixture to the saucepan and simmer it for 5 minutes.

Add the diced peppers and mix them in well.

Serve with a dollop of sour cream.

serves 6

Corona Beer Batter Fried Shrimp

1	cup flour
1	cup Corona beer
2	eggs
1	teaspoon salt
½	teaspoon pepper
1	tablespoon paprika
3	cups vegetable oil *(or as needed)*
24	medium shrimp, shelled and deveined

In a medium bowl place the flour, beer, eggs, salt, pepper, and paprika. Mix the ingredients together until they are well blended.

In a deep-fryer or large frying pan place the oil and heat it until it is very hot. Dip the shrimp into the batter and fry it in the hot oil for 2 minutes, or until it is crisp. Drain the shrimp well.

serves 4

Sopapillas

1	cup white flour
1	teaspoon baking powder
¼	teaspoon salt
2	tablespoons lard
⅓	cup water *(plus 1 tablespoon, or as needed)*
	vegetable oil *(as needed)*
	honey

Sift together the flour, baking powder, and salt. Add the lard and work it in well with a pastry cutter. Add the water and mix it in until the dough is of a smooth consistency *(not crumbly, and not sticky)*.

On a floured cutting board roll out the dough until it is ⅛" thick. Cut the dough into 4" triangles.

In a deep saucepan pour the oil so that it is 4" deep. Heat it to 400°. Very carefully deep-fry the sopapillas on both sides until they are golden brown. Drain them on paper towels. Serve them with the honey.

"One of my chefs came up with this recipe. It's a very basic batter that is almost like a tempura. And you can use it on almost anything..... vegetables, white fish, or whatever you like. It's wonderful, nice and crunchy, and it seals in the flavor. One thing – be careful that the oil doesn't smoke. If it does, turn down the heat!"

"We serve this with black beans and Spanish rice, along with green chile, salsa, and chile con queso. So, there are three condiments that go with this shrimp."

"These are very tricky to make. It's difficult to get them to come out correctly. You must be quite gentle, especially when you flip them over. Some practice will be needed, so don't get discouraged!"

Migas

1	**tablespoon butter**
2	**eggs, beaten**
1	**tablespoon scallions, chopped**
1	**tablespoon longhorn cheese, grated**
1	**tablespoon Monterey Jack cheese, grated**
1	**tablespoon green chile pepper, chopped**
½	**handful tortilla chips, crumbled**

In a small skillet place the butter and melt it over medium heat.

Add the eggs, scallions, cheeses, and chile. Scramble the ingredients together until they are cooked.

Add the tortilla chips and mix them in.

serves 1

"This recipe was suggested by a young girl from Texas.....it's something her mother used to make. So, we tried it out and everyone loved it. The tortilla chips are what make it so delicious. They add a nice crunchiness."

Simple Green Chile Sauce

5	**7-ounce cans mild green chiles, diced**
2	**7-ounce cans hot green chiles, diced**
1	**clove garlic, minced**
3	**cups water**
	salt *(to taste)*
½	**cup vegetable oil**
½	**cup flour**

In a medium saucepan place the chiles *(and their liquid)*, garlic, water, and salt. Bring the mixture to a boil and remove it from the heat.

In a small saucepan place the oil and heat it on medium. Gradually add the flour, while stirring constantly, to form a paste.

Reheat the chile mixture to a simmer. Very slowly add the flour paste while stirring constantly. Add more water if necessary.

makes 4 cups

"With this chili sauce you can make great enchiladas, burritos, or whatever you want. The recipe is designed for people who don't have access to fresh chiles."

Mexican Chicken Salad
with Guadalupe Salsa

Mexican Chicken Salad

3   cups white chicken, cooked and sliced
1   red bell pepper, seeded, washed, and diced
3   stalks celery, diced
2   cups mayonnaise
1   tablespoon fresh lime juice
1   tablespoon sour cream
2   tablespoons red chile powder
1   cup piñon *(or pine)* nuts, roasted
1   avocado, sliced
1   lime, wedged
     Guadalupe Salsa *(recipe follows)*

In a medium bowl place all of the ingredients *(except for the avocado, lime, and salsa)*. Mix them together.

Serve with the avocado slices, limes, and Guadalupe Salsa.

serves 4

Guadalupe Salsa

4   cups crushed tomatoes
2   green bell peppers, seeded, washed, and chopped
1   medium onion, chopped
2   tablespoons garlic salt
4   jalapeño peppers, boiled for 15 minutes, cooled and chopped
¼   cup green chile, chopped
1   tablespoon crushed red chile
1   teaspoon cumin
2   teaspoons oregano

In a medium bowl place all of the ingredients and mix them together.

Cover, and refrigerate over night.

"The piñon nuts must be roasted so that they are nice and crunchy. They are what makes this dish so special, no two ways about it!"

"We serve this in a tortilla basket, which I invented a way to make. Take a coffee can and punch holes into the bottom. Put the flour tortilla into the deep-fryer and then very carefully, using long tongs, press the bottom of the coffee can into the center of the tortilla and hold it there until the tortilla is cooked. But, this is very dangerous and you have to stand way back!"

"This salsa is very zesty and fresh tasting. It's also quite thick, so that when you dip a tortilla chip into it, the salsa adheres to the chip. The fresh jalapeños really make it good."

"The crushed tomatoes must be pure, with no basil or oregano added."

Benedict Mexican with Con Queso Sauce

1	**pound Velveeta cheese, cubed**
½	**cup Simple Green Chile Sauce** *(see page 117)*
1	**dash Worcestershire sauce**
6	**English muffins, halved and toasted**
12	**slices ham, sautéed in butter**
12	**eggs, poached**

In a double boiler place the cheese, chile sauce, and Worcestershire sauce. Simmer the ingredients until the cheese is melted.

Place both halves of an English muffin on each individual serving plate.

Place one slice of ham on top of each English muffin half.

Place one poached egg on top of each slice of ham.

Pour the cheese sauce over the top, and serve immediately.

serves 6

"We love to do Benedicts here, and they are very popular for brunch. We do mushroom Benedicts, turkey Benedicts.....and we serve them with a Hollandaise sauce, or a con queso sauce, or with green chile and melted cheese. Whatever! The English muffins and the poached eggs are the only constants."

"The Velveeta I apologize for, but I've found that it's the only cheese that stays smooth and creamy, and doesn't get grainy."

Breast of Chicken Relleno

6   large, whole chicken breasts, cooked, with bones and skin removed
2   cups Monterey Jack cheese, grated
3   eggs, lightly beaten
1   cup milk
2   cups flour
2   cups yellow cornmeal
1   cup vegetable oil *(or as needed)*
2   cups Simple Green Chile Sauce *(see page 117)*
½   cup Monterey Jack cheese, grated

Cut a pocket into the middle of each chicken breast. Pack in the two cups of grated cheese.

In a small bowl place the eggs and the milk. Beat them together.

Dip the stuffed chicken breasts in the flour and then in the egg batter. Roll them in the cornmeal.

In a large heavy skillet place the vegetable oil and heat it until it is hot. Add the chicken breasts and sauté them on both sides until they are golden brown.

Place the sautéed, stuffed chicken breasts in a buttered baking dish.

Cover them with the Simple Green Chile Sauce and the ½ cup of Monterey Jack cheese.

Preheat the oven to 450°, and bake them for 6 to 8 minutes, or until the cheese is melted.

serves 6

"This recipe takes some time to make, although it's not difficult. The chicken must be rolled up very tightly, so that the cheese doesn't ooze out when you sauté it."

"The breading makes the chicken very crunchy, and then the chile softens it up a bit, but not too much. It's a wonderful, delicious dish!"

"It's a good idea to let the coated chicken breasts sit in the refrigerator for an hour or two. That way the batter will set before you sauté them."

Breakfast Burritos

2	tablespoons butter
4	cups mushrooms, sliced
3	bunches fresh spinach, washed, dried, stems removed, and chopped
6	medium flour tortillas
2	cups Simple Green Chile Sauce *(see page 117)*
2	cups Monterey Jack cheese, grated

In a large skillet place the butter and heat it on medium until it is melted.

Add the mushrooms and sauté them for 2 to 3 minutes, or until they are just tender.

Add the spinach and sauté it until the leaves are hot.

Divide the spinach mixture into 6 equal parts and spread it on each tortilla. Roll the tortillas up tightly.

In a shallow, buttered baking dish place each tortilla with the seam side down.

Cover the burritos with the Simple Green Chile Sauce.

Sprinkle the cheese over the top.

Preheat the oven to 450°.

Bake the burritos for 5 minutes, or until the cheese is melted.

serves 6

"This is just a very simple, basic recipe, that is wonderful tasting and easy to make."

"When people from Texas come here there is this confusion about our chile. They think that it is supposed to be pinto beans with red chile powder and great big hunks of meat, which, of course, it isn't. Our chile is entirely different."

"If a tourist expresses concern about the green chile being hot, we will just put on a little bit and then smother it with sour cream."

Heath Bar Pie
with Guadalupe Hot Fudge Sauce

Heath Bar Pie

1   box Famous Chocolate Wafers, crushed
1   teaspoon almond extract
⅓   cup butter, melted
1   pint Häagen Daz chocolate ice cream, softened
1   cup peanut butter chips
1   pint Häagen Daz vanilla ice cream, softened
3   Heath Bars, chopped
       Guadalupe Hot Fudge Sauce *(recipe follows)*

In a medium bowl place the crushed cookies, almond extract, and melted butter. Mix the ingredients together.

Press the mixture into a buttered pie pan and form a pie crust.

Preheat the oven to 350°. Bake the crust for 6 to 8 minutes. Let it cool, and then freeze it for 15 minutes.

Spread the chocolate ice cream evenly onto the bottom of the crust.

Sprinkle the peanut butter chips evenly on top of the chocolate ice cream.

Freeze the pie for 15 minutes, or until the ice cream is firm.

Spread the vanilla ice cream evenly on top.

Sprinkle on the chopped Heath Bars, and freeze. Serve with the Guadalupe Hot Fudge Sauce.

serves 6

Guadalupe Hot Fudge Sauce

2   cups semisweet chocolate chips
1   cup whipping cream
⅓   cup corn starch

In a double boiler place the chocolate chips and melt them.

Add the whipping cream and corn starch. Mix them together.

"This pie is very rich and very delicious. It's a little more time consuming to make than the Adobe Pie, but, then, I think that it's well worth the extra effort. If you want to use Amaretto instead of the almond extract, that's fine."

"Through a lot of experimentation we've found that the only cookies to use are the Nabisco Chocolate Wafers, which you can find anywhere. The chocolate flavor is just the best."

Adobe Pie

1¾   cups Famous Chocolate Wafer Cookies, crumbled
¼   cup butter, melted
1   teaspoon Amaretto
1   pint vanilla ice cream, softened
1   pint coffee ice cream, softened
2   ounces semisweet chocolate, grated

In a medium bowl place the cookie crumbs, melted butter, and Amaretto. Mix the ingredients together.

Press the mixture into a buttered pie pan to form a pie shell.

Preheat the oven to 350°. Bake the pie crust for 6 to 8 minutes. Let it cool, and then freeze it for 15 minutes.

Spread the vanilla ice cream evenly over the bottom of the pie crust.

Freeze the pie for 15 minutes, or until the ice cream is firm.

Spread the coffee ice cream on top of the vanilla ice cream.

Sprinkle the chocolate shavings over the top, and freeze.

serves 6

"When Häagen Daz first came to New Mexico I decided I wanted to use it in a dessert. My son and I were experimenting with different crusts because we liked the idea of an ice cream pie. We wanted a regional sounding name and he came up with the title 'Adobe Pie'. He also figured out the exact ingredients."

"You can put hot fudge sauce over the top, but I think that it's wonderful without. The Amaretto crust together with the ice cream is just exquisite!"

Adobe Gate Detail, Santa Fe, New Mexico

La Plazuela

Timeless charm with a commitment to excellence.....these are the words to describe the historic La Fonda, *"The Inn at the End of the Santa Fe Trail"*. La Plazuela, its colorful and decorative Mexican style restaurant, serves great American and Southwestern dishes.

Recipes

*Tomato Basil
Santa Fe Pizza*

*Southwestern Stuffed
Artichokes*

Avocado Gazpacho Soup

Santa Fe Black Bean Soup

*New Mexican
Chorizo Burrito*

*Swordfish Borracho
Salsa Fresca*

Basic Green Chile Sauce

Basic Red Chile Sauce

Blue Corn Husk Muffins

Natillas

Executive Chef Lela Cross and her Sous Chef brother, Thomas, form a winning team at La Plazuela. Lela says, *"This is an adaptation of a recipe from Sunset Magazine when they did an article on Santa Fe."*

Tomato Basil Santa Fe Pizza

2   teaspoons garlic, chopped
2   medium tomatoes, sliced
2   tablespoons olive oil
1   dash salt
1   dash pepper
6   ounces Mozzarella cheese, sliced
2   medium wheat flour tortillas, pierced with a fork
2   tablespoons fresh basil, minced
½   cup fresh Parmesan cheese, grated

In a small bowl place the garlic, tomatoes, olive oil, salt, and pepper. Thoroughly coat the tomatoes.

Place the cheese slices over the tortillas. Place the soaked tomatoes on top. Sprinkle on the basil and Parmesan cheese.

Preheat the oven to 350°. Place the tortillas on a cookie sheet and bake them for 8 minutes, or until the cheese is melted.

Cut the pizza into wedges.

serves 2

Southwestern Stuffed Artichokes

½   cup mayonnaise
½   cup sour cream
½   green chile, chopped
1   cup artichoke hearts, drained and chopped
½   cup fresh Parmesan cheese, grated
1   dash Worcestershire sauce
1   dash tabasco
    salt (to taste)
    pepper (to taste)
6   fresh artichokes, boiled until tender
1   small tomato, diced
    blue (or yellow) corn tortilla chips

In a medium bowl place the mayonnaise, sour cream, chile, artichoke hearts, Parmesan cheese, Worcestershire sauce, tabasco, salt, and pepper. Mix the ingredients together.

Carve out the middle of the cooked artichokes. Remove the hearts, chop them, and mix them into the dip.

Stuff the dip into the middle of the artichokes.

Place each artichoke on a plate. Sprinkle the diced tomatoes on top.

Serve the stuffed artichokes surrounded by the blue corn tortilla chips.

serves 6

"We've been using this recipe for several years in the restaurant. When I first found it we kept adding to it and changing it, and after awhile we ended up with a Southwestern version by adding the green chile, tabasco, and a couple of other items."

"What makes this dish so nice is that when you stuff the dip into the artichoke, it looks like a little cactus. And then when you sprinkle the tomatoes on top, it looks like a cactus in bloom in the spring. You can also use carrots or any bright, colorful vegetable."

"The leaves that you take out of the center you can spread around the plate to be eaten. This is a very good recipe.....people really seem to enjoy it!"

Avocado Gazpacho Soup

1	**large cucumber, peeled, seeded, and diced**
1	**large avocado, diced**
1	**large tomato, diced**
1	**medium green bell pepper, diced**
1	**medium red bell pepper, diced**
1	**cup celery, diced**
¼	**cup green onions, sliced**
¼	**cup white wine**
¼	**cup red wine vinegar**
2	**cups beef broth**
4	**cups crushed tomatoes**
1	**tablespoon fresh cilantro**
1	**teaspoon salt** *(or to taste)*
½	**teaspoon pepper** *(or to taste)*
1	**dash tabasco** *(or to taste)*

In a large glass or porcelain bowl place all of the ingredients and mix them together.

Cover, and refrigerate the soup overnight.

serves 6-8

"This is a very basic recipe that Tom worked on to make it more Southwestern. He added the avocado, cilantro, wine, and vinegar."

"This soup is so good that we serve it all year round. Normally a cold soup is served only in the warm months. But, here at La Fonda our Gazpacho is so popular that we can get away with serving it in the winter as well!"

"Remember, the longer it refrigerates, the better it tastes."

Santa Fe Black Bean Soup

2	tablespoons olive oil
3	slices bacon, cooked, drained, and diced
¼	pound smoked ham, diced
2	medium onions, diced
2	cloves garlic, minced
2	stalks celery, chopped
1½	cups dried black beans, washed, soaked overnight, and drained
2½	teaspoons dried red chile flakes
4	cups water
1	tablespoon beef base
1	teaspoon salt *(or to taste)*
½	teaspoon pepper *(or to taste)*
¼	cup sherry
⅛	cup white vinegar
1	tablespoon fresh cilantro, minced

In a large, heavy soup pot place the olive oil and heat it on medium. Add the bacon, ham, onions, garlic, and celery. Sauté them until the vegetables are tender.

Add the soaked black beans, red chile flakes, water, beef base, salt, and pepper.

Bring the soup to a boil, and then simmer it for 2½ to 3 hours, or until the beans are tender. Add more water if necessary. Occasionally skim the fat from the top.

Place the soup in a food processor or blender, and purée it until it is smooth.

Place the soup in a bowl, cover it tightly, and refrigerate it overnight.

When ready to serve, place the soup in a saucepan and heat it. Stir in the sherry and vinegar.

Garnish with the cilantro.

serves 6-8

"Although I didn't say so in this recipe, here at the restaurant we serve the soup inside a hollowed-out small round bread roll, like the Indians used to make. We put some grated cheese on top, melt it, and then put the top of the roll back on for a lid. So, when you are finished with the soup you can eat the bread. This adds a nice festive flair to the presentation."

New Mexican Chorizo Burrito

1	pound chorizo, peeled
8	eggs
4	tablespoons milk
2	tablespoons butter
2	tablespoons green chile, finely diced
1	tablespoon green onion, finely diced
4	flour tortillas
2	cups Basic Green Chile Sauce *(see page 132)*
2	cups Monterey Jack cheese, grated

In a medium skillet place the chorizo and sauté it until it is crumbled and done. Drain the chorizo thoroughly on paper towels and set it aside.

In a medium bowl place the eggs and the milk. Whip them together until they are well blended.

In a large skillet place the butter and heat it on medium until it is melted. Add the green chile and green onions, and sauté them for 2 to 3 minutes, or until they are tender.

Add the eggs and scramble them.

Add the chorizo and mix it into the eggs.

Heat the flour tortillas. Place ¼ of the egg mixture into each of the tortillas and roll them up.

Place each rolled tortilla on an oven-proof plate. Pour the Basic Green Chile Sauce over the top. Sprinkle the cheese on top.

Broil the burritos until the cheese melts.

serves 4

Swordfish Borracho
with Salsa Fresca

Swordfish Borracho

4	cups olive oil
1	cup white wine
2	dried chile pods, crushed
½	bunch cilantro, chopped
2	fresh lemons, squeezed
2	fresh limes, squeezed
2	teaspoons fresh basil, chopped
2	tablespoons fresh thyme, chopped
2	tablespoons fresh dill, chopped
2	tablespoons garlic, minced
4	8-ounce swordfish fillets
¼	cup tequila
	Salsa Fresca *(recipe on next page)*

In a medium bowl place all of the ingredients *(except for the swordfish, tequila, and the Salsa Fresca)* and mix them together.

Place the swordfish fillets in the mixture and coat them thoroughly. Cover, and refrigerate them for 4 hours.

Add the tequila and continue to marinate the swordfish for 1 hour more.

Preheat the oven to 350°.

Place the swordfish fillets on a flat sheet and bake them for 12 to 15 minutes, or until they are milky white and firm.

Top with the Salsa Fresca.

serves 4

"I wanted to make a swordfish that was marinated, so everyone in the kitchen more or less contributed to this recipe. We added a little of this and that, and someone suggested the tequila, which really made it excellent."

"It is important that you do not let the fish soak in the tequila for more than 1 hour, or it will get bitter. You can broil this, bake it, sauté it, or grill it.....do anything you want and it always will come out delicious."

"The flavor is very unusual.....it's kind of bitter and sweet at the same time, but the taste of the fish comes through nicely."

"Several years ago Santa Fe had a chile cook-off between some of the Southwestern states. La Fonda was the host for Tucson, and the chef came into our kitchen to cook his recipes. We watched him make this salsa, so we adopted it, and changed it more to our taste."

Salsa Fresca

6	tomatoes, diced
½	red onion, finely diced
1	bunch scallions, chopped
1	tablespoon garlic, chopped
1	jalapeño pepper, seeded and finely diced
1	tablespoon wine vinegar
1	tablespoon olive oil
½	bunch cilantro, chopped
1	teaspoon oregano
1	teaspoon salt
½	teaspoon pepper

In a medium mixing bowl place all of the ingredients and mix them together.

Cover, and refrigerate them for at least 2 hours.

"My brother Thomas and I work very well together. I give him the ideas, and then he goes into the kitchen and figures them out. His strengths balance out my weaknesses, and vice versa. And then, of course, we have our annual big fights, twice a year, to be exact. We do this without fail, and it works out perfectly, because we get all our problems worked out that way!"

Basic Green Chile Sauce

2   **tablespoons vegetable oil**
1   **cup onions, chopped**
4   **tablespoons flour**
2   **cups mild green chile, chopped**
2   **cups chicken broth**
½   **teaspoon garlic powder**
1½   **teaspoons salt**

In a medium saucepan place the oil and heat it on medium until it is hot. Add the onions and sauté them until they are tender.

Add the flour and cook it until it is browned, while stirring constantly to make a roux.

Add the remaining ingredients and simmer the sauce for 20 minutes.

makes 4 cups

"This is a very simple, basic recipe. But for some reason, if we have five different people in our kitchen make it, it will come out five different ways! This particular recipe calls for a mild chile, but you can combine that with some jalapeño to make it hotter."

"The trick to making this chile is to cook the roux until it gets really brown. That's what gives it the good flavor. You can simmer the sauce longer. I just gave you the minimum time to get rid of the flour taste in the roux."

Basic Red Chile Sauce

4	tablespoons vegetable oil
4	tablespoons flour
½	cup red chile powder
4	cups cold water
1½	teaspoons salt
1	teaspoon garlic salt
1	teaspoon oregano
1	teaspoon cumin

In a medium saucepan place the oil and heat it on medium until it is hot. Add the flour and cook it for 1 minute, while stirring constantly.

Add the chile powder and cook it for 1 minute, while stirring constantly.

Gradually stir in the water, being careful that no lumps form.

Add the salt, garlic salt, oregano, and cumin. Simmer the sauce for 15 minutes.

makes 4 cups

"In this recipe we were conservative with the amount of chile powder we used. You can use up to a cup, if you want. The sauce should have a medium consistency, not too thin or too thick."

"My brother and I grew up in Santa Fe. A lot of our recipes we try to do the way our mom and grandmother made them. We use the flavors that we loved as children."

Blue Corn Husk Muffins

8	corn husks, separated and soaked in boiling water until they are pliable
1	cup all purpose flour
1	cup atole *(blue corn meal)*
1	tablespoon baking powder
¾	cup Monterey Jack cheese, grated
¼	cup butter, melted
2	tablespoons honey
2	eggs, beaten
1	cup milk
½	cup green chile, diced
¼	cup Monterey Jack cheese, grated

Drain the corn husks and pat them dry. Cut them into 1½" wide strips.

In a medium bowl place the flour, corn meal, baking powder, and the ¾ cup of cheese. Mix everything together.

In another medium bowl place the butter, honey, eggs, milk, and green chile. Mix the ingredients together and add them to the flour mixture. Stir all of the ingredients together until they are well combined.

In a lightly greased muffin tin place 2 to 3 strips of the corn husks, crosswise, into the bottom of each muffin cup.

Pour in the batter, until the cups are ¾ full. Sprinkle the ¼ cup of grated cheese over the tops.

Preheat the oven to 350°. Bake the muffins for 20 to 25 minutes, or until they are done and nicely browned.

serves 6

"We took about three different recipes and combined them into one. To make the muffins a little more Southwestern, we added the blue corn meal, or atole. Of course, if you can't find the blue corn meal, just substitute the yellow. You should be able to get the corn husks in your grocery store."

"The taste is kind of like a sweet cornmeal with a touch of cheese and green chile for flavor. You can serve these muffins with the swordfish, or a soup or salad. They would also be delicious for a breakfast muffin."

Natillas

4	egg yolks
¼	cup corn starch
4	cups condensed milk
¾	cup sugar
¼	teaspoon vanilla
4	egg whites
	cinnamon *(as needed)*

In a small bowl place the egg yolks, corn starch, and 1 cup of the condensed milk. Stir the ingredients together to make a smooth paste.

In a medium saucepan place the remaining 3 cups of condensed milk, sugar, and vanilla. Stirring constantly, heat over a medium heat until the milk is scalded.

Add the egg yolk and cornstarch mixture. Continue to cook until the mixture thickens, stirring constantly.

Let the mixture cool to room temperature.

In a small bowl place the egg whites and beat them until they are stiff, but not dry. Fold them into the custard.

Place the custard in individual goblets, and chill.

Sprinkle the cinnamon on top.

serves 6-8

"This is a traditional New Mexican dish that Thomas and I grew up with. Everyone loves this dessert, and we have very strong memories of it as children. In the restaurant we serve the Natillas with an almond lady finger and a little raspberry sauce on top."

Detail of Mission Church, Laguna Pueblo, New Mexico

Mañana

With an intimate, warm, *at home* atmosphere, the Inn of the Governors strives to be known as the friendliest hotel in Santa Fe. The Mañana restaurant contributes to this goal by offering excellent food served in a happy, airy, and tastefully decorated dining room.

Recipes

Crab and Avocado
Quesadilla

Mañana Tortilla Soup

Poulet Dijon

Poached Salmon
Cucumber Buerre Blanc

Al Mayo de Ajo

Milagro Bread Pudding
Warm Whiskey Sauce

Chef Kelly Rogers says, *"This is an excellent appetizer. It takes only a few minutes to prepare, and people love it."*

"These quesadillas are mild, but they still have a good kick to them. Just be sure not to let them burn under the broiler."

Crab and Avocado Quesadilla

½   pound crab meat, cooked
1   ripe avocado, diced
2   tablespoons sour cream
1   green chile, chopped
     salt *(to taste)*
     pepper *(to taste)*
4   tablespoons vegetable oil
4   medium flour tortillas
½   cup Monterey Jack cheese, grated

In a medium bowl place the crab, avocado, sour cream, green chile, salt, and pepper.

In a medium skillet place the oil and heat it on medium until it is hot. Place each tortilla in the pan for 10 seconds and then turn it over. Remove it after another 10 seconds.

Spread ¼ of the mixture on one half of each tortilla and fold it over.

Place the filled, folded tortillas on a baking sheet. Sprinkle the cheese on top and broil the quesadillas in the oven until it melts.

Cut the quesadillas into 4 triangles and serve them immediately.

serves 4

Mañana Tortilla Soup

1   **quart chicken stock**
1   **cup cooked posole**
1   **cup cooked pinto beans**
1   **cup red chile sauce**
¼   **cup fresh cilantro, chopped**
¼   **pound butter, melted**
8   **tablespoons flour**
½   **cup cheddar cheese, grated**
½   **tomato, diced**
      corn tortilla chips

In a large, heavy pot place the chicken stock, posole, pinto beans, red chile sauce, and cilantro. Heat the soup on medium until it reaches a boil. Reduce the soup to simmer.

In a small saucepan place the butter and heat it on medium until it melts. While stirring constantly, add the flour to create a roux. Continue to stir and cook on low heat for 5 minutes.

Add the roux to the soup and stir it in. Cook the soup until it thickens.

Place ¼ of the cheese in the bottom of each individual soup bowl, and fill them up with hot soup.

Garnish with the tomatoes and the corn tortilla chips.

serves 4

"Tortilla soup is a regional favorite, and this particular recipe is one that I developed as far as what the specific ingredients are."

"This is a hearty soup, kind of like a stew. The blue and yellow corn chips really freshen it up. By the way, there are two ways to do the tortilla chips. You can buy any flavored chips you want in your grocery store, or you can buy fresh corn tortillas and fry them in vegetable oil yourself."

"If you want to cook the posole and beans yourself, then simmer them in water with salt, pepper, and some chile, until they are tender."

Poulet Dijon

½	cup Dijon mustard
½	cup yellow mustard
2	tablespoons safflower oil
2	tablespoons soy sauce
½	lemon, juiced
1	tablespoon fresh dill, minced
½	teaspoon tabasco
½	teaspoon salt
½	teaspoon pepper
4	chicken breasts, boned, with skin on

In a medium bowl place all of the ingredients except for the chicken breasts. Mix everything together.

Add the chicken breasts and thoroughly coat them with the sauce on both sides.

Cover, and refrigerate for 2 to 6 hours.

Preheat the oven to broil.

Place the chicken breasts in a pan and broil them in the center of the oven for 8 minutes, with the skin side up. Turn, and broil them for 6 minutes more, or until the chicken is done.

serves 4

"This is a very popular recipe in our restaurant. We marinate the chicken for at least twenty-four hours to ensure the good taste. In fact, we let this chicken sit for three to four days.....so you don't need to worry!"

"When you grill this chicken the sugar crystallizes and the outside gets real crispy, with the skin kind of burnt.....this adds flavor!"

"This is a perfect dish to grill at an outside barbecue. It goes great with rice, pasta, or potato salad."

Poached Salmon
with Cucumber Buerre Blanc

Poached Salmon

1   quart water
1   lemon, juiced
½   cup white wine
1   tablespoon black peppercorns
4   8-ounce salmon fillets
     Cucumber Buerre Blanc *(recipe on next page)*
8   cucumber slices

In a medium saucepan place the water, lemon juice, wine, and peppercorns. Bring the mixture to a boil and then reduce it to medium.

Add the salmon fillets and poach them for 5 to 7 minutes, or until they are firm.

Serve with the Cucumber Buerre Blanc laced over the fish.

Garnish with the cucumber slices.

serves 4

"When you poach the salmon you should have no trouble. It's very easy, and all you need to do is to check them for doneness, so that the flesh is pink and flaky, instead of red."

"Actually, any kind of nice fish will work well with this recipe.....halibut, swordfish, mahi-mahi or tuna."

"Here at Mañana we try to reflect the lifestyle of Santa Fe itself. Our food is unique and fun for our customers, just like Santa Fe is unique and fun. I'm sure that if we were in New York or San Francisco we would have a different style."

"This sauce is very delicate and to make it correctly you have to pay careful attention to what you are doing. So read the recipe over several times before you start. Get your ingredients all ready, and then go ahead!"

"It is important that the heat stays on low, or at least that it doesn't go over medium. At the end the heat should be turned off. The trick is to not let the sauce get too hot or too cold, or else the butter will separate. If this happens then the sauce won't look right, but it will still taste good."

"In our kitchen we have a special little spot where we keep the sauce warm. It's kind of a ledge between our grill and our sauté area. There's no draft.....it's just a nice cozy little area that's the perfect temperature."

Cucumber Buerre Blanc

½ cup white wine
1 cucumber, peeled, seeded, and diced
1 shallot, diced
½ cup heavy cream
¼ lemon, juiced
6 tablespoons butter, softened

In a medium skillet place the wine, cucumber, and shallots. Heat the ingredients on medium and cook them for 2 to 3 minutes, or until the liquid reduces and slightly thickens.

Add the cream and the lemon juice. Continue to cook until the sauce thickens even more.

Turn the heat to low and whisk in the butter, 1 tablespoon at a time, until it is dissolved.

Remove the sauce from the heat and strain it.

Al Mayo de Ajo

2	teaspoons garlic, minced
½	lemon, juiced
1	tablespoon parsley, chopped
1	dash salt *(or to taste)*
1	dash pepper *(or to taste)*
½	pound butter, softened
⅓	cup olive oil
1	pound large shrimp, peeled and deveined
½	cup sherry
1	tomato, diced
2	stalks green onions, diced
2	tablespoons capers
½	pound fettucini, cooked al dente

In a small bowl place the garlic, lemon juice, parsley, salt, pepper, and butter. Mix the ingredients together.

In a large, heavy skillet place the olive oil and heat it on medium until it is hot. Add the shrimp and sauté them for 2 minutes, or until they are white and firm.

Add the sherry and continue to cook until the liquid is reduced by half.

Add the tomatoes, green onions, and capers. Cook for 1 minute, while tossing the ingredients about.

Carefully spoon the garlic butter evenly over the shrimp.

Add the pasta and swirl it about in the pan until everything is coated evenly by the butter.

serves 4

"Definitely, this is one of our most popular dinner entrées because people love garlic, they love shrimp, and they love all of that luscious sauce. This dish is very rich..... it's not for dieters! I actually toned down the butter in this recipe, because we really put in a LOT! But then that's what makes it so good."

"Don't sauté the shrimp too long, because you don't want it to get tough. Also, don't overcook the pasta. Remember, you are cooking it a little bit longer when you put it into the sauce."

"This is a quick dish to make. Once you have all of your ingredients prepared you can put it together in five minutes."

Milagro Bread Pudding
with Warm Whiskey Sauce

Milagro Bread Pudding

1	12" French baguette, torn into 2" chunks
3	cups milk
2	eggs
4	ounces raisins
2	tablespoons vanilla extract
1	cup sugar
1	tablespoon butter, melted
	Warm Whiskey Sauce (recipe follows)

In a medium bowl place the French bread pieces. Add the milk and soak them for 1 hour, or until all of the chunks are completely saturated. If necessary, add more milk.

In a small bowl place the eggs, raisins, vanilla, sugar, and butter. Lightly beat everything together. Pour this mixture over the soaked bread chunks.

Preheat the oven to 325°.

Pour the mixture into a greased 8" by 8" casserole dish. Bake for 1 hour, or until it is golden brown.

Serve with the Warm Whiskey Sauce poured over the top.

serves 4

Warm Whiskey Sauce

½	pound butter
1	cup powdered sugar
1	egg, beaten
4	tablespoons whiskey
1	tablespoon apricot brandy

In a double boiler place the butter and melt it on medium until it is hot. Add the powdered sugar and stir until the mixture is very smooth.

Remove the pan from the heat. Add the egg and whip it in. Cool it for 15 minutes.

Whip in the whiskey and apricot brandy, 1 tablespoon at a time.

"This is a regional recipe that is a classic among Mexican-American people. Like a lot of recipes it derived out of necessity.....or, what to do with your stale bread! I imagine that the Spanish brought the idea over from Europe hundreds of years ago."

"This is our most popular dessert, and it won the 1988 Taste of Santa Fe award."

"The warm whisky sauce is a French recipe. We added the apricot brandy which we think enhances the flavor and makes it a little different tasting."

"Anybody can make this recipe. Just make sure that the pudding is firm, and nice and brown on top."

Adobe Architecture with Skull, Santa Fe, New Mexico

Maria's New Mexican Kitchen

Typical of an old Mexican style cantina, Maria's is a rambling adobe building, complete with a view of fresh tortillas being made in the main dining room. They specialize in fajitas and northern New Mexican food, and you can be assured that anything you order will be completely authentic!

Recipes

Maria's Blue Corn
Enchiladas

Maria's Red Chile Sauce

Maria's Old Santa Fe
Style Soupy Beans

Maria's Beef Fajitas

Maria's Guacamole

Maria's Pico de Gallo

Maria's Bizcochitos

Maria's New Mexican Kitchen is owned by Al Lucero and his wife, Laurie. Al says, *"The word enchilada means 'in chile' in Spanish. So, the chile is the most important ingredient in this recipe. It's what makes this dish so delicious!"*

Maria's Blue Corn Enchiladas

¼   cup vegetable oil
8   blue corn tortillas
1   cup diced onions
2   cups cheddar cheese, grated
2¼ cups tomatoes, diced
5   cups Maria's Red Chile Sauce *(recipe on next page)*
4   fried eggs
2   cups lettuce, shredded

In a medium skillet place the oil and heat it until it is hot. One at a time, place each tortilla in the oil and then immediately turn it over. Drain the tortillas on paper towels and keep them warm.

Place one tortilla on an individual serving plate. In this order, sprinkle on ⅛ cup of the onions, ⅛ cup of the cheese, and ¼ cup of the tomatoes. Add ¼ cup of Maria's Red Chile Sauce.

Place another tortilla on top and repeat the process for the onions, cheese, and tomatoes.

Add ¾ cup of the chile sauce and then sprinkle on ¼ cup of the cheese. Broil the enchilada in the oven until the cheese melts.

Place one fried egg on top. Add ¼ cup of the chile sauce.

Add the lettuce and garnish with some of the diced tomatoes.

serves 4

Maria's Red Chile Sauce

½   cup vegetable oil
1   cup red New Mexico chile powder
2   tablespoons flour, sifted
6   cups water
1   teaspoon salt
2   cloves garlic, minced

In a large saucepan place the oil and heat it on medium until it is hot.

Add the chile powder, 1 tablespoon at a time, while whisking constantly, until all of the chile powder is dissolved and a paste is formed. Add water as needed to maintain a pasty consistency.

Add the flour and whisk it for 3 to 4 minutes, or until the entire mixture thickens. Add the water, salt, and garlic, and whisk them in.

Simmer the sauce for 1 hour. Stir occasionally so that it doesn't cake on the bottom of the pan.

Maria's Old Santa Fe Style Soupy Beans

4   cups pinto beans
12   cups water
½   pound salt pork, cut into ½" cubes
     salt *(to taste)*

Clean the beans to remove the pebbles and debris. Rinse the beans thoroughly.

In a large, heavy saucepan place the pinto beans and the water. Let the beans soak overnight.

Bring the beans to a boil and then reduce them to a simmer.

Add the salt pork cubes and simmer for 3 hours, or until the beans are tender and will mash easily. Add salt to taste.

serves 8-10

"Red chile powder is not a spice like most people think. It's actually a vegetable. It is a red chile pepper that has been dried and then pulverized. So, when you add a cup of chile powder to a recipe, don't think that you are adding a cup of spice! Also, you should be aware that New Mexican chile powder can be mild, medium, or hot."

"The recipe here is a vegetarian one, but if you wish you can add beef or pork to the sauce before you simmer it. You should sauté the meat first, however. The meat will be delicious in the Blue Corn Enchilada."

"If you lightly mash these beans up and fry them with a little shortening, then you will have made re-fried beans. Add a little of the broth if they seem too dry."

Maria's Beef Fajitas

24	ounces top sirloin steak, trimmed and cut into 4 steakettes
½	cup silver tequila
⅛	cup fresh lime juice
⅛	cup soy sauce
3	dashes tabasco sauce
½	teaspoon black pepper, freshly ground
8	tablespoons vegetable oil
2	cups green bell pepper slices
2	cups onion slices
2	cups tomato chunks
8	flour tortillas, warmed
	Maria's Pico de Gallo (recipe on next page)
	Maria's Guacamole (recipe on next page)

Charbroil the steakettes until they are rare. Cut them into ¼" strips.

In a medium bowl place the tequila, lime juice, soy sauce, tabasco, and the black pepper. Mix them together.

Add the beef slices and coat them well. Cover, refrigerate, and marinate them for 24 hours. Turn them occasionally.

Remove the beef strips from the marinade.

For one serving, place 2 tablespoons of oil in a large skillet and heat it until it is hot. Add ½ cup of the green peppers, onions, and tomatoes. Sauté them for 2 to 3 minutes.

Add ¼ of the beef strips and sauté them for 2 to 3 minutes.

Preheat a well-seasoned, dry, cast iron fajita pan (or a small cast iron skillet) to 450°, or until it is as hot as possible.

Pour the sautéed ingredients into the hot cast iron pan and serve them immediately with 2 warm flour tortillas, Maria's Pico de Gallo, and Maria's Guacamole.

Do this for each serving.

serves 4

"Fajitas are a Tex-Mex dish. Years ago when the migrant workers would come across the border into southern Texas, they were able to buy only the very cheapest cuts of meat, which were quite tough. So, they would marinate the meat to tenderize it. Then they would eat the meat with guacamole and tortillas. They would also add pico de gallo, because they loved hot sauce."

"To eat the fajitas you should generously spread guacamole over half of the tortilla. Add the strips of beef and vegetables, and then the Pico de Gallo, and roll it up. Eat it with your hands."

Maria's Guacamole

4	ripe California Haas avocados
¾	cup onion, finely chopped
1	tomato, finely chopped
¾	cup green chiles, finely diced
2	tablespoons garlic, finely minced
1	tablespoon Worcestershire sauce
1	teaspoon salt
½	lemon, juiced
	corn tortilla chips

Remove the skins from the avocados *(save the pits)*.

In a medium bowl place the avocados and mash them with a fork, leaving some small chunks.

Add the onion, tomato, and green chile. Gently mix them in.

Add the garlic, Worcestershire sauce, salt, and lemon juice. Gently blend them in *(do not purée)*.

Place the avocado pits in the guacamole *(to help retard browning)* and store it in the refrigerator, covered.

Serve with the corn tortilla chips.

"Guacamole is a kind of California tradition. But avocados have become part of modern New Mexican cooking since they were able to transport them here."

"There are a lot of variations that you can do with guacamole. You can add or delete whatever – just don't overwhelm the flavor of the avocados. And, I recommend using only California Haas avocados.....they are the best!"

Maria's Pico de Gallo

¼	cup fresh New Mexican green chiles, finely chopped
¼	cup jalapeño peppers, finely chopped
¼	cup tomatoes, finely chopped
¼	cup onions, finely chopped
1	teaspoon tabasco
1	clove garlic, finely minced

In a medium bowl place all of the ingredients and mix them together by hand.

Cover, and refrigerate the sauce for 1 hour.

"Laurie has a good saying.....'Add your Pico de Gallo to your Fajitas like you add your vermouth to a dry martini – very sparingly!' It is liquid fire, so be careful!"

Maria's Bizcochitos

1	cup sugar
1¼	cups shortening
1	egg
1	teaspoon vanilla
⅛	cup brandy
2	teaspoons anise seed
3	cups flour
½	teaspoon baking powder
¼	teaspoon salt
	warm water *(as needed)*
½	teaspoon cinnamon
¾	cup sugar

In a large bowl place the 1 cup of sugar, shortening, egg, vanilla, and brandy. Cream them together until they are well mixed.

Add the anise seed and mix it in.

In another large bowl place the flour, baking powder, and salt. Mix them together.

Add the flour mixture to the sugar mixture. Slowly add warm water and mix everything together by hand until the dough is flaky and soft, with the consistency of a pie dough.

On a floured cutting board roll out the dough into a ¼" thick sheet. Cut out 2" squares. On one side of the squares make ¼" cuts along the edge.

Place the cookies on a buttered baking sheet.

In a small bowl place the cinnamon and the ¾ cup of sugar. Mix them together.

Sprinkle the cinnamon and sugar mixture on top of the cookies.

Preheat the oven to 350°. Bake the cookies for 12 to 15 minutes, or until they are golden.

makes 2 dozen

Adobe and Wood Arch, Pojoaque, New Mexico

Nectarine

Nectarine. The name reflects the essence of its cuisine.....sensual, sweet, fresh, and delectable. With a decor that is elegant and slightly French, this restaurant is earning a fast growing reputation for excellence in both food and service.

Recipes

Owner and creator of these recipes, French-born Alain Grizard is a master at his craft.

"This recipe is simple, but you must use the very best ingredients you can find."

Tomato Goat Cheese Salad

2   cloves garlic, peeled
8   Roma tomatoes, sliced
1   bunch fresh basil, chopped
2   medium red onions, thinly sliced
2   cups virgin olive oil
     salt *(to taste)*
     pepper *(to taste)*, freshly ground
1   eggplant, cut into ⅜" slices
1   log Montrachet goat cheese, cut into 8 pieces
2   tablespoons balsamic vinegar

In a small saucepan blanch the garlic by placing it in boiling water for 30 seconds. Drain the water and repeat the process. Mince the blanched garlic.

In a medium bowl place the garlic, tomatoes, basil, onions, oil, salt, and pepper. Cover the ingredients with the mixture, and let them marinate at room temperature for 1 hour.

In a heated teflon skillet place the eggplant slices and sauté them for 2 to 3 minutes on each side, or until they are golden brown and tender.

On individual serving plates, artfully arrange *(in this order)* the tomatoes, basil, garlic, with the onions arranged on top.

Place two slices of the goat cheese next to the tomatoes.

Place two slices of the eggplant next to the goat cheese.

Sprinkle the balsamic vinegar over the tomatoes and eggplant. Grind the fresh black pepper over everything.

serves 4

Oyster Ravioli

1	tablespoon olive oil
1	bunch spinach, washed, dried, with stems removed
	salt *(to taste)*
	pepper *(to taste)*
1	egg yolk
1½	cups water
24	won ton skins
12	oysters, shelled, with the juice passed through a sieve and reserved
2	shallots, finely chopped
1	tablespoon fresh thyme, finely chopped
1	tablespoon fresh parsley, finely chopped
1	tablespoon fresh basil, finely chopped
1	tablespoon fresh tarragon, finely chopped
8	cups water
1	tablespoon olive oil
1	tablespoon rock salt
½	cup heavy cream
1	teaspoon fresh thyme, chopped
1	medium tomato, diced

In a large skillet place the olive oil and heat it on medium until it is hot. Add the spinach and quickly sauté it for 1 minute, or until it is slightly tender. Season with the salt and pepper.

Let the spinach cool, and then chop it. Drain off the liquid.

In a small bowl place the egg yolk and the 1½ cups of water. Whisk them together until they are well mixed.

Place one won ton skin on a cutting board. Brush it with the egg yolk and water mixture.

Place a small amount of the spinach in the center of the won ton. Place one oyster on top, and then sprinkle it with the fresh herbs.

Place another won ton skin on top of the oyster and then press the edges together very tightly.

Cut the ravioli into a circle with a cookie cutter. *(Make certain that the edges are still firmly pressed together.)* Do this for 12 ravioli.

(continued on next page)

"The history of this recipe goes back many years. Long ago my wife and I ate in a Chinese restaurant in France where we had steamed dumplings stuffed with crab. They were very good, and remained in my mind. Then, later, on my birthday, a friend of mine who owned a restaurant prepared a special meal for me. He served a ravioli stuffed with duck liver and a truffle sauce.....and it was amazing! So, I became very interested in stuffing a ravioli with a shellfish, but after all of my experimentation I still was not satisfied. Then, I remembered that the Chinese dumplings were made with won ton skins, and I finally achieved success by using them instead of the ravioli dough."

"This recipe is very special to me, and I have carried it with me always."

In a large sauce pan place the 8 cups of water, olive oil, and rock salt. Bring the water to a high boil and then reduce it to a low boil. Very carefully drop in the ravioli.

Cook the ravioli for 3 to 4 minutes, or until the skin is translucent and you can see the green spinach through it.

Very carefully remove the ravioli with a slotted spoon. Place 3 ravioli on individual serving plates.

In a small saucepan place the reserved oyster juice, cream, the 1 teaspoon of fresh thyme, and salt and pepper to taste. Heat the sauce to medium, and cook it for 2 to 3 minutes, or until it is reduced by half.

Garnish with the diced tomatoes.

"The secret of this dish is that the oysters should be warm, but not cooked, so that when you bite into the ravioli you taste the sea!"

serves 4

Belon Oyster Corn Soup
with Red Chile Pesto

Belon Oyster Corn Soup

1	16-ounce can sweet kernel corn
1	onion, chopped
1	bay leaf
1	stalk fresh thyme
2	cups water
1	cup heavy cream
4	Belon oysters, shelled, with the juice passed through a sieve and reserved
	salt *(to taste)*
	pepper *(to taste)*
1	cup dry white wine
1	bunch fresh cilantro, finely chopped
	Red Chile Pesto *(recipe on next page)*

In a medium saucepan place the corn *(with its juice)*, onions, bay leaf, thyme, and water. Cook the ingredients over a medium heat for 5 minutes.

Add the cream and cook for another 5 minutes. Remove the sprig of thyme and bay leaf.

Pour the mixture into a food processor and purée it.

Pour the mixture into a blender and purée it further, until it is very thin and creamy.

Pour the puréed soup back into the saucepan. Add the juice from the oysters. Season it with the salt and the pepper.

In a small saucepan place the wine and bring it to a boil. Add the oysters and poach them for 5 seconds.

Roll the oysters in the fresh cilantro, until they are well coated.

Spoon the hot soup into individual serving bowls. Place one spoonful of the Red Chile Pesto in the center.

Place one poached oyster on the top of each serving of soup and serve immediately.

serves 4

"When I moved from Los Angeles to Santa Fe I became friends with Mark Miller, the owner of the Coyote Cafe. I liked his style.....it was something brand new for me. So, I decided to create a dish that I would dedicate to him, which is a blend between the Southwestern and American styles, but using my French technique. The corn soup is typically American, the red chile pesto is Southwestern, and the oysters make it a combination of the sea and the earth."

"The only difficult thing is opening the Belon oysters, which are considered to be the best in the world (they are also very expensive). The taste is incredible! You ladies should get your men to open them, although in my home my wife does it.....she is very good at it!"

"I believe that when you go out to eat you should spend a good evening in the restaurant. Don't go to fill yourself up, but go to have a pleasurable experience!"

Red Chile Pesto

1	**cup red chile powder**
½	**cup pine nuts**
½	**cup Parmesan cheese, freshly grated**
1	**cup pure, virgin olive oil**

In a blender place all of the ingredients and blend them until they form a pesto.

Salmon in Herb Crust

3   **egg yolks**
½   **cup olive oil**
2   **tablespoons fresh basil, chopped**
2   **tablespoons fresh parsley, chopped**
2   **tablespoons fresh tarragon, chopped**
2   **tablespoons fresh dill, chopped**
2   **tablespoons fresh cilantro, chopped**
½   **pound butter, softened**
2   **cups bread crumbs**
      salt *(to taste)*
      pepper *(to taste)*
4   **6-ounce salmon fillets, boned and skin removed**
1   **cup fish stock**
1   **cup cream**
1   **bunch basil, chopped**
½   **lemon, juiced**
1   **tablespoon fresh basil leaves**
½   **red bell pepper, diced**

In a blender place the egg yolks, olive oil, the two tablespoons of basil, parsley, tarragon, dill, cilantro, the butter, bread crumbs, salt, and pepper. Mix the ingredients together well. Add more olive oil if the mixture is too thick.

Place the mixture between 2 large pieces of saran wrap. Roll it out flat with a rolling pin. Cut out 4 pieces, the exact shape of the 4 fish fillets. Remove the saran wrap and place the crust on top of the fish fillets.

In a small saucepan place the fish stock and cream. Cook over medium heat for 3 to 4 minutes, or until the sauce is reduced by ½. Season it with salt and pepper.

In a blender place the sauce and the 1 bunch of basil leaves. Blend them until they are of a juice consistency. Add the lemon juice.

Preheat the oven to 400°. Place the salmon on a flat sheet and bake it for 6 minutes, or until the crust is crisp and the fish is just done.

Place the salmon fillets on individual serving plates. Pour the sauce around the fillets. Garnish them with the basil leaves and the red bell pepper.

serves 4

"There is another personal, long history to this recipe. My grandfather was a very well known chef in France. During his career he had the opportunity to cook for royalty, such as Queen Victoria and the Kaiser of Germany. When I first moved to Santa Fe I was Executive Chef at the Eldorado Hotel. At that time the King and Queen of Spain were here to visit, and I was responsible for preparing the dinner for the royal family. It was very scary.....I had to cook for five-hundred people, there were security people in the kitchen, and someone had to taste each dish to make certain it wasn't poisoned. It was quite an experience! But I was happy because I felt that my grandfather was upstairs watching me, and that he was proud to have a grandson who was following in his footsteps. So, this is a dish that I created for that dinner."

"This recipe is not difficult to execute. It has an interesting texture with the soft salmon and the crunchy crust."

Veal Medallions with Hazelnut Sauce

8	**4-ounce medallions of veal, 1" thick**

salt *(to taste)*
pepper *(to taste)*
1 **tablespoon unsalted butter**
1 **tablespoon dry white wine**
1 **cup veal stock** *(see page 71)*
½ **cup hazelnut oil**

Season the veal on both sides with the salt and pepper.

In a medium skillet place the butter and heat it on hot until it is melted. Sauté the veal medallions on each side for 1½ minutes.

Lower the heat and cook them for 1 minute more, or until the desired doneness is achieved.

Remove the veal medallions. Place them in a baking dish and cover with foil.

Pour the burned butter out from the skillet.

Place the skillet back on the heat and add the white wine to deglaze it. Add the veal stock and cook it for 2 to 3 minutes, or until the sauce is reduced by ⅔.

Add the hazelnut oil and whip it in until the sauce boils.

Place the veal medallions on a serving platter and pour the sauce over them. Serve immediately.

serves 4

"Milk fed veal is very sweet and tender, and it has a slight natural flavor of nuts. I have found that hazelnut oil is very good in this country. It has an incredible flavor that is sweet. The combination of the veal with the hazelnut is hard to describe. It literally just melts in your mouth.....exquisite!"

"The only difficulty with this recipe is that the sauce has to be made at the very last minute, very quickly, and served right away."

Vegetables Napoleon

4	medium potatoes, peeled and grated
8	medium carrots, peeled and grated
8	medium turnips, peeled and grated
3	eggs
	salt *(to taste)*
	pepper *(to taste)*
1	bunch fresh parsley, chopped
1	bunch dill, chopped
1	bunch chervil, chopped
3	tablespoons olive oil *(or as needed)*
4	bunches spinach, washed, dried, and stems removed
4	leeks, thoroughly washed, with the white part and the tender part of the green coarsely chopped
1	tablespoon olive oil
1	pound mushrooms
2	cups Chardonnay wine
1	cup heavy cream
1	bunch chives, chopped

In three small bowls place the potatoes, carrots, and turnips. Add 1 egg to each bowl and mix it in well. Season with the salt and pepper.

Add the parsley to the potatoes and mix it in.

Add the dill to the carrots and mix it in.

Add the chervil to the turnips and mix it in.

In a large skillet place 1 of the tablespoons of olive oil and heat it on medium until it is hot.

Place the potatoes in the skillet and flatten them out with a fork until they cover the bottom of the pan. Cook them over medium heat for 2 minutes on each side, or until they stick together and form a vegetable crêpe.

Remove the vegetable crêpe from the skillet and place it on a cutting board. Cut the crêpe into four 4" round pieces *(use a cookie cutter)*.

Repeat this process for the carrots and the turnips.

(continued on next page)

"This recipe I created for our restaurant. I was looking for something vegetarian that was tasty, interesting to eat, and looked nice on the plate, because it's very difficult to make a vegetarian dish that looks good."

"I never used to like pastries, or to make them, until I met Michel Richard, who is certainly one of the best pastry chefs in the country. Through him I discovered the love and techniques of pastry making. He made a wonderful Napoleon, with different layers of fruits and creams. So, I got the idea to do the same thing with vegetables, and that is how this dish was created."

"This dish is very popular at the restaurant. I took it off my springtime menu and the customers complained, so maybe I will put it back on the summer menu."

"This is a very light and wonderful vegetarian preparation."

In a large skillet place the 1 tablespoon of olive oil and heat it to medium. Add the spinach and leeks and sauté them for 2 to 3 minutes. Remove them from the heat.

In a medium saucepan place the mushrooms and the wine. Cook them over medium heat for 4 minutes, or until the mushrooms are tender.

Place the mushrooms and wine in a blender and purée them. Season with the salt and pepper.

Reheat the spinach and the leeks. Add the heavy cream and stir it in.

Reheat the vegetable crêpes.

In the middle of an individual plate place one potato crêpe. Place a spoonful of the spinach leek mixture on top. Place one turnip crêpe on top, and then another spoonful of the spinach-leek mixture. Top with the carrot crêpe. Do this 3 more times, to make 4 servings.

Pour the mushroom sauce around *(not on top of)* the stacked crêpes. Sprinkle the chives over the top.

serves 4

Warm Apple Tart

15	egg yolks
½	cup sugar
1	cup flour
2	cups milk
1	vanilla bean
2	cups decaffeinated espresso *(liquid)*
1	stick unsalted butter
1	cup sugar
4	Golden Delicious apples, peeled, cored, and cut into thin wedges
1	package phyllo dough
1	teaspoon butter, melted
1	teaspoon sugar
1	teaspoon powdered sugar

In a medium bowl place the egg yolks and the ½ cup of sugar. Whip them together until the yolks become white. Add the flour and whip it in.

In a small saucepan place the milk and the vanilla bean. Bring the milk to a boil and then remove the vanilla bean.

Very slowly pour the boiling milk into the egg and flour mixture, while whipping constantly. Whip for 5 minutes, or until the sauce is cool.

Strain the batter through a sieve into a medium bowl. Add the espresso and stir it in. Cover the bowl and refrigerate.

In a medium saucepan place the stick of butter and the cup of sugar. Heat them until the butter is melted and mix them together.

Add the apples and cook them on medium heat for 4 to 5 minutes, or until they are caramelized. Remove them from the heat.

Cut the phyllo dough into four 3" by 3" squares. Mix the 1 teaspoon of melted butter and the 1 teaspoon of sugar together, and brush it over the top layer.

Preheat the oven to 350° and bake the phyllo squares for 8 to 10 minutes, or until they are golden brown and glazed on top.

(continued on next page)

"This is a transcription of a very traditional French dessert called Tarte Tatin, which is an upside down tart. It was created by two sisters in France with the last name of Tatin, over a hundred years ago. They had a restaurant and one day one of the sisters forgot to put the dough under the fruit, as you do in a regular tart. She cooked the apples in a sauté pan with the sugar, but without the dough. When she realized her mistake (this was an order in the restaurant so she didn't have time to start over) she made a dough, put it on top of the fruit, and flipped it over. Now the upside down tart is a classic in France. This is a true story!"

"This dessert is very light and crunchy. The smoothness of the apple is wonderful with the crisp dough."

"When I was looking for a name for my restaurant, I wanted something that reflected the type of food that I was doing. So, I called my friend Michel in Los Angeles. He said to use a name that began with the letters A, B, or C, because when people are looking for a restaurant in the Yellow Pages they start at the beginning of the alphabet (the name of his restaurant is Citrus). So, I was looking for a fruit or an herb, and thought of the name Basil, but that wasn't quite right. Finally I thought of a nectarine, which was just perfect for the kind of food I'm doing. Of course, it's not so near to the front of the Yellow Pages as it could be!"

Place the apples on top of the phyllo squares and heat them in the oven for 1 minute, or until they are warm.

Pour some of the coffee sauce on individual serving plates.

Place the phyllo squares with the apples on top of the sauce.

Sprinkle the tops with the powdered sugar.

serves 4

Harvest Festival, Rancho de las Golandrinas, New Mexico

The Old House Restaurant

Located in the beautiful Eldorado Hotel, the Old House Restaurant offers an outstanding classic American cuisine. The ambiance of its dining rooms combines a modern day elegance with a vibrant tradition, and reflects the excellence of one of Santa Fe's finest restaurants.

Recipes

Roma Tomatoes with
Fresh Herbs

Crab Cakes
Remoulade Sauce

Boston Bibb Lettuce
with Roquefort
Old House
French Vinaigrette

Old House Mixed Grill
Veal Sausage

Breast of Chicken
with Three Peppers
Poblano Sauce

Croissant Bread Pudding

John Davis, the Executive Chef at the Eldorado, says, *"This tomato is delicious, and goes very well with grilled meats. You can vary the toppings by using olive oil with minced green chile, or freshly grated Parmesan cheese."*

Roma Tomatoes with Fresh Herbs

4	Roma tomatoes, sliced in half from stem to blossom
1	tablespoon clarified butter, heated
1	dash salt
1	dash pepper
1	teaspoon fresh oregano, minced
1	teaspoon fresh tarragon, minced
1	teaspoon fresh cilantro, minced
1	teaspoon fresh parsley, minced

Brush the tops of the tomatoes with the clarified butter.

Lightly sprinkle the tomato tops with the salt and pepper.

Sprinkle the herbs over the tomato tops.

Preheat the oven to 350°.

Place the tomatoes on a baking tray.

Bake them for 10 to 12 minutes, or until they are tender.

serves 4

Crab Cakes with Remoulade Sauce

Crab Cakes

1	pound snow crab meat, cooked
1	egg
1	tablespoon mayonnaise
½	teaspoon Dijon mustard
½	teaspoon Worcestershire sauce
¼	cup Old Bay Seasoning
1	pinch baking powder
3	pieces white bread, toasted and ground to crumbs
½	lemon, juiced
½	teaspoon salt
¼	teaspoon pepper
	corn meal
4	tablespoons clarified butter *(or as needed)*
	Remoulade Sauce *(recipe on next page)*

In a medium bowl place all of the ingredients *(except for the corn meal, clarified butter, and the Remoulade Sauce)* and mix them together well.

Form the mixture into small patties. Roll the patties in the corn meal and coat them thoroughly.

In a large, heavy skillet place the clarified butter and heat it on medium until it is hot. Add the crab cakes and sauté them until they are golden brown on both sides.

Serve with the Remoulade Sauce.

serves 6

"This recipe is a version of the classic east coast crab cakes. This specific dish, insofar as the exact ingredients and amounts go, is probably seventy-five percent of my own invention. But basically, it is a very old, classic recipe."

"You can find the Old Bay Seasoning in fish markets, or in grocery stores where they sell fresh fish. It's a popular spice in the east and goes very well with all types of seafood."

"The baking powder gives the crab cakes a nice lightness. And the corn meal really lends a nice touch.....it gives it a good crunchiness!"

Remoulade Sauce

2	egg yolks
½	cup olive oil
⅓	cup celery, minced
2	scallions, minced
1	teaspoon Dijon mustard
1	teaspoon lemon juice
1	teaspoon vinegar
1	pinch paprika
1	teaspoon tabasco sauce
1	dash salt
1	dash pepper

In a small bowl place the egg yolks and whisk them well.

Very slowly dribble in the oil, while vigorously whisking constantly to achieve a mayonnaise consistency.

Whisk in the rest of the ingredients.

"The Remoulade Sauce is very spicy and tart. It's a great compliment to the crab cakes. Feel free to reduce the vinegar or tabasco if you want to make it milder."

Boston Bibb Lettuce with Roquefort and Old House French Vinaigrette

Boston Bibb Lettuce with Roquefort

2　heads Boston bibb lettuce, washed and dried
1　tomato, diced
4　ounces Roquefort cheese, crumbled
2　ounces alfalfa sprouts
1　red onion, sliced paper thin, with ringlets separated
　Old House French Vinaigrette *(recipe on next page)*

Cut the bibb lettuce in half, through the core. Cut each half into 3 wedges *(these 3 wedges make one serving)*.

Place the 3 lettuce wedges on a salad plate, in a sun ray pattern.

Sprinkle ¼ of the diced tomatoes over the lettuce wedges.

Sprinkle ¼ of the Roquefort cheese on top of the tomatoes.

Place ¼ of the alfalfa sprouts in the center of the sun ray.

Place 2 of the onion rings, overlapping, in between the lettuce wedges, for a total of 6 rings per serving.

Dribble the Old House French Vinaigrette over the top.

Repeat this process for the remaining 3 servings.

serves 4

"The presentation of this salad, with the bibb lettuce cut into three wedges, makes it more visually appealing than just a regular tossed salad with iceberg lettuce. The bibb lettuce has a wonderful flavor, and it's very tender. Also, the Roquefort cheese adds a nice touch. But make sure that it is of a high quality."

Old House French Vinaigrette

⅓	cup white wine vinegar
⅓	cup salad oil
⅓	cup olive oil
2	cloves garlic, minced
1	tablespoon lemon juice
1	teaspoon fresh basil, minced
1	teaspoon fresh tarragon, minced
1	teaspoon fresh cilantro, minced
1	teaspoon fresh parsley, minced
½	teaspoon salt
¼	teaspoon pepper

In a small bowl place the vinegar and very slowly add the oils, while whisking constantly.

Stir in the remainder of the ingredients. Cover, and refrigerate the dressing for 12 hours.

"It's important to let the dressing sit in the refrigerator for at least twelve hours so that the flavor of the fresh herbs will come through. We mix the olive oil with the salad oil so that the strong taste of the olive oil will not overpower the delicacy of the herbs."

"If you can't find the fresh herbs, it's fine to substitute dry herbs. But if you do so, be sure to add slightly smaller amounts, since dry herbs are stronger in their flavor."

Old House Mixed Grill
with Veal Sausage

Old House Mixed Grill

1   **veal sausage** (recipe follows)
4   **lamb rib chops**
4   **3-ounce petit beef fillets**

Snip the sausage into 4 pieces, where it is tied off.

Broil or grill the meats until the desired doneness is achieved.

Serve with the baked Roma Tomatoes with Fresh Herbs (see page 163)

serves 4

Veal Sausage

2   **sprigs parsley**
6   **peppercorns**
1   **large bay leaf**
10   **coriander seeds**
6   **ounces veal, cubed**
½   **cup red wine**
2½   **ounces fat back** (or salt pork), **cubed**
2   **ounces port butt** (or pork shoulder), **cubed**
4   **juniper berries**
1   **teaspoon fresh cilantro, chopped**
1   **teaspoon fresh parsley, chopped**
1   **teaspoon fresh sage, chopped**
½   **teaspoon salt**
¼   **teaspoon pepper**
1   **egg**
1½   **tablespoons flour**
2   **teaspoons brandy**
2   **teaspoons heavy cream**
1   **sausage casing**
2   **cups veal stock** (see page 71)

Using a square of cheese cloth, make a sachet of the parsley sprigs, peppercorns, bay leaf, and coriander seeds.

(continued on next page)

"If you wish, you can season the meats with salt and pepper before you cook them. And, of course, you can substitute other kinds of meats, chicken, or seafood. The key is to have variety."

"To make your own sausage may sound like an awesome task, but it's really not difficult at all. If you don't have a meat grinder, ask your butcher to grind the meats up for you. (It's always a smart idea to establish a good rapport with your butcher!) You also can get the casing and twine from the butcher. If you don't have a sausage funnel you can stuff the casing just by using a teaspoon. Just make sure that you pack it tightly."

"This particular recipe was put together by my Sous Chef, Ann Minty, and myself. It's not a spicy sausage, so if you want it hotter then you should add a little cayenne pepper."

"When you are poaching the sausage in the veal stock, be careful not to cook it too fast, or else the skin might break."

"Have your friendly butcher (with whom you have now established a great relationship) cut the veal bones into small pieces. The smaller they are the more the flavor will be extracted, and the better the stock will taste."

In a medium glass bowl place the sachet of herbs, veal, and red wine. Marinate the veal for 12 hours in the refrigerator.

Chill the meat grinder in the freezer. Chill the marinated veal, fat back, and pork butt in the refrigerator.

Run the veal, fat back, pork butt, juniper berries, cilantro, parsley, and sage through the meat grinder 3 times, using the large-holed plate.

Place the ground meat mixture in a bowl. Add the salt and pepper and mix them in well. Cover and refrigerate.

In a small bowl place the egg, flour, brandy, and cream. Mix them together to make a panada.

Using your hands, thoroughly mix the panada into the ground meat.

Using a sausage funnel, stuff the casing with the ground meat. With butcher's twine, twist, and then tie off the sausage into 4 equal parts. Tie off the ends.

In a medium saucepan place the sausage and the veal stock. Simmer the sausage for approximately 12 minutes, or until it is firm.

Breast of Chicken with Three Peppers and Poblano Sauce

Breast of Chicken with Three Peppers

4 8-ounce chicken breasts, boned and pounded
½ bunch cilantro, finely chopped
1 tablespoon cajun spice
2 tablespoons olive oil
1 green bell pepper, seeded, washed, and sliced
1 red bell pepper, seeded, washed, and sliced
1 yellow bell pepper, seeded, washed, and sliced
4 cups chicken stock
   Poblano Sauce (recipe on next page)

Season both sides of the chicken breast with the cilantro and the cajun spice.

In a large, heavy skillet place the olive oil and heat it on medium until it is hot. Add the bell peppers and sauté them for 2 minutes.

Cut 4 pieces of foil into 10" by 10" squares.

Place ¼ of the peppers on top of each chicken breast.

Roll the chicken breasts up, with the peppers inside.

Place each rolled chicken breast at the bottom of a piece of foil, and roll it up in the foil. Squeeze the ends of the foil together, so that the chicken is tightly packed inside the foil.

In a medium pot place the chicken stock. Add the rolled, foiled chicken.

Bring the stock to a boil, cover, and simmer for 12 minutes.

Remove the chicken from the foil.

Broil or grill the rolled breasts until they are done. Turn them frequently.

Slice the rolled chicken breasts into ¼" thick medallions and serve with the Poblano Sauce.

serves 4

"This is a good recipe for several reasons. First, you can prepare it ahead of time, and then grill it to order. Second, even though it might be considered to be a gourmet dish, it is very healthy.....low in cholesterol and calories. Third, it tastes delicious!"

"This is a very simple recipe that is quick and easy to make. It comes out moist, and it's delicious!"

Poblano Sauce

2   **cups veal stock** *(see page 71)*
¼   **cup red wine**
2   **dried red chiles, seeded, deveined, and chopped**
2   **Guallio chiles, seeded, deveined, and chopped**
2   **shallots, minced**

In a medium saucepan place the veal stock, wine, chiles, and shallots.

Simmer them until the sauce is reduced by ½.

Strain the sauce.

Croissant Bread Pudding

2   **large, dried-out croissants, cut into ¼" cubes**
3   **eggs, slightly whipped**
13   **ounces milk**
1   **teaspoon cinnamon**
5   **tablespoons sugar**
1   **teaspoon pure vanilla extract**

In a large bowl place all of the ingredients and mix them together.

Pour the mixture into a buttered baking dish.

Preheat the oven to 350°.

Bake for approximately 15 minutes, or until the pudding is done *(a toothpick inserted should come out dry)*.

serves 4

"Visually this is very colorful. You have the three colors of the peppers – red, yellow, and green. Also, there is the white of the chicken, and the dark brown of the sauce."

"The liquid mixture should just cover the top of the croissants. So, you may have to use a little more, or a little less, depending upon the size of your croissants."

"The cuisine of the Old House Restaurant is based on classical American cooking, blended with modern trends. We also have an upscale Southwestern menu in our other restaurant, The Eldorado Court. So, the two styles compliment each other nicely."

Detail of Adobe House, Santa Fe, New Mexico

Ore House on the Plaza

Overlooking the plaza in the heart of Santa Fe, the Ore House is a popular eating place for locals and tourists alike. The decor is a cheerful mixture of Southwestern and Mexican styles and the food is consistently excellent.....always cooked to order with the best ingredients possible.

Recipes

Ore House Salsa

Teriyaki Salmon

Ore House Blackn'd Trout

Sea Food Tacos
Veracruz Sauce

Steak Ore House
Béarnaise Sauce

Ore House Green Chile Stew

Margarita Mousse

Owner John Beaupre recommends the use of Machacado tomatoes and says, *"They have the best taste that we have found. But you also can use regular crushed tomatoes if you want. And, add some cumin if it sounds good to you."*

Ore House Salsa

2½ cups canned Machacado tomatoes, crushed
2½ cups fresh tomatoes, finely chopped
1 medium white onion, finely diced
½ cup green chile, finely diced
1 bunch cilantro, finely chopped
1 bunch parsley, finely chopped
2 tablespoons fresh lemon juice
12 cloves garlic, mashed and finely diced
1 cup water

In a medium bowl place all of the ingredients and mix them together well.

Place the salsa in the refrigerator for 2 hours.

Teriyaki Salmon

2	cups Kikkoman soy sauce
¾	cup brown sugar
1	teaspoon dry mustard
4	cloves garlic, mashed and finely diced
½	bunch parsley, finely diced
¼	cup burgundy wine
6	8-ounce boneless salmon fillets
¼	pound butter
2	tablespoons fresh lemon juice
2	lemons, wedged

In a small saucepan place the soy sauce, brown sugar, dry mustard, garlic, and parsley.

Heat the mixture over a low heat until the sugar is dissolved. Add the burgundy.

Pour the sauce into a large bowl. Add the salmon fillets and coat them thoroughly.

Marinate the salmon in the refrigerator for 4 hours.

In a small sauce pan place the butter and the lemon juice. Heat them until the butter is melted.

Grill the salmon (skin side down) for 5 minutes, or until it is just done. Baste both sides with the warm butter and lemon mixture. Turn the salmon once.

Garnish with the lemon wedges.

serves 6

"This is a good way to serve salmon in the winter, when you can't get it fresh, only frozen. The marinade is a great way to zing it up! Swordfish and halibut also taste great with the teriyaki sauce."

"The absolute best way to make this is to get a whole side of salmon and marinate it for six hours. Cook the whole slab on the barbecue. Get an extra grill, and when you are ready to turn it over, put it on top of the fish and flip it over, like a sandwich. That way the salmon won't break. Start with the skin side down and cook it until it is about one third done before you turn it. Also, be sure to baste it well with the lemon butter."

Ore House Blackn'd Trout

½ cup Hungarian paprika
1 tablespoon cayenne pepper
1 teaspoon salt
1 teaspoon onion salt
1 teaspoon onion powder
1 teaspoon powdered thyme
1 teaspoon powdered oregano
1 teaspoon powdered garlic
1 teaspoon white pepper
1 teaspoon coarse black pepper
6 10-ounce trout, boned and split
3 limes, halved
3 tablespoons butter, melted
2 limes, wedged

On a flat dish place the spices and mix them together. Press the trout down into the spices until both sides are well coated.

Heat a large, heavy, seasoned, dry cast iron skillet until it is as hot as possible. *(Turn on the exhaust fan!)*

Cook the trout for 2 to 3 minutes on each side. If they curl up then press them back down.

Squeeze one half of a lime over each trout. Dribble on a small amount of the melted butter.

Garnish with the lime wedges.

serves 6

"This is a New Orleans style recipe. I had tasted it several times in different restaurants and just loved it. The classic way is to use a red fish, but we've had some fun using different kinds of fish in our restaurant. One of our favorites is a blackn'd blue fish! Salmon, swordfish, and halibut are all delicious. And blackn'd prawns are just delicious!"

"It is essential that you have a good exhaust system because this really makes a lot of hot, spicy smoke. Your eyes will tear and you may cough, so be forewarned!"

"I think that normally trout is kind of boring. The beauty of this recipe is that it really makes the trout sing! You can also barbecue with this spice. Sprinkle it on about half way through."

"One tip.....most fish are easier to cook if they sit in the refrigerator for a couple of hours so that they stabilize."

Sea Food Tacos
with Veracruz Sauce

Sea Food Tacos

½   cup flour
1   teaspoon savory salt
1   teaspoon white pepper
1½   pounds firm-fleshed whitefish, sliced ¼" thick
2   tablespoons olive oil *(or as needed)*
12   flour tortillas, heated
   Veracruz Sauce *(recipe on next page)*
½   cup cilantro, minced

In a small bowl place the flour, savory salt, and white pepper. Mix them together. Coat the fish with the seasoned flour.

In a large skillet pour the olive oil and heat it on medium until it is hot. Add the coated fish and sauté them until they are golden brown.

Divide the fish into 12 portions and place a portion on one half of each of the tortillas. Roll the tortillas up and cover them with the Veracruz Sauce.

Garnish with the cilantro.

serves 6

"When I lived in Sun Valley, Idaho, there was this little fish restaurant that I liked, and they had a fish taco which was really good. So, we came up with a combination of a seafood Veracruz and a taco."

"You don't need a real fancy fish to make this. Monkfish is good because when it cooks up it tastes like lobster, and it's fairly inexpensive to buy. If you use a bland fish then you should add some spices to the flour."

Veracruz Sauce

4	tomatillos, peeled and finely diced
2	ripe red tomatoes, finely diced
6	jumbo cocktail green olives, thinly sliced
2	tablespoons capers
2	teaspoons olive oil
2	teaspoons cilantro, diced
1	teaspoon fresh lemon juice

In a medium bowl place all of the ingredients. Let them sit for 2 hours in the refrigerator.

"This sauce is supposed to be very piquant, so it's okay to use extra olives and capers because they really impart a lot of flavor."

"The sauce keeps well, but you should be aware that the longer it sits, the stronger the taste of the olives and the capers becomes."

"A trick to keeping the tortillas warm is to wet a kitchen towel, wring it out, and fold it in between the individual tortillas. Use more towels if you need to. Then put them in the oven for five minutes. This gets the tortillas really hot. But it also makes them slightly limp, so if you want them crisper then just cover a whole stack of them with one wet towel. That way only the top tortilla will be limp, but they will all be hot."

Steak Ore House
with **Béarnaise Sauce**

Steak Ore House

6	**strips bacon**
6	**6-ounce prime center cut beef fillets**
12	**ounces crab meat**
1½	**cups Béarnaise Sauce** *(recipe on next page)*
4	**tablespoons butter**
1	**pound button mushrooms**
	salt *(to taste)*

Wrap the bacon strips around the fillets. Secure them with a small wooden skewer.

Grill the steaks to almost the desired doneness *(remove them 1½ minutes before they are done)*.

In a medium skillet place the butter and heat it on medium until it melts. Add the mushrooms and sauté them for 2 to 3 minutes, or until they are tender. Add salt to taste.

Place the steaks on individual serving plates.

Top each steak with 2 ounces of the crab meat. Pour 2 ounces of the Béarnaise over the top.

Garnish with the button mushrooms.

serves 6

"Years ago at my restaurant in Sun Valley we wanted to expand upon a simple grilled steak. There was a Steak Oscar, and so we went just a step further by adding the bacon strips and the sautéed mushrooms."

"This is something you don't want to eat every day.....it's really a treat! And you may think that six ounces of beef is pretty skimpy, but believe me, if you get the absolute core of the fillet, and then add the crab meat and the bacon with the Béarnaise Sauce, I can guarantee that there will be plenty of food for each person!"

Béarnaise Sauce

1   **teaspoon butter**
3   **shallots, diced fine**
4   **tablespoons tarragon vinegar**
4   **egg yolks**
½   **pound butter, melted**
1   **small bunch fresh tarragon, finely chopped**
      salt *(to taste)*
      white pepper *(to taste)*

"This is pretty much a classic recipe. A copper pan is the most efficient for heat regulation when you are dealing with eggs. The rate at which you pour in the butter, and the way that you whip it, all adds up to a better, smoother sauce."

In a medium saucepan place the 1 teaspoon of butter and melt it over a medium heat. Add the shallots and sauté them for 2 minutes.

Add the vinegar and heat it for 3 to 5 minutes, or until the sauce is reduced by ½.

In a heated double boiler place the egg yolks and whip them vigorously with a wire whisk for 1 minute, or until they are the consistency of a thick cream. Remove the egg yolks from the heat.

Very slowly and consistently dribble in the ½ pound of melted butter. Whip constantly until the mixture is smooth.

Strain the vinegar into a medium bowl. Add the egg and butter mixture and whip it in.

Add the fresh tarragon. Season with the salt and pepper.

"Actually, you are starting with a Hollandaise Sauce, and when you add the tarragon vinegar, it becomes a Béarnaise Sauce."

Ore House Green Chile Stew

2	tablespoons olive oil
1	pound top sirloin steak, cut into ½" cubes
2	yellow onions, diced
1	cup red wine
8	cups water
2	carrots, diced
2	russet potatoes, diced into ½" cubes
½	cup green chile, diced
1	cup beef stock
1½	teaspoons cumin
1½	teaspoons coriander
2	cups Ore House Salsa (see page 173)
	salt (to taste)
	pepper (to taste)
36	large garlic croutons
3	ounces sharp cheddar cheese, grated
3	ounces Monterey Jack cheese, grated
	sour cream
	red chile powder

In a large heavy saucepan pour the oil and heat it on medium until it is hot. Add the steak and onions, and sauté them for 2 to 3 minutes.

Add the wine and water. Bring them to a boil and then simmer them for 15 minutes.

Add the carrots and potatoes. Bring the stew to a boil and then reduce it to a simmer.

Add the green chile, beef stock, cumin, coriander, and the Ore House Salsa. Simmer the stew for one hour. Season with the salt and pepper.

Place the stew in individual serving bowls. Place 6 large garlic croutons on top.

Sprinkle on the 2 cheeses, and broil in the oven until the cheese melts.

Top with a dollop of sour cream, and sprinkle on some red chile powder.

serves 6

"This is really a great tasting dish! We use the same preparation as for a French onion soup, along with our extremely potent garlic bread croutons. How do you make them? Well, melt up a stick of butter and add a huge amount of minced garlic, some parsley, a good dose of white pepper, and some salt. Pour this over some large French bread cubes and bake them in the oven until they are brown and crunchy."

Margarita Mousse

2	eggs, separated
1	ounce Herradura gold tequila
¼	lime, juiced
1	orange, zested
¼	cup sugar
½	cup whipping cream
6	mint sprigs
6	lime slices

In a double boiler place the egg yolks and beat them over a medium heat for 1 minute, or until they are creamy.

Add the tequila, lime juice, and orange zest. Stir them in for 1 minute, or until everything is creamy. Refrigerate the mixture for 20 minutes.

In a small bowl place the egg whites and whip them until they are foamy *(not stiff)*.

Very slowly add the sugar and whip until the egg whites are firm, but before any peaks form.

In a small bowl place the whipping cream and beat it until peaks are formed.

Remove the egg yolks from the refrigerator. Gently fold in the egg white mixture and the whipped cream.

Pour the mousse into goblets and refrigerate them for 2 hours.

Garnish with the mint sprigs and lime slices.

serves 6

"I personally don't eat desserts, so this recipe is from my manager, Eric Sanders. He loves it, and so does almost everyone else. It's a good Southwestern version of a mousse."

"My belief is that when a person goes out to eat he should leave the restaurant feeling that he has had a good experience at a reasonable price. And then, hopefully, he will want to come back!"

Inn at Loretto, Santa Fe, New Mexico

The Palace

A reconstruction of a once famous Santa Fe saloon and bordello, The Palace restaurant is an expression of *Old West* opulence and luxury, from its red velvet wallpaper to the gold leaf chandeliers. It's a real treat to enjoy the contemporary Italian and Continental cuisines in such lush surroundings!

Eugen Bingham is the new Head Chef at the Palace. Before moving to Santa Fe he worked with Fred Halpert at The Portman in San Francisco. Fred is one of the current top chefs in the Bay Area. Eugen says, *"Serve this with champagne!"*

Olive Crostini

¼   **cup olive oil**
1   **clove garlic, chopped**
10   **ounces fresh porcini mushrooms, washed and sliced**
  salt *(to taste)*
  fresh ground pepper *(to taste)*
½   **cup Calamata olives, seeded**
½   **teaspoon fennel seed**
6   **slices coarse-textured bread**

In a medium skillet place ½ of the oil and heat it on medium until it is hot. Add the garlic and mushrooms and sauté them for 5 minutes, or until the mushrooms are tender. Add the salt and pepper.

In a food processor place the olives, fennel seed, and the remaining oil. Finely chop the olives.

In a small bowl place the chopped olives and the mushrooms, and mix them together.

Toast the bread in a 350° oven until it is golden.

Spread the mixture on top of the toast.

serves 6

Chilled Chardonnay and Strawberry Soup

12	ounces strawberries, washed and hulled
¼	cup honey, soft
1½	cups Chardonnay wine
1	teaspoon fresh lime juice
2	tablespoons heavy cream
4	sprigs mint leaves

In a food processor place the strawberries, honey, and Chardonnay. Purée the ingredients until the mixture is smooth. Pour the mixture in a bowl and refrigerate it for 3 hours.

Add the lime juice and heavy cream. Mix them in well.

Pour the soup into individual serving bowls. Garnish with the mint sprigs.

serves 4

"This is a very refreshing soup, especially for Santa Fe, because it's so hot here. I especially like it because I just moved from San Francisco and I'm not used to the heat, so it's nice to have a cold soup. The flavor is sweet and the lime gives it a nice acidic bite. Also, it's quick and easy to make."

Red Cabbage Salad with Goat Cheese and Duck

½	small head red cabbage, julienned
3	ounces soft goat cheese, crumbled
2	duck breasts, roasted, skinned, and julienned
½	bunch thyme, finely chopped
¼	cup balsamic vinegar
1	cup extra virgin olive oil
	salt *(to taste)*
	pepper *(to taste)*

In a medium bowl place the cabbage, goat cheese, duck, and thyme. Toss them together.

In a small saucepan place the vinegar, oil, salt, and pepper. Heat it on medium until it is warm. Pour the warm dressing over the cabbage mixture and mix well.

serves 4

"The ingredients in this dish may seem unusual, but they all go great together. It's a delicious, tangy salad, and a great way to spice up cabbage, which most people think is somewhat boring."

Fettucini Estate was created at The Palace by the Pertusini brothers, who are the owners of the restaurant. They grew up in Lake Como, Italy, and learned their cooking skills from their father, who was the premiere chef at the Villa D'Esta.

"This dish tastes wonderful! In fact, Gourmet Magazine just requested the recipe for it."

Fettucini Estate

4	**artichokes, washed**
¼	**cup dry porcini mushrooms, soaked in 2 cups of water for 1 hour** *(reserve the water)*
2	**tablespoons olive oil**
2	**shallots, finely chopped**
½	**teaspoon fresh basil, finely minced**
¼	**teaspoon fresh rosemary, finely minced**
¼	**teaspoon fresh sage, finely minced**
	salt *(to taste)*
	pepper *(to taste)*
1	**tablespoon dry white wine**
1	**cup chicken stock**
¼	**cup butter**
1	**cup heavy cream**
½	**cup Pecorino cheese, grated**
1	**pound fettucini, cooked al dente**
¼	**cup Parmesan cheese, freshly grated**

Peel off the leaves of the artichokes and remove the hearts. Cut the hearts into julienne strips.

Squeeze the excess water out of the soaked mushrooms and finely chop them.

In a medium saucepan place the olive oil and heat it on medium until it is hot. Add the shallots and sauté them for 1 minute. Add the artichoke hearts and sauté them for 3 minutes.

Add the mushrooms, basil, rosemary, sage, salt, pepper, wine, and chicken stock. Simmer everything for 10 minutes, or until the artichokes are tender.

Add the butter, cream, and Pecorino. Stir the sauce until the butter has melted and the sauce is nice and creamy. Thin it out with the mushroom water, if necessary.

Pour the sauce on top of the fettucini. Sprinkle on the grated Parmesan cheese.

serves 4

Roasted Quail
with Fava Bean Ragoût
and Thyme Sauce

Roasted Quail

4	quails, cleaned
	salt *(to taste)*
	pepper *(to taste)*
8	tablespoons olive oil
	Fava Bean Ragoût *(recipe follows)*
	Thyme Sauce *(recipe on next page)*
2	sprigs fresh thyme, finely chopped

Season the quails with the salt and pepper.

In a medium saucepan place 2 tablespoons of the olive oil and heat on medium until it is hot. One at a time, sauté each quail on all sides until it is nicely browned, adding more oil as needed.

Preheat the oven to 375°. Place the 4 quails in a roasting pan and bake them for 10 minutes, or until they are done.

On individual serving plates place the Fava Bean Ragoût. Place a roasted quail on top. Spoon the Thyme Sauce around the quail. Garnish with the thyme.

serves 4

Fava Bean Ragoût

2	tablespoons butter
4	shallots, minced
3	cloves garlic, minced
2	cups fava beans, peeled
½	cup heavy cream
	salt *(to taste)*
	pepper *(to taste)*

(continued on next page)

"Cooking the quail is the simplest part of this recipe. By sautéing it you are enhancing the flavor and getting it nice and brown."

"Fava beans are very Italian. I love them! They make excellent mousses if you add olive oil and different fresh herbs. But, they have a very tough, thick skin, so you must be sure to peel them."

In a medium saucepan place the butter and heat it on medium until it is melted. Add the shallots and garlic and sauté them for 2 minutes.

Add the beans and sauté them until they are soft. Remove the beans and set them aside.

Add the cream and cook it for 5 to 7 minutes, or until it is reduced by ⅔.

Add the beans and cook them for 3 to 5 minutes, or until they are well coated. Add the salt and pepper to taste.

Thyme Sauce

2   **tablespoons butter**
6   **shallots, minced**
2   **cloves garlic, minced**
2   **tomatoes, quartered**
½   **bunch fresh thyme, minced**
1   **cup Chardonnay wine**
2   **cups chicken stock**
    salt *(to taste)*
    pepper *(to taste)*

In a medium saucepan place the butter and heat it on high until it is melted. Add the shallots and garlic, and sauté them for 2 minutes.

Add the tomatoes, thyme, and wine. Cook them on medium heat for 10 minutes, or until the liquid is reduced by ⅔.

Add the chicken stock and cook the sauce for 15 to 20 minutes, or until the sauce is slightly thickened.

Add the salt and pepper to taste. Strain the sauce.

"As long as you have all of the ingredients prepared, then this recipe is quick and easy to make. It's a nice, basic sauce, and the thyme really adds a lot of flavor."

"The consistency of the sauce that you are trying to achieve is hard to explain. It should be thinner than melted chocolate, but thicker than a heavy cream. If you mess up and get it too thick, then just add some water."

Sautéed Red Snapper
with Artichoke Mousse
and Light Tomato Sauce

Sautéed Red Snapper

2	pounds Florida red snapper, boned and cut into 4 pieces *(remove the skins if they are not small fish)*
4	tablespoons olive oil
	Artichoke Mousse *(recipe follows)*
	Light Tomato Sauce *(recipe on next page)*
4	sprigs fresh basil

In a large skillet place the olive oil and heat it on medium until it is hot. Sauté the snapper on both sides *(skin side first)* for a total of 6 to 8 minutes, or until it is just done.

Place some heated Artichoke Mousse on a plate. Place the fish on top. Pour the Light Tomato Sauce around the fish. Garnish with a sprig of basil.

serves 4

"I like to buy red snapper when they are small, because then the skin is tender and you can eat it. You should sauté the skin side first and it will get all delicious and crunchy. However, if you are using a bigger snapper, then you should first remove the skin, because it will be too tough to eat. In this case you should cook the meat side first. Don't ask me why, just do it!"

Artichoke Mousse

6	fresh, raw artichoke hearts, cooked in lemon water and drained
¼	cup olive oil
	salt *(to taste)*
	pepper *(to taste)*
2	teaspoons olive oil
6	sprigs fresh thyme, chopped
¼	cup Calamata olives, pitted and quartered

In a blender place the cooked artichoke hearts and purée them. Slowly add the ¼ cup of olive oil while slowly blending. Add the salt and pepper, and blend them in.

(continued on next page)

"Be sure that you blend the artichokes so that they are nice and fine. Add the oil very slowly so that it will bind with the artichokes. By the way, if you don't like artichokes, don't make this recipe!"

Remove the mousse from the blender and place it in a bowl.

In a small skillet place the 2 teaspoons of olive oil and heat it on medium. Add the thyme and sauté it for 2 minutes.

Add the sautéed thyme to the mousse and stir it in. Add the olives and stir them in.

Before serving the mousse reheat it in the oven.

Light Tomato Sauce

4	cups white wine
¼	cup dry vermouth
2	shallots, finely chopped
1	cup fish stock
½	cup prepared tomato sauce
½	pound unsalted butter, cut into small pieces
	salt *(to taste)*
	pepper *(to taste)*

In a medium saucepan place the wine, dry vermouth, and shallots. Cook the ingredients on a medium heat for 3 to 4 minutes, or until the liquid is reduced by ⅔.

Add the fish stock and tomato sauce and cook for 25 minutes, or until the sauce is reduced by ⅔.

Pour the sauce into a food processor and add the butter, piece by piece, while blending constantly.

Strain the sauce through a fine sieve. Add the salt and pepper.

"This is a very delicious, light sauce that is simple to make. Again, it should be a little thicker than heavy cream."

"In most cases I make up my own recipes instead of taking them from a book. Basically I just combine ingredients together any way I see fit."

Palace Lamb Roast

1	leg of lamb
	salt *(as needed)*
	pepper *(as needed)*
1	tablespoon olive oil
1	whole bulb garlic, slightly smashed so that the cloves separate
3	sprigs fresh thyme
3	fresh rosemary sprigs
¼	cup veal stock *(see page 71)*
2	cups chicken stock
2	tablespoons butter
1	tablespoon fresh thyme, chopped
1	tablespoon fresh rosemary, chopped

Season the lamb with the salt and pepper.

Preheat the oven to 450°.

In a large roasting pan place the lamb and the olive oil. Roast the lamb for 15 minutes *(turn it frequently)*.

Add the garlic cloves *(skins on)*, thyme sprigs, and rosemary sprigs. Bake the lamb for 1¼ hours, or until it is done.

Remove the lamb from the pan. Add the veal stock to the pan and cook it on the stove until it is reduced by ½.

Add the chicken stock and cook it for 10 minutes, or until it is reduced by ⅔.

Add the butter and whisk it in.

Strain the sauce.

Serve the lamb with the sauce poured over it. Garnish with the chopped thyme and rosemary.

serves 8

"This is a very simple, Mediterranean dish. I love lamb because it's very aromatic and has a lot of flavor."

"When you crush the bulb of garlic you just want the cloves to separate, but you don't want to peel the skins. By leaving the skins on the flavor will really be enhanced. When the lamb is cooked the garlic flavor will be nice and subtle."

"This dish takes some skill to make. The main thing is not to overcook the rice, which should be al dente, or firm on the inside. So, don't add so much liquid that the rice gets mushy. Be sure to stir constantly so that the rice doesn't stick to the bottom of the pan and burn. If you don't get it just right it will still taste great!"

"In Italy there are different kinds of rice that you can make risotto with, but in this country it is only Aborrio rice that is available to us."

"Risotto is very Italian, very ricey, and very delicious. Buen appetito!"

Mussel Risotto

3	tablespoons olive oil
2	pounds mussels, beards removed and washed
3	cloves garlic, finely chopped
6	tablespoons butter
½	small onion, chopped
2	tablespoons olive oil
1¾	cups Aborrio rice, uncooked
	salt *(to taste)*
	freshly ground pepper *(to taste)*
⅛	teaspoon saffron
6	cups fish stock *(or as needed)*
2	cups spinach, chopped and blanched

In a large pot place the 3 tablespoons of olive oil and heat it on low. Add the mussels and half of the garlic. Cook them for 4 to 5 minutes, or until the mussels have opened. Remove the mussels from their shells and set them aside.

Strain the cooking liquid from the mussels and reserve it.

In a large pot place 4 tablespoons of the butter and the 2 tablespoons of olive oil. Heat them on medium. Add the rest of the garlic and the onions and sauté them for 1 minute.

Add the rice, salt, pepper, and saffron. Add the fish stock, one ladle at a time, stirring frequently, over a 20 minute period, or until the rice is cooked al dente.

Remove the rice from the heat. Add the spinach, mussels, strained mussel juice, and the remaining butter. Stir everything together well.

serves 6

Cantaloupe-Muscat Tart

1   **ripe cantaloupe, peeled, seeded, and cut into ¼"**
        slices
1   **cup muscat wine**
½   **cup sugar**
4   **egg yolks**
½   **cup cream**
¼   **cup milk**
3   **tablespoons all-purpose flour**
½   **cup apricot jam**
1   **pre-baked tart shell** *(recipe on next page)*

In a medium bowl place the cantaloupe slices. Mix 5 tablespoons of the wine with 5 tablespoons of the sugar and pour it over the melon slices. Cover, and refrigerate them for 12 hours. Drain them and pat them dry.

In a medium bowl place the egg yolks and 2 tablespoons of the sugar. Whisk them together until the yolks are pale.

In a small saucepan place the cream, milk, and flour. Heat the ingredients on medium and whisk them together until the mixture is smooth. Bring the mixture to a boil.

Gradually add the hot cream mixture to the egg yolks and whisk it in. Return the mixture to the saucepan and cook it on medium heat for 4 minutes, whisking constantly, until the mixture is slightly thickened.

Remove the pan from the heat and add ⅓ cup of the wine. Stir it in.

In another small saucepan place the apricot jam with the remaining sugar and wine. Bring the mixture to a boil and strain it. Let it cool.

Brush a thin layer of the apricot glaze over the pre-baked tart shell. Place the egg and cream mixture evenly in the bottom of the shell.

Place the melon slices in a pinwheel design on top. Reheat the apricot glaze and brush it onto the melon slices.

serves 6

"Melons are very popular in Italy, and this recipe is very traditional. It's a nice light dessert that is good to serve in the summer."

"My basic philosophy of cooking is: if it's not fresh, then don't use it! Be creative, and don't limit yourself to cookbooks. Remember, there are a hundred roads that lead to Rome, so don't always take just one way. The final criteria is, if it tastes good, then you've succeeded!"

"When you roll the dough out it must be only one quarter inch thick and it should be even all over. When you roll it, roll it in a circle, and never lift the pin from the dough until you are completely finished."

"The thing that might seem strange is placing the foil on top of the dough and then filling it with the dried beans. The purpose of this is to weigh the dough down so that it doesn't rise."

"Our restaurant has a line of seasonings, called The Palace Seasonings, which are sold internationally. You can find them in the gourmet sections of major department stores. We also sell them at the restaurant."

Tart Shell

1⅓ cups all purpose flour, sifted
1   tablespoon sugar
¼   teaspoon salt
1   stick butter, softened and broken into pieces
1   egg, lightly beaten

In a food processor place the flour, sugar, and salt. Mix them together. Add the butter, piece by piece, and mix it in. Add the eggs and mix until the dough is smooth, like a pie dough.

Place the dough on a floured cutting board and form it into a ball. Wrap it in plastic and refrigerate it for 2 hours.

Preheat the oven to 375°.

Roll out the dough on a floured surface. Add more flour as needed to prevent sticking.

Place the dough in a 9" buttered tart pan. Set it in the refrigerator for 30 minutes.

Line the pastry shell with foil. Fill the bottom with dried beans. Bake the shell for 10 minutes. Remove the beans and foil. Pierce the bottom with a fork.

Bake the shell for another 15 minutes, or until it is light brown. Let it cool.

Saint Francis Cathedral, Santa Fe, New Mexico

Piñon Grill

Located in the new Hilton of Santa Fe, the Piñon Grill captures all of the charm, style, and grace of New Mexico. Customers can relax in the elegant ambiance, while enjoying a classic Continental cuisine prepared with a Southwestern twist.

Recipes

Apple Pecan Chutney

Stuffed Chile
Jalapeño Cheese Sauce

Hot Duck Salad
Piñon Grill
Raspberry Vinaigrette

Piñon Grill Tortilla Soup

Pork Chops Calvados

Chicken Breast Roberto
Jalapeño Jelly
Blue Corn Crêpes

Piñon Nut Tart

Sous Chef James Lamoureux recommends making this chutney three days before you are ready to use it so that the flavors will really develop. *"This is kind of an un-classic chutney in that it is fairly subtle and has no overtones of the Far East."*

Apple Pecan Chutney

3   Granny Smith apples, peeled, cored, and sliced
¼   cup fresh lemon juice
1   cup water
⅓   cup Calvados *(apple brandy)*
2   tablespoons white vinegar
2   tablespoons orange juice concentrate
¼   teaspoon garlic, minced
¼   teaspoon nutmeg
¼   teaspoon cinnamon
2   tablespoons white sugar
2   tablespoons brown sugar
2   tablespoons pecan pieces
⅓   cup raisins

In a medium saucepan place all of the ingredients. Bring them to a boil over medium heat. Cook them for 20 minutes, or until the apples are al dente.

Cool the chutney to room temperature. Cover, and refrigerate it overnight.

Stuffed Chile
with Jalapeño Cheese Sauce

Stuffed Chile

1	cup water
1	pound chicken breast, skinned, boned, and ground
½	onion, finely diced
1	pound mushrooms, washed and finely diced
¼	teaspoon nutmeg
1	tablespoon salt
¼	teaspoon cumin
1	teaspoon red chile powder
1	teaspoon garlic, minced
1	teaspoon oregano
½	teaspoon cayenne pepper
3	eggs
6	tablespoons pimientos, diced
⅓	cup fresh parsley, chopped
2	teaspoons salt *(or to taste)*
1½	cups bread crumbs
6	large Anaheim chiles, roasted, peeled, seeded, and deveined
	Jalapeño Cheese Sauce *(recipe on next page)*

In a large saucepan place the water and bring it to a boil. Add the chicken, onion, mushrooms, nutmeg, the 1 tablespoon of salt, cumin, chile powder, garlic, oregano, and cayenne pepper. Simmer the ingredients for 3 minutes.

Strain off the liquid and let the ingredients cool to room temperature. Add the eggs, pimientos, parsley, the 2 teaspoons of salt, and the bread crumbs. Mix everything together well.

Slice open the Anaheim chiles lengthwise and stuff them with the mixture. Leave the slices slightly separated so that the stuffing shows. In a baking pan add water so that it is ¼" deep. Place the chiles in the pan.

Preheat the oven to 375° and bake the chiles for 7 to 10 minutes, or until they are thoroughly heated. Pour the Jalapeño Cheese Sauce on a platter and place the chiles on top.

serves 6

"This is a recipe that I came up with. The Executive Chef, Steve Johnston, had the idea, and he told me to go for it!"

"The stuffed chiles are quite easy to make. They're not spicy, but rather, they are subtle in taste. The spiciness of the Jalapeño Cheese Sauce just accents them enough to make it happen!"

"The cheese sauce is really good and we designed it so that it would be very easy to make. It holds up nicely and the stuffed green chiles look quite pretty sitting on top of the white cheese sauce."

"The recipe is pretty much middle of the road as far as how hot it is. If you want to make it snappier then you can hit it with a little bit more of the tabasco sauce, and that will wake it right up!"

Jalapeño Cheese Sauce

½	pound cream cheese, cut into 1" cubes
1	cup whipping cream
1	teaspoon shallots, minced
1	teaspoon garlic, minced
1	teaspoon Worcestershire sauce
1	teaspoon tabasco sauce
1	teaspoon fresh lemon juice
1	teaspoon white vinegar
1	pinch salt
¾	cup jalapeño Jack cheese, grated

In a medium saucepan place all of the ingredients except for the jalapeño Jack cheese.

Heat the ingredients on medium for 3 to 5 minutes, stirring occasionally, until the cheese is melted.

Add the jalapeño Jack cheese and mix it in until it is melted.

Hot Duck Salad
with Piñon Grill Raspberry Vinaigrette

Hot Duck Salad

¼	cup salt
2	tablespoons sugar
1	tablespoon thyme
1	tablespoon rosemary
1	tablespoon black pepper
1	teaspoon paprika
2	ducklings
1	orange, halved
1	lemon, halved
2	bay leaves
1	large head romaine lettuce, washed, dried, and shredded
	Piñon Grill Raspberry Vinaigrette *(recipe on next page)*
1	12-ounce can mandarin oranges, strained

In a small bowl place the salt, sugar, thyme, rosemary, pepper, and paprika. Mix them together. Thoroughly season the ducklings, inside and out, with the seasonings.

Place the orange, lemon, and bay leaves into the cavity of the ducklings. Place them in a baking pan.

Preheat the oven to 400°. Bake the ducks for 15 minutes. Reduce the heat to 325° and bake them for 1 hour.

Bone the ducks and slice the meat into ½" by 2" strips. Divide the meat into 6 equal parts of the thigh, leg, and breast.

On individual serving plates place the romaine lettuce. Pour the Piñon Grill Raspberry Vinaigrette over the top. Artfully arrange the duck slices on top.

Arrange the mandarin orange pieces around the rim.

serves 6

"The roasted duck with the seasoning mixture and the aromatics that you put inside the cavity make it really tasty. The citrus juices penetrate the duck and when you serve it with the mandarin oranges the flavors compliment each other perfectly."

"I came up with the idea for the preparation of the duck a long time ago. I've been making it for years, it's so good!"

Piñon Grill Raspberry Vinaigrette

2	egg yolks
4	ounces raspberries, puréed
⅓	cup white vinegar
¼	cup white wine
½	cup raspberry vinegar
2	teaspoons sugar
2	teaspoons fresh lemon juice
½	teaspoon salt
1	tablespoon shallots, minced
2	teaspoons Dijon mustard
¾	cup olive oil

In a medium bowl place the egg yolks and whip them until they are light and thick.

Add the remainder of the ingredients *(except for the olive oil)* and beat everything together.

Gradually add the oil in a thin stream while whisking constantly.

Strain the dressing through a fine sieve.

"This is a great dressing and I've been using it for a long time, too. It lasts very well and is wonderful with just a plain green salad."

"It's a light egg emulsified dressing which is very easy to make. You can use a blender, a hand mixer, or whip it by hand. If you are worried about cholesterol you can eliminate the egg."

Piñon Grill Tortilla Soup

2	tablespoons vegetable oil
1	medium onion, diced
1	tablespoon red chile powder
1	tablespoon garlic, minced
1	teaspoon coriander
1	teaspoon cumin
2	teaspoons white pepper
1	teaspoon paprika
2	bay leaves
1½	quarts chicken stock
2	tablespoons vegetable oil
2	medium flour tortillas
½	cup cheddar cheese, grated

In a medium saucepan place the 2 tablespoons of vegetable oil and heat on medium until it is hot. Add the onions and sauté them for 1 to 2 minutes, or until they are translucent.

Add the chile powder and sauté it for 1 minute. Add the remainder of the spices and mix them in well.

Add the chicken stock and simmer the soup for 20 minutes.

In a medium skillet place the other 2 tablespoons of the vegetable oil and heat on medium until it is hot. Place one tortilla in the skillet and sprinkle ¼ cup of the cheese over the top.

Gently sauté the tortilla for 2 to 3 minutes, or until the cheese has melted. Drain the tortilla on paper towels.

Repeat this process for the other tortilla.

Cut the tortillas in half, and then cut them into ¼" strips.

Place the cheese tortilla strips in the bottom of individual soup bowls and pour the hot soup on top.

serves 6

"This is a soup that Steve introduced here. The tortillas with the melted cheese on top really make the dish happen! If you have a homemade chicken stock, so much the better, but canned stock that you buy in the store works out fine, too."

"The softer the tortillas the better, because if they get crisp then they tend to break up when you cut them."

Pork Chops Calvados

1	**tablespoon olive oil**
1	**tablespoon shallots, minced**
2	**teaspoons garlic, minced**
1	**ounce brandy**
1	**ounce calvados** *(apple brandy)*
2	**ounces apple juice**
2	**cups whipping cream**
1	**cup veal stock, reduced to ¼ cup** *(see page 71)*
2½	**tablespoons butter**
	salt *(to taste)*
	white pepper *(to taste)*
12	**3-ounce center cut pork chops**
	Apple Pecan Chutney *(see page 195)*

In a medium saucepan place the olive oil and heat it on medium until it is hot. Add the shallots and the garlic. Sauté them for 1 to 2 minutes.

Add the brandy and calvados, and flame.

Add the apple juice and shake the pan for 1 to 2 minutes, or until it is reduced to a glaze.

Add the cream and cook the sauce for 3 to 4 minutes, or until it is reduced by ½.

Add the veal stock and stir it in.

Add the butter in small pieces, one at a time, until it is melted.

Add salt and pepper to taste. Keep the sauce warm.

Preheat the oven to broil and place the pork chops in a baking pan. Broil them for 2 to 3 minutes on each side, or until they are done.

Place the sauce on a serving platter. Place the broiled pork chops on top. Serve with the Apple Pecan Chutney.

serves 6

"The sauce for the pork is fairly straightforward. The reduced veal stock gives it more body. The butter and cream make it a rich sauce, and it is also slightly sweet. It really goes well with the Apple Pecan Chutney. If you barbecue your pork chops, they will be even more delicious."

"We have to please large crowds of people of all ages from all over the country (or the world). They want to taste some Southwestern cooking, but they don't want it every day. So, we try to come up with interesting, well-balanced items, that have just a slight indigenous Southwestern twist."

Chicken Breast Roberto
with Jalapeño Jelly
and Blue Corn Crêpes

Chicken Breast Roberto

24	ounces beer
4	ounces rosé wine
1	tablespoon garlic, minced
2	tablespoons salt
½	cup red wine vinegar
1	teaspoon tarragon
1½	tablespoons thyme
2	tablespoons Worcestershire sauce
1	cup olive oil
6	chicken breasts, boned
	Jalapeño Jelly *(recipe on next page)*
	Blue Corn Crêpes *(see page 204)*

In a large bowl place the beer, wine, garlic, salt, vinegar, tarragon, thyme, Worcestershire sauce, and olive oil. Mix everything together well.

Add the chicken breasts and cover them completely with the marinade.

Cover and refrigerate the marinated chicken for 1 to 3 days.

Remove the chicken from the marinade and place it in a baking pan.

Preheat the oven to broil, and cook the chicken *(turn it twice)* for 10 to 12 minutes, until it is done and the skin is crispy.

Serve with the Jalapeño Jelly and the Blue Corn Crêpes.
serves 6

"This is another recipe from Steve, the Executive Chef. The marinade is one he got from another chef years ago, who made him promise that he would never use it! But we decided to resurrect it from the grave, so to speak, and it is probably our best seller, along with the Pork Chops Calvados."

"This is so good, and so simple to make. You can marinate it for up to a week. It's a great thing to take camping because you can marinate the chicken at home and then wrap it up and take it with you."

"The chicken tastes the best if you barbecue it. The skin will get very dark but it won't be burnt.....and it's great!"

Jalapeño Jelly

1	cup green bell pepper, chopped
4	jalapeño peppers, chopped
6	cups sugar
1¼	cups white vinegar
3	ounces Certo pectin
½	red bell pepper, seeded, washed, and minced
½	green bell pepper, seeded, washed, and minced
½	yellow bell pepper, seeded, washed, and minced

In a medium saucepan place the 1 cup of chopped bell pepper, the jalapeños, sugar, and vinegar. Cook them on a low boil for 15 minutes.

Strain the liquid into another saucepan. Add the pectin and stir it in. Let it cool to room temperature.

Blanch the red, green, and yellow peppers for 30 seconds in boiling water.

Strain them through a sieve and immediately place them in ice water. Strain the peppers again and mix them in the cooled jelly.

Pour the jelly into 6 individual serving cups.

Refrigerate the jelly overnight.

"The recipe is not complex at all, and you can buy all of the ingredients at the grocery store."

"The only thing I like to stress is that the blanched peppers should be added to the jelly after it has cooled to room temperature. If you add them while the jelly is still hot then the peppers will continue to cook and they won't look as nice because the color will fade."

"I had a very sophisticated woman from Chicago ask for this recipe. She loved it so much she was eating it with her fingers!"

Blue Corn Crêpes

3   eggs
½   cup water
½   cup flour
½   cup blue corn meal
1   teaspoon salt
3   tablespoons butter, melted
¼   cup vegetable oil *(or as needed)*

In a medium bowl place the eggs and the water, and beat them together.

Add the flour, blue corn meal, salt, and butter.

Mix everything together well.

Cook the crêpes, using the vegetable oil *(see page 72 or 94)*.

"The blue corn crêpes give a Southwestern twist to the recipe and they make a nicer presentation. You can definitely make yellow corn crêpes as well, and they will be just as good. They go great with the Jalapeño Jelly, so it's nice to give people three or four crêpes apiece to eat on the side."

"It's really a good idea to use a non-stick pan because then the crêpes come right out with no problem at all. Easy money!"

Piñon Nut Tart

1¼ **cups sugar**
2½ **tablespoons butter**
1 **teaspoon salt**
6 **eggs**
1½ **cups dark corn syrup**
2 **teaspoons vanilla**
1½ **cups piñon nuts**
1 **10" unbaked pie shell**
1 **cup heavy cream** (unsweetened), **whipped**

In a medium bowl place the sugar, butter, and salt. Beat them together well.

While beating constantly, add the eggs, one at a time, until they are absorbed into the mixture.

Add the corn syrup and vanilla, and blend them in.

Place the piñon nuts on the bottom of the pie shell. Add the filling.

Preheat the oven to 450°. Bake the tart for 10 minutes.

Reduce the heat to 350°. Bake the tart for 40 minutes, or until it is set.

Cool it to room temperature and serve with the whipped cream.

serves 6

"This recipe is very similar to a pecan pie filling except that it has the addition of piñon nuts. And they don't necessarily have to be toasted because they brown up pretty well in the oven."

"It's a simple dessert to prepare and people love it. It's also very rich, especially if you serve it with the unsweetened whipped cream. But it's worth it!"

Adobe House, Tesuque Pueblo, New Mexico

Rancho Encantado

Rancho Encantado, the *"Enchanted Ranch"*, is a blend of Southwestern elegance and warm hospitality, a true haven in the rolling hills north of Santa Fe. The gourmet restaurant offers an original cuisine, combining European, American, and New Mexican tastes.....all enjoyed in a truly enchanting place!

Recipes

Roasted Oysters Encantado

Sautéed Beef and
Lamb Medallions
Piñon Tomatillo Sauce

White and Blue
Corn Chowder

Blood Orange and
Watercress Salad
Mint Vinaigrette

Baked Breast of Duck
Raspberry Port Sauce

Lobster Enchiladas
Green Chile Piñon Sauce

Wild Rice with Piñons

Savory Black Beans

Poached Anjou Pears
Chantilly Cream

Ed Turk, the Executive Chef at Rancho Encantado, received his training in the creole tradition, in the deep south.

Roasted Oysters Encantado

24	oysters, washed and shelled
2	sticks butter, melted
8	cloves garlic, finely minced
1	tablespoon fresh parsley, minced
1	teaspoon salt
½	teaspoon white pepper
¼	cup Pernod
½	cup fresh Parmesan cheese

In a baking pan place the oysters, in the half shell.

In a medium skillet place the butter and heat it on medium until it is hot. Add the garlic, parsley, salt, and pepper. Sauté them for 2 minutes.

Add the Pernod and shake the pan until it flames up *(use a match if you have an electric stove)*. Shake until the flames subside.

Pour equal amounts of the butter mixture into the oysters. Sprinkle the tops with the Parmesan cheese.

Preheat the oven to 450°. Bake the oysters for 5 minutes, or until the butter bubbles and the cheese is browned.

serves 4

Sautéed Beef and Lamb Medallions with Piñon Tomatillo Sauce

Sautéed Beef and Lamb Medallions

12   ounces beef tenderloin, peeled and cut into 12 slices
12   ounces lamb tenderloin, peeled and cut into 12 slices
½   **cup flour** *(or as needed)*
2   **tablespoons olive oil** *(or as needed)*
2   **fresh tomatillos, thinly sliced**
12   **piñon nuts, roasted**
     Piñon Tomatillo Sauce *(recipe follows)*

Lightly pound the beef and lamb slices. Coat them with the flour.

In a large, heavy skillet place the olive oil and heat it until it is hot *(just before it smokes)*. Sauté the meat on both sides, until the desired doneness is achieved.

Pour the Piñon Tomatillo Sauce on a serving platter. Arrange the medallions in a fan-like pattern over the sauce, alternating the beef and the lamb.

Garnish with the tomatillo slices and the piñon nuts.

serves 6

Piñon Tomatillo Sauce

6   **fresh tomatillos, quartered**
¼   **cup sunflower seeds, roasted**
¼   **cup piñon seeds, roasted**
1   **clove garlic, chopped**
¼   **bunch cilantro, finely diced**
     salt *(to taste)*
     pepper *(to taste)*

Place all of the ingredients in a blender and purée them.

Season the sauce with the salt and pepper.

"Try to get center cuts for the beef and the lamb. Ask your butcher to take the lamb off the rack, and to peel and clean the meats. If you are feeling a little more daring, you can ask him to explain how to do it yourself. But it's simpler just to leave it to him."

"This is an offshoot of a traditional sauce from Mexico. The piñon nuts give it a more Southwestern flavor."

"In the old days, the people were very limited in what they could grow in the arid climate of New Mexico. The things that did well were beans, corn, tomatoes, piñon nuts, chile, and root vegetables.....so that's how the Southwestern style of cooking developed."

White and Blue Corn Chowder

4	tablespoons sweet butter
½	medium onion, finely chopped
2	cloves garlic, minced
3	cups fresh *(or frozen)* white corn
1½	tablespoons cornstarch, mixed in ¼ cup water
2	cups milk
2	chipotle peppers *(smoked jalapeños)*, finely chopped
1	cup whipping cream
1	teaspoon salt
4	large fresh oysters, washed and shelled *(reserve the liquid)*
½	cup blue corn kernels, soaked 1 hour, and then boiled 30 minutes until tender
2	teaspoons cilantro, minced

In a medium saucepan place 2 tablespoons of the butter and heat on medium until it is hot. Add the onions and sauté them for 5 minutes, or until they are soft.

Add the garlic and sauté the mixture for 1 minute.

Purée the white corn in a food processor and then place it in a large soup pan. Add the sautéed onion and garlic.

Add the cornstarch mixture and the remaining 2 tablespoons of the butter to the soup and whisk them in.

Whisking constantly, add the milk, chipotles, cream, and salt. Simmer until the soup thickens.

In a small saucepan poach the oysters in their own liquid, until the gills start to curl slightly.

Ladle the soup into individual bowls. Place one oyster in the center of each bowl. Sprinkle the blue corn kernels around the oysters.

Sprinkle the cilantro over the top.

serves 4

"We took a basic white corn chowder, which is indigenous to this area, and asked ourselves what we could do to give it some flair. So we came up with the idea of the chipotles, which give it a unique, smoky flavor, and the blue corn kernels, which add a nice color. The poached oyster is basically a garnish.....just like a little pearl in a beautiful sea of white, with little flecks of blue!"

"Visually, this soup is very pleasing. And it has a nice combination of textures and tastes."

"If you can't get a hold of the blue corn, go ahead and make the soup anyway. It will still taste great!"

Blood Orange and Watercress Salad with Mint Vinaigrette

Blood Orange and Watercress Salad

4   bunches watercress, washed, dried, with leaves cut off just above the stems
4   blood oranges, peeled and sliced into thin wheels
1   medium Bermuda onion, sliced paper thin
8   button mushrooms
     Mint Vinaigrette *(recipe follows)*

Place the watercress on 4 salad plates.

Place the orange and onion slices on top of the watercress by overlapping them and alternating them, to form a half circle.

Place the mushrooms on the other half of the salad.

Sprinkle with the Mint Vinaigrette.

serves 4

Mint Vinaigrette

¼   cup red wine vinegar
1   bunch fresh mint, finely minced
¼   teaspoon salt
¼   teaspoon white pepper
¾   cup good olive oil

In a small bowl place the vinegar, mint, salt, and pepper.

Let them sit at room temperature for 1 to 2 hours.

Slowly whisk in the olive oil.

"This was created by my Sous Chef, Tim Buchser. He is a native of Santa Fe, but has trained in classical French cooking. So, with his Southwestern and Continental background, along with my Cajun influence, we have created a rather unique interpretation of food.....both with the flavors and the presentation. We make a good team!"

"This salad is very good for cleansing the palate, and should be served after the entrée. The mint and the blood orange have a nice, refreshing feel."

"Blood oranges have an interesting bitter and sweet taste to them. They are bright red in color..... visually they really demand your attention."

Baked Breast of Duck
with Raspberry Port Sauce

Baked Breast of Duck

4   **6-ounce duck breasts, boned**
1   **cup flour**
2   **tablespoons vegetable oil**
½   **cup Tawny Port**
    Raspberry Port Sauce (recipe follows)

Lightly dredge the duck breasts in the flour. In a large, heavy skillet place the oil and heat it on medium until it is hot. Sauté the breasts, meat side down, until they are lightly browned.

Preheat the oven to 450°. Place the duck breasts in a roasting pan with the meat side up. Bake them for 8 to 10 minutes. Remove the duck. Add the port to the roasting pan and place it over a high heat to deglaze the pan.

Slice the duck into thin pieces. Layer it in a fan shaped pattern on individual serving plates. Pour the Raspberry Port Sauce over the top.

serves 4

Raspberry Port Sauce

¼   **cup raspberry preserves**
2   **tablespoons port wine**
1   **teaspoon lemon juice**
6   **ounces fresh raspberries** (or frozen)
1   **teaspoon cornstarch**
1   **tablespoon water**
1   **dash salt**
1   **dash white pepper**

In a small saucepan place the raspberry preserves, port, lemon juice, and raspberries. Simmer them until the mixture is well heated. Place the mixture in a blender and purée it. Run the mixture through a fine sieve and pour it back into the saucepan. Return the mixture to a medium heat.

In a small bowl mix the cornstarch and water and add it to the raspberry mixture. Simmer, stirring constantly, until the sauce thickens.

"Duck is one of my specialties! When I used to work in Colorado I had a friend who grew fresh raspberries, and I would use them in a cream sauce for the duck. So, when I came to Santa Fe, I wanted to find another way to use these berries, and came up with this recipe."

"Raspberries and duck go extraordinarily well together. And the port, with its fruity flavor, blends in perfectly. This is one of our most popular dishes."

"Try to find a low sugar or a natural sugar raspberry preserve. By using cornstarch instead of flour to thicken the sauce, you save a few calories. Every little bit helps!"

Lobster Enchiladas
with Green Chile Piñon Sauce

Lobster Enchiladas

¼ cup clarified butter
4 8-ounce lobster tails, shelled and cut into small pieces
4 scallions, thinly sliced
½ teaspoon salt
½ teaspoon white pepper
¼ teaspoon cayenne pepper
¼ cup dry sherry
½ cup vegetable oil
8 blue corn tortillas
¼ pound Gruyère cheese, thinly sliced
Green Chile Piñon Sauce *(recipe on next page)*

In a large, heavy skillet place the clarified butter and heat it on high. Add the lobster and sauté it for 1 minute.

Add the scallions, salt, white pepper, and cayenne pepper. Sauté until the lobster is just cooked.

Add the dry sherry. Shake the pan until the sherry flames up. Continue shaking until the flames die down, and then remove the pan from the heat.

In another large, heavy skillet place the vegetable oil and heat it until it is hot. Flash fry the tortillas, one at a time, until they are very soft, but not crispy. Drain them on paper towels.

Place the lobster in the tortillas and roll them up. Place the rolled enchiladas in a baking pan.

Pour the Green Chile Piñon Sauce over the enchiladas. Place the cheese on top. Broil in the oven until the cheese melts.

serves 4

"Here is another creation by my Sous Chef, who was given the task of dealing with an overstock of lobster tails. It's a nice variation from the traditional lobster served with drawn butter, or from the usual beef or chicken enchiladas. People really love this dish."

"Keep your lobster tails moving in the pan so that they don't stick. Don't leave them even for a minute, or they might burn."

"When one cooks as much as a professional chef does, one tends to get tired of cooking the same dishes over and over. So that's why chefs are always creating, and coming up with new versions of old recipes. The boredom inspires the creativity!"

"The wild rice and black beans go perfectly with the Lobster Enchiladas. It's what we serve in the restaurant."

"We have many celebrities that come to Rancho Encantado. It's such a beautiful setting! The architect who designed the dining room has won many awards, but I think that this is one of his best works."

"The owners, John and Betty Egan, are wonderful to work with. There is a growing sense of family with employees here. We all realize that Rancho Encantado is something very special."

Green Chile Piñon Sauce

1	tablespoon olive oil
2	cloves garlic, minced
2	shallots, minced
2	cups green chile, chopped
1	cup chicken stock
½	cup piñon, roasted
½	teaspoon salt
½	teaspoon white pepper
½	teaspoon ground coriander

In a large heavy skillet place the olive oil and heat it on medium. Add the garlic and shallots, and sauté them for 2 minutes.

Add the remaining ingredients and simmer them for 5 minutes.

Place the mixture in a blender and purée it.

Wild Rice with Piñons

1	cup wild rice
2	cups water
2	tablespoons butter
½	small onion, diced
¼	cup piñons
1	tablespoon cilantro, minced

In a medium saucepan place the rice and the water. Bring the water to a boil, cover, and simmer for 45 minutes, or until the rice is just tender. Strain out the excess water.

In a small skillet melt the butter. Add the onion and sauté it for 4 minutes, or until it is tender.

Add the piñons and cilantro. Sauté them until the nuts are light brown.

Add this mixture to the rice and stir it in.

serves 4

Savory Black Beans

½ pound black beans, washed
1 quart water
¼ cup olive oil
½ large onion, minced
2 cloves garlic, minced
1 ham bone
½ teaspoon salt
½ teaspoon oregano
2 bay leaves
1 teaspoon cumin

In a large, heavy pot place the beans and the water. Soak the beans overnight.

In a medium skillet place the oil and heat it on medium. Add the onions and sauté them for 4 minutes, or until they are tender.

Add the garlic and sauté it for 1 minute.

Add the onion, garlic, ham bone, salt, oregano, bay leaves, and cumin to the beans and water.

Simmer the beans over low heat until they are tender. Stir occasionally. Add more water if necessary.

serves 4

"This recipe is very simple to make, but it really tastes good. Black beans together with rice make a healthy combination."

"Speaking of health, we are always working to make our recipes as good for you as possible. For instance, we lower the calories and fat content whenever it is possible, as long as the flavor isn't sacrificed. A lot of thought and time goes into our recipes."

Poached Anjou Pears
with Chantilly Cream

Poached Anjou Pears

1 **quart water**
1 **tablespoon vanilla**
2 **tablespoons honey**
¼ **cup white wine**
1 **cinnamon stick**
⅛ **teaspoon coriander**
1 **lemon, zested** (yellow part of skin grated off)
4 **fresh Anjou pears, peeled, halved, and cored**
8 **dried figs**
1 **pint raspberries**
1 **pint strawberries**
Chantilly Cream (recipe follows)

In a medium saucepan place the water, vanilla, honey, wine, cinnamon stick, coriander, and zest of lemon.

Heat up the mixture and add the pears. Poach them for 5 minutes, or until they are tender. Remove the pears and let them cool.

Add the figs to the mixture and poach them until they are plump and tender (like fresh figs). Remove the figs and let them cool.

Place 2 of the pear halves in an individual serving bowl. Place 2 figs on each side of the pear halves. Add some of the raspberries and strawberries. Place the Chantilly Cream over the top. Repeat this for each serving.

serves 4

Chantilly Cream

1 **pint whipping cream**
1 **teaspoon vanilla**
1 **teaspoon Grand Marnier**
¼ **cup powdered sugar**

In a bowl place the cream and whip it until soft peaks form. Add the vanilla, Grand Marnier, and powdered sugar. Whip until the soft peaks become stiff.

"This is a very pleasing and palatable dessert. It is rather Italian in style because it is a simple fruit dessert, as opposed to a heavy, sweet, American cake or pie. It makes a nice presentation with the fresh fruit, pears, and whipped cream, and has an interesting combination of tastes and textures."

"Although this recipe might sound exotic, it's not. Possibly the only hard part is poaching the pear. Other than that it's just a question of arranging the fruits and putting the whipped cream on top. You can use whatever fruits are in season."

"If you really want to get wild, you can dip the pear into a hot chocolate sauce, and then let it harden."

Horno Oven, Taos Pueblo, New Mexico

Rincon del Oso

Rincon del Oso, or *"Corner of the Bear"*, is a place where one can relax with friends, and expect to be served generous portions of tasty, well-prepared, Southwestern food. The service is cheerful, the decor is warm, and locals strive to keep its special charm a secret from the tourists. Good luck!

Owners Debby and Richard Casillas make this a true family-run restaurant. Richard does the cooking and Debby takes care of the customers. Most of the recipes were handed down from Richard's father, who had his own restaurant in Clovis, New Mexico.

Guacamole Salad

4	medium ripe avocados, mashed
2	tablespoons green chile, finely chopped
4	serrano chiles, minced
2	limes, juiced
½	teaspoon salt
½	teaspoon garlic powder
½	head iceberg lettuce, shredded
2	tomatoes, wedged
	tortilla chips

In a medium bowl place the avocados, green chile, serrano chiles, lime juice, salt, and garlic powder. Mix the ingredients together well.

On individual salad plates place the shredded lettuce with the guacamole on top.

Garnish with the tomato wedges and the tortilla chips.

serves 4

Green Chile Burrito
with Shredded Beef

Green Chile Burrito

4 flour tortillas
2 cups pinto beans, cooked and slightly mashed
1 cup Shredded Beef *(recipe follows)*
2 cups Rincon del Oso Green Chile Sauce *(recipe on next page)*
1 cup Monterey Jack cheese, grated

On one half of each flour tortilla place ½ cup of pinto beans. Place ¼ cup of the Shredded Beef on top of the beans.

Roll the tortillas up and place each one on an individual serving plate with the seams down.

Cover each one with the Rincon del Oso Chile Sauce. Sprinkle the Monterey Jack cheese on top.

Preheat the oven to 350°. Bake the burritos until the cheese is melted and the sauce is bubbly.

serves 4

Shredded Beef

2½ pounds chuck roast *(or top round)*
    salt *(as needed)*
    thyme *(as needed)*
    red chile powder *(as needed)*
½   onion, chopped
1   clove garlic, chopped
1   teaspoon salt *(or to taste)*

With a damp towel wipe the chuck roast. Sprinkle the salt, thyme, and red chile powder on both sides. Rub the seasonings in well.

In a large, heavy casserole place the seasoned chuck roast, onion, and garlic. Fill it half way up with water, and cover.

Preheat the oven to 250°. Bake the roast for 6 hours. Raise the heat to 325° for the last half hour. Add more water if needed. Remove the roast, shred it, and toss it together with the salt.

According to Richard, *"Burritos are standard in northern New Mexico, but the flavors are always a little different. The pinto beans are really important to the taste. You should cook them until they are just tender, and then slightly mash them. They should be somewhat juicy. Be sure you don't fry them to make re-fried beans!"*

"We make our own shredded beef. It's very flavorful and tender, and not much seasoning is needed."

"When I was a kid our family would travel in Mexico, and whenever my father had a dish that he liked he would go back to the kitchen and talk to the cook and ask for the recipe. Then, when we would return home he would play around with it. So, that's how he got a lot of his recipes."

Rincon del Oso Green Chile Sauce

6	tablespoons butter
6	tablespoons flour
1	tablespoon diced onions
2½	cups chicken broth *(or as needed)*
4	cups green chiles, chopped
1	teaspoon salt *(or to taste)*

In a medium saucepan place the butter and melt it over medium heat. Add the flour and stir it with a wire whisk for 2 minutes.

Add the onions and chicken broth. While constantly whisking, cook it for 5 minutes, or until the sauce is thick and smooth.

Add the green chiles and simmer on low heat for 10 minutes. Add more chicken broth if necessary. Add the salt and stir it in.

Mexican Rice

¾	cup canned plum tomatoes
½	clove garlic, chopped
¼	onion, chopped
1¼	cups chicken broth *(or as needed)*
2	tablespoons peanut oil
1	cup long grain white rice
1	teaspoon salt
½	teaspoon pepper

In a blender place the tomatoes, garlic, and onion. Purée them until they are well blended. Add enough of the chicken broth to make a cup of liquid, and blend it in.

In a medium saucepan place the peanut oil and heat it on medium until it is hot. Add the rice and stir it in the oil until it is golden. Add the puréed tomato mixture, salt, and pepper.

Bring the ingredients to a boil, cover tightly, and simmer for 25 minutes, or until the liquid is absorbed.

serves 4

"This green chile sauce is a little different in that we use butter to make the roux, instead of lard, which is more common. You can use the sauce for a lot of different things. It's good for enchiladas."

"When my father first started his restaurant he hired some Mexican ladies who were his neighbors. They loved to use a lot of cilantro, green onions, black beans, and other fresh items that are popular in Mexico and Central America. So, he turned the cooking over to them and they made very traditional Mexican dishes."

"This is Debby's recipe for the Mexican rice. The peanut oil gives it a somewhat different flavor. It's not really spicy.....just pleasantly subtle."

Flan

¾   **cup sugar**
3   **eggs**
⅛   **teaspoon salt**
2   **cups milk, scalded**
½   **teaspoon Mexican vanilla**

In a small saucepan place ½ cup of the sugar and heat it on low until it caramelizes. Spoon it into 6 individual custard cups.

In a medium bowl place the eggs and salt. Beat them together slightly.

Add the remaining ¼ cup of sugar and beat it in well.

Gradually add the hot milk while stirring constantly. Add the vanilla and stir it.

Strain the sauce and pour it into the custard cups. Cover the lids with foil.

Preheat the oven to 325°.

Place the custard cups in a baking dish that is half filled with hot water. Bake them for 30 to 35 minutes, or until they are just set. If the water bubbles, then add some ice cubes.

serves 6

"Debby has tried a lot of flan recipes with different additions like cinnamon, orange, or lemon. But everyone seems to like this more simple recipe the best. Be careful not to overcook the flan. That's the most common mistake that everyone makes."

"My father gave us a lot of help when we first opened this restaurant. All of the recipes were in his head.....he had nothing written down. So, I followed him around in the kitchen and watched him make the dishes and wrote down the recipes. Later, when I would get into trouble, I would call him and say, 'Hey, Dad, my rice is lumpy, what am I doing wrong?', and he would tell me how to correct the problem."

"I'm really into cleanliness! My philosophy is – great food, great service, good atmosphere, and a really clean facility. All of these aspects are a number one priority to me."

Mexican Marble Cheesecake

1½   **cups graham cracker crumbs**
¼   **cup sugar**
6   **tablespoons butter, melted**
4   **triangles Mexican chocolate** (*Abuelita*)**, or 2 ounces semisweet chocolate**
1   **teaspoon water**
24   **ounces cream cheese, softened**
1   **cup sugar**
3   **eggs**
3   **tablespoons flour**
2   **tablespoons heavy cream**
1   **teaspoon vanilla**
¼   **teaspoon almond extract**

In a medium bowl place the graham cracker crumbs, sugar, and butter. Mix the ingredients together with a fork.

Press the mixture into a buttered, 9" springform pan to form a crust.

Preheat the oven to 350° and bake the crust for 10 minutes. Remove the crust and let it cool.

In a double boiler place the chocolate and melt it over low heat. Add the water and stir it in.

In a medium bowl place the remainder of the ingredients and mix them together well.

Remove 1 cup of the cream cheese mixture and add it to the melted chocolate. Mix it in well.

Pour half of the remaining cream cheese mixture into the crust.

Pour the chocolate mixture over the top.

Pour the remaining cream cheese mixture over the top of the chocolate.

Take a sharp knife and swirl it through the pie filling, bringing the chocolate to the top for a marbled effect.

Preheat the oven to 450° and cook the cheesecake for 10 minutes.

Lower the heat to 250° and cook it for 25 minutes, or until it is set. Chill the cheesecake before serving.

serves 10

The First Mission Church, Taos Pueblo, New Mexico

Rosedale SW Seafood Shop

This popular Santa Fe fish market and restaurant is the third-generation descendant of the award winning Rosedale Fish Market in New York City. The SW, logically, stands for *Southwest*. Fish lovers who dine here can relax, knowing that they are in *seaworthy* hands!

Recipes

Rosedale's Guacamole

Savory Boiled Shrimp
Cocktail Sauce
Tartar Sauce

Nova Scotia Smoked
Salmon Dip

Mediterranean Salad
Rosedale's Vinaigrette

Seafood Quiche

Rosedale Fish Stew

Grilled Tuna Fajitas

Swordfish Burgers

Chef Jim Lang says, *"Rosedale started out as a fish market only. Then we discovered that a lot of our customers were unfamiliar with many of the types of fish we offered. So, we decided to put in a few tables and sell small appetizers, thus giving people a chance to familiarize themselves with strange sounding fish."*

Rosedale's Guacamole

2   **ripe avocados**
1   **small tomato, finely diced**
1   **small onion, finely diced**
1   **clove garlic, minced**
2   **teaspoons lemon juice** *(or to taste)*
1   **jalapeño pepper, finely minced**

In a small bowl place the avocados and mash them. Add the remainder of the ingredients and mix them well.

Savory Boiled Shrimp with Cocktail Sauce and Tartar Sauce

Savory Boiled Shrimp

1   **pound large shrimp**
2   **quarts water**
½   **lemon, juiced**
2   **bay leaves**
6   **peppercorns**
      vegetable scraps *(optional)*
      Cocktail Sauce *(recipe follows)*
      Tartar Sauce *(recipe on next page)*

In a large pot place the water, lemon juice, bay leaves, peppercorns, and vegetable scraps.

Bring the water to a boil. Add the shrimp. Bring to a boil again and immediately remove the shrimp. Place the shrimp in a strainer. Cover with crushed ice and rinse under cold water until the ice melts.

Serve with the Cocktail Sauce and the Tartar Sauce.

serves 4

Cocktail Sauce

1   **cup catsup**
2   **tablespoons lemon juice**
1   **dash Worcestershire sauce**
⅓   **cup horseradish** *(or to taste)*

In a small bowl place the catsup, lemon juice, and Worcestershire sauce. Mix them together.

Gradually add the horseradish until the desired hotness is achieved.

"This is the only way to cook shrimp so that they come out perfect every time. Customers are always complaining to me that when they make shrimp cocktail at home, it never tastes as good as what we serve at Rosedale. I tell them the problem is that they overcook the shrimp. They are delighted when they discover how simple the secret is!"

"Brands of horseradish vary in their degree of hotness and moistness. We recommend using prepared horseradish, as it is less biting. Our cocktail sauce is HOT! If you are sensitive to spicy foods, be conservative when adding the horseradish."

Tartar Sauce

1	cup mayonnaise
2	tablespoons sweet pickle relish
2	tablespoons lemon juice *(or to taste)*
1	teaspoon dill weed
1	clove garlic, minced
1	teaspoon white pepper
1	dash tabasco sauce

In a small bowl place all of the ingredients and mix them together thoroughly.

Nova Scotia Smoked Salmon Dip

"Nova bits, or the scraps from smoked salmon slices used for lox and bagels, are perfect for this recipe. They are usually less than half the price of the nice salmon sheets, with one hundred percent of the wonderful flavor. If your local fish market doesn't offer these bits for sale, ask the owner if he can save them for you."

½	pound smoked salmon
⅓	cup mayonnaise
⅓	cup sour cream
1	clove garlic, minced
2	dashes white pepper
1	dash dry dill weed
1	tablespoon lemon juice

Place the salmon in a food processor or blender, and purée it.

In a medium bowl place the puréed salmon, mayonnaise, and sour cream. Mix the ingredients together until they are well blended.

Add the garlic, white pepper, dill, and lemon juice. Mix them together thoroughly.

serves 6

Mediterranean Salad
with Rosedale's Vinaigrette

Mediterranean Salad

2	quarts water
2	bay leaves
½	fresh lemon, squeezed
¾	pound fresh sea scallops, cut into small pieces
¾	pound raw squid, cleaned
¾	pound small, raw shrimp
¾	cup Rosedale's Vinaigrette *(recipe on next page)*
½	green bell pepper, thinly sliced
½	red bell pepper, thinly sliced
½	yellow bell pepper, thinly sliced
½	bermuda onion, thinly sliced
4	leaves red lettuce, washed and dried
1	lemon, cut into wedges

"This is a favorite with the lunch crowd. It has a wonderful flavor, is quite filling, but low on calories!"

In a large pot place the water, bay leaves, and the lemon juice. Bring them to a boil.

Add the scallops and squid. Bring to a boil again and then reduce the heat. Poach the scallops and squid for 2 to 3 minutes more.

Pour the scallops and squid into a strainer *(save the hot water)*. Cover them with crushed ice, and rinse with cold water until the ice is melted. Cover and chill in the refrigerator.

Reheat the water that the seafood was cooked in and bring it to a vigorous boil.

Add the shrimp. Bring the water to a boil again.

Immediately remove the shrimp and put them into a strainer.

Cover the shrimp with crushed ice and rinse with cold water until the ice is melted.

"Our fish comes from both the Atlantic and Pacific oceans. We fly it in fresh each day. We do a very healthy retail and wholesale business."

Place the shrimp in a bowl, cover tightly, and chill in the refrigerator for at least ½ hour.

Peel and clean the chilled shrimp.

Place the shrimp, scallops, and squid in a large bowl.

(continued on next page)

Add the vinaigrette and toss everything thoroughly.

Add the bell peppers and onion to the seafood. Toss them thoroughly. Cover and chill for 8 to 12 hours. Stir occasionally.

Place each lettuce leaf in the bottom of a chilled bowl. Put the marinated seafood mixture on top. Decorate with the lemon wedges.

serves 4

Rosedale's Vinaigrette

1	cup soybean oil
⅓	cup red wine vinegar
¾	teaspoon sugar or warmed honey
2	teaspoons Italian seasoning
1	teaspoon sweet basil
1	clove garlic, finely minced
½	teaspoon black pepper
1	egg
3	teaspoons Dijon mustard

In a medium bowl place all of the ingredients. Mix them vigorously with a wire whip until the egg and mustard are well blended with the oil and vinegar.

Cover tightly and refrigerate.

makes 1 pint

"If this dressing is too tart, you can add a dash of olive oil. The raw egg and mustard help to keep the oil and vinegar from separating. The Dijon mustard really adds a great flavor!"

Seafood Quiche

½   pound fresh or frozen shrimp, cooked, shelled, and
     deveined
¼   pound crab meat or surimi
1   tablespoon butter
½   yellow onion, finely diced
2   cloves garlic, minced
2   dashes white pepper
4   large eggs
⅓   cup heavy cream
1   9" unbaked pie shell
¼   cup Swiss cheese, grated

Cut the shellfish into small pieces and place them in a
medium bowl.

In a small skillet place the butter and heat it on medium until
it is melted. Add the onion, garlic, and white pepper. Sauté
them until the onions are golden brown.

Add the onions to the shellfish mixture and stir them in.

In another medium bowl place the eggs and whip them
vigorously. Add the cream and beat it in.

Add the egg and cream mixture to the seafood. Mix
everything well.

Preheat the oven to 350° and bake the pie shell (prick holes on
the bottom) for 6 to 8 minutes.

Pour the shellfish mixture into the pie shell. Sprinkle the
cheese on top.

Bake the quiche for 45 minutes, or until it is set. Let it cool for
10 minutes.

serves 6

*"This quiche can easily
be reheated in the
microwave."*

*"Surimi is a
manufactured shellfish,
chiefly made from
reprocessed pollack and
snow crab. The
ingredients are all
natural, and it's a good
substitute when you can't
find fresh crab. It's also
three times as cheap, but
very tasty! If you are
skeptical, ask for a
sample taste before you
buy it."*

Rosedale Fish Stew

3	tablespoons olive oil
½	medium yellow onion, diced
3	teaspoons garlic, finely minced
2	stalks celery, chopped
2½	teaspoons black pepper
1	bay leaf
1	teaspoon thyme
1	tablespoon Old Bay Seasoning
3	cups fish stock, heated
1	large carrot, sliced
½	cup red wine
1	large Idaho potato, cubed and covered with cold water
¾	pound fresh swordfish, cut into cubes
½	bell pepper, cubed
1	dash cayenne pepper
1	dash lemon juice

In a large, heavy pot place 1 tablespoon of the olive oil and heat it on medium until it is hot. Add the onions and 1 teaspoon of the garlic.

Sauté them for 2 minutes. Add the celery and sauté it for 2 minutes. Add 1½ teaspoons of the black pepper, the bay leaf, thyme, and Old Bay Seasoning. Sauté for 2 to 3 minutes, or until the onions are a golden brown.

Add the heated fish stock, carrots, wine, potatoes, and the water that the potatoes were stored in. Bring the stew to a boil, cover, and simmer it for 20 minutes, or until the potatoes are just done.

In a large skillet place the other 2 teaspoons of olive oil and heat it on medium until it is hot. Add the rest of the garlic and the black pepper. Add the fish and sauté it for 5 minutes.

Drain the fish and add it to the stew. Bring the stew to a boil. Add the bell pepper, cayenne, and lemon juice.

Simmer the stew for 5 minutes. Correct the seasoning if necessary.

serves 6

"*If you are wondering how to get the fish stock, there are several ways. Sometimes you can find a local delicatessen or fish market that makes its own. Or, you can make it yourself, similar to making chicken or other soup stock. Markets are usually happy to donate fish bones. Bottled clam juice, probably found in the gourmet section of your supermarket, is an alternative. But, maybe the easiest way is to buy a bottle of concentrated fish sauce (look in the Oriental section) and mix one tablespoon to a quart of water.*"

Grilled Tuna Fajitas

1   tablespoon olive oil
1   large yellow onion, thinly sliced
1   large green bell pepper, thinly sliced
2½   teaspoons garlic, finely minced
1   teaspoon black pepper
        salt *(to taste)*
2   pounds fresh yellow fin tuna cut into ¼" steaks
2   tablespoons butter, melted
1   tablespoon vegetable oil
8   flour tortillas, heated
¾   cup longhorn cheese, grated
1   cup lettuce, shredded
1   cup tomatoes, diced
        salsa *(hot or medium)*
        sour cream
        Rosedale's Guacamole *(see page 223)*

In a large skillet place the olive oil and heat it on high. Add the onions and bell peppers and sauté them for 2 minutes.

Add the garlic, pepper, and salt. Sauté them for 3 minutes, or until the onions are golden.

Preheat the oven to broil with the broiler pan in the oven.

Brush the tuna with the melted butter. Brush the broiler pan with the vegetable oil. Broil the tuna for 3 to 4 minutes, or until it is done.

Cut the broiled tuna into long, thin strips, and place them on one half of each warmed tortilla. Sprinkle on the grated cheese.

Place the sautéed onions and peppers on the other half of each tortilla.

Broil the tortillas, open faced, until the cheese melts. Fold them over and serve with shredded lettuce, tomatoes, salsa, sour cream, and Rosedale's Guacamole.

serves 8

"These fajitas are always a big hit. The salsa gives them a Southwestern flair, but you can be creative and garnish them with whatever is available. This is a fun and flexible recipe."

"Our recipes are very healthy. The focus is on high-fiber, low sodium dishes. And, of course, all the ingredients must be fresh."

Swordfish Burgers

1½	**pounds fresh swordfish, skin removed and cut into small pieces**
1	**small yellow onion, diced**
1	**egg**
1	**teaspoon olive oil**
1	**clove garlic, minced**
½	**teaspoon black pepper**
2	**dashes celery salt**
¼	**cup bread crumbs**
	vegetable oil *(as needed)*
6	**slices Swiss cheese**
6	**sourdough rolls or hamburger buns**
6	**tomato slices**
6	**onion slices**
6	**lettuce pieces**
6	**lemon wedges**
	salsa

Run the swordfish and onions through a meat grinder, or chop them in a food processor, until the consistency is like hamburger meat.

Place the ground swordfish and onion in a strainer. Balance the strainer over a bowl. Cover it with saran wrap and refrigerate for 1 hour, allowing the moisture to drain out.

In a large bowl place the egg, olive oil, garlic, pepper, and celery salt. Beat everything together. Add the swordfish and bread crumbs. Mix everything together with your hands. Add more bread crumbs if necessary.

Form the mixture into six hamburger sized patties.

In a large skillet place the oil and heat it on low until it is hot. Fry the patties for 4 to 5 minutes on each side with the lid on.

Place the cheese slices on top of the patties and broil them until the cheese melts.

Heat the rolls and serve them with the patties. Garnish with the tomato, onion, and lettuce slices, the lemon wedges, and salsa.

serves 6

"If you love a good burger, but are trying to avoid red meat, here is a delicious alternative. You can add guacamole or whatever else sounds good."

Historic Home on Canyon Road, Santa Fe, New Mexico

San Francisco Street Bar & Grill

An American version of a local French *bistro* or an Italian *trattoria*, the San Francisco Street Bar and Grill serves consistently good meals at affordable prices. The dishes are simple and straight-forward, with only fresh, quality ingredients.....a winning combination!

Recipes

Italian Sausage Sandwich

Chicken Pasta Salad
San Francisco Vinaigrette

Catalonian Fish Stew

Spinach Fettucini with
Italian Sausage and
Bell Pepper Sauce

Owner Robbie Day is a native of Santa Fe, but worked for three years in Italy and Switzerland.

Italian Sausage Sandwich

2   **tablespoons olive oil**
2   **bell peppers, seeded, washed, and diced**
2   **medium yellow onions, diced**
1   **baguette French bread, cut into 4 pieces**
1   **cup San Francisco Vinaigrette** (see page 235)
4   **Italian sausages, cut in half lengthwise and cooked**
1   **cup feta cheese**
6   **ounces provolone cheese, cut into 8 slices**

In a large, heavy skillet place the olive oil and heat it on medium until it is hot. Add the peppers and onions and sauté them until they are soft.

Slice the French bread in half, the long way down.

Sprinkle the San Francisco Vinaigrette over the inside of both bread slices for each sandwich.

Place the peppers, onions, sausage, feta cheese, and 2 slices of provolone on one slice of the bread. Place the other slice on top. Do this for each sandwich.

Preheat the oven to 350°.

Place the sandwiches on a baking sheet and heat them in the oven until the cheese is melted.

serves 4

Chicken Pasta Salad
with San Francisco Vinaigrette

Chicken Pasta Salad

1	green bell pepper, seeded, washed, and minced
1	red bell pepper, seeded, washed, and minced
1	bunch celery stalks, minced
1	bunch fresh dill, minced
2	teaspoons olive oil
3	cups mayonnaise
¼	cup Dijon mustard
	salt *(to taste)*
	pepper *(to taste)*
1	pound chicken breast, cooked, skinned, boned, and cubed
2	pounds shell pasta, cooked al dente
1½	cups San Francisco Vinaigrette *(recipe on next page)*
1	cup fresh Parmesan cheese, grated
1	cucumber, peeled and thinly sliced
1	green bell pepper, washed, seeded, and julienned
8	mushrooms, julienned
16	cherry tomatoes, halved
2	avocados, peeled and sliced
	black bread

In a large bowl place the minced green and red peppers, celery, dill, olive oil, mayonnaise, mustard, salt, and pepper. Mix the ingredients together.

Add the chicken and mix it in.

Add the pasta and mix it in.

Add the San Francisco Vinaigrette and mix the ingredients together thoroughly. Correct the seasoning.

Place the salad on individual serving plates and sprinkle it with the Parmesan cheese.

Garnish with slices of cucumber, green pepper, mushrooms, the cherry tomatoes, and the avocado slices.

Serve with a good black bread.

serves 8

"This is our application of a straightforward, cold pasta salad, which is very popular in this country. You can use almost any pasta you like."

"The recipe is very simple.....cook the pasta, add the ingredients, toss it, chill it, and eat it. For variations you can add prosciutto or boiled ham, feta cheese, black olives, sun-dried tomatoes, balsamic vinegar or fresh cilantro. Fresh lemon juice is also very good, and so is Parmesan or Romano cheese. The sky's the limit! You just need the confidence to be creative."

"Be sure that the pasta is al dente, firm to the teeth.....otherwise it will tend to fall apart. Rinse it in cold water."

San Francisco Vinaigrette

1	**bunch parsley, coarsely chopped**
2	**cloves garlic**
¼	**red bell pepper, seeded, washed, and chopped**
1	**teaspoon thyme**
½	**cup red wine vinegar**
2	**teaspoons Dijon mustard**
½	**cup olive oil**
1	**cup vegetable oil**
1	**teaspoon sugar**
1	**teaspoon salt**
½	**teaspoon pepper**

In a food processor or blender place the parsley, garlic, bell pepper, thyme, vinegar, and mustard. Mix them together.

While blending on a low speed, slowly add the olive and vegetable oils, until the desired consistency is achieved.

Add the sugar, salt, and pepper, and mix them in.

Cover, and refrigerate.

"We use this dressing in a lot of our other dishes, which is just a variation of a classic vinaigrette. You can vary the herbs and spices any way you like. Balsamic vinegar is also nice to use, although if you do use it then I would recommend adding only a little fresh ground black pepper, and maybe a bit of mustard, because the flavor of the balsamic is already so complex."

"My mother is an artist, and she has always enjoyed cooking. She would spend a lot of time making meals for our family, and for a while she had her own restaurant, so I picked up much of what I know from her."

Catalonian Fish Stew

4	tablespoons olive oil
1	bunch celery stalks, diced
2	large carrots, diced
1	large onion, diced
1	24-ounce can tomatoes, diced
1	quart fish stock
3	bay leaves
	salt *(to taste)*
	pepper *(to taste)*
2	pounds fresh Boston blue fish *(pollack)*, cut into ½" cubes
2	cups red wine
1	pinch saffron
2	lemons, wedged

In a large, heavy pot place the oil and heat it on medium until it is hot. Add the celery and carrots and sauté them until they are soft.

Add the onions and sauté them until they are transparent.

Add the tomatoes and cook them for 15 minutes.

Add the fish stock, bay leaves, salt, and pepper. Cover and simmer for 10 to 15 minutes.

Add the fish and simmer, until it flakes easily.

Add the wine and saffron. Add more salt and pepper to taste.

Serve in individual soup bowls with a wedge of lemon.

serves 8

"The essential ingredients in this recipe are the saffron, tomatoes, garlic, and red wine. Otherwise, you can vary it in any way you want. We often add clams, mussels, shark, mahi-mahi, or whatever kind of good, fresh fish we have that day."

"There are no tricks to this dish. It is better the second day, so you can put it into the refrigerator and then reheat it. But, be sure to bring it to a boil, so that any possible bacteria will be destroyed."

"The bar & grill phenomenon is best reflected in the city of San Francisco. It is derived from a simple European style that offers affordable meals in a friendly, home style atmosphere.....and there is always a delicious soup or stew simmering on the stove in the back room."

Spinach Fettucini with Italian Sausage and Bell Pepper Sauce

"Actually, any kind of fettucini or pasta will do. This particular recipe is reflective of some of our favorite ingredients."

6	tablespoons olive oil
6	bell peppers, seeded, washed, and diced
2	tablespoons garlic, minced
1	24-ounce can stewed tomatoes, diced
2	tablespoons fresh oregano, finely chopped
2	tablespoons fresh ground black pepper
2	teaspoons sugar
1	teaspoon salt
4	cups chicken stock
1	cup red wine vinegar
7	Italian sausages, halved and thinly sliced
24	ounces spinach fettucini
8	quarts water
1	tablespoon rock salt
½	cup fresh parsley, finely chopped
½	cup fresh Parmesan cheese, grated

"We just drain our pasta and serve it immediately. Or, you can put the pasta into a bowl, add a little butter, and toss it. This keeps it from sticking and adds a little flavor."

In a large, heavy skillet place the olive oil and heat it on medium until it is hot. Add the bell peppers and garlic. Sauté them until they are tender.

Add the tomatoes and cook them for 10 to 12 minutes.

Add the oregano, pepper, sugar, and the 1 teaspoon of salt.

Add the chicken stock and vinegar. Simmer over low heat for 15 to 20 minutes, or until the sauce has reduced by ½.

Add the sausage and cook on medium heat for 10 minutes. Cover, and let the sauce simmer on low heat until it is ready to be used.

In a very large, heavy pot bring the water to a boil.

"We people who are in the service business are all sort of neurotic by nature, because we are always trying to satisfy the demanding customer, and every customer is different. But this neurosis is what inspires us to seek perfection!"

Add the fettucini and the rock salt to the boiling water. Return the water to a boil and cook until the fettucini is almost done, *(al dente)*, stirring occasionally.

Pour the fettucini into a large colander and rinse it quickly with warm tap water. Thoroughly shake out all of the excess water.

Pour the fettucini on a large platter. Pour the sauce over the top. Sprinkle with the parsley and the Parmesan cheese.

serves 6-8

Adobe Gate in Winter, Santa Fe, New Mexico

Santacafe

The cuisine of Santacafe is an original combination of regional Southwest and Asian influences, providing subtle, yet exciting flavors. Enjoying rave reviews by food critics, the Santacafe is a fast rising star in the world of fine restaurants.....and especially in this town!

Recipes

Grilled Clams
Santa Casino Sauce

Roasted Japanese Eggplant
Wasabi-Serrano
Lime Butter

Watercress-Endive-
Radicchio Salad
Oriental Citrus Vinaigrette
Fried Won Tons

Crispy Duck with
Flour Tortillas
Cary's Dipping Sauce

Ginger Ice Cream
Bittersweet Chocolate Sauce

The beautiful interior of Santacafe is a credit to the talent of Jim Bibo, owner and architect. Jim also had the wisdom to hire Michael Fennelly, the Head Chef, who is largely responsible for the innovative cuisine. Michael is the creator of this recipe, as well as the others that are included here.

Grilled Clams
with Santa Casino Sauce

Grilled Clams

20	little neck, cherrystone, or Manilla clams, washed
	Santa Casino Sauce *(recipe on next page)*
½	cup sweet cream butter, melted
1	lemon, wedged

Open the clams on the half shell with a clam knife.

Preheat the broiler.

Place a heaping tablespoon of the Santa Casino Sauce on each clam.

Drizzle the clams with the butter.

Grill or broil them for 3 minutes.

Serve with the lemon wedges.

serves 4

Santa Casino Sauce

3	tablespoons sun-dried tomatoes, soaked in olive oil and chopped
1	teaspoon fresh basil, chopped
1	teaspoon fresh parsley, chopped
1	teaspoon fresh cilantro, chopped
1	teaspoon fresh thyme, chopped
½	teaspoon fresh rosemary, chopped
1	tablespoon red onion, finely chopped
1	tablespoon garlic, chopped
6	anchovies, chopped
2	strips bacon, lightly browned, drained, and crumbled
2	hot Italian sausages, cooked and coarsely chopped
5	dashes tabasco sauce
1½	teaspoons fresh lemon juice
¼	teaspoon kosher salt
¼	teaspoon fresh ground pepper
3	tablespoons bread crumbs

In a medium bowl place all of the ingredients and mix them together thoroughly.

"I've always liked to mix different foods, such as seafood with sausage, just being careful that the flavors are not too strong so that they don't work well together."

"This recipe was an experiment of mine.....kind of an adaptation of the classic Clams Casino. Working with clams is great.....they are so tender, mild, and succulent. I wanted to create something more interesting than simply grilling clams with melted butter and lime, and finally came up with this fresh herb and sausage combination. They taste great!"

Roasted Japanese Eggplant with Wasabi-Serrano Lime Butter

"Cooking has always been very relaxing for me. When I create new dishes I don't use a lot of pre-determined thought. Rather, I work spontaneously, using my intuition. I'm at my best when I don't worry about what I'm doing."

Roasted Japanese Eggplant

7	Japanese eggplants, cut lengthwise into ¼" slices
3	tablespoons olive oil
2	cloves garlic, finely chopped
½	teaspoon kosher salt *(coarse)*
½	teaspoon pepper, freshly ground
	Wasabi-Serrano Lime Butter *(recipe follows)*

Place the eggplant slices in a medium bowl. Toss them with the olive oil, garlic, salt, and pepper until the eggplant is thoroughly coated.

Preheat the oven to 375°. Place the eggplant slices on a baking sheet. Cover them with foil. Roast the eggplant for 10 minutes.

Remove the foil and continue to roast for another 10 minutes. The eggplant should be tender, and slightly browned.

Serve with a small dollop of Wasabi-Serrano Lime Butter.

serves 4

Wasabi-Serrano Lime Butter

2	limes
3	Serrano chile peppers *(or 2 jalapeño peppers)*
½	pound sweet cream butter, softened
1	tablespoon Wasabi powder
½	teaspoon kosher salt
½	teaspoon pepper, freshly ground

In a medium bowl finely grate the outer green skin of the limes. Do not grate the white pith.

Add the remainder of the ingredients and mix everything together well.

Watercress-Endive-Radicchio Salad with Oriental Citrus Vinaigrette and Fried Won Tons

Watercress-Endive-Radicchio Salad

2   bunches watercress, washed, dried, with heavy
     stems removed
2   heads Belgian endive, washed, dried, and cut
     lengthwise into ¼" julienned strips
1   head butter lettuce, washed, dried, and ripped
1   head radicchio, washed, dried, and ripped
     Oriental Citrus Vinaigrette *(recipe follows)*
     Fried Won Tons *(recipe on next page)*

In a large bowl gently toss the watercress, endive, butter
lettuce, and radicchio. Very lightly coat the salad with the
Oriental Citrus Vinaigrette dressing. Toss by hand until the
dressing is evenly distributed.

Place the salad in chilled serving bowls. Garnish with the
Fried Won Tons.

serves 4

"If you toss the lettuce by hand you can really feel the way the dressing goes on, so that the leaves don't get weighed down. The citrus dressing is very light and should be used sparingly."

Oriental Citrus Vinaigrette

¼   cup seasoned rice vinegar
1   orange, juiced
½   lime, juiced
½   lemon, juiced
1   shallot, finely chopped
½   teaspoon Szechwan peppercorns, freshly ground
½   teaspoon kosher salt
1   cup good olive oil

In a medium bowl place the rice vinegar, citrus juices,
shallots, pepper, and salt. Whisk them together. Very slowly
drizzle in the oil, while continuously whisking, until a smooth
emulsion is formed.

"All lettuce is extremely tender.....it's easily bruised or damaged. To me, the nicest salad is one where the leaves are all intact, just like they came out of the garden."

Fried Won Tons

peanut oil *(as needed)*
½ **package won ton skins, cut cross-wise into triangles.**

In a large heavy skillet or wok heat 3" of peanut oil to 375°.

Fry 6 to 8 won ton pieces at a time, until they are crispy.

Drain them on paper towels.

"I'm strongly influenced by Japanese food. I love its simplicity and the manner of Japanese presentation. I've tried to combine the Oriental philosophy of cooking with Southwestern ingredients, because the American palate demands a stronger sensory input.....and more excitement!"

"Szechwan peppercorns are reddish-brown, with a somewhat sweet, complex flavor. But, if you can't find them in a specialty store, just use black peppercorns."

Crispy Duck with Flour Tortillas and Cary's Dipping Sauce

Crispy Duck with Flour Tortillas

1	5 pound duck
¼	teaspoon ground ginger
¼	teaspoon ground cinnamon
¼	teaspoon ground nutmeg
½	teaspoon ground red chile, medium hot
¼	teaspoon ground cloves
2	tablespoons tamari or soy sauce
1½	tablespoons honey
2	bunches scallions
	peanut oil *(as needed)*
2	tablespoons butter
4	flour tortillas
	Cary's Dipping Sauce *(recipe on next page)*

Split the duck down the middle. Separate the wings, breasts, and legs.

In a small bowl place the ginger, cinnamon, nutmeg, chile, cloves, tamari, and honey. Mix everything together.

Brush the mixture over the pieces of duck. Be certain to cover all areas.

Let the duck sit in the refrigerator for 4 hours.

Using a medium pot, place the duck in a vegetable steamer. Scatter one bunch of the scallions over the duck. Cover, and steam for 20 minutes.

Remove the duck and cool to room temperature.

Prick the duck all over with a fork.

Preheat the oven to 500°.

Roast the duck in the preheated oven for 10 minutes.

Remove the duck and cool to room temperature.

In a large, heavy skillet *(or wok)*, place 2" of peanut oil and heat it to 375°. Fry the pieces of duck for approximately 5 minutes, or until they are nice and crispy.

(continued on next page)

"Our duck recipe is a vague adaptation of a Chinese Peking Duck. It seems complicated, and admittedly there are a lot of steps, but they can be done at different times of the day, or even the day before, so that the procedure really isn't as laborious as it appears."

"At the Santacafe there is really a nice harmony between the food and the ambiance. This is a subtle restaurant, but with some extremes, like Santa Fe itself. For example, some of our food items are very electric in taste, color, and presentation. Other dishes are much more subtle.....soothing and refined." Also, notice the contrast of the large playful papers and crayons on top of the elegant linen tablecloths!

"The marinade ensures that the seasonings will seep into the meat. The steaming helps to melt the fat away. A Peking duck is traditionally served with thin pancakes, but we decided to use flour tortillas to give it a Southwestern flavor."

Bone the duck. Cut it into 4" by ½" strips.

In a large skillet place the butter and melt it over a medium heat. Fry the tortillas for 30 seconds on each side.

Fold each tortilla into quarters.

Place the duck pieces on the tortillas. Garnish with the remaining scallions and serve with Cary's Dipping Sauce.

serves 4

Cary's Dipping Sauce

½	**cup pure maple syrup**
1½	**tablespoons Worcestershire sauce**
¼	**cup tamari**
1½	**tablespoons Japanese seasoned rice vinegar**
¼	**cup magi sauce** *(or 2 tablespoons tamari, 1 tablespoon water, and 1 tablespoon molasses)*

Mix all of the ingredients in a steel bowl with a wire whisk.

"The scallions used for the garnish should be thinly sliced down from the bulb, and then stored in ice water so that they curl up. Rip pieces of the scallions and tortillas off to eat with the duck, and dip into the sauce. Delicious!"

"Cary Clark, who is one of our most gifted cooks, developed this recipe. It's a nice, light sauce that compliments the aromatic spiciness of the duck."

246

Ginger Ice Cream
with Bittersweet Chocolate Sauce

Ginger Ice Cream

4   cups heavy cream
8   egg yolks
1   cup sugar
2   tablespoons fresh ginger, grated
1   teaspoon vanilla extract
    Bittersweet Chocolate Sauce *(recipe on next page)*

In a double boiler place ½ of the heavy cream *(2 cups)* and heat it until it is hot.

In a medium bowl place the egg yolks and beat them with a mixer until they are thick and pale.

Add the sugar to the egg yolks and beat on low speed for 3 minutes.

Add half of the scalded cream *(1 cup)* to the yolk mixture and stir it in.

Add the yolk and cream mixture back to the remainder of the scalded cream *(1 cup)* in the double boiler. Add the ginger.

While stirring constantly, reheat the mixture until it reaches 178° to 180° *(use a candy thermometer)*.

Remove the mixture and stir until it has cooled to room temperature.

Add the vanilla extract and the rest of the cream *(2 cups)*.

Chill in the refrigerator for 4 hours.

Freeze in an ice cream maker, according to the manufacturer's instructions. Serve with the Bittersweet Chocolate Sauce.

serves 4

"The ginger flavor here is very subtle, with a slight aftertaste of hot and sweet. As the ice cream sits in the freezer, the taste of the ginger becomes more apparent. The contrast of the light spice of the ginger and the rich, sweet of the chocolate is wonderful!"

"What I try to do in my cooking is to be aware of trends that are going on. But essentially I go with my own instinct of what good food is, and try not to be too worried about what is currently in fashion. Jim Bibo has been wonderful in giving me total freedom of expression in the kitchen."

Watch for the beautiful new cookbook by Jim Bibo and Michael Fennelly, *East Meets Southwest,* published by Chronicle Books in San Francisco. It is loaded with gorgeous pictures, and more wonderful recipes!

Bittersweet Chocolate Sauce

¾   cup sugar
3   cups water
½   cup corn syrup
1   pound bittersweet chocolate
1   cup heavy cream, scalded

In a double boiler place the sugar, water, corn syrup, and chocolate. Bring the ingredients to a boil while stirring occasionally.

Stir in the scalded cream.

Cool the sauce to room temperature.

Adobe Dwellings, Taos Pueblo, New Mexico

The Shed

The Shed is a tradition in Santa Fe, with a history as colorful as the town itself. In the midst of rapid growth and change, it has remained a constant, true in the simplicity and honesty of its cuisine. Be prepared to wait in line!

Recipes

Ensalada de Garbanzos
Posole
Huevos á la Mexicana
Carne Adovada
Chocolate-Coffee Soufflé

Owner Courtney Carswell says, *"Many years ago, wood gatherers would come down from the mountains to Burro Alley, a block long street in the heart of Santa Fe. They would leave their burros in a shed, and go around the corner to the cantina to have a few drinks. They always threw a blanket over the head of their donkey, so that later, when they staggered back, they could identify it by the blanket. That shed is where my family started the restaurant thirty-six years ago."*

Ensalada de Garbanzos

1	teaspoon sugar
1	tablespoon Dijon mustard
½	cup cider vinegar
1	clove garlic, crushed
1	teaspoon oregano
¾	cup extra virgin olive oil
2	12-ounce cans garbanzo beans (*chick peas*)
1	cup celery, chopped
½	cup fresh parsley, chopped
½	cup green onions, chopped

In a medium large bowl place the sugar, mustard, and vinegar. Whisk them together until the sugar and mustard are dissolved.

Add the garlic, oregano, and oil. Whisk them together.

Add the garbanzo beans and stir until the beans are well coated with the dressing.

Cover tightly and marinate in the refrigerator overnight.

Just before serving, add the celery, parsley, and onions.

serves 6

Posole

2	cups dry lime hominy *(posole)*
2	quarts water
1	pound lean pork shoulder
1	lime, juiced
4	dry, red chile pods
3	cloves garlic, chopped
¼	teaspoon oregano
3	teaspoons salt *(or to taste)*

In a medium bowl place the hominy and the water. Soak the hominy overnight.

Drain the water from the hominy.

In a large heavy pot place the pork, hominy, lime juice, and chile pods. Add enough water to cover the ingredients.

Bring to a boil and then cover. Simmer for 3 hours, or until the hominy pops open. Add more water as needed, always keeping the ingredients covered. Stir occasionally.

Remove the pork and shred it.

Return the pork to the pot. Add the garlic, oregano, and salt.

Simmer, covered, for 30 minutes.

serves 8

"The chile pods in our recipes are the dry, red chiles, about 6" to 8" long. They are packaged in large plastic bags, and you can find them in the Mexican section of your grocery store. Southwestern cooking is so popular now that, hopefully, they can be found in most cities."

"Posole was a main staple of the Pueblo Indians. It was taken up by the Spaniards, who used it as a stew for special holiday occasions. Here at The Shed, we found posole so special and workable, that many years ago we put it on our regular menu, when the other restaurants were serving only beans and rice as a side dish. Our recipe is as good as posole comes."

"Hominy is starchy, and careful attention should be paid to seasoning it sufficiently without overpowering it."

Huevos á la Mexicana

3   **medium tomatoes, diced**
6   **pickled jalapeño chiles, diced**
4   **green onions, diced**
2   **tablespoons vegetable oil** *(or as needed)*
8   **blue or yellow corn tortillas**
8   **large eggs**
1½   **cups Monterey Jack cheese, grated**

In a medium bowl place the tomatoes, jalapeños, and green onions.

In a large skillet place the vegetable oil and heat it on medium until it is hot.

Quickly fry 1 tortilla at a time on each side until it blisters, but does not stiffen. Add more oil as needed.

Blot the fried tortillas on paper towels. Keep them warm.

Fry or poach the eggs until the whites are firm and the yolks are soft.

Place 2 tortillas on each plate.

Top each tortilla with an egg. Sprinkle on the cheese and top with a spoonful of the tomato and chile mixture *(salsa)*.

Serve the remaining salsa in a bowl.

serves 4

"I went to the university in Mexico City, and it was there that I got the inspiration for this recipe. The pickled jalapeños make an outstanding sauce. This is a spicy dish!"

"Our recipes are traditionally based, with a lot of my mother's enhancement. She had a wonderful talent with cooking.....a good sense for the balance, color, and texture of food. Most of our recipes are from the Pueblo Indians, with a Spanish influence, and then refined to my mother's taste."

Carne Adovada

16	dried, red chile pods
3	teaspoons salt
4	cloves garlic
2	teaspoons oregano
5	pounds pork *(any tender cut)*

Preheat the oven to 225°.

Remove the stems from the chile pods.

Place the pods in a pan and bake them for 5 to 10 minutes, stirring occasionally, until the chiles are lightly roasted. Leave the oven door open. Don't breathe the fumes!

Place the pods in a medium bowl and cover them with boiling water. Let them sit for 30 minutes.

Drain the water from the chile pods.

Place the pods in a blender. Add the salt, garlic, and oregano.

Barely cover the mixture with water. Blend well for 2 minutes, or until the skins of the pods virtually disappear.

Cut the pork in strips that are 2" wide and 4" long.

Place the pork in a plastic container. Add the sauce and thoroughly coat the pork.

Cover and refrigerate for 24 hours.

Preheat the oven to 325°.

Place the marinated pork and sauce in a baking dish. Cover, and bake for 4 hours, or until the meat is quite tender.

serves 6-8

"This is a basic recipe that is simple and direct. I believe that a lot of the best recipes in the world are simple, using good ingredients that have been well taken care of. For instance, the chile that we use at The Shed has been kept cool, and away from light. There has been no deterioration from the time that it is dried to the time that we grind it, soak it, blend it, or roast it."

"A lot of chiles are dried on ristras, hung on roofs, or in sheds. The more freshly ground the chile, the better it is."

"I make my own contacts for chile in the farm country, and store it myself. That's the only way I can be assured that we are getting the freshest, highest quality chile. Plus, it's interesting, and I enjoy dealing with the local farmers."

Chocolate-Coffee Soufflé

2	tablespoons sweet butter, softened
1	cup sugar
1	teaspoon vanilla
4	eggs, separated
2	ounces bittersweet chocolate
2	tablespoons flour
1	cup coffee
½	cup half and half
¼	teaspoon salt

In a medium bowl place the butter and cream it.

Add the sugar and stir until the butter is fluffy.

Add the vanilla and mix it in.

Beat in the 4 egg yolks, one at a time.

In a double boiler melt the chocolate and then add it to the mixture. Stir it in.

Blend in the flour, coffee, and the half and half.

In a separate bowl place the 4 egg whites and the salt. Beat them until soft peaks are formed.

Fold the egg whites into the chocolate mixture. Gently stir the mixture until all of the ingredients are well integrated.

Preheat the oven to 425°.

Turn the mixture into buttered soufflé cups.

Place the soufflé cups in a baking pan with 1" of hot water lining the bottom. Bake them for 20 minutes, or until the soufflés are completely puffed up.

serves 4-6

"This is a spectacular dessert! At home you can serve it right out of the oven, when it is still really puffy. In the restaurant the soufflés might have to sit for awhile, and then they sag slightly. But at home, you can make sure that they come out perfect."

With brightly painted, crooked adobe-walled rooms, wood floors, and tiny doorways, The Shed is rich in local flavor. Also, it is one of the only restaurants in town that is quite successful serving only lunches.

Adobe Gate, Santa Fe, New Mexico

Shohko Cafe

Serving both Japanese and Chinese fare, the Shohko Cafe is probably the world's only sushi bar with vigas and adobe walls! Its extreme popularity is a testament to the impeccability with which the excellent dishes are prepared.

Recipes

Daikon Miso Soup
Egg Rolls
Combination Tempura
Vegetable Chirashi
California Roll
Sushi Rice
Curry Scallops
Chicken Fried Rice
Szechwun Beef
Sunomono
Fruit Kanten

Manager Kazuyoshi Nakagome says that in Japan the people eat some kind of miso soup every day. *"Make sure that you use the Bonito flakes. And don't boil the miso!"*

Daikon Miso Soup

4½   **cups water**
¾   **level cup dried Bonito fish flakes** (Katsuobushi)
1¾   **cups daikon** (Japanese radish)**, peeled and shredded**
¾   **cup white or red traditional Japanese miso**

In a medium saucepan place the water and bring it to a boil.

Add the fish flakes and cook them on medium for 3 minutes.

Strain the broth into another medium saucepan. Squeeze the moisture out of the fish flakes with a wooden spatula.

Add the daikon and cook it on medium (*do not boil*) for 20 minutes, or until the daikon is transparent and tender.

Place the miso in a fine metal strainer and lower it into the broth. Push it through with a wooden spoon.

Taste for seasoning and add more miso if needed.

serves 4

Egg Rolls

15	black dried mushrooms
4	cups water
2	tablespoons sesame oil
1	teaspoon sesame oil
1	clove garlic, finely minced
1	tablespoon ginger, finely minced
6	ounces lean, ground pork
1	large onion, sliced paper thin
2	medium carrots, finely sliced
½	teaspoon salt
2	cups cabbage, finely shredded
½	cup bamboo shoots, minced
2	cups bean sprouts
2	tablespoons brown sugar
3	tablespoons tamari
1	tablespoon ginger, finely minced
½	teaspoon salt
½	cup sake
4	ounces bean thread noodles *(broken into 2" long pieces)*
1	egg, beaten
¼	cup water
12	egg roll skins
8	cups vegetable oil

"Egg rolls are a Chinese dish. This recipe is exactly how we make it in the restaurant. But we make it in huge quantities, so this reduced version might come out a little different. But this is the best I can do for such a small amount! It will still be delicious, I know that."

In a medium bowl place the mushrooms and the water, and soak them for 1 hour. Remove the mushrooms, squeeze out the excess water, and mince them. Reserve the water.

Heat a very large, heavy pot *(preferably cast iron)* until it is very hot. Add the 2 tablespoons of sesame oil and swirl it around until the pot is well coated and the oil smokes. Remove the pot from the heat and let it sit until the smoke settles. Pour out the oil.

Add the 1 teaspoon of sesame oil and heat it on medium until it is hot. Add the garlic and the 1 tablespoon of ginger.

When the garlic and ginger start to move add the pork. Stir-fry for 3 to 5 minutes, or until the pork is done and crumbled up. Stir constantly and do not let the pork stick to the bottom.

"Please follow the instructions exactly the first time you make this, because I want you to learn how to make the rolls and cook it right. Then the next time you can vary the ingredients as you wish."

(continued on next page)

Turn the heat up to high and add the onions, carrots, and the ½ teaspoon of salt. Stir-fry for 2 minutes, or until the onions are translucent and the carrots are softened. Reduce the heat to medium.

Add the cabbage and stir-fry it until it is soft.

One at a time, add the bamboo shoots, bean sprouts, and the minced mushrooms. Mix them in while stirring constantly.

Add the water from the soaked mushrooms. Turn the heat to high. Add the brown sugar, tamari, the 1 tablespoon of ginger, the ½ teaspoon of salt, and the sake. Reduce the liquid by ½.

Add the bean thread noodles and cook them for 3 to 5 minutes, or until most of the liquid is absorbed.

Remove the wok from the heat and strain off the excess liquid. Let the mixture cool for 30 minutes.

In a small bowl place the beaten egg and the water and mix them together. Paint 3 edges of each egg roll skin with the egg and water mixture, ½" wide.

Divide the egg roll mixture into 24 equal portions. Place 2 portions on the unpainted edge of the egg roll skin, 1½" away from the end. Leave a small space between the 2 portions.

Roll up the egg rolls and press the edges together so that they are well sealed. Use more of the egg and water mixture if necessary.

In a heavy, large, deep pot place the vegetable oil and heat it on medium until it is medium-hot.

Place the egg rolls in the hot oil and cook them for 3 to 5 minutes, or until they are crisp and golden brown. Drain them on paper towels.

Serve with hot mustard or soy sauce.

serves 4

"Don't have the oil too hot or you will burn the crust and the inside won't get heated."

Combination Tempura

6	cups unbleached baker's flour, sifted
1	cup cornstarch, sifted
6	cups ice cold water
8	cups vegetable oil
8	scallops
8	medium shrimp, peeled, deveined, and butterflied
4	large mushrooms
4	green chile peppers, cut in half the long way
4	cauliflower florets
4	slices acorn squash (⅛" thick)
4	green bell pepper slices (1" wide by 4" long)
4	carrot slices (⅛" thick by 1" wide by 4" long)
4	zucchini slices (⅛" thick by 1" wide by 4" long)
4	green beans
1	bunch watercress, divided into 4 equal parts
½	cup tamari
4	tablespoons daikon, finely grated
1	teaspoon ginger, finely grated

In a large bowl place the flour, cornstarch, and ice cold water. Mix them together until they are the consistency of a pancake mix. Add more water if necessary.

In a large wok place the oil and heat it on medium until it is hot. Dip the shellfish and vegetables into the batter and cook them for 3 minutes, or until the batter is crisp and golden brown. Drain them on paper towels.

In a small bowl place the tamari, daikon, and ginger. Serve in 4 tiny containers for a dipping sauce.

serves 4

"The ingredients are very simple, especially for the batter. But you must experience making it and practice to get it to come out right. No matter how hard I try to explain how to do it, people will still burn it or undercook it."

"We use a special flour from Japan that is unavailable here in the U.S. However, a good white pastry flour should work fine."

"I will tell you the real secret of making a good tempura.....the batter must be as cold as possible before you use it."

"Please be careful with the oil! If you get burned it's no joke. I know this to be true from personal experience."

Vegetable Chirashi

3   **cups water**
15   **black dried mushrooms**
1   **cup carrots, cut into slices** (⅛" thick by ½" wide by 1" long)
1   **cup bamboo shoots**
1   **cup water chestnuts**
⅓   **cup sugar**
¼   **cup Japanese sweet rice wine**
¼   **cup tamari**
20   **spears asparagus** (cut 6" from the top and then cut in half), **steamed**
1   **teaspoon fresh lemon juice**
4   **cups cold prepared sushi rice** (see page 261)

In a medium saucepan place the water and the dried mushrooms. Let them soak for 1 hour.

Remove the mushrooms and squeeze out the excess water into the saucepan. Cut off the tough stems and slice the mushrooms in half. Reserve the water.

Put the mushrooms back in the water and boil them for 1 minute.

Add the carrots, bamboo shoots, water chestnuts, sugar, wine, and tamari. Cook them on medium for 2 to 3 minutes, or until the carrots are just tender.

Add the asparagus and cook them for 30 seconds, or until they are just heated.

Remove the vegetables with a slotted spoon and let them drain. Cool them to room temperature.

Add the lemon juice to the vegetable water. Correct the seasoning if necessary.

Place the sushi rice on a platter. Arrange the vegetables on top, and pour the sauce over them.

serves 4

"Chirashi means 'to arrange vegetables or other foods on top of sushi rice'. This is a very traditional Japanese dish. I grew up eating it but usually I had it with raw fish."

"Once you get the sushi rice done, which is tricky (I talk about that in the California Roll recipe), the preparation is very easy."

California Roll
with Sushi Rice

California Roll

4   sheets roasted Nori seaweed *(cut into 5" by 8" pieces)*
        Sushi Rice *(recipe on next page)*
⅛   cup wasabi, mixed with water to make a paste
½   cup crab meat, cooked, and chilled
½   cup cucumber, shredded
4   slices avocado
4   teaspoons toasted sesame seeds

Place one Nori sheet on a flat surface with the shiny side down and the coarse side up.

Place the rice ½" from the bottom, 2" from the top, ½" thick, and completely covering the Nori from side to side.

Spread some wasabi paste across the center of the rice, from side to side.

Spread the crab on top of the wasabi. Place the cucumber on top, and sprinkle with the sesame seeds.

Fold the bottom of the Nori towards the center, just so that the ingredients are covered. Roll it up. Seal the roll by placing 4 grains of rice along the top edge of the Nori, and press them together.

Cut the roll into 4 pieces. Repeat the process.

serves 4

"The only hard part here is the making of the sushi rice.....and that's hard. You probably couldn't do it to my satisfaction, but it will still taste good!"

"It's like if you try to make a real fancy dinner for your friends.....no matter how it turns out they will think you did well and they will appreciate your efforts. So, I definitely think that you should try making this recipe!"

Sushi Rice

2   **cups short grain Japanese white rice, raw**
2   **quarts water**
2   **cups Japanese rice vinegar**
¾   **cup raw sugar**
⅓   **cup salt**

"It takes a lot of experience to learn how to mix in the vinegar and separate the rice. You can't damage the grains, and if you are too slow then the rice will get cold and the grains won't separate."

In a large bowl place the rice. Add the water and very gently wash the rice with your hands. Do this for 15 minutes, or until the liquid becomes clear.

Cook the rice in a rice cooker, according to the manufacturer's directions. When the rice is done do not open the lid, but let it sit for 20 minutes.

In a small saucepan place the vinegar and the sugar. Heat on low until the mixture is warm. Add the salt, and remove the saucepan from the heat. Let it cool to room temperature.

Working very quickly, place 2 cups of the warm rice on a cookie sheet. Take ⅓ cup of the sauce and pour it over the rice. Using a wide, wooden spatula, flatten out the rice. Cut it and turn it over so that the grains separate and mix well with the sauce *(be careful not to damage the rice grains)*.

On another cookie sheet quickly repeat the process, until all of the rice Is saturated and the grains are separated.

Let the rice sit for 10 minutes.

serves 6

"I don't mean to scare you, but even with professional chefs it takes about one year to make a perfect sushi rice. But like I said, no matter how it turns out, it still will be good.....so go for it!"

Curry Scallops

36	large sea scallops
1	tablespoon sea salt
1	egg white, lightly beaten
1	tablespoon cornstarch
	vegetable oil *(as needed)*
2⅔	cups onions *(cut into 1" squares)*
1	cup carrot slices *(cut 1" wide by 2" long by ⅛" thick)*
2	cups green bell peppers *(cut 1" wide by 2" long)*
½	teaspoon vegetable oil
½	teaspoon garlic, minced
2	cups chicken broth
4	teaspoons salt
7	teaspoons sugar
4	tablespoons Japanese curry powder
3	tablespoons coconut milk

Season the wok *(see page 263)*.

In a medium bowl place the scallops and the salt. Carefully stir them for 5 minutes.

Add the cornstarch and the egg white. Mix them in well.

Fill up a large wok with the vegetable oil until it is 2½" from the top. Heat the oil over medium until the oil is medium hot.

Add the scallops and fry them for 3 minutes.

Add the onions, carrots, and peppers, and then immediately pour the contents of the wok through a sieve that is placed over a saucepan *(be careful)*. Drain the scallops and vegetables on paper towels.

Add the ½ teaspoon of oil and reheat the wok to high. Add the garlic and stir-fry it for 30 seconds. Add the chicken broth and heat it for 30 seconds.

Add the scallops and vegetables, and cook them for 30 seconds.

In this order, and while stirring constantly, add the salt, sugar, curry powder, and coconut milk.

Correct the seasoning with more salt or sugar if needed.

serves 4

"The key to the success of this recipe lies in the curry powder. We use a Japanese curry which is roasted, as opposed to a regular curry powder, which is not. If you do use a regular curry then you must roast it yourself. However, to teach you how to do that is another big process that would take a long time to explain. So, I highly recommend that you find some Japanese curry powder!"

Chicken Fried Rice

½	cup vegetable oil
1	tablespoon vegetable oil
4	cups cooked white rice
½	cup carrots, minced
½	cup onion, minced
½	cup mushrooms, minced
½	cup peas, cooked
6	ounces chicken breast, boned, skin removed, cooked, and diced
4	eggs, scrambled and chopped
2	teaspoons salt
1	teaspoon white pepper
¼	teaspoon sugar
1	tablespoon tamari
1	teaspoon sesame oil
¼	cup scallions, minced

Season a large wok by placing it on a high heat until it is very hot. Remove the wok and pour in the ½ cup of vegetable oil *(the oil should smoke)*. Swirl the oil around until the wok is completely coated. Let the wok sit for 1 minute and then pour out the oil. *(This process should be repeated each time the wok is used.)*

Place the one tablespoon of vegetable oil in the wok and heat it on medium until it is hot.

Add the rice and quickly cut it *(to separate the grains)* and stir-fry for 1 minute.

In this order add the following ingredients, briefly stir-frying each one: the carrots, onions, mushrooms, peas, chicken, and eggs.

Stir-fry everything together for 5 minutes, or until the vegetables are cooked and everything is well mixed and hot.

In this order add the following ingredients, briefly stir-frying each one: the salt, white pepper, sugar, tamari, sesame oil, and scallions.

serves 4

"To correctly season the wok is extremely important. You should do this each time you use the wok, without fail."

"Another important point is to separate the rice. You should push it down with the spoon, cut it, and stir constantly."

"This dish is not spicy or hot.....it's just right! You know, like a good hamburger isn't spicy or hot.....it's hard to describe what it tastes like, except that it's a perfect taste!"

"The recipe isn't hard to make. Once you learn how to season the wok, and you get the hang of separating the rice and stir-frying, the possibilities of different applications are endless."

Szechwan Beef

    vegetable oil *(as needed)*
12 **ounces top sirloin, cut into strips** *(¼" thick, ¾" wide, and 1¼" long)*
4   **cups bamboo shoots**
¼   **cup Szechwan bean paste**
1   **tablespoon Japanese red pepper powder**
1   **tablespoon sesame oil**
2   **cloves garlic, mashed and minced**
2   **cups carrots, cut into match sticks**
2   **cups tree ear mushrooms, soaked and cut into match sticks**
2   **cups chicken broth**
2   **teaspoons salt**
2½ **tablespoons sugar**
¼   **cup tamari**
¼   **cup sake**
1   **teaspoon sesame oil**

Season the wok *(see page 263)*.

Fill up a large wok with vegetable oil until it is 2½" from the top. Heat the oil until it is hot.

Add the sirloin and cook it for 2 minutes, making sure that the pieces separate.

Add the bamboo shoots and cook them for 2 minutes.

Place a strainer over a large pot. Very carefully pour the contents of the wok through the strainer so that the oil goes into the pot. Drain the beef and bamboo shoots on paper towels.

In a small bowl place the bean paste and the red pepper powder. Mix them together.

Reheat the wok to high. Add the 1 tablespoon of sesame oil and swirl it around.

Add the garlic and stir-fry it for 1 minute, or until it is brown.

Add the bean paste and pepper mixture. Stir-fry for 2 minutes and mix it in well.

Add the deep-fried sirloin and bamboo shoots. Stir-fry them for 30 seconds.

(continued on next page)

"Szechwan Beef is a Chinese dish. It is not difficult to make, so please try it!"

"The secret to the perfect taste for this recipe is the combination of the Szechwan bean paste and the Japanese red pepper powder. Once you have all of these ingredients, congratulations!"

"The recipe here is quite hot, so if you are worried, then cut down on the red pepper powder."

Add the carrots and the tree ears, and stir-fry them for 2 to 3 minutes, or until the carrots are soft.

In this order add the following ingredients, while stirring constantly to mix them in: the chicken broth, salt, sugar, tamari, and sake.

Cook until the sauce is reduced so that it covers only the bottom half of the ingredients.

Add the 1 teaspoon of sesame oil and stir it in.

serves 4

Sunomono

1   **cup water**
⅓   **cup Bonito flakes**
⅛   **cup sweet Japanese rice cooking wine** *(Mirin)*
¼   **cup raw sugar**
¾   **cup rice vinegar**
1½ **teaspoons sea salt**
1   **large English cucumber** *(peeled lengthwise in four ¼" strips)*
1   **quart water**
1   **teaspoon salt**
26   **medium shrimp**
1   **lemon quarter, thinly sliced**

"This is a very, very good dish. It has a strong sweet and sour flavor. The recipe is very typical of Japan and it is hundreds of years old."

In a small saucepan place the water and bring it to a boil. Add the Bonito flakes and cook them over medium heat for 3 minutes.

Strain the broth into a medium saucepan. Squeeze out the excess moisture from the Bonito flakes with a wooden spoon.

Add the wine to the broth and cook it on medium for 5 minutes *(don't boil)*. Remove the broth from the heat. Add the sugar and whisk it until it is completely absorbed. Cool the broth to room temperature.

Add the vinegar and the ½ teaspoon of the sea salt. Correct the seasoning if necessary by adding more sugar, salt, or vinegar.

Slice the cucumber into the thinnest possible pieces, so that you can see through them *(use a food processor)*. Add the cucumber slices to the broth. Cover, and refrigerate the marinade for 6 hours.

"It is important that the cucumbers are sliced as paper thin as possible. No one has knives as sharp as we have, so you should use the food processor with the blade. Also, be sure that you use an English cucumber. The regular kind has too many seeds."

Remove the marinated cucumber slices and divide them into 4 equal parts. Wash your hands very well so that there is no oil on them. Very carefully squeeze the moisture out of the cucumber slices. Place them into individual serving bowls.

In a large saucepan place the water and the 1 teaspoon of salt and bring to a boil. Add the shrimp and bring to a boil again. Remove the shrimp.

Peel and devein the shrimp, and then chop them up. Sprinkle the shrimp over the cucumbers. Garnish with a lemon slice.

serves 4

Fruit Kanten

2	pieces *(0.4 ounces)* **agar agar squares**	
2¾	cups water	
1	cup brown rice syrup	
4	tablespoons fresh lemon juice	
¼	cup raspberries	
¼	cup peeled orange slices	
¼	cup strawberries, sliced	
1	kiwi, peeled and sliced	
3	tablespoons fresh mint, chopped	
1	lemon, sliced	

In a medium saucepan place the agar agar and the water.

Heat the water on medium until the agar agar melts.

Add the brown rice syrup, lemon juice, raspberries, orange slices, strawberries, and kiwi. Cook the ingredients on low heat for 15 minutes.

Pour the Kanten into a square baking dish and let it cool. Place it in the refrigerator and chill for 1 hour, or until it sets.

Cut the Kanten into squares. Garnish with the chopped mint sprinkled on top, and the lemon slices.

serves 4

"This is a very traditional, Japanese dessert. It is light, and refreshing to your mouth, especially because of the lemon and mint. Serve this after a heavy meal."

"When you buy the agar agar, follow the instructions on the package, because they all differ slightly. Never stir it!"

"Cooking for others must come from the heart. One of the most wonderful moments in life is eating a meal out. So, we are accepting a very important role in other people's lives."

Mission Church, Zuni Pueblo, New Mexico

The Staab House Restaurant

A hidden garden oasis in the heart of Santa Fe, La Posada is truly a unique accommodation. The Staab House Restaurant occupies part of the European style mansion built in 1882, and offers a traditional Southwestern cuisine along with an exotic Middle Eastern fare.

Recipes

Mediterranean Beet Salad

Muhammara

La Posada Lentil Soup

Pita Bread Salad

Middle Eastern
Eggplant Salad

Tabouli

Crème Caramel

Ruta Jundi, who is the creator of these recipes, lived in Syria for ten years, and that's where she acquired her taste for Middle Eastern food.

"I like this recipe.....it's simple, straightforward, healthy, and low in calories!"

Mediterranean Beet Salad

12 medium cooked beets, shredded, drained, and squeezed dry
2   cups yogurt
½   teaspoon salt
3   cloves garlic, minced
2   tablespoons fresh lemon juice
½   cup tahini
1   bunch parsley, finely chopped

In a medium bowl place all of the ingredients and mix them together.

Sprinkle the parsley over the top.

serves 4-6

Muhammara

2½ pounds red bell pepper, seeded and coarsely
     chopped
1½ cups walnuts
½   cup bread crumbs
2   tablespoons pomegranate concentrate
1½ tablespoons fresh lemon juice
¾   teaspoon salt
1   teaspoon cumin
½   cup olive oil

Place the red bell peppers in a blender and chop them.

Place the chopped peppers in a medium bowl.

Place the walnuts in the blender and chop them. Add them to the chopped red bell peppers.

Add the bread crumbs, pomegranate concentrate, lemon juice, salt, and cumin. Mix all of the ingredients together.

Place the Muhammara on a plate and pour the olive oil over the top.

serves 4-6

"This is my favorite recipe and I eat it with everything! You can serve it with pita bread, or as a side vegetable dish with a meat entrée."

"The flavor of the Muhammara is quite delicious.....it is almost sweet, with a nuttiness, and also a tartness caused by the pomegranate concentrate."

"If you don't want to pour the olive oil over the top, that's okay, but it really adds a good flavor, and I think it tastes much better if you use it."

La Posada Lentil Soup

4	cups lentils, washed
10	cups water
1	onion, chopped
2	large potatoes, diced
2	fresh lemons, juiced
1	tablespoon cumin
1	tablespoon allspice
1	teaspoon salt
1	teaspoon pepper
½	cup olive oil
2	bunches cilantro, chopped
2	cloves garlic, minced

In a large, heavy pot place the lentils, water, onions, and potatoes. Bring them to a boil and then simmer for 2 hours, or until the lentils and potatoes are tender. Add more water as needed.

Add the lemon juice, cumin, allspice, salt, and pepper. Simmer for 15 minutes.

In a large skillet place the olive oil and heat it on medium. Add the cilantro and garlic, sauté for 2 minutes, and add to the soup.

serves 4-6

"I believe that the classic recipe for lentil soup originated in the Arab world. Here, I have taken the basic recipe, but have added and subtracted some ingredients so that it is more to my personal liking."

"You can eat this soup hot or cold. The cilantro is really what gives it the unique flavor, and personally, I would add one more bunch. It doesn't hurt!"

"When you fry the cilantro it gives off an aroma that is just..... ummmm! People love it!"

Pita Bread Salad

2 cucumbers, peeled, seeded, and finely diced
4 tomatoes, finely diced
1 head romaine lettuce, washed, dried, and finely diced
1 bunch parsley, minced
1 bunch fresh mint, minced
2 bunches green onions, finely chopped
1 tablespoon dried mint
2 tablespoons sumac (optional)
2 cloves garlic, minced
½ cup fresh lemon juice
1 cup olive oil
1 teaspoon salt
½ teaspoon pepper
½ cup vegetable oil
1 slice pita bread, diced into ¼" pieces

In a medium bowl place the cucumbers, tomatoes, and the romaine. Mix them together.

In a small bowl place the parsley, fresh mint, green onions, dried mint, sumac, garlic, lemon juice, olive oil, salt, and pepper. Whisk the ingredients together until they are well blended.

Add the dressing to the salad and toss it thoroughly.

In a medium skillet place the vegetable oil and heat it on medium until it is hot. Add the pita bread pieces and fry them quickly, until they are crisp. Drain them well on paper towels.

Toss the fried pita bread pieces into the salad. Serve immediately.

serves 4-6

"This is a very popular salad in Lebanon and Syria. Pour the dressing on just before you are ready to serve it. The pita bread should not get soggy. It really adds a wonderful taste."

"When I lived in Syria I had a cook and a maid, so I never did any housework or cooking. Although, just before the maid was ready to serve the meal, I would go into the kitchen and make certain that the dishes were seasoned and presented to my liking. I was thoroughly pampered over there, and I'm a little ashamed to admit that I completely enjoyed it!"

Middle Eastern Eggplant Salad

2	medium eggplants, peeled and cut into ¼" slices
1	tablespoon salt
2	cups vegetable oil, or as needed
2	tablespoons pomegranate concentrate
2	cloves garlic, minced
2	medium tomatoes, diced
1	cup parsley, minced
1	teaspoon salt
½	teaspoon pepper

In a large colander place the eggplant slices and sprinkle them with the salt. Let them sit for 1 hour, until the moisture drains out. Squeeze out any excess moisture with your hands, and pat them dry with a paper towel. *(This removes the bitterness.)*

In a large, heavy skillet place the oil and heat it on medium until it is very hot. Fry the eggplant slices on both sides until they are golden brown and tender. Drain them thoroughly on paper towels.

Place the eggplant slices on a serving platter.

In a small bowl place the pomegranate concentrate and the garlic, and stir them together. Sprinkle the mixture over the eggplant slices.

Sprinkle the tomatoes and the parsley on top.

Sprinkle on the salt and the pepper.

serves 4-6

Tabouli

5	bunches parsley, finely chopped
1	bunch fresh mint, finely chopped
2	bunches green onions, finely chopped
4	tomatoes, finely chopped
½	cup fine cracked wheat, washed
2	tablespoons dry mint
1	cup olive oil
½	cup fresh lemon juice
1	teaspoon salt
½	teaspoon pepper

In a large bowl place the parsley, fresh mint, green onions, tomatoes, cracked wheat, and dry mint. Mix the ingredients together.

In a small bowl place the olive oil, lemon juice, salt, and pepper, and whisk them together.

Add the dressing to the tabouli and mix it in thoroughly.

serves 4-6

"Tabouli is very famous in the Middle East, especially in Lebanon where it is their main salad. This recipe is a classic one. Diced cucumbers can be added if you aren't too concerned about not sticking to the exact original. I personally think that they make a very good addition."

"This is a very healthy salad.....and it's probably the most popular one with our guests."

"At the Staab House we are known for our salad bar, which my daughter likes to call the 'un-salad bar'. Our concept is somewhat different.....in addition to the traditional salad items and dressings, we also have Middle Eastern vegetarian dips and unusual salad type dishes."

Crème Caramel

10   eggs
5   cups milk
2   cups sugar
2   teaspoons vanilla
1   **lemon, zested** (yellow part of skin grated off)
1   cup sugar

In a medium bowl place the eggs, milk, and 2 cups of the sugar. Mix the ingredients together thoroughly.

Add the vanilla and the lemon zest.

In a small saucepan place the 1 cup of sugar, and heat it on low. Cook it until the sugar melts and turns dark brown.

Pour the caramelized sugar into the bottom of a well buttered baking mold.

Pour the egg and milk mixture on top.

Preheat the oven to 300°.

Place the baking mold in a pan filled with water. Bake for 1½ hours, or until the custard is set.

When you are ready to serve the custard, place it in a pan of hot water for 1 minute.

Shake the mold to loosen the custard. Place a serving dish on top of the mold and flip it over so that the custard sits on the plate. The sauce should run down over the sides.

Chill in the refrigerator before serving.

serves 4-6

"There are actually many ways of making a crème caramel. This is my own recipe, and one that I actually did make in Syria because I occasionally enjoyed making a dessert over there."

"I tried many recipes and this is the one that always comes out perfect for me. It's just delicious! Also, it's easy to make, but it looks like you worked for hours at it. It's a very elegant looking dish."

"If you wish, you can serve this with whipped cream and some fresh strawberries."

Lilacs in Bloom, Santa Fe, New Mexico

Swiss Bakery and Restaurant

A warm, cozy chalet nestled in the high mountain Alps, with tantalizing aromas emanating from the kitchen.....this is the experience of the Swiss Bakery and Restaurant. Offering exquisite pastry items and delicious homemade meals, everything here is authentically Swiss.

Recipes

Fondue au Fromage

Soupe de Chalet

Chicken Salad in Stuffed Artichoke

Pâté en Croute

French-Swiss Pizza Pecan Pesto

Broccoli Bacon Quiche

Florentine Cookies

Marie-Jeanne and Gerard Chaney are from the French part of Switzerland, and they have brought with them the skills and secrets of their country's cuisine. Gerard is the head baker, and Marie-Jeanne runs the restaurant. She assures us that this classic recipe will not fail!

Fondue au Fromage

1	clove garlic
1⅓	cups dry white wine
1	pound Gruyère cheese, grated
1	pound Appenzeller cheese, grated
1	teaspoon cornstarch
⅓	cup kirschwasser
3	cloves garlic, pressed
2	French baguettes, cut into bite size cubes

Rub the clove of garlic on the bottom of a cheese fondue pot.

Place the wine in the fondue pot. Squeeze the garlic with a press and add it to the wine. Bring the wine to a boil *(on the stove)*.

While stirring constantly, add half of the cheese. When it begins to melt down, add the rest of the cheese. Continue to stir until the cheese is melted and thickened.

Add the cornstarch, kirschwasser, and the 3 garlic cloves. Stir them in.

Set the hot fondue on a table gas burner, on low heat.

Serve with the French bread cubes.

(Note: Serve this with dry white wine, not water.)

serves 4

Soupe de Chalet

2½ quarts water
2   pounds potatoes, peeled and thinly sliced
1   cup carrots, sliced
1   cup parsnips, sliced
½   cup whole spinach leaves, washed and stems removed
1   cup leeks, sliced
1   cup fava beans *(peeled if necessary)*
1   tablespoon salt *(or to taste)*
1   teaspoon pepper, freshly ground
1   quart milk
1   cup tiny macaroni noodles, uncooked
¾   pound Gruyère cheese, grated
1   tablespoon heavy cream
½   bunch fresh parsley, chopped
½   bunch fresh chives, chopped

In a large, heavy soup pot place the water, potatoes, carrots, parsnips, spinach, leeks, beans, salt, and pepper. Simmer the ingredients for 3 hours.

Add the milk and simmer for 1 hour. Add the pasta and cook until it is done.

Pour the soup into a large, wooden bowl. Add the cheese, cream, parsley, and chives. Stir them in.

Serve immediately.

serves 6

Marie-Jeanne says that this is a typical soup from where she grew up. *"It's a very thick, country soup that you eat mainly in the winter, because it is so hearty. Serve it with fried ricotta cheese and a fruit tart for dessert."*

"Fava beans are very similar to lima beans, which you can substitute with no problem."

"I recommend sticking to these exact ingredients (with the exception of the fava beans) if you want the true flavor of the soup. Preferably the vegetables should be purchased from the farmer rather than the grocery store, but this may be unrealistic for most people."

Chicken Salad in Stuffed Artichokes

3	chicken breasts, skinned, boned, cooked, and cut into small pieces
3	shallots, minced
1	tablespoon fresh parsley, minced
1	tablespoon capers
1	cup canned corn, drained
3	tomatoes, diced
1½	medium carrots, grated
½	bunch celery stalks, finely diced
3	cloves garlic, minced
2	lemons, juiced
1	teaspoon olive oil
⅔	cup mayonnaise
1	dash tabasco sauce
1	pinch salt
6	artichokes, cooked, drained, and cooled
1½	cups vinaigrette

In a medium bowl place all of the ingredients *(except for the artichokes and vinaigrette)* and mix them together well.

Spread out the leaves of the artichokes and core out their centers, leaving the bottoms intact.

Stuff the centers with the chicken salad.

Serve each artichoke on an individual plate with a small container of vinaigrette.

serves 6

"This dish is one of my very best sellers. The shallots, celery, corn, and capers all give the salad a wonderful taste."

"A lot of people do not know how to eat artichokes. The flesh of the leaves should be scraped off (preferably with your teeth!), and the bottom of the artichoke should be treasured. It's the most tender and succulent part. Be sure that you eat it because I get very upset when I see the best of the artichoke returned to the kitchen!"

"The vinaigrette is for you to dip the artichoke leaves in. Use your favorite recipe."

Pâté en Croute

¾	pound veal, ground
¾	pound lean pork, ground
¼	cup brandy
3	shallots, chopped
2	tablespoons fresh parsley, chopped
1	tablespoon fresh chives, chopped
¼	teaspoon thyme
¼	teaspoon Worcestershire sauce
1	dash tabasco
1	teaspoon salt
½	teaspoon pepper
4½	cups flour, sifted
2	teaspoons salt
1⅛	sticks butter, softened
2	eggs
3½	tablespoons water
1	pound bacon, thinly sliced
½	pound ham, cut into eighteen 4" slices
1	egg, beaten
1	quart meat aspic

In a large bowl place the veal, pork, brandy, shallots, parsley, chives, thyme, Worcestershire sauce, tabasco, the 1 teaspoon of salt, and the pepper. Mix the ingredients together well.

Cover and refrigerate the mixture for 6 to 12 hours.

In a food processor place the flour, the 2 teaspoons of salt, butter, eggs, and water. Mix everything together.

Knead the dough lightly, and roll it into a ball. Place the dough in a bowl, cover it, and let it sit in a cool place for 2 hours.

On a floured cutting board roll out the dough until it is ⅛" thick.

In a buttered and floured round or oval pâté mold place ⅔ of the dough. Pat it into place so that it covers the bottom and sides, with 1" extra overlapping on the sides.

Line the bottom and sides of the dough with the bacon slices. Push them into the sides so that they stay. Cut the bacon to the proper lengths if necessary.

(continued on next page)

"This is a very popular dish in Europe. It goes especially well in the summer, and it can be used as an appetizer or as an entrée."

"I grew up eating this recipe. It's good for special occasions, mainly because it's somewhat expensive to make, and it's really a lot of work. But, it's worth it!"

Swiss Bakery and Restaurant

Santa Fe Recipe

"I love to make this dish! At the beginning when we first offered it, the people in Santa Fe were very apprehensive of the meat aspic. Now, all of a sudden they are loving it, and I can't figure out what happened."

"A little secret is to add a dash of port into the aspic because that really gives it a good flavor. You can find the aspic in the grocery store and you just mix it up according to the directions. Let it cool, and then add it to the pâté, which should be very cold."

Divide the ground meat mixture into 4 equal parts.

Pat ¼ of the meat mixture into the bottom of the mold. Place 6 strips of ham on top. Do this twice more, and finish with the ground meat on top.

Place the remaining dough very loosely on the top, with 1" extra remaining around the sides.

Pinch the excess dough together with your fingers so that it is well sealed.

In the center of the top of the dough make a hole the size of a quarter.

Cut a piece of glazed baking paper into a 6" by 6" square. Roll it up and insert it into the hole, to make a chimney *(for a steam vent)*.

Glaze the top of the pastry with the egg.

Use the remainder of the dough to form decorative patterns for the top. Glaze again with the egg.

Preheat the oven to 375°.

Place the pâté in the middle of the oven and bake it for 1¼ hours, or until it is a golden brown.

Remove the pâté from the oven and remove the chimney vent. Let it cool, and refrigerate overnight, or until it is very cold.

Pour the aspic into the hole, until it fills up the space between the meat and the pastry.

Place the pâté in the refrigerator and chill it for at least 1 hour.

Slice the pâté and place it on a serving platter.

serves 6

French-Swiss Pizza
with Pecan Pesto

French-Swiss Pizza

5¼   cups flour
4   teaspoons salt
5   teaspoons fresh *(not dried)* yeast
¼   cup olive oil
2   cups water
1⅓   cups tomato sauce
2   cups Mozzarella cheese, grated
2   tomatoes, sliced into 12 pieces
8   ounces Brie cheese, cut into 16 strips
      Pecan Pesto *(recipe on next page)*

In a food processor place *(in this order)* the flour, salt, yeast, and oil. Blend everything together. Gradually add the water and blend it in until the mixture has become a soft, oily dough.

On a floured cutting board roll the dough out into 4 rounds, to fit into four 9" pie tins.

Place the dough into 4 oiled and floured 9" pie tins. Let them sit for 5 minutes, and then refrigerate them for 30 minutes.

Remove the pie shells from the refrigerator.

Spread ⅓ cup of the tomato sauce on the bottom of each pizza.

Sprinkle ½ cup of the cheese on each pizza.

Place 3 tomato slices on top of each pizza.

Arrange four slices of the Brie cheese in a star pattern on top of each pizza.

Dribble the Pecan Pesto over the Brie cheese slices.

Preheat the oven to 350°.

Bake the pizzas for 8 minutes, or until the cheese is bubbly.

serves 4

"I came up with this recipe when I was trying to create a new and different pizza for our restaurant. It is now my most popular pizza."

"The purpose of refrigerating the dough is to prevent it from rising further. Take the dough out of the refrigerator just before you are ready to use it, or else the crust might come out hard."

Pecan Pesto

1	cup pecan pieces, chopped
½	bunch basil
4	cloves garlic
4	shallots, cut into 4 pieces each
2	teaspoons fresh parsley
1	teaspoon salt
1	teaspoon pepper
¼	teaspoon tabasco
1	cup olive oil
2	tablespoons fresh Parmesan cheese, grated

In a food processor, one at a time, place the pecans, basil, garlic, shallots, parsley, salt, pepper, and tabasco. Blend the ingredients together thoroughly.

Pour the mixture in a bowl. Add the olive oil and Parmesan cheese. Mix them in well.

"If you use a food processor this is very easy to make. I love the taste of pecans, and they are wonderful with the fresh basil."

"This pesto is excellent with a pasta. Just cook your pasta, and heat the pesto separately with some heavy cream. Mix everything together, and voilà!"

Broccoli Bacon Quiche

1	15" pie shell, uncooked
1	medium onion, chopped
2	cloves garlic, minced
1	tomato, sliced
1	bunch broccoli, cut into florets
6	strips bacon, fried, drained, and crumbled
1	teaspoon fresh parsley, chopped
2	cups Swiss cheese, grated
4	cups milk
7	medium eggs
¼	cup flour
4	teaspoons salt
¼	teaspoon pepper

In a 10" buttered quiche dish place the pie shell. Punch holes in the bottom with a fork.

In the pie shell place (*in this order*) the onion, garlic, tomato slices, broccoli, crumbled bacon, parsley, and Swiss cheese.

In a large bowl place the milk, eggs, flour, salt, and pepper. Mix them together well.

Pour the egg and milk mixture into the quiche.

Preheat the oven to 350°.

Cover the quiche with foil and bake for 1 to 1¼ hours, or until it is set.

serves 6

"A quiche is a typical Swiss, or French-Swiss dish. However, this particular recipe is my idea, because broccoli is not well known in Switzerland. In fact, I never heard of it before I came to America."

"The combination of the broccoli, bacon, and onions is really excellent. This quiche has a wonderful taste."

Florentine Cookies

¾   cup heavy cream
1¼   cups sugar
⅔   cup corn syrup
⅓   cup honey
7   tablespoons butter
2¼   cups blanched almond slivers
1⅛   cups candied fruits
⅓   cup powdered sugar
½   pound dark, semisweet chocolate
     powdered sugar *(as needed)*

In a medium saucepan place the cream, sugar, corn syrup, honey, and butter. Heat the ingredients until the sugar and butter melt, and the mixture comes to a boil. Stir constantly.

Add the almonds and candied fruits. Continue to boil and stir until the mixture reaches the temperature of 226° *(use a candy thermometer)*.

Preheat the oven to 350°. Cover a baking sheet with baking paper. Sprinkle the powdered sugar evenly over the paper.

Make the batter into approximately 1½" balls and drop them onto the cookie sheet, 4" apart. Flatten the balls out with a fork to form approximately 3" diameter circles.

Bake the cookies for 5 to 7 minutes.

Dip a round 4" pastry cutter into some oil and work it around the edges of the cookies to form nice round shapes.

Let the cookies cool.

Turn the cookies over so that the flat side is facing up.

In a double boiler melt the chocolate. Spread some of the chocolate on top of the cookies. Turn the cookies over and let the chocolate harden.

Turn the cookies back over with the chocolate side up. Spread another coat of chocolate on top.

Make a design on the chocolate with a fork while the chocolate is still warm. Sprinkle some powdered sugar on top.

makes 20 cookies

"We make these cookies a lot in Switzerland, although I think that they originated in Italy. This is not an easy cookie to make, but I frankly believe that it is completely worth the trouble. Although, to be truthful, I probably wouldn't make them myself.....I would rather go out and buy them!"

"This is a wonderful, exquisite cookie that is almost like a candy. The key is to get the mix at the exact temperature so that the consistency is correct. A copper pot is best, and you should stir it constantly with a wooden spoon. If the cookies don't come out perfect, don't worry.....they will still be delicious!"

"We have wonderful cakes and pastries. Many times people from out-of-state come to Santa Fe to get married and they call ahead to order one of our wedding cakes." (See page 300.)

Gate Detail, Santuario de Chimayo, New Mexico

Zia Diner

The Zia Diner offers a unique variety of dishes, ranging from basic American food (the way mom used to cook it!) to some exotic interpretations of classic New Mexican cuisine. Elegant, light, and airy, with an old fashioned soda fountain in front, it could be described as *"Southwestern deco"*.

Recipes

Polenta

*Roasted Poblano
Potato Soup*

Grilled Vegetable Sandwich

*Black Currant Turkey
with Cassis Mole Sauce*

*Pecan Smoked Chicken
Maple-Orange Sauce*

Zia's Meat Loaf

*Santa Fe Ravioli
Basil Cream Sauce*

*Lamb Tacos with
Goat Cheese
Tomatillo Salsa*

*Black Midnight Cake
Chocolate Frosting*

Head Chef Michael Nelsen is primarily responsible for designing the interesting menu at the Zia Diner. His Sous Chef, Sarah Alvord, also has contributed to the creation of some of the following recipes.

Polenta

5	cups water
1	teaspoon salt
1½	cups polenta *(coarse cornmeal)*

In a medium saucepan place the water and bring it to a boil over medium heat.

Add the salt. Add the polenta in a slow, steady stream while whisking constantly.

Reduce the heat to low and cook very slowly, for 40 minutes, or until the polenta begins to pull away from the sides of the pan.

Lightly oil a 9" by 5" baking sheet and pour the polenta on to it. Make sure that it is spread out evenly.

Place the polenta in the refrigerator for 4 hours.

Remove the chilled polenta from the refrigerator and cut it into six squares.

Preheat the oven to 350°. Place the polenta squares on an oiled baking sheet and bake them for 5 to 8 minutes, or until they are done.

Roasted Poblano Potato Soup

6	Poblano chiles
8	medium Russet potatoes, peeled, boiled *(retain water)*, and mashed
½	stick butter
1	8-ounce package cream cheese
1	quart milk
¼	cup fresh lemon juice
½	teaspoon white pepper
½	teaspoon garlic powder
	salt *(to taste)*
2	teaspoons summer savory
1	teaspoon paprika

Roast the chiles over an open flame until they are black all over. Wrap them in a wet towel and set them aside for 20 minutes.

Peel and seed the chiles. Coarsely chop them.

In a large pot place the chiles and the remainder of the ingredients *(except for the summer savory and the paprika)*. With a hand held blender purée everything until the mixture is smooth *(a regular blender may also be used)*.

Add the water that the potatoes were boiled in to achieve a nice, slightly thick consistency.

Add salt to taste.

Garnish with the summer savory and the paprika.

serves 6

Michael says, *"This is my creation, motivated by a lot of good quality, leftover mashed potatoes. It has really caught on and people seem to love it."*

"It's a hot soup! Roasting the chiles is probably the most important thing. The skins should be nicely burned. The poblano chiles are essential to the correct flavor. You can use another kind of green chile but it won't be quite the same."

Grilled Vegetable Sandwich

⅓	cup olive oil
2	garlic cloves, minced
1	teaspoon fresh basil, chopped
1	teaspoon fresh oregano, chopped
1	teaspoon fresh summer savory, chopped
8	red onion slices
16	Roma tomato slices
8	long zucchini slices *(lengthwise)*
8	long carrot slices *(lengthwise)*
8	broccoli florets, halved
8	slices good bread
1	cup white cheddar cheese, grated

In a medium bowl place the olive oil, garlic, basil, oregano, and summer savory. Mix them together well. Add the onions, tomatoes and zucchini. Marinate the ingredients for ½ hour.

Remove the vegetables from the marinade and broil them for 2 to 3 minutes. Turn them once.

Lightly steam the carrots and broccoli.

On each bread slice artfully arrange the vegetables.

Sprinkle the cheese on top.

Preheat the oven to 350° and bake the sandwich halves until the cheese melts.

serves 4

Black Currant Turkey with Cassis Mole Sauce

2	tablespoons vegetable oil
16	medium dried New Mexican chiles, seeded, deveined, and chopped
8	dried Pasilla chiles, seeded, deveined, and chopped
4	dried chipotle chiles, seeded, deveined, and chopped
	water (as needed)
2	tablespoons vegetable oil
½	white onion, chopped
2	cloves garlic
½	cup raisins
¼	cup sesame seeds
⅓	cup almonds
2	medium tomatoes, chopped
1	cup Crème de Cassis
1	tablespoon cumin
⅛	teaspoon ground cloves
1	teaspoon cinnamon
¼	teaspoon black pepper
½	teaspoon coriander
¼	cup unsweetened cocoa powder
1½	cups turkey (or chicken) stock
3	cups turkey meat, cooked and chopped
½	cup dried black currants
	Polenta (see page 287)
	sour cream

In a large skillet place the 2 tablespoons of vegetable oil and heat on medium until it is hot. Add the chiles and sauté them for 3 to 5 minutes, or until they are a toasty brown.

Strain off the excess oil. Add enough water to barely cover the peppers. Simmer the chiles on low heat for 1 hour. Strain off the liquid.

In another large skillet place the 2 tablespoons of vegetable oil and heat on medium until it is hot. Add the onions and garlic, and sauté them for 2 to 3 minutes, or until the onions are translucent.

(continued on next page)

"Sarah is the creator of this recipe. Mole is one of her favorite sauces, and whenever she goes out to eat Mexican food, that is what she looks for to order."

"The cassis makes the sauce just a little bit different. The berry flavor really compliments the chocolate and the green chiles."

"There are about twenty different flavors in the mole sauce, so when you taste it your mouth will experience some varied sensations. There is a little hotness, the muskiness of the chocolate, and the sweetness of the cassis. The flavor is complex, but very, very good!"

"Some people are scared of mole sauce because there's chocolate in it, but I think that it really is one of the best sauces that there is. The little currants add a nice packet of sweetness to counteract the hotness of the sauce."

"This recipe is quite long, but actually it is simple to make. Just get all of your ingredients together and prepped before you start, and then things will go much easier."

Add the raisins, sesame seeds, and almonds. Sauté them for 2 to 3 minutes, or until the seeds are brown.

In a food processor place the cooked chiles, the raisin, onion and seed mixture, the tomatoes, Crème de Cassis, cumin, cloves, cinnamon, pepper, coriander, cocoa, and the turkey stock.

Blend all of the ingredients together until they are smooth.

Pour the sauce in a medium pan and cook on low heat for 40 minutes.

Add the turkey and currants to the mole sauce, and cook for 5 minutes.

Place the polenta squares on individual serving plates. Pour the turkey and mole mixture over the polenta.

Garnish with a large dollop of sour cream.

serves 6

Pecan Smoked Chicken
with Maple-Orange Sauce

Pecan Smoked Chicken

2	cups pecan shells
¼	cup sherry
2	frying chickens, split in half
	Maple-Orange Sauce *(recipe follows)*
2	scallions, slivered
1	orange, segmented

Soak the pecan shells in the sherry and use them to smoke the chicken, until it is almost done.

Preheat the oven to 350°.

Baste the chicken in the Maple-Orange Sauce. Bake for ½ hour to 45 minutes, or until it is done.

Spoon on more of the sauce. Garnish with the scallions and orange segments.

serves 4

Maple-Orange Sauce

¼	cup orange juice concentrate
⅓	cup maple syrup
¾	cup water
1	tablespoon balsamic vinegar
2	tablespoons sherry
2	tablespoons soy sauce
¼	teaspoon Worcestershire sauce
1	pinch white pepper
¼	teaspoon salt
2	tablespoons cornstarch, mixed with 2 tablespoons of cold water

In a small sauce pan place all of the ingredients *(except for the cornstarch mixture)*. Whisk in the cornstarch mixture.

Simmer the sauce for 10 minutes. Add water if necessary.

"I love this chicken, and it has been really well received. This is an original recipe, pretty much developed from scratch. The sweet citrus flavor of the sauce works well with the smoked chicken. This sauce is more than adequate to thoroughly glaze the chicken. There should be enough left over to pour on to some rice."

"To smoke the chicken you need to find a crummy pan that you don't love. Put the pecan shells and the sherry in it, and set it directly on the coals of your barbecue, or on the lowest level of your gas grill. The heat will burn away the sherry, which gives the smoke a really nice, sweet flavor. Put the chicken directly above the pecan shells. You need the coals to be going pretty well.....they shouldn't be on their dying legs. Let the chicken cook for up to two hours. Turn it and check it frequently. It should be almost, but not quite done, because then you bake it some more. Don't let it dry out!"

Zia's Meat Loaf

2	pounds ground beef
1	pound ground pork
3	teaspoons garlic, minced
1	large onion, diced
1	large green bell pepper, seeded, washed, and diced
1	cup mild green chile, diced
½	cup pine nuts, toasted
¾	cup tomato sauce
3	tablespoons tomato paste
2½	teaspoons salt
1½	teaspoons black pepper
1	teaspoon thyme
3	eggs, beaten
6	bacon strips

In a large bowl place all of the ingredients *(except for the bacon strips)*. Mix everything together thoroughly with your hands.

Place the mixture in a loaf pan. Place the bacon strips on top. Cover the pan with foil.

Preheat the oven to 400° and bake for 1 to 1½ hours, or until the meat has reached 175°.

Pour off the grease before serving.

serves 6

"This is probably the most requested item on our menu. It's kind of a Southwestern style meat loaf. It's not hot, but it has a little spice in it just for interest. And it still goes well with catsup, which is important!"

"Before you serve this be sure to pour off all of the grease, of which there will be plenty!"

Santa Fe Recipe

Zia Diner

Santa Fe Ravioli
with Basil Cream Sauce

Santa Fe Ravioli

1½   cups French white goat cheese, softened
¼   cup mild green chiles, diced
4   ounces prosciutto, thinly sliced and diced
2   pounds fresh tomato ravioli pasta sheets
2   quarts water
½   teaspoon salt
     Basil Cream Sauce *(recipe on next page)*

In a food processor place the goat cheese, chiles, and prosciutto ham. Briefly blend them together until the chiles and ham are in small but recognizable pieces.

Cut the ravioli pasta into 1" squares. Place a small spoonful of the filling in the center of each square.

Moisten the edges with water, and place the second ravioli square on top. Seal the ravioli at the edges so that there is no air in the middle.

Let the ravioli sit at room temperature for 20 to 30 minutes, or until they are slightly dry.

In a large saucepan place the water and bring it to a boil. Add the salt.

Carefully place the ravioli in the boiling water and cook them for 6 to 8 minutes, or until they rise to the top.

Gently remove the ravioli with a slotted spoon and place them on a serving platter. Pour the Basil Cream Sauce over the top.

serves 4-6

"This is another creation by Sarah. She wanted to make a ravioli that was Southwestern. Previously she had made a lasagna with goat cheese and prosciutto, so she expanded upon that theme and added some green chiles to make it more Santa Fe!"

"This is a very tasty dish. The ravioli are only slightly spicy. They have a real Mediterranean flavor to them in spite of the green chiles."

"The recipe is not that difficult to make as long as you take it in steps. The hardest part is assembling the ravioli. Just make sure that the edges are well sealed, and treat them gently!"

"The sauce is nice and delicate, and is a wonderful complement to the goat cheese and prosciutto flavors."

Basil Cream Sauce

4	teaspoons sweet butter
2	cloves garlic, minced
1	teaspoon basil, chopped
1	cup heavy cream
¼	cup Parmesan cheese, freshly grated

In a small saucepan place the butter and heat on medium until it is melted.

Add the garlic and basil, and sauté them for 30 seconds.

Add the cream and stir it in. Reduce the heat and let the sauce cool to a slow boil. Simmer it for 2 minutes.

Remove the sauce from the heat and add the Parmesan cheese. Whisk it until the sauce is smooth.

"I think that what people look for in a restaurant is something that they wouldn't do at home, like deep-frying, or preparations that take a lot of time. Also, they go out to enjoy the creativity of a different cook."

Lamb Tacos with Goat Cheese and Tomatillo Salsa

Lamb Tacos with Goat Cheese

2	tablespoons oil
1	small yellow onion, julienned
1	tablespoon vinegar
1	tablespoon sugar
2	tablespoons vegetable oil
1	pound lamb, diced
3	cloves garlic, minced
12	corn tortillas, steamed
½	pound Chevre (goat cheese), softened and crumbled
	Tomatillo Salsa (recipe on next page)

In a medium skillet place the 2 tablespoons of vegetable oil and heat on medium until it is hot. Add the onions and sauté them for 3 to 5 minutes, or until they are golden.

Add the vinegar and sugar, and mix them in well. Remove the onions from the heat and keep them warm.

In a large skillet place the other 2 tablespoons of oil, and heat on medium until it is hot. Add the lamb and sauté it for 5 minutes, or until it is done.

Add the garlic and sauté it for 1 minute.

Remove the lamb from the heat and keep it warm.

On one half of each steamed tortilla place a spoonful of the crumbled goat cheese, lamb, caramelized onion, and Tomatillo Salsa.

Serve the tacos immediately.

serves 6

"Whenever we have any kind of leftover roasted meats we make them into tacos with goat cheese. People just love them, especially when they are served with the Tomatillo Sauce and the caramelized onions. They are very easy to make, and you can use either fresh meat or leftovers."

Tomatillo Salsa

6	**tomatillos, peeled**
	water *(as needed)*
1	**clove garlic**
2	**serrano chiles, seeded and deveined**
⅛	**teaspoon sugar**
1	**tablespoon olive oil**
2	**tablespoons cilantro**
¼	**teaspoon salt**
¼	**teaspoon pepper**

In a small saucepan place the tomatillos and cover them with water. Gently simmer them for 20 minutes or until they are tender. Do not let the skins break.

Remove the tomatillos from the water.

In a food processor place the tomatillos and the remainder of the ingredients, and blend them.

Cover the salsa and refrigerate it.

"Tomatillos are those little green tomatoes that come in a leafy skin that you need to peel off. They are kind of sticky and sugary underneath, so you need to wash them and core them."

"The salsa is fairly easy to make. As long as you don't burn it, then it is almost impossible to fail at."

Black Midnight Cake
with Chocolate Frosting

Black Midnight Cake

1   cup shortening
2   cups sugar
5   eggs, warmed to room temperature
1   cup cocoa
2   cups flour
1¾ teaspoons baking soda
1½ teaspoons salt
1½ teaspoons vanilla
2   cups water
    Chocolate Frosting *(recipe on next page)*

In a medium bowl place the shortening, sugar, and eggs. Cream everything until the mixture is fluffy. Beat for 5 minutes more on high.

In a medium bowl place the cocoa, flour, baking soda, and salt. Mix them together.

In a small bowl place the vanilla and water.

Alternately add a small amount of the flour mixture and then a small amount of the water mixture to the creamed egg mixture. Beat constantly until all of the ingredients are added and well mixed.

Preheat the oven to 350°.

Pour the batter into 3 greased and floured cake pans. Line the bottoms with wax paper. Bake for 35 to 40 minutes.

Ice the cakes with the Chocolate Frosting.

serves 8

"It amazes me that more people don't make cakes from scratch, because they are really easy to do, and then you know exactly what the ingredients are."

"Just follow the instructions exactly, and it works. I've even done it and I'm not a baker. Just don't stomp around the kitchen when the cake is in the oven!"

Chocolate Frosting

12   **tablespoons sweet butter, softened**
1½ **cups cocoa**
5½ **cups powdered sugar**
⅔   **cup milk**
2   **teaspoons vanilla extract**

In a medium bowl place the butter and cream it.

In a small bowl place the cocoa and sugar and mix them together.

In another small bowl place the milk and vanilla and mix them together.

Alternately add a small amount of the cocoa mixture and then a small amount of the water mixture to the butter, whipping constantly, until everything is well mixed.

"The cake and frosting are extremely rich, and they are a favorite with the chocoholics. It doesn't require one, but it stands up well to a big dish of vanilla ice cream!"

Supplemental Information

The Chile Shop

For a catalogue of special Southwestern ingredients that can be purchased through mail order, write to:

The Chile Shop/SFR
109 East Water Street
Santa Fe, NM 87501

Phone: (505) 983-6080

Grant Corner Inn Breakfast & Brunch Cookbook

To order a copy of this cookbook send a check or money order for $10.95, plus $3.00 shipping and handling for each book. (New Mexico residents enclose $.53 per book for sales tax.) Mail to:

Grant Corner Inn Cookbook
122 Grant Avenue
Santa Fe, NM 87501

Swiss Bakery and Restaurant

To obtain information on wedding and special order cakes please contact:

Swiss Bakery and Restaurant
320 Guadalupe
Santa Fe, NM 87501

Phone: (505) 988-3737

Index

COOKBOOK ORDER FORMS

Please send me the book(s) which I have indicated below. For shipping charges I am enclosing $2.75 for the first book, and $1.50 for each additional book.

Quantity	Book Title	Price	Total
_____	Santa Fe Recipe	$13.95	_____
_____	*Taos Recipe (softbound)	$11.95	_____
_____	** Southern California Beach Recipe (hardbound)	$17.95	_____
		Shipping total:	_____
		TOTAL AMOUNT ENCLOSED:	_____

Ship to: _____

Address: _____

City: _____

State: _____ Zip: _____

Make check or money order payable to **Tierra Publications**. Send it to:

Tierra Publications
2801 Rodeo Road, Suite B-612
Santa Fe, New Mexico 87505
(505) 983-6300

(Master Card and Visa phone orders accepted)

Please send me the book(s) which I have indicated below. For shipping charges I am enclosing $2.75 for the first book, and $1.50 for each additional book.

Quantity	Book Title	Price	Total
_____	Santa Fe Recipe	$13.95	_____
_____	*Taos Recipe (softbound)	$11.95	_____
_____	** Southern California Beach Recipe (hardbound)	$17.95	_____
		Shipping total:	_____
		TOTAL AMOUNT ENCLOSED:	_____

Ship to: _____

Address: _____

City: _____

State: _____ Zip: _____

Make check or money order payable to **Tierra Publications**. Send it to:

Tierra Publications
2801 Rodeo Road, Suite B-612
Santa Fe, New Mexico 87505
(505) 983-6300

(Master Card and Visa phone orders accepted)

---

* *Taos Recipe* "A Cookbook of Recipes from Restaurants in Taos, New Mexico" • 170 recipes • 177 pages
** *S.C. Beach Recipe* "Recipes from Favorite Coastal Restaurants - Malibu to Laguna Beach" • 335 recipes • 352 pages

The
Great Turkey
Cookbook

The
Great Turkey
Cookbook

385 Turkey Recipes for
Every Day and Holidays

BY
VIRGINIA AND ROBERT HOFFMAN

Crossing Press
Freedom, CA 95019

WE WISH TO ACKNOWLEDGE . . .

Our appreciation for the help that we have received in the past three years, in the writing of this book.

Dr. Francine Bradley, Ph.D., Extension Poultry Specialist of the Avian Sciences Department, The University of California at Davis, for her many contributions, and The American Poultry Historical Society, for information on the early days of American turkey production.

The National Turkey Federation, who supplied us with recipes and material from which we prepared the sections on selection and preparation of turkey.

The California Poultry Industry Federation who generously shared many of their prize-winning recipes with us.

Ms. Anne Salisbury, of the R.C. Auletta Company, our source of recipes and cooking instructions from The Perdue Farms, Incorporated, one of America's leading turkey producers.

The Louis Rich Company, whose turkey products are found throughout the United States, for recipes and nutritional information.

Foster Farms, the leading poultry producer in California, who provided us with many "uniquely California" recipes.

Ms. Denise O'Meara of the British Turkey Information Service, who generously shared some of their best recipes with us.

Pinpoint Publishing, Santa Rosa, CA, for their nutritional analysis program "Micro Cookbook 4.0 for Windows © 1995."

Library of Congress Cataloging-in-Publication Data

The great turkey cookbook : 385 turkey recipes for every day and holidays
     by Virginia and Robert Hoffman.
       p. cm.
     Includes index.
     ISBN 0-89594-792-7 (paper)
      1. Cookery (Turkeys)   I. Hoffman, Virginia.   II. Hoffman, Robert.
TX750.5 T87G74 1995   95-19835
641.6'6592—dc20   CIP

CONTENTS

INTRODUCTION

How To Use This Cookbook

Each recipe is identified on the upper corner of the page as to the type of food (soup, salad, et cetera) and which part of the turkey can be used (leftovers, turkey breast, and so forth).

Ingredients in all the recipes are available in most grocery stores and/or supermarkets. In certain cases, we have named alternatives that are equally satisfactory.

Each recipe has a nutritional analysis based upon the larger number of servings noted. The editors and the publisher accept no responsibility for the accuracy of these analyses. There are many variations in ingredients, which can change these figures substantially.

What's So Special About Turkey

Today, nearly 60 percent of the U.S. population is made up of one- or two-person households. This is a dramatic change from the large families of previous generations. Now, career-minded singles, dual-income couples, single parents, "empty-nest" parents and seniors are the majority. Turkey is the right choice for today's lifestyle.

First, it is convenient. Turkey is available in more than thirty different forms at the market. You can buy it fresh, frozen, already cooked or smoked. It comes in portions for one or two, and for larger families.

Second, it is so easy and quick to prepare.

Third, it is delicious. Whether it be a slice of plain white breast of turkey, a drumstick or a plate of traditional roast turkey, it is moist, tender and rich in flavor.

Fourth, it is the most versatile of all meats. Turkey has the unique ability to take on and absorb seasonings and flavors, so you may use it instead of beef, pork and lamb in most, if not all, of your favorite recipes.

Fifth, it is good for you. Turkey has fewer calories, less fat and less cholesterol than beef, pork or lamb. See the Nutritional Comparison chart on page 9.

Sixth, it is much less expensive than beef, pork or lamb. It not only costs less per pound, but there is far less waste in the form of fat and bones.

Convenient, easy to prepare, delicious, versatile, healthy, economical—that's turkey!

There Are Many Kinds of Turkey Meat

Not so long ago, "turkey for dinner" meant buying and roasting a whole bird for Thanksgiving and Christmas. Today, you can choose from many different forms of turkey for any meal at any time of the year. Here's what is available, fresh or frozen:

Whole turkeys, ranging in size from 6 to 24 pounds. You can buy them pre-stuffed and pre-basted, even with a pop-out thermometer.

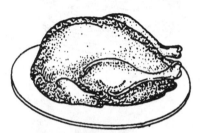

Whole Turkey

Half turkeys, with half breast, one drumstick, one thigh and one wing. Perfect for smaller families.

Whole or half breast. This is all white meat. Particularly good to substitute for pork.

Whole Turkey Breast

Thighs, the second joint of the leg, have juicy dark meat, are very simple to use and are low in price. Use them instead of beef, particularly in Italian dishes.

Drumsticks, the first joint of a turkey leg, are all dark meat and, like the thighs, are very versatile for a wide variety of dishes.

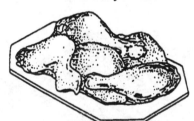

Turkey Thighs, Wings, Drumsticks

Wings, available whole or with the wing tip removed, are the least expensive turkey part. For many years, they were used only in making soups. Today, there are exciting recipes for turkey wings.

Roasts, both breast and hindquarters, are specially boned and bound with string, with a choice of white or dark meat, or both, in sizes from 2 to 8 pounds. The skin has been removed.

Turkey Hindquarter Roast

Turkey Breast Slices or Steaks

Ground Turkey

Turkey Ham, Bologna, Salami,
Pastrami, Franks and Weiners

Slices or steaks. These are cut from the tender white breast meat, to be used as you would use veal or tender beef steaks.

Tenderloin. The best cut of the turkey breast. Use as you would veal, pork or lamb.

Ground turkey. Probably the kind of turkey used most. Can be used in any recipe that calls for ground beef, pork or lamb.

Turkey sausage. Comes ground or as links. Like all turkey products, sausages are lower in fat content than their traditional source—pork. The giblets, which include the heart, liver, gizzard, necks and tails, are now available separately for making soups and stews. (The English make a fabulous pâté with the liver.)

Cooked turkey is also available. The white meat, available in both thick and thin slices, is ideal for sandwiches, salads and recipes calling for cooked turkey.

Turkey ham is boneless turkey thigh meat, rolled, cured and seasoned. It is available in the Deli section of your market.

Bacon-like turkey strips are fully cured and cooked and take just seconds to heat.

Turkey bologna, salami, pastrami, franks and corn dogs are available in most Deli departments. All have one-third less fat than the originals, and many people prefer them.

Smoked turkey, available as whole turkeys, breasts, wings, drumsticks and slices, is fully cooked and has a robust hickory smoked flavor.

NUTRITIONAL COMPARISON

Product	Calories	Total Fat	Saturated Fat	Cholesterol	Sodium	Protein	Iron
Whole Turkey Per 3-oz. Roasted, skinless	**129**	**2.6 gm**	**0.9 gm**	**64 mg**	**59 mg**	**25 gm**	**1.5 mg**
Beef Per 3-oz. Roasted, trimmed	192	9.4 gm	4.2 gm	73 mg	57 mg	25 gm	2.6 mg
Pork Per 3-oz. Roasted, trimmed	198	11.1 gm	3.8 gm	79 mg	59 mg	23 gm	1.1 mg
Lamb Per 3-oz. Roasted, trimmed	176	8.1 gm	3.0 gm	78 mg	71 mg	24 gm	1.7 mg
Ground Turkey Per 3-oz. Braised	**195**	**11 gm**	**3.2 gm**	**58 mg**	**70 mg**	**21 gm**	**1.6 mg**
Ground Beef 76% lean Per 3-oz. Broiled, trimmed	251	16.9 gm	6.5 gm	86 mg	71 mg	23 gm	2.6 mg
Ground Beef 82% lean Per 3-oz. Broiled, trimmed	233	14.4 gm	6.0 gm	86 mg	69 mg	24 gm	2.6 mg

Source: United States Department of Agriculture

Turkey, A Native American

Turkeys have played an important role in American and world history. Although popular American history places the discovery of turkey with the first Thanksgiving in America, the turkey was in the New World long before the Pilgrims.

Recent archaeological studies show that turkeys have roamed the Americas for ten million years. When Christopher Columbus came to the New World in 1492, turkeys were here to greet him. The name "turkey" came from Columbus, who, thinking that the New World was connected to India, named them "tuka," the East Indian Tamil language name for the peacock. (Actually, the turkey is a variety of pheasant.)

A few years later Cortez, the conqueror of Mexico, sent some turkeys to King Charles of Spain as part of his agreement to repay his Majesty with "One fifth of all the spoils taken in the New World." The turkeys then were called "tukki" by the Sephardic merchants of Spain, from their Hebrew word for the peacock.

By 1530, turkeys were being raised domestically in England, France and Italy, and soon were being exported to America, where the settlers bred them with the wild turkey to produce the magnificent Bronze and Narragansett breeds, which became the foundation of the American turkey industry.

Because wild turkeys were so plentiful in America, there were very few domesticated flocks. It was not until the early 1900s, when practically all wild turkeys had ceased to exist, that turkeys were raised domestically.

One of the few exceptions were the California missions, where as early as 1816 flocks of turkeys were being raised.

Transporting turkeys in those days was by herding a flock, sometimes as many as 500 birds, to market. In the late 1800s, turkey growers in Northern California herded their flocks to market, a 250-mile trip, which took 75 to 100 days.

Benjamin Franklin, who proposed the turkey as the official United States bird, was deeply disappointed when the bald eagle was chosen instead. In a letter to his daughter he wrote, "I wish the bald eagle had not been chosen as the Representative of our country! The Turkey is a much more respectable Bird, and therefore a true original native of America."

In England, turkeys raised in Suffolk were herded to London, and, in inclement weather, had their feet bound in cloth, over which leather shoes were laced. The 50-mile trip took three to four weeks and required five to ten persons and dogs.

Turkey production in the United States soared in the early part of the twentieth century. In the 1990s, nearly 300 million turkeys are raised in the U.S. each year.

Because turkey is now a year-round meat, no longer used only for Thanksgiving, Christmas and other special occasions, its consumption has risen to more than 20 pounds per person each year in the United States. (The French consume 13 pounds, Italians 11, Germans 8 and English 7, per person.)

J. A. Brillat-Savarin, in his book *The Physiology of Taste*, published in 1791, wrote of the American turkey as being "One of the most beautiful presents which the New World has made to the Old."

Now, on to the recipes . . . .

APPETIZERS

Ginger Turkey Wontons

Make and freeze up to 3 weeks ahead; do not thaw before frying.

1 1/4 pounds turkey breast tenderloins
2 cloves garlic
1 bunch green onions, chopped
2 tablespoons chopped fresh ginger

3 tablespoons Madeira wine or sherry
Salt and pepper to taste
1 package (14 ounces) wonton wrappers
3 cups oil, for frying

Put turkey, garlic, onion, ginger, Madeira, salt and pepper in food processor; process until smooth. Put 1 teaspoon of this filling in center of each wonton wrapper. Wet edges with water; fold to form triangle. Press around edges to seal. Wet both side points and pinch together over center. Freeze on baking sheet.

Heat oil to 375 degrees. Fry wontons a few at a time until golden brown, about 2 minutes. Drain on paper towels. Serve hot with dipping sauces.

Makes approximately 50 wontons.

SHERRY ORANGE SAUCE:
Combine 1 can (6 ounces) frozen orange juice concentrate, 1 tablespoon minced fresh ginger and 1/3 cup sherry in saucepan and bring just to a boil. Serve hot or cold.

SESAME SCALLION SAUCE:
Whisk together 1/2 cup rice vinegar, 2 tablespoons sesame oil, 2 tablespoons oyster sauce,* 5 green onions, chopped, and 2 tablespoons vegetable oil.

*Note: Oyster sauce can be found in the Oriental section of food stores.

Per Wonton (approx) excluding dipping sauces:
Calories 143   *Protein 3 gm*   *Fat 14 gm*
Carbohydrate 2 gm   *Sodium 32 mg*   *Cholesterol 9 mg*

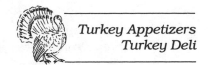

Eggplant Turkey Stacks

Lining your baking sheet with aluminum foil makes cleanup easy.

8 ounces turkey ham, sliced
8 ounces provolone cheese,
  thinly sliced
1 large eggplant, sliced to
  1/8 inch thick

4 eggs, lightly beaten
1 cup seasoned bread crumbs
1/4 cup olive oil

Layer turkey ham and cheese on half the eggplant slices. Top with remaining eggplant slices. Dip "sandwiches" in eggs, then coat with bread crumbs. Place on foil-covered baking sheet. Drizzle with olive oil. Bake in 300 degree oven for 25 minutes; turn over halfway through cooking time. Cut into quarters to serve.   Makes about 86 appetizers.

Per Appetizer (approx):
Calories 26   *Protein 2 gm*   *Fat 2 gm*
Carbohydrate 1 gm   *Sodium 61 mg*   *Cholesterol 13 mg*

Smoked Turkey Quesadillas

Messy to eat, but so good! Serve with plenty of napkins.

2 cups shredded Cheddar cheese
12 flour tortillas (8 inches)
1 1/2 pounds smoked turkey breast,
  shredded

3/4 cup diced mild green chilies
Oil, for frying
1 1/2 cups guacamole
1 1/2 cups sour cream

Sprinkle cheese on half the tortillas. Top with turkey and chilies. Cover with remaining tortillas. Heat lightly oiled skillet over medium-high heat. Cook each quesadilla until golden brown and crisp, about 2 to 3 minutes per side. Cut into 8 wedges and serve with guacamole and sour cream.   Makes 48 appetizers.

Per Appetizer (approx):
Calories 123   *Protein 7 gm*   *Fat 6 gm*
Carbohydrate 11 gm   *Sodium 269 mg*   *Cholesterol 14 mg*

Country Pâté

3 pounds turkey drumsticks
Water or broth as needed
4 shallots, chopped
2 cloves garlic
1/4 teaspoon each ground
    allspice and mace
2 teaspoons fresh minced thyme
    or 1 teaspoon dried

1 teaspoon fresh minced
    marjoram or 1/2 teaspoon
    dried
2 tablespoons brandy
1 cup heavy cream
Salt and pepper to taste

Poach turkey drumsticks in water or broth to cover, gently simmering until meat is tender, about 1 1/2 hours. Pull turkey meat from bones; discard skin and bones.

Place turkey, shallots, garlic, spices, herbs and brandy in food processor; process for 1 minute. With motor running add cream slowly. Season with salt and pepper. Spoon into crock and refrigerate overnight. Serve with toasted baguette slices or crackers.   Makes approximately 3 cups.

Per 1/4-cup Serving (approx):
Calories 237	*Protein 23 gm*	*Fat 15 gm*
Carbohydrate 1 gm	*Sodium 101 mg*	*Cholesterol 95 mg*

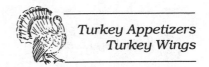
Ginger-Orange Turkey Wings

If the Chinese had turkey (they didn't, until very recent times), they probably would have invented this zesty treatment of turkey wings, fit for an emperor.

4 turkey wings
1 bay leaf
1 clove garlic
3 1/2 cups orange juice
2 tablespoons grated orange
   zest

1/2 cup firmly packed brown
   sugar
2 tablespoons shredded fresh
   ginger
1 tablespoon soy sauce

Poach turkey wings in simmering water with bay leaf and garlic for 35 minutes. Drain water and arrange wings in baking dish. Combine juice, zest, sugar, ginger and soy sauce; bring to a boil. Simmer for 20 minutes. Pour over wings and bake at 350 degrees for 1 hour, basting occasionally.

Makes 4 servings.

Per Serving (approx):
Calories 680
Carbohydrate 62 gm

Protein 56 gm
Sodium 386 mg

Fat 23 gm
Cholesterol 145 mg

Turkey Liver Pâté

You'll probably have to order turkey livers from your market butcher a couple of days in advance. Very few butchers have them on hand, unless it is during a holiday period when they have lots of turkeys. If you think of it then, buy several pounds, freeze them and defrost when you are ready to make pâté.

8 tablespoons butter or
  margarine
1 large or 2 medium onions,
  very finely chopped
1 clove garlic, very finely
  minced

1 pound turkey livers, trimmed
  and quartered
1/4 teaspoon each black
  pepper, dried thyme, dried
  tarragon and salt
1/2 ounce brandy or Cognac

Melt 3 tablespoons of the butter in large frying pan over medium-low heat. Cook onions until soft and translucent, about 6 minutes. Add garlic and cook for another minute or two. Pour into blender or food processor. Puree for a minute.

Melt remaining butter in same pan and add livers. Sauté over medium-high heat until slightly browned on outside, rosy red on inside, about 4 to 5 minutes. Sprinkle livers with spices, herbs and brandy; cook for another minute or two. Be sure to scrape up browned residue in pan.

Add all this to onion-garlic puree in blender and puree until absolutely smooth.

Put in serving bowl, cover tightly and refrigerate for 8 hours or overnight. Serve with toast points or melba toast.   Makes 8 servings.

Per Serving (approx):
Calories 181
Carbohydrate 5 gm

Protein 9 gm
Sodium 226 mg

Fat 13 gm
Cholesterol 215 mg

Party Meatballs

1 pound ground turkey
1 egg, lightly beaten
1/3 cup finely chopped onion
1/3 cup dry bread crumbs

1 tablespoon dried parsley flakes
1 teaspoon instant beef bouillon
1/4 teaspoon salt
1/4 teaspoon black pepper

Combine all ingredients. Shape into 1-inch meatballs; place on shallow greased baking pan. Bake in 350 degree oven for 20 minutes.

Meanwhile, prepare Cranberry-Horseradish Sauce. Pour sauce over meatballs; serve hot.

Makes 3 dozen appetizers.

CRANBERRY-HORSERADISH SAUCE:
Combine 1 can (8 ounces) jellied cranberry sauce and 1 tablespoon prepared horseradish or 1 teaspoon grated orange zest in saucepan. Warm over medium heat, stirring until smooth.

Per Appetizer (approx):
Calories 34
Carbohydrate 3 gm

Protein 3 gm
Sodium 45 mg

Fat 1 gm
Cholesterol 15 mg

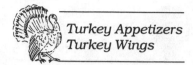
Crunchy Oven-Baked Turkey Drumettes

1 1/3 cups Grape-nuts
  cereal
2 teaspoons dried Italian seasoning
1/2 to 3/4 teaspoon red pepper
  flakes

1/2 cup buttermilk
2 pounds turkey drumettes

In food processor fitted with metal blade, process cereal, Italian seasoning and red pepper flakes for 30 seconds or until mixture is coarsely chopped. Transfer mixture into gallon-sized, self-closing plastic bag.

Pour buttermilk into 9-inch pie plate. Dip each turkey drumette into buttermilk, coating completely. One at a time, add drumettes to cereal mixture in plastic bag. Shake bag to completely coat drumette with cereal mixture. Remove drumette from bag. Repeat to coat remaining drumettes. Place drumettes in refrigerator for 30 to 45 minutes to allow coating to adhere better.

On 2- x 10- x 15-inch jelly-roll pan sprayed with nonstick spray, arrange drumettes. Bake, uncovered, at 400 degrees for 30 minutes. Cover drumettes loosely with foil and continue baking for 15 minutes or until meat thermometer reaches 170 degrees when inserted in thickest part of drumettes.   Makes 4 servings.

Per Serving (approx):
Calories 455	*Protein 44 gm*	*Fat 15 gm*
Carbohydrate 35 gm	*Sodium 370 mg*	*Cholesterol 160 mg*

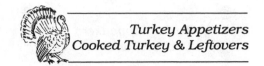

Parmesan Turkey Cubes

2 egg whites
2 tablespoons oil
1/3 cup seasoned bread crumbs
2 cloves garlic, minced
1 teaspoon dried parsley flakes

1 teaspoon dried dill, rosemary
  or basil
1 pound cooked turkey breast,
  cubed
1/4 cup grated Parmesan cheese
Pimiento-stuffed olives

Whisk egg whites and oil just to blend. Combine bread crumbs with garlic and herbs. Dip turkey in egg mixture, then coat with bread crumb mixture. Bake in preheated 450 degree oven until golden and crisp, about 8 to 10 minutes. Roll in Parmesan. Skewer with pimiento-stuffed olives.

Makes approximately 30 skewers.

Per Skewer (approx):
Calories 37   *Protein 5 gm*   *Fat 1 gm*
Carbohydrate 1 gm   *Sodium 35 mg*   *Cholesterol 13 mg*

**Expenditures for Turkey
Per Person**

Year	Dollar Amount
1986	14.21
1987	15.09
1988	15.04
1989	16.47
1990	17.35
1991	17.77
1992	17.40

Cheese-n-Turkey Bundles

1 sheet puff pastry
Dijon-style mustard
Chopped fresh herbs
1/2 cup shredded cooked turkey
   breast

1 slice turkey ham
1 slice Swiss cheese
4 strands chives
1 egg, lightly beaten
1 1/2 teaspoons sesame seeds

Spread puff pastry sheet with mustard and sprinkle with herbs. Cut in quarters. Top each piece with 2 tablespoons shredded turkey and quarter slice of turkey ham and cheese. Bring edges of pastry together and tie each packet with chive. Brush with egg; sprinkle with sesame seeds and bake in preheated 425 degree oven until browned.

Makes 4 appetizers.

Per Appetizer (approx):
Calories 79
Carbohydrate 2 gm

Protein 9 gm
Sodium 126 mg

Fat 4 gm
Cholesterol 72 mg

Sesame Turkey Cubes

1/4 cup sesame seeds
1 cup dry bread crumbs
2 pounds smoked or oven-roasted
   turkey breast, cut in 3/4-inch cubes

5 eggs, lightly beaten
3 cups oil, for frying

Mix sesame seeds and bread crumbs together. Dip turkey in egg, then roll in bread crumb mixture. Heat oil to 375 degrees. Deep-fry turkey until golden brown, about 2 minutes. Serve with Honey Mustard.

Makes 60 appetizers.

HONEY MUSTARD:
Combine 3/4 cup Dijon-style mustard with 1/3 cup honey.

Per Appetizer (approx):
Calories 159
Carbohydrate 3 gm

Protein 5 gm
Sodium 101 mg

Fat 14 gm
Cholesterol 26 mg

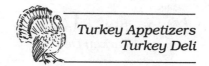

Quick Turkey Appetizers

6 flour tortillas (10 inches)
4 teaspoons olive oil
1 cup salsa
1 pound deli smoked turkey, sliced
    and cut into 1/4-inch strips
1 medium tomato, chopped

2 tablespoons chopped cilantro
1 1/2 tablespoons chopped
    black olives
1/2 teaspoon crushed red
    pepper flakes
1 cup grated Monterey jack
    cheese

Place tortillas on two 12- x 14-inch baking sheets. Lightly brush both sides of tortillas with oil. Bake tortillas at 400 degrees for 3 minutes; remove from oven.

Spread salsa evenly over center of each tortilla, to within 1/2 inch of edge. Sprinkle turkey, tomato, cilantro, olives, red pepper and cheese evenly over salsa on each tortilla. Bake tortillas for 10 to 12 minutes longer or until cheese melts.

To serve, slice tortillas in eighths.   Makes 48 appetizers.

Per Appetizer (approx):
Calories 55
Carbohydrate 6 gm

Protein 4 gm
Sodium 163 mg

Fat 2 gm
Cholesterol 6 mg

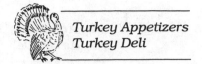
Turkey Jack Appetizers

Turkey ham and turkey breast are combined in this recipe to make either appetizers or a main dish.

8 ounces turkey ham, sliced
8 ounces oven-roasted
  turkey breast, sliced
8 slices (1 ounce each)
  Monterey jack cheese
16 slices whole wheat bread

4 eggs, lightly beaten
2 tablespoons flour
3/4 cup milk
Oil, for deep-frying
1 cup sour cream
1 cup strawberry jam

Place 1 slice each turkey ham, turkey breast and cheese on 8 slices bread. Top with remaining bread; cut in quarters and secure with toothpicks. Whisk eggs, flour and milk together. Dip each minisandwich in batter. Deep-fry for 40 to 60 seconds at 375 degrees until golden brown, turning halfway through. Serve with sour cream and strawberry jam.

Makes 24 appetizers.

Per Appetizer (approx):
Calories 227
Carbohydrate 20 gm

Protein 10 gm
Sodium 268 mg

Fat 12 gm
Cholesterol 60 mg

SOUPS

Golden Turkey Soup

Not too long ago the only way you could buy turkey for making soup was to buy a whole turkey and use the carcass. Now, you can buy turkey parts, such as thighs, wings or drumsticks, and simmer them to make a broth. Use your favorite turkey parts and yellow vegetables to make this golden turkey soup.

2 1/2 pounds turkey thighs
6 cups chicken broth
6 cups water
2 onions, sliced
4 carrots, chopped
2 pounds yams, thinly sliced
3 cloves garlic

1 cup yellow split peas
2 cups half-and-half
2 tablespoons curry powder
2 tablespoons brandy
Salt and pepper to taste
Croutons and chopped parsley,
   for garnish

Remove skin from turkey thighs. Combine broth, water, onions, carrots, yams, garlic and yellow split peas in large pot. Add turkey thighs. Bring to a boil; simmer for 1 hour. Remove turkey from pot. Cut meat from bones; discard bones and reserve meat.

Puree broth and vegetable mixture in batches in blender or food processor. Return puree to heat; add turkey meat and remaining ingredients except garnish. Simmer for 15 minutes or until heated through. Garnish with croutons and chopped parsley.   Makes 12 servings.

Per Serving (approx):
Calories 358
Carbohydrate 38 gm

Protein 27 gm
Sodium 875 mg

Fat 10 gm
Cholesterol 73 mg

Turkey Stock

There is probably no more useful item to have in your freezer than turkey soup stock. This stock becomes the base for many, many soups and stews. You may add noodles, rice, beans, potatoes, vegetables or bits and pieces of turkey. You may serve it piping hot to "cure" a cold, or chilled as a jellied aspic. The choices are endless and are limited only by your creativity.

5 pounds turkey backs, bones,
   necks, wings (but not liver)
   and/or any other turkey parts
2 large onions, coarsely chopped
3 large carrots, coarsely chopped
2 stalks celery with leaves,
   coarsely chopped

3 sprigs fresh thyme or
   1/2 teaspoon dried
5 sprigs parsley
2 bay leaves
12 black peppercorns

Put turkey pieces in stockpot or large pan with enough cold water to cover bones by an inch. Bring to a boil over medium heat. Skim off foam as it forms.

Reduce heat to medium-low, add remaining ingredients and simmer, partially covered, for 2 hours. If necessary, add more water to keep ingredients covered.

Strain through fine sieve or cheesecloth. When cool, skim off any fat from surface and store in freezer.   Makes approximately 1 quart.

Per Cup (approx):
Calories 187
Carbohydrate 38 gm

Protein 6 gm
Sodium 421 mg

Fat 0 gm
Cholesterol 0 mg

Amish Vegetable and Noodle Soup

1 turkey carcass with neck and
    giblets (except liver), chopped
    into large pieces (optional)
3 medium ribs celery, cut into
    1/2-inch slices
2 medium carrots, cut into
    1/4-inch rounds
1 large onion, chopped
1 can (46 ounces) chicken broth
    (about 6 cups)

1 tablespoon chopped parsley
1/2 teaspoon salt
1/2 teaspoon dried thyme
1 bay leaf
1/4 teaspoon black peppercorns
2 medium boiling potatoes,
    scrubbed and cut into 1-inch
    pieces
1/2 pound wide egg noodles
2 to 3 cups coarsely chopped
    cooked turkey

In large stockpot or Dutch oven over high heat, combine carcass pieces, celery, carrots, onion, broth and enough water to cover carcass; bring to a boil, skimming off foam. Reduce heat to low. Add parsley, salt, thyme, bay leaf and peppercorns. Simmer, partially covered, for 2 to 3 hours; if not using carcass, reduce to 30 minutes.

With tongs, remove pieces of carcass. Cut off meat and add to soup; discard bones. Increase heat to medium; add potatoes and cook for about 10 minutes or until almost tender. Add noodles; cook for about 10 minutes longer or until noodles are tender. Add turkey; cook for 2 minutes longer or until turkey is heated through.   Makes about 6 to 8 servings.

Per Serving (approx):
Calories 386
Carbohydrate 52 gm

Protein 30 gm
Sodium 801 mg

Fat 6 gm
Cholesterol 156 mg

Acorn Squash Soup

This rich, elegant soup is the perfect preface for a very special dinner, or as the main course for a luncheon.

3 cups cooked, peeled and diced
   acorn squash
2 cups turkey stock or chicken broth
1 cup whipping cream*
1/2 teaspoon ground nutmeg

2 cups cubed cooked turkey
1/4 cup dry sherry
Salt and pepper to taste
Minced parsley (optional)

Puree cooked squash in food processor or blender. Transfer squash to medium saucepan; stir in stock. Place over medium heat and cook for 5 to 10 minutes. Stir in cream and nutmeg. Reduce heat to medium-low. Add turkey and continue cooking for 5 to 6 minutes or until slightly thickened. Add sherry. Season with salt and pepper. To serve, sprinkle with parsley, if desired.   Makes 6 servings.

*Note: Half-and-half may be substituted for the heavier whipping cream.

Per Serving (approx):
Calories 258
Carbohydrate 9 gm

Protein 16 gm
Sodium 602 mg

Fat 18 gm
Cholesterol 90 mg

Turkey Corn Chowder

What's a tailgate picnic or after-game get-together without a mug of steaming hot soup? Add garlic French bread and fresh fruit to complete the menu.

1 large onion, chopped	1 1/2 teaspoons salt
3 tablespoons oil	1/2 teaspoon black pepper
1 pound ground turkey	2 teaspoons sugar
1 can (12 ounces) whole kernel corn	3 cups boiling water
1 large potato, diced	2/3 cup canned evaporated
1 can (16 ounces) tomatoes	milk

Sauté onion in oil in Dutch oven until transparent. Push to one side. Add turkey and cook, stirring, until lightly browned. Add remaining ingredients except canned milk.

Stir well. Cover and bring just to a boil; reduce heat and simmer for 30 minutes or until potatoes are tender.

Just before serving remove from heat and slowly stir in evaporated milk.

Makes 6 generous servings.

Per Serving (approx):
Calories 331
Carbohydrate 30 gm

Protein 19 gm
Sodium 695 mg

Fat 15 gm
Cholesterol 63 mg

Hearty Turkey-Vegetable Soup

Leftovers of turkey are the basis of this fall and winter standby. Double this recipe and freeze the extras.

2 cups turkey stock
1/4 cup regular pearl barley
Salt to taste
1/4 teaspoon black pepper
1 small onion, chopped
1/4 cup chopped parsley

1/2 cup chopped celery
1/2 cup sliced carrots
1/2 cup drained canned
  whole kernel corn
1 cup cubed cooked turkey

Combine stock, barley, salt, pepper, onion and parsley in 3-quart saucepan. Bring to a boil; reduce heat, cover and simmer for 40 minutes, stirring occasionally. Add more stock if necessary. Add celery and carrot; cook for an additional 20 minutes, stirring frequently. Add corn and turkey; bring to a boil. Boil for 2 minutes to heat through.

Makes 4 servings.

Per Serving (approx):
Calories 170
Carbohydrate 23 gm

Protein 14 gm
Sodium 878 mg

Fat 3 gm
Cholesterol 27 mg

Turkeys are fed a balanced diet of corn and soybean meal mixed with a supplement of vitamins and minerals. Fresh water is always available. It takes about 84 pounds of feed to raise a 30 pound tom turkey.

Wild Rice and Turkey Bacon Soup

1 pound turkey bacon, cooked
    to package directions and
    chopped
1 medium onion, chopped
1 medium carrot, chopped
1 medium potato, chopped
1 cup water

4 cups milk
2/3 cup wild rice, cooked and
    drained
1 can (10 3/4 ounces) cream of
    potato soup
1/2 cup shredded American
    cheese

In 3-quart saucepan over high heat, combine turkey, bacon, onion, carrot, potato and water; boil until vegetables are tender.

Reduce heat to medium-low; add milk, wild rice and potato soup. Simmer mixture for 6 minutes or until soup is heated through, stirring frequently.

Just before serving, fold in cheese. Garnish each serving with additional cheese, if desired.   Makes 6 servings.

Per Serving (approx):
Calories 435
Carbohydrate 40 gm

Protein 23 gm
Sodium 1026 mg

Fat 20 gm
Cholesterol 88 mg

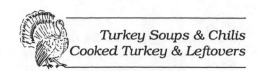

New England Turkey Chowder

1 cup finely chopped celery
1/2 cup chopped onion
1 tablespoon margarine
2 cups turkey broth or
   reduced-sodium chicken bouillon
2 1/2 cups potatoes cut into
   1/2-inch cubes

1 teaspoon salt
1/4 teaspoon white pepper
Dash cayenne pepper
2 cups cooked turkey cut into
   1/2-inch cubes
2 cups cold skim milk
1/4 cup cornstarch

In 5-quart saucepan over medium-high heat, sauté celery and onion in margarine for 2 to 3 minutes, or until vegetables are tender-crisp.

Add broth, potatoes, salt, pepper and cayenne; bring to a boil. Reduce heat to low. Once mixture is at a simmer, cover and cook mixture for 8 to 10 minutes or until potatoes are tender. Stir in turkey.

In medium bowl gradually add milk to cornstarch. Stir mixture into soup. Increase heat to medium. Cook for 6 to 8 minutes or until mixture thickens.

Makes 4 servings.

Per Serving (approx):
Calories 316
Carbohydrate 32 gm

Protein 28 gm
Sodium 510 mg

Fat 8 gm
Cholesterol 56 mg

By the early 1800s, entire flocks were being wiped out by the hunters. By 1840, wild turkeys had become rare even in their former haven of New England.

Turkey Tortilla Soup

This hearty soup, which takes just a few minutes to prepare, has a base of leftover turkey.

1 cup chopped onion
2 teaspoons olive oil
1 can (4 ounces) chopped
   green chilies
1 package (1 1/4 ounces) taco
   seasoning mix
1 can (16 ounces) tomatoes,
   undrained
6 cups turkey broth or reduced-
   sodium chicken bouillon

1 package (10 ounces) frozen
   corn, thawed
2 cups cooked turkey cut into
   1/2-inch cubes
1/3 cup chopped cilantro
4 ounces unsalted tortilla chips,
   broken into pieces
1/2 cup shredded Monterey jack
   cheese

In 5-quart saucepan over medium heat, sauté onion in oil for 3 to 4 minutes or until translucent. Stir in chilies and taco seasoning mix; cook for 1 minute. Add tomatoes, breaking them up with spoon. Stir in turkey broth; bring to a boil. Add corn and turkey; reduce heat to low and simmer for 5 minutes. Add cilantro.

To serve, spoon 1 1/3 cups soup in each bowl. Top each serving with 1/2 ounce tortilla pieces and 1 tablespoon cheese.   Makes 8 servings.

Per Serving (approx):
Calories 244
Carbohydrate 24 gm

Protein 18 gm
Sodium 1053 mg

Fat 9 gm
Cholesterol 33 mg

Hot-n-Sour Turkey Soup

The Orient comes into your kitchen with this broth of drumsticks, Chinese vegetables and zestful seasonings.

2 turkey drumsticks
   (approximately 1 pound each)
2 1/2 quarts water
1 can (14 ounces) chicken broth
1 tablespoon coarsely chopped
   fresh ginger
1/4 cup soy sauce
2 green onions, chopped

1 ounce dry Chinese
   mushrooms,* soaked in
   1 cup water
1/2 cup sliced bamboo shoots
7 ounces tofu, diced
1/4 cup white vinegar
4 drops hot chile oil,* or to taste

In large pan over medium heat, cook turkey with 2 1/2 quarts water, broth, ginger, soy sauce and onions for 1 1/2 hours. Remove turkey meat from bones and return meat to pot.

When mushrooms have soaked for 20 minutes, slice and add to soup along with any remaining liquid. Add all remaining ingredients; cook for 20 minutes over medium-low heat.   Makes 8 servings.

*Note: Chinese mushrooms and hot chile oil may be found in Oriental section of grocery stores.

Per Serving (approx):
Calories 168	*Protein 20 gm*	*Fat 8 gm*
Carbohydrate 5 gm	*Sodium 866 mg*	*Cholesterol 52 mg*

Oriental "Flower" Soup

1 can (46 ounces) chicken broth
3 cups water
6 green onions, chopped
2 medium ribs celery, cut into
    1/2-inch slices
3 tablespoons minced fresh ginger
3 cloves garlic, crushed
2 to 3 cups coarsely chopped
    cooked turkey

16 ounces frozen Oriental vege-
    tables, without sauce, thawed
1/2 cup sliced water chestnuts
    (optional)
2 tablespoons soy sauce,
    or to taste
3 large eggs, well beaten
Salt and pepper to taste

In large stockpot or Dutch oven, combine broth and water. Place over high heat and bring to a boil. Add onions, celery, ginger and garlic. Return to a boil. Reduce heat to low and simmer, partially covered, for 30 minutes.

Increase heat to medium and add cooked turkey, Oriental vegetables, water chestnuts and soy sauce. Bring to a boil and simmer for 2 minutes.

Stirring soup, slowly add eggs. Remove from heat immediately and let stand for 1 minute or until "egg flowers" form. Season with salt and pepper to taste.   Makes 6 to 8 servings.

Per Serving (approx):
Calories 210
Carbohydrate 17 gm

Protein 22 gm
Sodium 1327 mg

Fat 6 gm
Cholesterol 120 mg

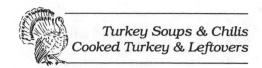

Turkey Divan Soup

Classic Turkey Divan makes an elegant entree. But if all you have are bits of leftover turkey or drumsticks, you can make this main-dish soup, duplicating the same flavors and providing the same elegance, for far less money.

1/2 cup chopped onion
1 tablespoon butter
2 1/2 cups chicken or turkey stock
   or 2 cans (10 1/2 ounces each)
   chicken broth
1 clove garlic, minced
2 cups heavy cream
1/8 teaspoon each white pepper
   and ground nutmeg

2 1/2 cups shredded Cheddar
   cheese
2 stalks broccoli, blanched and
   cut up
2 cups leftover cooked turkey
   turkey chunks*
4 ounces turkey ham, cut into
   strips

Sauté onion in butter; add stock and garlic. Stir in cream and seasonings. Heat for 10 minutes without boiling. Add cheese, broccoli, turkey and turkey ham; warm over low heat until cheese melts Serve immediately. Top with additional shredded cheese, if desired.

Makes 4 servings.

*Note: Two turkey drumsticks could be substituted for leftover turkey. Poach in simmering water until tender, about 1 hour. Remove meat from bones and cut up.

Per Serving (approx):
Calories 729
Carbohydrate 9 gm

Protein 39 gm
Sodium 1406 mg

Fat 60 gm
Cholesterol 247 mg

Moroccan Crockpot Soup

For Moroccans, a favorite meal includes the hearty, spicy soup they call Harira, served with honey cakes and dates. This crockpot version could simmer through any busy day, ready for a sunset supper.

2 pounds turkey thighs
1 1/2 cups lentils, rinsed and
   picked over
1 cup chopped onion
1 cup chopped celery
   with leaves

2 tablespoons tomato paste
1 teaspoon ground turmeric
3/4 teaspoon ground cinnamon
7 cups chicken broth or water
2 to 3 tablespoons lemon juice
Salt and pepper to taste

Place thighs in crockpot. Add lentils, onion, celery, tomato paste, turmeric, cinnamon and chicken broth; stir. Place lid on pot and set temperature to high or low. Allow soup to cook until thighs are tender, 3 to 5 hours on high, or 7 to 9 hours on low.

Transfer thighs from soup to cutting board; remove and discard skin and bones. Cut meat into bite-sized pieces; return to soup. Season to taste with lemon juice, salt and pepper. Serve hot.   Makes 6 servings.

*Note: For a special treat, serve with oranges and cinnamon. Peel and section 6 small oranges. Add 2 teaspoons lemon juice and sprinkle with sugar and ground cinnamon to taste. Chill and serve.

Per Serving (approx):
Calories 380
Carbohydrate 33 gm

Protein 45 gm
Sodium 478 mg

Fat 8 gm
Cholesterol 93 mg

Turkey Vegetable Chowder

1 1/2 pounds boneless turkey thighs
2 medium onions, chopped
3 cups chicken broth
2 tablespoons dry sherry
  (optional)
1 bay leaf
1 teaspoon dried thyme

Salt to taste
1/4 teaspoon black pepper
3 carrots, thickly sliced
  (about 1 cup)
2 ribs celery, thickly sliced
  (about 3/4 cup)
2 potatoes, cubed (about 2 cups)

In Dutch oven combine thighs, onions, broth, sherry, bay leaf, thyme, salt and pepper. Over high heat bring to a boil. Reduce heat to low; cover and simmer for 35 minutes.

Remove turkey and cut into chunks; return to pot and add carrots, celery and potatoes. Over high heat bring to a boil. Reduce heat to low; cover and simmer for 20 to 25 minutes longer or until turkey and vegetables are tender.
                                      Makes 6 servings.

Per Serving (approx):
Calories 198
Carbohydrate 16 gm

Protein 22 gm
Sodium 849 mg

Fat 5 gm
Cholesterol 71 mg

Portuguese Sopa

The Portuguese love soup! And you will, too, with their recipe of a delightful blending of herbs and garlic, which transforms smoked turkey breast, simmered in chicken broth, into a culinary adventure.

1 onion, chopped	2 cans (14 1/2 ounces each)
2 stalks celery with leaves,	chicken broth
chopped	1 teaspoon dried summer savory
1 clove garlic, minced	Salt and pepper to taste
2 tablespoons oil	2 cans (15 1/2 ounces each)
1 pound smoked or cooked	garbanzo beans, drained
turkey breast, cubed	1/4 head cabbage, chopped
4 cups water	

Sauté onion, celery and garlic in oil for 3 minutes. Add turkey, water, broth and seasonings; simmer for 30 minutes. Add garbanzo beans and cabbage; cook for 15 minutes.   **Makes 8 servings.**

Per Serving (approx):
Calories 360   *Protein 25 gm*   *Fat 9 gm*
Carbohydrate 45 gm   *Sodium 1034 mg*   *Cholesterol 22 mg*

U.S. Turkey Exports*			
Year	Whole Body	Parts & Cut-up	Total
1986	7.0	18.5	25.5
1987	7.9	25.2	33.1
1988	7.4	43.5	50.9
1989	8.9	31.7	40.6
1990	13.7	40.2	53.9
1991	16.6	86.8	103.4
1992	20.3	150.3	170.6
1993**	21.0	166.0	187.0

*In millions of pounds
**Estimated

Harvest Soup

2 pounds turkey wings
6 cups water
2 tablespoons instant chicken
  bouillon
1 teaspoon dried poultry seasoning

Salt to taste
1/4 teaspoon black pepper
1 package (16 ounces) frozen
  vegetable blend, thawed
1/4 cup uncooked pasta

Place turkey in stockpot or Dutch oven with water, bouillon and season-ings. Bring to a boil; reduce heat, cover and simmer for 2 hours. Remove turkey and add vegetables and pasta. Bring to a boil; reduce heat, cover and simmer for 10 minutes more. Meanwhile, remove turkey skin and discard. Remove turkey from bones and cut into bite-sized pieces. Add turkey to soup before serving.   Makes 6 servings.

SLOW-COOKER METHOD:
Place turkey in slow cooker with bouillon, seasonings and 4 1/2 cups water. Cover. Cook on low setting for 10 hours. Remove turkey. Add veg-etables and pasta. Cover and cook on high setting for 30 minutes. Mean-while, remove turkey skin and discard. Remove turkey from bones and cut into bite-sized pieces. Add turkey to soup before serving.

Per Serving (approx):
Calories 296
Carbohydrate 12 gm

Protein 32 gm
Sodium 340 mg

Fat 14 gm
Cholesterol 88 mg

Rich Turkey Soup

Use economical turkey parts for this low-cost, tasty soup.

2 pounds turkey necks and
   backs
1 teaspoon salt
1 bay leaf
1 sprig parsley

3 onions
4 stalks celery
1 1/2 cups diced or sliced carrot
1 1/2 cups diced potato
1 1/2 cups sliced zucchini

Place turkey necks and backs in large kettle. Add water to cover, salt, bay leaf, parsley, 2 onions (quartered) and 2 stalks celery. Bring to a boil; cover, reduce heat and simmer for 2 hours.

When cool enough to handle, strain and measure broth (there should be at least 2 quarts); discard cooked vegetables. Pick meat from turkey bones and add to strained broth. Chop remaining onion and celery stalks. Add to broth along with diced carrot and potato.

Simmer for 15 minutes. Add zucchini and continue simmering until vegetables are tender. Taste, and add a little additional salt, if needed.

Makes about 2 1/2 quarts, 6 servings.

Per Serving (approx):
Calories 403
Carbohydrate 44 gm

Protein 38 gm
Sodium 991 mg

Fat 9 gm
Cholesterol 93 mg

Santa Fe Chili

2 tablespoons oil
2 pounds ground turkey
1/2 cup chopped onion
2 cloves garlic, minced
2 tablespoons chili powder,
    or to taste
1 tablespoon paprika

2 teaspoons ground cumin
1/2 teaspoon salt
Freshly ground pepper to taste
1 can tomatoes (28 ounces),
    drained
2 cans red kidney beans
    (15 ounces each), drained

In large skillet over medium heat, warm oil. Add turkey and onion; cook, stirring, for about 4 to 5 minutes or until turkey is no longer pink.

Stir in garlic, chili powder, paprika, cumin, salt, pepper and tomatoes; cover. Increase heat to high and bring to a boil. Reduce heat and simmer for 1 to 2 hours. Add beans and cook until heated through. May be prepared a day ahead.   Makes 8 servings.

Per Serving (approx):
Calories 344
Carbohydrate 24 gm

Protein 28 gm
Sodium 641 mg

Fat 16 gm
Cholesterol 76 mg

California Turkey Chili

Californians have been using turkey in everything since the 1700s, when wild turkeys were domesticated by the Franciscan monks at the monasteries. We use canned tomatoes and kidney beans instead of fresh, for your convenience.

1 cup chopped green bell pepper	1 tablespoon chili powder
1 1/4 cups chopped onion	1 tablespoon chopped cilantro
2 cloves garlic, minced	or 1 teaspoon dried coriander
3 tablespoons oil	1 teaspoon crushed red pepper
1 can (28 ounces) kidney beans,	flakes
drained	1/2 teaspoon salt
1 can (28 ounces) stewed tomatoes	Grated cheese, chopped onion
1 cup red wine or water	or chopped cilantro, for
3 cups cubed cooked turkey	garnish (optional)

Sauté bell pepper, onion and garlic in oil until soft. Add beans, tomatoes, wine, turkey and seasonings. Simmer for 25 minutes. Serve topped with grated cheese, chopped onion or cilantro, if desired.

Makes 6 servings.

Per Serving (approx):
Calories 718	*Protein 55 gm*	*Fat 11 gm*
Carbohydrate 93 gm	*Sodium 610 mg*	*Cholesterol 53 mg*

The first authenticated reference to turkey production in California is in a letter from Fray Pedro Munoz at Mission San Fernando to Fray Antonio Ripoll at Mission Santa Barbara. He wrote that he could not send any turkeys to Santa Barbara for all his hens were sitting on nests. The letter was dated May 9, 1816.

Texas Turkey Chili

2 pounds turkey thighs
2 teaspoons oil
1 cup water
2 large onions, cut into chunks
2 medium green bell peppers, cut
   into chunks
1 can (28 ounces) tomatoes,
   with liquid

2 cloves garlic, minced
2 tablespoons chili powder
2 teaspoons ground cumin
1 teaspoon salt
1/4 teaspoon cayenne pepper
1/4 cup shredded Cheddar
   cheese

Remove skin from turkey thighs. Cut the meat away from the bones using a sharp knife. Cut into 1-inch chunks. Brown in oil in stockpot or Dutch oven over medium heat.

Add remaining ingredients except cheese. Bring to a boil; reduce heat, cover and simmer for 1 hour. Remove cover and simmer for about 15 minutes more or to desired thickness. Ladle into bowls; sprinkle with cheese.   Makes 4 servings.

Per Serving (approx):
Calories 452
Carbohydrate 23 gm

Protein 51 gm
Sodium 815 mg

Fat 17 gm
Cholesterol 147 mg

Easy Turkey Chili

1 pound ground turkey
1 medium onion, chopped
1/2 medium green bell pepper,
  chopped
1/4 cup sliced celery
1 tablespoon vegetable oil
1 can (15 1/2 ounces)
  kidney beans, with liquid
1 can (14 1/2 ounces) stewed
  tomatoes

1 can (12 ounces) tomato juice
1 can (6 ounces) tomato paste
1 tablespoon Worcestershire
  sauce
1 teaspoon ground cumin or
  chili powder
1/2 teaspoon salt
1/4 teaspoon garlic powder

Place turkey and fresh vegetables in large skillet with oil. Cook over medium heat for 10 minutes, stirring and separating turkey as it cooks. Add remaining ingredients. Bring to a boil; reduce heat and simmer for at least 30 minutes, stirring occasionally.   Makes 6 servings.

Per Serving (approx):
Calories 460
Carbohydrate 61 gm

Protein 35 gm
Sodium 673 mg

Fat 9 gm
Cholesterol 55 mg

Crockpot Chili

Chili fans, like chili, run from mild to volcanic. This is a medium-to-hot dish meant to be prepared early and left to perk as a warm welcome at the end of the day.

1 to 1 1/2 pounds turkey thigh cutlets
1 can (16 ounces) pinto, red kidney or black beans, drained
1 can (14 ounces) Italian plum tomatoes, undrained*
1/2 cup chopped onion
1/2 cup chopped green bell pepper

3 tablespoons chili powder
1 tablespoon ground cumin
2 cloves garlic, minced
1/2 to 1 teaspoon hot pepper sauce (optional)
Salt and pepper to taste
Sour cream (optional)
Chopped green onion (optional)

Trim turkey cutlets and cut into 1-inch pieces. Add turkey, beans, undrained tomatoes, onion, bell pepper, chili, cumin, garlic and hot pepper sauce to crockpot; stir to combine. Cover crockpot and set temperature control to high or low. Allow chili to cook until meat is tender, 3 to 5 hours on high, or 7 to 9 hours on low. Season with salt and pepper to taste.

Serve chili topped with dollop of sour cream and chopped green onion, if desired.   Makes 4 to 6 servings.

*Note: For thicker chili, use only half the juice from the tomatoes.

Per Serving (approx):
Calories 244
Carbohydrate 18 gm

Protein 28 gm
Sodium 483 mg

Fat 7 gm
Cholesterol 70 mg

Black Bean Chili

1/4 cup oil
3/4 cup chopped onion
2 cloves garlic, minced
4 to 6 tablespoons chili powder,
  or to taste
1 tablespoon dried oregano
2 teaspoons ground cumin
1 teaspoon salt
3 cups chopped cooked turkey

1 can (28 ounces) crushed
  tomatoes
1/2 to 1 cup water
2 cans (16 ounces each) black
  beans, drained
Shredded Monterey jack cheese,
  chopped onion and sour cream
  (optional)

In large skillet or Dutch oven over medium heat, warm oil. Add onion, garlic, chili powder, oregano, cumin and salt. Sauté for 5 minutes or until onion is tender. Stir in turkey, tomatoes and 1/2 cup water. Simmer, uncovered, for 15 minutes, adding water if needed.

Stir in beans; cook for 15 minutes longer or until slightly thickened. Serve chili topped with shredded Monterey jack cheese, chopped onion and sour cream, if desired.   Makes 6 servings.

Per Serving (approx):
Calories 462   *Protein 36 gm*   *Fat 14 gm*
Carbohydrate 48 gm   *Sodium 1150 mg*   *Cholesterol 53 mg*

White Turkey Chili

The name of this recipe comes from the white cannellini beans, which are used instead of the customary red kidney beans.

1 1/2 cups coarsely chopped onion
2 cloves garlic, minced
1 tablespoon olive oil
1 jalapeño pepper, minced
1 can (4 ounces) chopped mild
   green chilies
1 teaspoon ground cumin
1/2 teaspoon dried oregano
1/4 teaspoon cayenne pepper
1/4 teaspoon salt

1 cup reduced-sodium chicken
   bouillon
1 can (19 ounces) white kidney
   beans (cannellini), drained
   and rinsed
2 cups cooked turkey cut into
   1/2-inch cubes
1/4 cup coarsely chopped
   cilantro
1/2 cup reduced-fat Monterey
   jack cheese

In 3-quart saucepan over medium-high heat, sauté onion and garlic in oil for 5 minutes or until onion is tender. Add jalapeño pepper, chilies, cumin, oregano, cayenne pepper and salt. Cook for 1 minute.

Stir in bouillon, beans and turkey. Bring to a boil; reduce heat and simmer, uncovered, for 20 to 25 minutes or until slightly thickened. Stir in cilantro.

To serve, ladle into bowls and top each with 2 tablespoons cheese.

Makes 4 servings.

Per Serving (approx):
Calories 323
Carbohydrate 23 gm

Protein 34 gm
Sodium 798 mg

Fat 10 gm
Cholesterol 65 mg

Vintner's Turkey Chili

The red wine is essential to the success of this chili—and a glass or two with it is nice, too!

1 cup chopped green bell pepper	3 cups cooked turkey cut into
1 1/4 cups chopped onion	1/2-inch cubes
2 cloves garlic, minced	1 tablespoon chili powder
3 tablespoons oil	1 tablespoon cilantro or
2 cans (15 1/2 ounces each)	1 teaspoon dried
kidney beans, drained	1 teaspoon crushed red pepper
1 can (28 ounces) stewed	flakes
tomatoes, crushed	1/2 teaspoon salt
1 cup red wine	

In 3-quart saucepan over medium-high heat, sauté bell pepper, onion and garlic in oil for 5 minutes or until vegetables are tender-crisp.

Add beans, tomatoes, wine, turkey, chili powder, cilantro, red pepper and salt. Increase heat to high and bring mixture to a boil; reduce heat to low and simmer mixture, uncovered, for 25 minutes.

To serve, garnish with additional chopped onion or cilantro, if desired.

Makes 6 servings.

Per Serving (approx):
Calories 356 *Protein 30 gm* *Fat 11 gm*
Carbohydrate 35 gm *Sodium 1094 mg* *Cholesterol 54 mg*

SALADS

Curried Turkey Pasta Salad

A colorful presentation and well worth the effort.

1 pound turkey breast cutlets
  or tenderloins, cut into
  1/2- by 2-inch strips
2 teaspoons peanut oil
1/4 teaspoon garlic powder
1/4 teaspoon curry powder
1/8 teaspoon ground ginger
Nonstick vegetable cooking spray
2 ounces fresh snow peas,
  blanched

1/2 cup sliced mushrooms
8 cherry tomatoes, halved
1/4 cup red bell pepper cut
  into 1/4- by 2-inch strips
1/4 cup green bell pepper
  cut into 1/4- by 2-inch strips
2 cups rotini pasta, cooked
  to package directions and
  drained

In medium bowl combine turkey, oil, garlic powder, curry powder and ginger. Cover and refrigerate for 30 minutes. Coat large nonstick skillet with vegetable cooking spray. Over medium-high heat, sauté turkey mixture for 4 to 5 minutes or until turkey is no longer pink in center.

Prepare Chutney Salad Dressing. In large bowl combine cooked turkey mixture, snow peas, mushrooms, tomatoes, bell peppers, pasta and Chutney Dressing. Cover and refrigerate for 20 minutes to allow flavors to blend.   Makes 6 servings.

CHUTNEY SALAD DRESSING:
In blender combine 1/3 cup peanut oil, 1/3 cup mango chutney, 2 tablespoons fresh lemon juice, 1 1/2 teaspoons curry powder, 1/2 teaspoon salt and 1/2 teaspoon hot pepper sauce. Blend until mixture is smooth.

Per Serving (approx):
Calories 387
Carbohydrate 37 gm

Protein 23 gm
Sodium 242 mg

Fat 16 gm
Cholesterol 42 mg

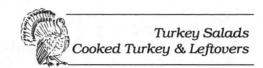

Mandarin Salad

1/3 cup mayonnaise
1 tablespoon Dijon mustard
1/2 teaspoon ground ginger
1/2 teaspoon sesame seeds
1 can (11 ounces) mandarin
   orange segments, drained
   (liquid reserved)
2 cups chopped cooked turkey

1 cup diagonally sliced celery
1/4 cup thinly sliced green
   onion
1/2 cup coarsely chopped
   pecans
Spinach or lettuce leaves
Toasted coconut, for garnish

In small bowl stir together mayonnaise, mustard, ginger, sesame seeds and 1/4 cup reserved mandarin orange liquid.

In large bowl mix turkey, celery, green onion and chopped pecans. Pour mayonnaise mixture over turkey mixture; stir to combine. Add mandarin orange segments, tossing well. Refrigerate until well chilled. Serve on bed of greens and top with coconut. **Makes 4 servings.**

Per Serving (approx):
Calories 428
Carbohydrate 18 gm

Protein 24 gm
Sodium 328 mg

Fat 29 gm
Cholesterol 60 mg

Many precocial birds, such as the turkey, experience a short period of rapid learning just after hatching. This is called the imprinting sensitive period. During this short time the animal forms a long-lasting memory or template of its immediate environment. It earns the characteristics of its mother and hence its species. This information directs the animal's behavior in later life. It may choose to mate with an animal that resembles this "mother" even if the "mother" has been a human keeper. Also, the mature bird may later prefer the kind of environment he was exposed to during this early imprinting period.

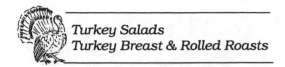

Salad Niçoise #1

3 to 4 pounds boneless turkey
  breast
7 tablespoons extravirgin olive
  oil
2 tablespoons dried *herbs de
  Provence**
1 tablespoon lemon juice
1 tablespoon balsamic vinegar
1 tablespoon red wine vinegar
1 teaspoon Dijon mustard
1 clove garlic, minced

1 teaspoon anchovy paste
  (optional)
Salt and pepper to taste
Romaine lettuce leaves
10 red new potatoes, boiled
  until tender, cooled and sliced
6 tomatoes, cut into wedges
1 1/4 pounds fresh green beans,
  cooked until tender-crisp
1 cup Niçoise olives

Prepare outdoor grill for cooking or preheat broiler. Pat turkey dry and rub with 1 tablespoon of the olive oil and the *herbs de Provence*. Grill or broil turkey 6 to 8 inches from heat source for about 20 minutes per pound or until cooked through, turning occasionally.

Meanwhile, in small bowl combine lemon juice, vinegars, mustard, garlic, anchovy paste, salt and pepper to make dressing. Slowly whisk in remaining 6 tablespoons oil.

To assemble salad, line large platter with lettuce. Slice grilled turkey and arrange on lettuce. Surround turkey with sliced potatoes, tomatoes, green beans and olives. Drizzle with dressing and serve.

Makes 12 servings.

*Note: *Herbs de Provence* are the herbs typical of southern France: thyme, summer savory, basil and rosemary. Commercial blends are available.

Per Serving (approx):
Calories 418
Carbohydrate 32 gm

Protein 44 gm
Sodium 244 mg

Fat 12 gm
Cholesterol 106 mg

Salad Niçoise #2

This version of salad Niçoise has no garlic.

1/4 cup olive oil
3 tablespoons wine vinegar
1 to 2 cloves garlic, minced
2 tablespoons minced fresh
  basil
2 teaspoons Dijon mustard
1/2 teaspoon salt
1/4 teaspoon black pepper
2 cups diced cooked turkey

3 cups cooked, peeled and diced
  potato
2 cups green beans, cooked
  tender-crisp
1/3 cup sliced red onion
1/2 cup pitted Niçoise or
  oil-cured olives
2 tomatoes, quartered
Lettuce leaves (optional)

In small bowl combine oil, vinegar, garlic, basil, mustard, salt and pepper to make dressing; mix well and set aside. In salad bowl combine turkey, potato, beans, onion and olives; toss gently. Garnish with tomatoes, drizzle with dressing and serve on bed of lettuce, if desired.

Makes 4 to 6 servings.

Per Serving (approx):
Calories 318
Carbohydrate 26 gm

Protein 17 gm
Sodium 696 mg

Fat 16 gm
Cholesterol 35 mg

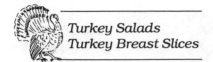
Nouvelle Salade

This should be served really hot so the dressing, turkey and greens are properly blended.

1 pound turkey breast slices
8 cups mixed greens
2 medium tomatoes, cut into
   wedges
1 tablespoon oil

2 tablespoons chopped green
   onion
1 medium green bell pepper, cut
   into thin strips

Cut turkey slices into thin strips; set aside. Arrange 2 cups greens and the tomatoes on each of 4 dinner plates. Warm oil in skillet over medium-high heat. Add turkey strips, onion and bell pepper. Stir-fry for about 8 minutes. Place hot turkey mixture over greens.

Combine dressing ingredients; add to skillet. Heat for about 1 minute or until boiling. Drizzle over salads.

Makes 4 servings.

DIJON SALAD DRESSING:
Combine 1/3 cup oil, 1/3 cup red wine vinegar, 1/3 cup water, 2 tablespoons Dijon mustard, 1 tablespoon sugar, 1/4 teaspoon garlic powder and 1/4 teaspoon black pepper.

Per Serving (approx):
Calories 426	*Protein 27 gm*	*Fat 29 gm*
Carbohydrate 11 gm	*Sodium 256 mg*	*Cholesterol 61 mg*

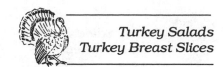

Minted Turkey Salad

The cuisine of Southeast Asia lends mint to turkey in this delightful salad. It is worthy of being served to your most discriminating guest or family member for lunch or as a light supper entree!

1 pound turkey breast slices
1/3 cup lemon juice
1/4 cup soy sauce
1/4 cup oil
1/4 teaspoon garlic powder
Salt and pepper to taste
1 can (15 1/2 ounces) garbanzo
   beans, drained

1 can (14 ounces) artichoke
   hearts, drained and
   quartered
3 green onions, chopped
1 red bell pepper, chopped
1 head butter lettuce

Marinate turkey slices in mixture of lemon juice, soy sauce, oil, garlic powder, salt and pepper for about 1 hour. In shallow pan bake marinated turkey for 15 minutes at 350 degrees, turning halfway through. Let cool. Meanwhile, prepare Minted Mayonnaise.

Slice turkey into strips; combine with garbanzo beans, artichoke hearts, onion, bell pepper and Minted Mayonnaise. Serve on bed of lettuce.

Makes 6 to 8 servings.

MINTED MAYONNAISE:
In blender, mix 3 egg yolks with 1/4 cup lemon juice. With blender running, slowly drizzle in 1 cup olive oil or vegetable oil. Stir in 2 tablespoons chopped fresh mint and salt to taste.

Per Serving (approx):
Calories 709	*Protein 33 gm*	*Fat 50 gm*
Carbohydrate 30 gm	*Sodium 1074 mg*	*Cholesterol 165 mg*

Turkey Taco Salad

1 pound ground turkey
1 package (1 1/4 ounces)
   taco seasoning mix
3/4 cup water
1 small head lettuce, torn into
   bite-sized pieces
1 cup corn chips

1 cup (4 ounces) shredded
   Cheddar cheese
1 tomato, chopped
1/4 cup sour cream
Sliced ripe olives, chopped
   onion, chopped avocado and
   taco sauce (optional)

Cook turkey in skillet over medium heat for 8 to 10 minutes or until no longer pink, stirring and separating turkey as it cooks. Stir in seasoning mix and water. Bring to a boil; reduce heat and simmer for 10 minutes, stirring occasionally.

Place lettuce on 4 plates. Top each with corn chips, cheese, turkey mixture, tomato, sour cream and other toppings as desired.

Makes 4 servings.

Per Serving (approx):
Calories 525
Carbohydrate 16 gm

Protein 30 gm
Sodium 973 mg

Fat 26 gm
Cholesterol 118 mg

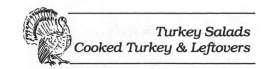

Pasta Primavera Salad

This makes a spectacular dish, especially for a buffet. The green, white and red of the ingredients are particularly cheery on a dark fall or winter evening.

4 cloves garlic, minced
1 medium zucchini, cut in thin
   2-inch sticks
2 cups snow peas, stringed
   and stemmed
1/2 cup chopped red onion
4 green onions, chopped
Approximately 1/2 cup plus 2
   tablespoons olive oil
1 pound pasta (shell, macaroni
   or corkscrew), cooked and well
   drained

1/4 cup chopped sun-dried
   tomatoes
1 cup chopped parsley
1/2 cup chopped fresh basil or
   2 tablespoons dried
1 package (10 ounces) frozen
   petite peas, thawed
2 cups cubed roasted turkey
   breast
Salt and pepper to taste

Sauté garlic, zucchini, snow peas, red onion and green onions in the 2 tablespoons olive oil until tender-crisp. In large bowl, toss pasta with sautéed vegetables, tomatoes, parsley, basil, petite peas, the 1/2 cup olive oil, turkey, salt and pepper. Add more olive oil if needed. Serve at room temperature.   Makes 8 to 10 servings.

Note: If you like a bit of tartness or a sharper flavor in this salad, try adding balsamic or red wine vinegar, a bit at a time, to this salad.

Per Serving (approx):
Calories 320
Carbohydrate 34 gm

Protein 14 gm
Sodium 107 mg

Fat 14 gm
Cholesterol 48 mg

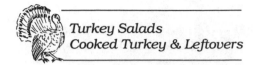

Gingery Stir-Fry Salad

1/3 cup chicken broth or water
1 tablespoon dry sherry
1 teaspoon cornstarch
3 tablespoons oil
1 1/2 tablespoons minced
  fresh ginger
2 green onions, finely chopped
1 clove garlic, minced

1 cup broccoli florets
1 carrot, sliced diagonally
  1/4 inch thick
1 medium zucchini, halved
  lengthwise and sliced
  diagonally 1/2 inch thick
2 cups cooked turkey cut into
  thick strips
Chinese cabbage leaves

In small bowl combine broth and sherry. Add cornstarch; stir to dissolve and set aside.

In large skillet or wok over high heat, warm oil. Add ginger, onion and garlic; stir-fry until fragrant, about 30 seconds. Add broccoli and carrot; stir-fry for 1 minute. Add zucchini; stir-fry for 1 minute longer. Add turkey strips; stir-fry for 1 minute.

Stir broth mixture to blend. Add to skillet and stir for about 30 seconds until vegetables are coated with sauce. Serve warm on cabbage leaves.

Makes 4 servings.

Per Serving (approx):
Calories 348
Carbohydrate 20 gm

Protein 32 gm
Sodium 511 mg

Fat 15 gm
Cholesterol 53 mg

New Potato and Turkey Ham Salad

This is a terrific salad for a potluck because it holds up well. Keep it chilled until ready to serve.

1/4 cup herbed wine vinegar
3 tablespoons salad oil
1/2 teaspoon each salt and
  dried basil
1/8 teaspoon black pepper
2 pounds small red potatoes,
  cooked and cubed
1 1/4 cups diced celery

1 cup chopped red or green
  bell pepper
1/4 cup chopped green onion
3 hard-cooked eggs, chopped
1/4 cup each mayonnaise and
  sour cream
2 cups cubed turkey ham

Whisk together vinegar, oil, salt, basil and black pepper. Add potatoes, celery, bell pepper and green onion; let marinate for 1 hour. Combine eggs, mayonnaise and sour cream; add to potato mixture and fold in gently. Fold in turkey ham. Serve immediately or refrigerate for up to a day. Serve on lettuce-lined platter.   Makes 6 to 8 servings.

Per Serving (approx):
Calories 420
Carbohydrate 40 gm

Protein 16 gm
Sodium 784 mg

Fat 22 gm
Cholesterol 139 mg

Only one of every six turkeys is sold whole, for roasting. The other five are sold as parts, or processed into turkey products such as ham, sausages, frankfurters, salami, etc.

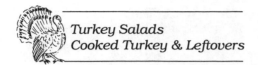
Colorful Turkey Pasta Salad

This is one of those dishes that you can prepare a day or two in advance, refrigerate, and have ready as soon as you get home from work or play. Looks great, too, for a buffet.

2 cups cubed oven-roasted turkey breast
2 1/2 cups tricolored rotini pasta, cooked and drained
1/2 cup thinly sliced onion
1/4 cup thinly sliced celery
1/4 cup chopped parsley

1 tablespoon oil
1 1/2 teaspoons chopped fresh tarragon or 1/2 teaspoon dried
2 tablespoons tarragon vinegar
1 tablespoon lemon juice
2 tablespoons reduced-calorie mayonnaise

In large bowl combine turkey, pasta, onion, celery, parsley, oil, tarragon, vinegar, lemon juice and mayonnaise. Mix thoroughly; cover and refrigerate for 1 to 2 hours or overnight.

Makes 4 servings.

Per Serving (approx):
Calories 458
Carbohydrate 60 gm

Protein 30 gm
Sodium 119 mg

Fat 10 gm
Cholesterol 56 mg

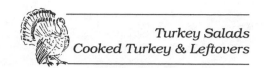

Waldorf Turkey Salad

The Waldorf part of the name comes from a salad that originated at the Waldorf Hotel in New York City many years ago. The salad became a regular item on the menu of hundreds of diners and restaurants in small towns across America in the 1940s and '50s. It's an easy way to feed a lot of people because you can make it ahead. The turkey mixture will keep up to four days in the refrigerator.

6 ounces cubed cooked turkey breast

1/2 cup diced celery

1 small Red Delicious apple, cut into small cubes

2 tablespoons chopped walnuts

1 tablespoon reduced-calorie mayonnaise

1 tablespoon nonfat yogurt

1/8 teaspoon ground nutmeg

1/8 teaspoon ground cinnamon

4 lettuce leaves

In medium bowl combine turkey, celery, apple, walnuts, mayonnaise, yogurt, nutmeg and cinnamon. Cover and refrigerate for at least 1 hour or overnight to allow flavors to blend.

To serve, arrange lettuce leaves on 4 plates. Spoon 3/4 cup turkey mixture over each lettuce leaf. This makes a good sandwich on raisin bread.

Makes 4 servings.

Per Serving (approx):
Calories 130
Carbohydrate 10 gm

Protein 14 gm
Sodium 59 mg

Fat 4 gm
Cholesterol 36 mg

Smoked Turkey and Fresh Vegetable Salad

If salt is a problem in your diet, use oven-roasted turkey instead of smoked turkey.

1/2 pound smoked turkey breast, cut into 1/2-inch cubes
1 cup broccoli florets
1/2 cup thinly sliced yellow squash
1/2 cup coarsely grated carrot
1/4 cup thinly sliced red bell pepper
1/4 cup thinly sliced green onion

1/3 cup reduced-calorie mayonnaise
1 teaspoon Dijon-style mustard
1 teaspoon lemon juice
1/2 teaspoon dried dill weed
1/4 teaspoon dried parsley flakes
1/8 teaspoon garlic powder

In medium bowl combine turkey, broccoli, squash, carrot, bell pepper and onion. In small bowl combine mayonnaise, mustard, lemon juice, dill, parsley and garlic powder. Fold mayonnaise mixture into turkey and vegetables. Cover and chill for at least 1 hour.

Makes 2 servings.

Per Serving (approx):
Calories 269
Carbohydrate 13 gm

Protein 27 gm
Sodium 1378 mg

Fat 13 gm
Cholesterol 48 mg

White Bean and Smoked Turkey Salad

Substitute canned white beans, rinsed and drained, for dried beans if you prefer. You could also make this salad with garbanzo beans.

1 pound dried white beans
1 pound smoked turkey breast, cubed
1 cup thinly sliced red onion

1 cup chopped Italian parsley
Salt and pepper to taste
1 1/2 cups chopped tomato
1 cup imported black olives

Soak beans overnight in cold water to cover; drain. Place beans in saucepan and add cold water to cover. Bring to a boil. Cook until tender, about 45 minutes, skimming any scum that forms on surface. Meanwhile, prepare Mustard Garlic Dressing. Drain beans and combine with 1 cup dressing.

To bean mixture add turkey, onion, parsley, salt and pepper. Refrigerate, covered, for at least 2 hours. To serve, bring to room temperature; toss with chopped tomato and with more dressing if necessary. Garnish with olives.   Makes 8 servings.

MUSTARD GARLIC DRESSING:
Combine 1 egg yolk, 1/4 cup Dijon-style mustard and 1/2 cup red wine vinegar in food processor or blender. Process for 1 minute. While motor is running, add 4 cloves garlic and then 1 1/2 cups olive oil in slow, steady stream. Season to taste with salt and pepper. Refrigerate until ready to use.

Per Serving (approx):
Calories 584
Carbohydrate 21 gm

Protein 18 gm
Sodium 1106 mg

Fat 46 gm
Cholesterol 50 mg

Tuscany Bean Salad

1 pound turkey ham, diced
1 pound white beans, cooked and
  cooled
3 cups diced tomato
1 cup chopped parsley
1/3 cup chopped fresh mint

6 green onions, chopped
1 teaspoon salt
1/2 teaspoon black pepper
1/2 teaspoon dry mustard
1/3 cup Champagne vinegar
2/3 cup olive oil

In large bowl combine turkey ham, beans, tomato, parsley, mint and onions. In small bowl mix together salt, pepper, mustard and vinegar for dressing. Whisk in oil. Pour dressing over salad; mix well. Refrigerate for 30 minutes before serving.
Makes 12 servings.

Per Serving (approx):
Calories 229
Carbohydrate 13 gm

Protein 11 gm
Sodium 674 mg

Fat 14 gm
Cholesterol 21 mg

Chutney Turkey Salad

1 1/2 pounds smoked or
  oven-roasted turkey, cubed
2 cups seedless red or green
  grapes
1 1/2 cups chopped celery
1 cup slivered almonds,
  lightly toasted

1/2 cup sour cream
1/2 cup mayonnaise
1/2 cup mango chutney,
  chopped
1/2 teaspoon curry powder,
  or to taste)
Salt and pepper to taste

In large bowl combine turkey, grapes, celery and almonds. In medium bowl whisk together sour cream and mayonnaise; stir in chutney, curry powder, salt and pepper; toss gently with turkey mixture.
Makes 6 to 8 servings.

Per Serving (approx):
Calories 539
Carbohydrate 26 gm

Protein 28 gm
Sodium 1344 mg

Fat 36 gm
Cholesterol 63 mg

Pizzeria Salad

1 package (10 ounces)
  tagliarini pasta
2 cups cubed turkey ham or
  turkey pastrami
1 cup chopped tomato

1 cup sliced mushrooms
1 cup cubed mozzarella cheese
1/2 cup sliced ripe olives
1/4 cup sliced green onion

Prepare Italian Dressing. Cook tagliarini according to package directions; drain and transfer to a bowl. Pour Italian Dressing over pasta while still warm. Add remaining ingredients; toss gently. Serve immediately or chill.

Makes 6 to 8 servings.

ITALIAN DRESSING:
Whisk together 1/2 cup red wine vinegar, 1/2 cup oil, 1 clove garlic, minced, 1 teaspoon sugar, 1 teaspoon Dijon-style mustard, 1/2 teaspoon dried Italian seasoning, 1/2 teaspoon seasoned salt and 1/4 teaspoon black pepper.

Per Serving (approx):
Calories 371
Carbohydrate 30 gm

Protein 15 gm
Sodium 769 mg

Fat 20 gm
Cholesterol 31 mg

Arizona Turkey Salad

Smoked turkey is the key to this easy-to-make salad because the turkey is precooked and ready to use. The dressing is something special.

1 pound smoked turkey breast,
   cut in 1/2-inch strips
1 head red leaf lettuce, torn
   into bite-sized pieces

1/2 bunch watercress
1 cup halved red seedless grapes
1/2 cup walnuts, toasted

Toss all ingredients together. Serve with Creamy Cheese Dressing.

Makes 6 servings.

CREAMY CHEESE DRESSING:
In blender whirl together 1 egg yolk, 2 ounces Roquefort or blue cheese, 2 tablespoons Champagne vinegar and 1 teaspoon Dijon-style mustard. Slowly add 1/3 cup oil while blender is running. Stir in 1/4 cup cream and salt and pepper to taste.

Per Serving (approx):
Calories 349
Carbohydrate 6 gm

Protein 19 gm
Sodium 978 mg

Fat 27 gm
Cholesterol 82 mg

The wild turkey roamed from the Atlantic coast to as far west as Arizona, from the Great Lakes down south into Central America.

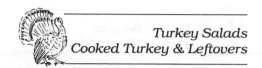

Curried Turkey Salad Amandine

Those Thanksgiving turkey leftovers earn a place for themselves in this crisp and crunchy salad, with a dressing lightly sparked by curry.

2 to 3 cups cooked turkey pieces
2 cups sliced celery
1/3 cup sliced green onion
1/2 cup blanched almonds, toasted

Lettuce
Toasted coconut chips
Raisins

Toss turkey, celery, onion and almonds together. Add Curry Mayonnaise and mix well. Serve on crisp lettuce. Top with coconut chips and raisins.

Makes 4 servings.

CURRY MAYONNAISE:
Combine 1/2 cup mayonnaise, 1 teaspoon lemon juice, 1/2 teaspoon curry powder and 1/2 teaspoon salt; mix well.

Per Serving (approx):
Calories 482
Carbohydrate 8 gm

Protein 30 gm
Sodium 572 mg

Fat 37 gm
Cholesterol 77 mg

Getting Enough z z Z's

Many people report drowsiness after eating Thanksgiving dinner. Recent studies suggest that the composition of a meal (particularly the ratio of carbohydrate to protein) influences the production of brain neurotransmitters which are involved in sleep, mood and depression.

Neurotransmitters in the brain are produced by the amino acid, tryptophan. A carbohydrate-rich–not a protein-rich–meal increased the level of tryptophan in the brain.

Since many people eat an unusually large, many-coursed, carbohydrate-rich meal at Thanksgiving, they often associate the drowsiness they feel with the turkey. To be more accurate, they should associate their sleepy feelings to the increased amount of carbohydrates consumed.

Fruitful Turkey Salad

3 tablespoons oil
1 pound turkey breast slices,
   cut into 1-inch strips
1/2 cup mayonnaise
1/4 cup sour cream
2 tablespoons honey
1 tablespoon lime juice

1 teaspoon chopped fresh dill,
   plus more for garnish
1 cup seedless grapes, halved
1 red Delicious apple, chopped
1/2 cup chopped pecans
Lettuce leaves

Warm oil in medium skillet over medium heat. Add turkey and cook for 5 to 7 minutes or until turkey is no longer pink; stir occasionally. Drain and chill.

In large bowl combine mayonnaise, sour cream, honey, lime juice and dill. Add turkey, grapes, apple and pecans; toss. Serve turkey mixture over lettuce leaves. Garnish with dill.   Makes 4 servings.

Per Serving (approx):
Calories 671	*Protein 26 gm*	*Fat 52 gm*
Carbohydrate 24 gm	*Sodium 219 mg*	*Cholesterol 77 mg*

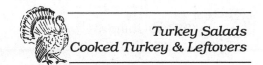
Szechuan Turkey Salad

A spicy peanut dressing makes this cabbage salad special.

4 ounces snow peas, stringed
  and stemmed
4 ounces bean sprouts
1 pound oven-roasted turkey
  breast

1 red bell pepper, cut in long
  thin strips
1 1/2 cups shredded Chinese
  cabbage
1/2 cup sliced cucumber

Blanch snow peas and bean sprouts in boiling salted water for about 30 seconds. Drain in sieve under cold running water; drain again and pat dry. Combine all salad ingredients; toss with Szechuan Dressing.

Makes 6 servings.

SZECHUAN DRESSING:
Whisk together 1/3 cup oil, 1/4 cup white vinegar, 1/4 cup soy sauce, 3 tablespoons peanut butter and 2 teaspoons red pepper flakes.

Per Serving (approx):
Calories 300
Carbohydrate 8 gm

Protein 21 gm
Sodium 734 mg

Fat 21 gm
Cholesterol 41 mg

Hollywood Turkey Salad

Belgian endive or spinach could take the place of some of the leaf lettuce.

1 pound smoked turkey breast,
   cut in 1/2-inch strips
1/2 head red leaf lettuce
1/2 head green leaf lettuce
1/2 bunch watercress

1 cup each red and green
   seedless grapes
2/3 cup slivered almonds
   or chopped walnuts, toasted

Toss all ingredients together. Serve with Blue Cheese Dressing.

Makes 6 servings.

BLUE CHEESE DRESSING:
In blender puree 1 ounce blue cheese, 2 tablespoons white white wine vinegar and 1 teaspoon Dijon-style mustard. With motor running, slowly add 1/3 cup salad oil. Transfer to bowl; whisk in 1/4 cup heavy cream and salt and pepper to taste.

Per Serving (approx):
Calories 375
Carbohydrate 10 gm

Protein 20 gm
Sodium 912 mg

Fat 29 gm
Cholesterol 50 mg

Affluent, traditional families are the most likely to consume turkey at least once in a two-week period. Double-income families with no children, affluent empty-nesters and working parents also head the list of those who have made turkey a regular part of their lifestyles.

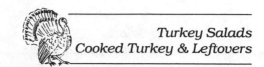

Chinese Turkey Salad

4 cups shredded cooked
   turkey
1 head lettuce, shredded
4 green onions, thinly sliced
1 bunch cilantro, chopped
   (reserve a few leaves for garnish)
1/4 cup sesame seeds, toasted
1 cup chopped peanuts,
   cashews or slivered almonds

2 cups seedless red or green
   grapes, halved or whole
3 cups bean threads or rice
   sticks, fried in salad or
   sesame oil* (cooked white
   rice may be used)
1 carrot, thinly sliced diagonally
Additional whole nuts (optional)
Small clusters of grapes

Mix together turkey, lettuce, onions, cilantro, seeds, nuts and grapes. Pour Lemon Dressing over top and toss to coat. Place a nest of bean threads on each plate. Spoon turkey mixture over top.

Garnish with reserved cilantro, a few carrot slices, additional nuts, if desired, and small clusters of grapes.   **Makes 4 to 6 servings.**

LEMON DRESSING:
Blend together 1/2 teaspoon dry mustard, 1 teaspoon sugar, 3 tablespoons lemon juice, 1 clove garlic, minced, 1 teaspoon soy sauce and 1/4 cup sesame oil or salad oil.

*Note: Deep-fry bean threads or rice sticks, a bunch at a time, until light and puffy. Do not burn. Drain on paper towels.

Per Serving (approx):
Calories 691
Carbohydrate 20 gm

Protein 54 gm
Sodium 353 mg

Fat 44 gm
Cholesterol 106 mg

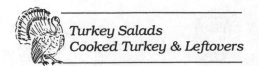

Rice Salad with Pesto Dressing

If you like pesto with pasta, you'll love pesto with rice.

3 tablespoons chopped fresh
   basil or 1 tablespoon dried
1/4 cup grated Parmesan cheese
3 tablespoons lemon juice
1/2 cup olive oil
1 pound turkey breast, cooked
   and shredded

3 cups cooked long-grain rice
1 cup cooked wild rice
1 green bell pepper, chopped
1 red bell pepper, chopped
1/2 cup chopped red onion
3/4 cup sliced ripe olives
Salt and pepper to taste

In blender combine basil, Parmesan and lemon juice. With motor running, slowly add olive oil to make a creamy dressing. Combine remaining ingredients in bowl. Add dressing and toss gently with fork to blend.

Makes 6 to 8 servings.

Per Serving (approx):
Calories 561
Carbohydrate 85 gm

Protein 6 gm
Sodium 316 mg

Fat 22 gm
Cholesterol 3 mg

Kansas City Salad

3 cups diced cooked turkey
1/2 cup bottled French dressing
2 tablespoons mayonnaise
1 tablespoon lemon juice
1/4 cup thinly sliced green onion

4 to 6 Bibb or iceberg lettuce
   cups
4 to 6 slices bacon, cooked crisp
   and crumbled

In medium bowl combine turkey and dressing. Cover and let marinate in refrigerator for 1 to 2 hours. Drain excess marinade; fold in mayonnaise, lemon juice and onion. To serve, spoon salad into lettuce cups; top with bacon.

Makes 4 to 6 servings.

Per Serving (approx):
Calories 292
Carbohydrate 5 gm

Protein 23 gm
Sodium 564 mg

Fat 20 gm
Cholesterol 74 mg

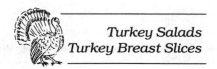

Turkey Spinach Salad

1 pound turkey breast slices,
  cut into 1-inch strips
3 tablespoons oil
2 bunches spinach, torn and chilled

1 cup sliced mushrooms
  (optional)
1/2 cup chopped walnuts
1 tomato, chopped

Prepare Apple-Soy Marinade; marinate turkey for at least 15 minutes. Cook turkey in medium skillet in hot oil for 5 to 7 minutes or until no longer pink, stirring occasionally. Drain and set aside.

Prepare Sweet & Sour Dressing. Mix remaining ingredients with cooked turkey and toss with dressing. Serve immediately.

Makes 6 to 8 servings.

APPLE-SOY MARINADE:
Combine 1/4 cup soy sauce, 1/4 cup apple juice, 2 sliced green onions and 1 clove garlic, minced.

SWEET & SOUR DRESSING:
Combine 1/3 cup oil, 1/4 cup cider vinegar, 2 tablespoons brown sugar and 1/2 teaspoon onion powder.

Per Serving (approx):
Calories 288
Carbohydrate 7 gm

Protein 15 gm
Sodium 554 mg

Fat 22 gm
Cholesterol 31 mg

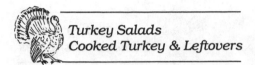
Apple Pie Turkey Salad

2 1/4 cups cubed cooked turkey
2 cups diced celery
2 cups diced unpeeled Granny Smith
   apples
1/4 cup raisins
2 tablespoons reduced-calorie
   mayonnaise

2 tablespoons plain low-fat
   yogurt
1/4 teaspoon ground nutmeg
1/4 teaspoon ground cinnamon
Salt and pepper to taste
Lettuce leaves
Grated Cheddar cheese, for
   garnish (optional)

In large bowl combine turkey, celery, apples and raisins. In small bowl combine mayonnaise, yogurt, nutmeg and cinnamon; fold into turkey mixture. Season to taste with salt and pepper. Serve on lettuce leaves and garnish with grated Cheddar cheese, if desired.   Makes 6 servings.

Per Serving (approx):
Calories 157
Carbohydrate 14 gm

Protein 16 gm
Sodium 115 mg

Fat 4 gm
Cholesterol 42 mg

Turkey and Corn Bread Salad

2 cups cooked turkey cut into
   1/2-inch cubes
1 cup corn bread stuffing mix
1/2 cup drained whole kernel
   corn
1/4 cup coarsely chopped
   green bell pepper

1/4 cup finely chopped onion
1 jar (2 ounces) chopped
   pimiento, drained
1/2 cup reduced-calorie
   cucumber or buttermilk
   salad dressing

In large bowl combine turkey, 3/4 cup of the corn bread stuffing mix, turkey, the corn, bell pepper, onion, pimiento and dressing. Cover and refrigerate for 4 hours or overnight. To serve, top salad with remaining 1/4 cup stuffing mix.   Makes 4 servings.

Per Serving (approx):
Calories 294
Carbohydrate 26 gm

Protein 24 gm
Sodium 728 mg

Fat 10 gm
Cholesterol 54 mg

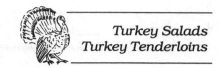

Tender-ness Turkey Stir-Fry Salad

1 pound turkey breast tenderloins
6 tablespoons peanut oil
1 small bunch green onions, cut diagonally into 1-inch pieces
1 red bell pepper, julienned
1 medium zucchini, julienned
1 can (8 ounces) water chestnuts, drained and sliced
1 clove garlic, minced
1 tablespoon reduced-sodium soy sauce
2 cups shredded Chinese cabbage
4 cups cooked Asian noodles or other pasta (8 ounces uncooked)
1/3 cup light teriyaki sauce
Cilantro sprigs (optional)

Slice tenderloins lengthwise in half along natural crease. Cut into 1-inch chunks. In wok or large nonstick skillet over medium-high heat, warm 2 tablespoons of the oil. Add turkey and stir-fry for 2 to 3 minutes.

Add onions and bell pepper; cook for 1 minute longer, stirring constantly.

Add zucchini, water chestnuts and garlic; stir-fry for 1 minute longer or until vegetables are tender-crisp and turkey is cooked through. Stir in soy sauce and set aside.

In large bowl combine shredded cabbage and noodles. In small bowl whisk together remaining peanut oil and teriyaki sauce. Add turkey mixture to bowl; toss with teriyaki mixture. Garnish with cilantro and serve with Oriental-style corn or rice chips and iced tea.   Makes 6 servings.

Per Serving (approx):
Calories 457
Carbohydrate 33 gm

Protein 24 gm
Sodium 1168 mg

Fat 26 gm
Cholesterol 46 mg

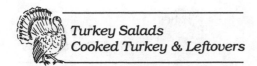
Curried Salad Bombay

1/2 cup reduced-calorie
   mayonnaise
1/2 cup plain low-fat yogurt
1 tablespoon peach or mango
   chutney
2 to 3 teaspoons curry powder
Salt and pepper to taste
1 1/2 pounds cubed cooked turkey
   breast

1 red apple, unpeeled and sliced
1 green apple, unpeeled
   and sliced
3/4 cup red and/or green
   seedless grapes
2 tablespoons snipped chives
Curly green or Bibb lettuce

In medium bowl combine mayonnaise, yogurt, chutney, curry, salt and
pepper. Add turkey, then add apples, grapes and chives; toss gently to
coat ingredients with dressing. Serve salad on bed of lettuce.

Makes 6 servings.

Per Serving (approx):
Calories 241
Carbohydrate 14 gm

Protein 28 gm
Sodium 263 mg

Fat 8 gm
Cholesterol 78 mg

Deluxe Turkey Salad

1 cup cubed cooked turkey
2 cups crisp lettuce torn in
   bite-sized pieces
1/4 cup golden raisins
1/2 cup red grapes, halved
   and seeded if necessary
1 sweet gherkin, chopped

1/4 cup chopped pecans
2 tablespoons chopped red
   onion
1/4 cup cubed mild Cheddar
   cheese
1/2 cup salad dressing or
   mayonnaise

In large bowl combine turkey, lettuce, raisins, grapes, gherkin, pecans,
onion and cheese. Toss with salad dressing.   *Makes 2 servings.*

Per Serving (approx):
Calories 776
Carbohydrate 31 gm

Protein 27 gm
Sodium 704 mg

Fat 60 gm
Cholesterol 68 mg

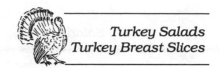

Fruit and Turkey Medley

4 cups torn mixed greens (Bibb, Romaine, leaf lettuce, spinach or cilantro)
1 orange, peeled and sliced crosswise
1/2 cantaloupe, cubed
1 cup seedless grapes
1 apple, thinly sliced into wedges and dipped in lemon juice

1 pear, cubed
1/4 cup chopped pecans or pecan halves
1 tablespoon margarine
1 pound turkey breast slices
Enoki mushrooms, for garnish (optional)

Arrange greens, fruit and pecans on 4 large plates. Combine dressing ingredients; set aside. Warm half the margarine in skillet over medium heat. When margarine begins to bubble, add half the turkey. Cook for 3 minutes; turn turkey over and cook for 2 minutes more. Remove from pan and repeat with remaining margarine and turkey.

Arrange warm turkey evenly among salads. Add Orange-Mint Dressing to skillet; bring to a boil. Pour hot dressing over salad; garnish with mushrooms, if desired. Serve immediately.   Makes 4 servings.

ORANGE-MINT DRESSING:
Combine 1/2 cup orange juice, 1/4 cup olive oil, 1 tablespoon Dijon mustard and 1 teaspoon dried mint.

Per Serving (approx):
Calories 452
Carbohydrate 35 gm

Protein 38 gm
Sodium 209 mg

Fat 23 gm
Cholesterol 94 mg

Caesar Turkey Salad

Here is our version of one of today's most popular salads.

Nonstick vegetable cooking spray
1 pound turkey breast slices,
   cut in strips
4 cups torn Romaine lettuce
1/2 cup thinly sliced red onion

1/2 cup croutons (Caesar salad
   or Parmesan cheese flavored)
2 tablespoons freshly grated
   Parmesan cheese
1 hard-cooked egg, cut into
   wedges (optional)

Spray large skillet with nonstick vegetable cooking spray. Warm over medium-high heat for about 30 seconds. Add turkey breast strips. Cook and stir for 2 to 4 minutes or until lightly browned. Remove from skillet and let cool slightly. Prepare dressing; set aside.

In large bowl combine lettuce, onion and warm turkey. Add dressing; toss gently to coat. Add croutons and toss gently. Sprinkle with cheese. Top with egg, if desired. Serve immediately.   Makes 6 servings.

CAESAR DRESSING:
In small bowl combine 3 tablespoons each fresh lemon juice and water, 2 teaspoons each Worcestershire sauce and olive oil, 2 cloves garlic, crushed, 1 teaspoon anchovy paste, 1/2 teaspoon grated lemon zest and 1/8 teaspoon black pepper. Mix well. Stir in 4 tablespoons low-fat sour cream 1 tablespoon at a time until smooth.

Per Serving (approx):
Calories 192
Carbohydrate 7 gm

Protein 21 gm
Sodium 148 mg

Fat 9 gm
Cholesterol 79 mg

ASIAN & INDIAN

Steaks Shanghai

*Add stir-fried vegetables, a steaming bowl of rice and a wedge of melon or a
scoop of sherbet for dessert, and you have a "company-quality" meal with a
Chinese accent.*

4 to 8 turkey breast steaks
   (1 1/2 pounds total),
   cut 1/4 to 1/2 inch thick
1/2 teaspoon salt
1/4 teaspoon black pepper
3 tablespoons peanut oil
1 1/2 tablespoons cornstarch
1 1/2 teaspoons chicken
   seasoned stock base

1/2 teaspoon ground ginger
1 teaspoon brown sugar
2 tablespoons sherry
1 tablespoon wine vinegar
1/4 cup soy sauce
1 1/2 cups water
Hot cooked rice (optional)
1/4 cup sliced green onion
   (optional)

Season steaks with salt and pepper. Cook in heated oil in skillet until
golden brown, turning once. Turkey steaks cook quickly, so be careful
not to overcook. Remove steaks from pan.

Combine all remaining ingredients except rice and onion in pan. Cook
and stir until sauce clears and thickens. Return turkey steaks to sauce
and reheat for a few minutes. Serve plain or with rice, and sprinkle with
green onion, if desired.   Makes 4 servings.

Per Serving (approx):
Calories 328
Carbohydrate 6 gm

Protein 42 gm
Sodium 1422 mg

Fat 15 gm
Cholesterol 94 mg

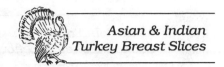

Ginger Turkey Stir-Fry

2 cups boiling water
1 cup bulgur
1/3 cup water
2 tablespoons fresh lemon juice
2 tablespoons honey
1 teaspoon fresh grated ginger,
   or 1/2 teaspoon
   ground ginger
1 tablespoon reduced-sodium
   soy sauce

1 large clove garlic, minced
2 tablespoons cornstarch
1 tablespoon oil
2 cups diagonally sliced carrot
2 cups broccoli florets
2 cups sliced mushrooms
1 can (8 ounces) water
   chestnuts, drained and sliced
1 pound turkey breast slices or
   cutlets, cut in strips

Pour boiling water over bulgur and let stand for 1 hour; drain and set aside.

Combine the 1/3 cup water, lemon juice, honey, ginger, soy sauce and garlic. Dissolve cornstarch in mixture; set aside.

Heat oil over high heat in wok or large skillet. Add carrot; stir-fry for 3 minutes or until tender-crisp. Add broccoli, mushrooms and water chestnuts; stir-fry for about 2 minutes more. Remove from pan.

Stir-fry turkey until lightly browned. Add soy sauce mixture and cook, stirring constantly, until thickened and translucent. Add reserved vegetables; heat through. Serve over drained bulgur.

Makes 6 servings.

Per Serving (approx):
Calories 303
Carbohydrate 45 gm

Protein 23 gm
Sodium 180 mg

Fat 4 gm
Cholesterol 47 mg

Turkey Chow Mein

Leftover turkey is the key to this familiar Chinese recipe for chow mein, American style.

2 to 3 cups cooked turkey pieces
1 can (13 3/4 ounces)
   chicken broth
3 tablespoons soy sauce
1/8 teaspoon ground ginger
1/8 teaspoon black pepper
1 cup sliced onion
1 clove garlic, minced
2 tablespoons oil
1 cup sliced celery

1/2 cup slivered bell pepper
2 tablespoons cornstarch
2 cups fresh bean sprouts
   or 1 can (16 ounces), drained
1 cup sliced fresh mushrooms
   or 1 can (4 ounces), drained
1 1/2 cups fresh Chinese pea
   pods or 1 package (6 ounces)
   frozen and thawed

Toss turkey with 1/2 cup of the broth, the soy sauce, ginger and black pepper; set aside. Sauté onion and garlic in oil for 3 minutes in large skillet with cover. Add celery, bell pepper and remaining broth. Bring to a boil, cover and cook over moderate heat for 2 to 3 minutes.

Drain turkey, saving marinade, and add to celery mixture. Mix cornstarch with drained marinade. Add to skillet and cook, stirring, until sauce thickens. Stir in bean sprouts, mushrooms and pea pods. Cover and cook for 2 to 3 minutes longer. Serve with rice.

Makes 6 servings.

Per Serving (approx):
Calories 336
Carbohydrate 42 gm

Protein 23 gm
Sodium 973 mg

Fat 8 gm
Cholesterol 44 mg

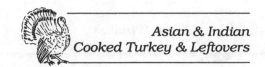

Curried Turkey Dinner

1 package (10 ounces) frozen
   broccoli spears, cooked
   and drained
2 cups cubed cooked turkey
1 can (10 1/2 ounces)
   reduced-sodium cream of
   mushroom soup

1/4 cup reduced-calorie
   mayonnaise
1 1/2 teaspoons lemon juice
1 teaspoon curry powder
1 cup seasoned croutons

In 8-inch-square baking dish, layer broccoli and turkey.

In small bowl, combine soup, mayonnaise, lemon juice and curry powder. Pour over turkey and top with croutons. Bake in preheated 350 degree oven for 20 to 25 minutes or until bubbly.

Makes 4 servings.

Per Serving (approx):
Calories 321	*Protein 24 gm*	*Fat 16 gm*
Carbohydrate 21 gm	*Sodium 720 mg*	*Cholesterol 63 mg*

Shanghai'd Turkey

1 pound skinless turkey
  tenderloins
1/2 cup white wine
3 tablespoons reduced-sodium
  soy sauce
1 tablespoon cornstarch
Black pepper to taste
1 tablespoon sugar
2 teaspoons rice vinegar or
  white vinegar
1 1/2 tablespoons oil
1 clove garlic, minced

1 teaspoon minced fresh ginger
2 carrots, shredded
1/3 pound green beans, split
  lengthwise and lightly steamed
1/2 cup thinly sliced green
  onion
2 cups hot cooked Chinese
  noodles (optional)
Carrots cut in flower shapes
  (optional)
Chopped green onion and
  cilantro sprigs (optional)

Slice turkey in thin strips and place in medium bowl. Sprinkle with 1/4 cup of the wine, 1 tablespoon of the soy sauce, the cornstarch and pepper. Toss to coat with mixture, then let marinate at room temperature for 15 minutes. In small bowl combine remaining 1/4 cup wine, remaining 2 tablespoons soy sauce, sugar and vinegar. Set aside.

Warm wok or large, heavy nonstick skillet over medium-high heat. Slowly add oil. Stir in garlic, ginger and turkey. Stir-fry for 3 to 4 minutes until turkey is cooked through. Add carrots, beans, green onions and reserved wine mixture. Cook for 1 to 2 minutes longer. Serve over Chinese noodles, garnished with carrot flowers, chopped green onion and cilantro sprigs, if desired.   Makes 4 servings.

Per Serving (approx):
Calories 246
Carbohydrate 13 gm

Protein 28 gm
Sodium 393 mg

Fat 7 gm
Cholesterol 70 mg

Sesame Turkey Cutlets

2 teaspoons lemon juice
1 teaspoon soy sauce
1 teaspoon honey
1/8 teaspoon black pepper

1 1/2 pound turkey breast
    cutlets or slices
1 tablespoon margarine
1 tablespoon sesame seeds,
    toasted*

In small bowl combine lemon juice, soy sauce and honey; set aside.

Lightly sprinkle pepper over cutlets. In skillet over medium-high heat, sauté cutlets in margarine for 1 to 2 minutes per side or until turkey is no longer pink in center. Pour lemon juice mixture over cutlets; heat through.

Serve cutlets garnished with sesame seeds.   Makes 2 servings.

*Note: To toast sesame seeds, warm large nonstick skillet over medium heat; toast sesame seeds until golden brown. Stir frequently. Do not allow to scorch.

Per Serving (approx):
Calories 220   *Protein 28 gm*   *Fat 10 gm*
Carbohydrate 5 gm   *Sodium 316 mg*   *Cholesterol 70 mg*

Armenian Turkey Dumplings

The cuisine of Armenia coupled with ground turkey results in a dumpling soup whose aroma alone will warm your heart on a cold, wet winter day.

1 pound ground turkey
2/3 cup Tabbouleh Salad Mix*
1/3 cup chopped parsley
   (reserve 1 tablespoon for garnish)
2 tablespoons chopped fresh
   mint or 1 teaspoon dried
1 teaspoon paprika

1/4 teaspoon ground cinnamon
Salt and cayenne to taste
3 cans (14 1/2 ounces each)
   beef broth
1 1/2 cups water
3 tablespoons tomato paste
1/2 cup plain yogurt

Knead turkey with tabbouleh mix, spices and seasonings. Form into 12 balls and chill.

Combine beef broth, water and tomato paste and bring to a boil. Drop dumplings in boiling broth about six at a time; cook for 5 minutes. Remove with slotted spoon; repeat with remaining dumplings. Serve dumplings in broth garnished with dollop of yogurt and sprinkle of parsley.

Makes 6 servings.

*Note: Prepare 1 box (7 ounces) Tabbouleh Salad Mix without tomato; retain unused portion for other use.

Per Serving (approx):
Calories 201
Carbohydrate 15 gm

Protein 19 gm
Sodium 799 mg

Fat 7 gm
Cholesterol 57 mg

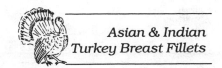

Turkey Fillets with Chutney Sauce

Ten minutes to make, twenty minutes to bake—what could be nicer for a busy yet hungry person?

4 turkey breast fillets
1 cup chicken broth
1 onion, chopped
1/2 cup mango chutney

2 cloves garlic, minced
2 teaspoons curry powder
Shredded coconut, chopped
   green onions and raisins,
   for garnish

Arrange turkey fillets in 9- x 12-inch baking dish. In small bowl mix broth, onion, mango chutney, garlic and curry powder; spoon over turkey. Cover and bake at 350 degrees for 20 minutes or more depending on thickness of the fillets. Meanwhile, prepare rice. Garnish turkey with shredded coconut, chopped green onion and raisins.

Makes 4 to 6 servings.

RICE:
Combine 1 1/2 cups basmati or white rice, 1 1/2 cups water, 4 green onions, chopped, and 1/2 cup chopped mushrooms. Cover, bring to a boil, reduce heat and simmer for 20 minutes. Add 1/2 cup frozen peas during last 5 minutes of cooking time.

Per Serving (approx) including rice:

Calories 408	*Protein 12 gm*	*Fat 2 gm*
Carbohydrate 86 gm	*Sodium 407 mg*	*Cholesterol 12 mg*

Mideast Fajitas

This marriage of two cuisines produces a new gourmet offspring.

1/4 cup oil
3/4 teaspoon ground ginger
3/4 teaspoon ground coriander
3/4 teaspoon ground cumin
Salt and coarsely ground black
   pepper to taste
3 pounds turkey breast fillets

18 lightly toasted pita breads
   (6 inches)
3 small cucumbers, thinly sliced
2 cups shredded Romaine
   lettuce
3 medium red onions, thinly
   sliced

In wide, shallow bowl combine oil, ginger, coriander, cumin, salt and pepper. Add turkey fillets; turn to coat with seasonings. Cover and let marinate in refrigerator for at least 1 hour. Meanwhile, prepare Mango Salsa and set aside.

Prepare outdoor grill for cooking or preheat broiler. Grill or broil fillets 5 to 6 inches from heat source for 3 to 5 minutes on each side or until cooked through. Remove fillets to cutting board and slice into 1/4-inch strips. To serve, split pita breads open to form pockets. Divide turkey, cucumbers, lettuce and onion among pita pockets. Serve with Mango Salsa.

Makes 12 to 14 servings.

MANGO SALSA:
In large bowl combine 3 large, ripe mangoes or peaches, peeled and diced, 1 can (4 ounces) chopped mild green chilies, 1/2 cup diced red bell pepper, 1/3 cup chopped green onion, 1/4 cup finely chopped cilantro, 3 tablespoons fresh lemon juice, 3/4 teaspoon ground ginger and salt and pepper to taste. Mix well.

Makes 3 cups salsa.

Per Serving (approx):
Calories 473
Carbohydrate 70 gm

Protein 36 gm
Sodium 682 mg

Fat 5 gm
Cholesterol 70 mg

Turkey Satay with Peanut Sauce

1 pound turkey tenderloins
3 tablespoons low-fat milk
1 tablespoon olive oil
1 teaspoon reduced-sodium
  soy sauce
1 tablespoon dried onion

1/2 teaspoon red pepper flakes
1/2 teaspoon lemon zest
1/4 teaspoon ground ginger
1/8 teaspoon coconut extract

Cut turkey tenderloins in half lengthwise. Between two 12-inch pieces of waxed paper, using a meat mallet, flatten each turkey half. Cut each turkey half into 1-inch-wide strips.

In self-closing plastic freezer bag, combine milk, oil, soy sauce, onion, pepper flakes, lemon zest, ginger and coconut extract. Add turkey strips; seal bag and turn bag to coat strips. Refrigerate for at least 4 hours. Meanwhile, prepare Peanut Sauce.

Remove grill rack from charcoal grill and lightly coat with vegetable cooking spray; set aside. Prepare grill for direct-heat cooking.

Soak bamboo skewers in water for 15 minutes. Weave turkey strips onto bamboo skewers. Discard marinade. Position grill rack over hot coals. Grill turkey for 2 to 3 minutes per side or until turkey is no longer pink in center. Serve with Peanut Sauce. Makes 4 servings.

PEANUT SAUCE:
In food processor fitted with metal blade and motor running, drop in 1 small clove garlic and 1 tablespoon chopped onion. Process for 10 seconds or until chopped. Add 1/4 cup creamy peanut butter, 1 1/2 teaspoons lemon juice, 1/4 teaspoon reduced-sodium soy sauce, 1/8 teaspoon cayenne pepper and dash of coconut extract. Process for 20 seconds or until blended. With motor running, slowly add 1/4 cup low-fat milk. Process sauce until smooth and well blended, scraping sides often. Heat until slightly thickened.

Per Serving (approx):
Calories 250
Carbohydrate 5 gm

Protein 33 gm
Sodium 180 mg

Fat 11 gm
Cholesterol 171 mg

Bombay Turkey

1/2 pound turkey tenderloins
   or slices, cut into 1/2-inch strips
1/2 cup cubed red Delicious apple

3/4 teaspoon curry powder
1 1/2 teaspoons margarine
1/4 cup mango chutney

In small bowl combine turkey, apple and curry powder; let stand for 10 minutes. In medium nonstick skillet over medium-high heat, stir-fry turkey mixture in margarine for 2 to 3 minutes or until turkey is no longer pink. Stir in chutney and continue to cook until heated through. Serve over rice, if desired. Makes 2 servings.

Per Serving (approx):
Calories 256
Carbohydrate 26 gm

Protein 27 gm
Sodium 178 mg

Fat 5 gm
Cholesterol 70 mg

Chinese Simmered Turkey Strips

1 pound turkey tenderloins,
  cut into strips
1 tablespoon oil
1/3 cup firmly packed brown sugar
3/4 cup water
1/3 cup soy sauce
2 tablespoons catsup
1 tablespoon cider vinegar

1/8 teaspoon ground ginger
1 green onion, sliced
1 clove garlic, finely chopped
1 tablespoon cornstarch
  dissolved in 1 tablespoon
  cold water

In medium skillet over medium-high heat, cook turkey in hot oil, stirring occasionally, for 5 to 8 minutes or until turkey is no longer pink. Add remaining ingredients except cornstarch and rice. Bring to a boil; cover, reduce heat and simmer for 10 minutes, stirring occasionally. Stir in cornstarch mixture; heat until thickened. Serve with hot cooked rice.

Makes 4 to 6 servings.

Per Serving (approx):
Calories 173
Carbohydrate 11 gm

Protein 17 gm
Sodium 1008 mg

Fat 7 gm
Cholesterol 41 mg

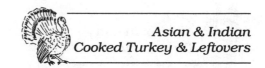

Quick Curry

1/4 cup oil
1 carrot, thinly sliced
1 small onion, thinly sliced
1 apple, thinly sliced
3 tablespoons flour
2 tablespoons curry powder
1/2 to 3/4 teaspoon cayenne
   pepper (optional)
1/4 teaspoon black pepper

1 can (13 3/4 ounces) chicken
   broth
1/2 cup whipping cream
3 cups chopped or shredded
   cooked turkey
Salt to taste
Hot cooked rice or baked
   pastry shells
Chutney, raisins and slivered
   almonds (optional)

In large skillet over medium heat, warm oil. Add carrot, onion and apple; sauté for 1 minute. Stir in flour, curry powder, cayenne and black pepper. Blend well; cook 1 to 2 minutes. Stir in broth and cream; cook 1 to 2 minutes until thickened, stirring often. Stir in turkey and heat through. Season to taste with salt.

Serve over rice or in baked pastry shells. Garnish with chutney, raisins and almonds, if desired.   Makes 6 servings.

Per Serving (approx):
Calories 534
Carbohydrate 28 gm

Protein 26 gm
Sodium 326 mg

Fat 36 gm
Cholesterol 80 mg

Madras Turkey with New Delhi Rice

This dish becomes a special event when served with chopped banana, toasted coconut and peanuts.

3 pounds turkey drumsticks
2 green apples, chopped
2 stalks celery, chopped
1 onion, sliced
2 tablespoons butter
3 tablespoons curry powder
1 cup chicken broth

1 cup whipping cream
Salt and pepper to taste
3 green onions, chopped
Toasted coconut, chopped peanuts, chopped banana and chopped cucumber

Poach turkey drumsticks in enough water to cover for 1 1/2 hours or until tender. Remove meat from bones; cut meat in bite-sized pieces and reserve.

Sauté apples, celery and onion in butter. Add curry, turkey meat, broth and cream. Simmer for 30 minutes. Season to taste with salt and pepper. Top each serving with chopped green onion. Serve with New Delhi Rice and condiments.

Makes 6 to 8 servings.

NEW DELHI RICE:
Combine 4 cups water, 2 cups rice, 3/4 cup currants and 3/4 teaspoon ground cardamom. Bring to a boil; cover and reduce heat to low. Simmer for 20 minutes.

Per Serving (approx):
Calories 819
Carbohydrate 81 gm

Protein 53 gm
Sodium 751 mg

Fat 31 gm
Cholesterol 180 mg

Cantonese Turkey Steaks

1 1/2 pounds turkey breast
   steaks, cut 1/2 to 3/4 inch
   thick*
2 teaspoons oil
1 can (6 ounces) pineapple juice
1/2 cup chicken or turkey broth
1 large clove garlic, mashed
2 1/2 tablespoons soy sauce
Pinch of fennel or anise seed

1/2 teaspoon light brown or
   granulated sugar
1 large Spanish onion, halved
and thinly sliced
1 medium green bell pepper,
   quartered and sliced 1/8 inch
   thick
2 tablespoons sliced pimientos

Rinse and pat turkey dry with paper towels. Warm oil over medium-high heat in skillet. Sear steaks quickly on both sides. Remove to plate. Add juice, broth and garlic. Boil about 8 minutes to reduce by half. Add soy sauce, fennel seed, sugar, vegetables and pimientos. Simmer for about 2 minutes or until vegetables start to soften.

Return steaks to pan. Spoon mixture over them and simmer over low heat for an additional few minutes or just until steaks are no longer pink. Serve steaks dressed liberally with vegetable mixture.

Makes 6 servings.

*Note: Steaks may be bone in or boneless. Your meat clerk may cut steaks for you from a whole, frozen or fresh turkey breast.

Per Serving (approx):
Calories 165
Carbohydrate 9 gm

Protein 25 gm
Sodium 721 mg

Fat 3 gm
Cholesterol 58 mg

Szechuan Stir-Fry

Some like it hot—and if you're one of them, this dish is for you.

1/4 cup soy sauce
1 teaspoon sugar
1 teaspoon cornstarch
1/2 teaspoon red pepper flakes
   (optional)
1/4 teaspoon ground ginger
1 clove garlic, finely chopped
1 pound turkey breast slices,
   cut into strips

2 tablespoons oil
1 red bell pepper, thinly sliced
4 green onions, cut into
   1/2-inch pieces
6 ounces pea pods (fresh, or
   frozen and thawed)

In medium bowl combine soy sauce, sugar, cornstarch, red pepper flakes, ginger and garlic. Add turkey; let marinate for at least 15 minutes. In large skillet or wok over medium-high heat, stir-fry turkey in 1 tablespoon of the oil for about 5 minutes or until turkey is no longer pink. Remove turkey from skillet.

Heat remaining 1 tablespoon oil in skillet and stir-fry vegetables until tender-crisp, 1 to 2 minutes. Return turkey to skillet; mix with vegetables. Serve over hot cooked rice.   Makes 4 to 6 servings.

Per Serving (approx):
Calories 175
Carbohydrate 5 gm

Protein 18 gm
Sodium 721 mg

Fat 9 gm
Cholesterol 41 mg

Modern turkeys have much more white breast meat than earlier turkeys; this makes them easier to carve.

Taj Kabobs

This classic recipe from India calls for chicken. We changed it to turkey and, quite honestly, like it better.

15 large cloves garlic
1 cup plain low-fat yogurt
3 tablespoons lemon juice
3 tablespoons minced fresh ginger
1 tablespoon curry powder
1 1/2 teaspoons ground
 coriander

1 1/2 teaspoons cayenne pepper
3 to 4 pounds skinless and
 boneless turkey thighs,
 cut into 2-inch cubes

Finely mince 3 cloves garlic. In wide, shallow bowl, combine yogurt, lemon juice, ginger, curry, coriander, minced garlic and cayenne. Add turkey to yogurt mixture, turning to coat well. Cover and let marinate in refrigerator for at least 1 hour.

Prepare outdoor grill for cooking or preheat broiler. On metal skewers, alternately thread turkey cubes and remaining 12 cloves garlic. Grill or broil 6 to 8 inches from heat source for 20 to 30 minutes or until turkey is cooked through, turning once or twice during grilling. Serve kabobs on bed of hot couscous or brown rice pilaf.   Makes 12 servings.

Per Serving (approx) excluding couscous or pilaf:
Calories 189   *Protein 29 gm*   *Fat 6 gm*
Carbohydrate 3 gm   *Sodium 122 mg*   *Cholesterol 107 mg*

Chinese Skillet Dinner

2 tablespoons oil
2 tablespoons minced fresh ginger
1 clove garlic, minced
1 cup chicken broth
1/4 cup soy sauce
2 tablespoons rice wine or
   dry sherry
5 teaspoons cornstarch
1 tablespoon wine vinegar

1 tablespoon sugar
Crushed red pepper flakes
   (optional)
3 cups shredded cooked turkey
2 cups shredded carrot
2 cups thinly sliced green onion
8 ounces water chestnuts,
   drained and sliced
8 ounces Chinese rice noodles,
   cooked

In large skillet over medium-high heat, warm oil. Add ginger and garlic; sauté briefly. In small bowl combine broth, soy sauce, rice wine, cornstarch, vinegar, sugar and red pepper flakes (if desired); pour into skillet and cook until sauce is slightly thickened.

Stir in turkey, carrot, green onion and water chestnuts. Sauté for 1 to 2 minutes longer. Add rice noodles; toss and serve hot.

Makes 6 to 8 servings.

Per Serving (approx):
Calories 330
Carbohydrate 29 gm

Protein 20 gm
Sodium 701 mg

Fat 15 gm
Cholesterol 40 mg

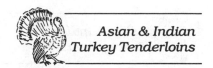

Turkey Teriyaki Tidbits
with Pennies and Rice

1 pound turkey breast tenderloins
3 tablespoons reduced-calorie,
    cholesterol-free mayonnaise

3/4 cup crushed chow mein
    noodles

Prepare Light Teriyaki Sauce. Slice tenderloins lengthwise in half along natural crease; cut into 1-inch chunks. In shallow bowl combine mayonnaise and 2 tablespoons Light Teriyaki Sauce; dip turkey chunks into mixture, then roll in crushed noodles. Place turkey on baking sheet. Bake in preheated 375 degree oven for 15 to 18 minutes or until crisp and cooked through. Serve with Pennies and Rice.

Makes 4 to 6 servings.

LIGHT TERIYAKI SAUCE:
Place 1/3 cup lemon juice in small bowl. Using garlic press, squeeze 1 piece (1 inch) diced fresh ginger over bowl to collect extract. Discard pulp. Press 1 clove garlic into bowl, then add 1 teaspoon Oriental chile paste (if used), pinch of sugar, 1 tablespoon reduced-sodium soy sauce and 2 teaspoons sesame oil. Stir well. Cover and store in refrigerator up to 1 week. Use as marinade, dipping sauce or salad dressing. Once used as marinade, discard sauce; do not reuse.   Makes about 1/2 cup.

PENNIES AND RICE:
In wok or large nonstick skillet over medium heat, melt 2 tablespoons margarine. Add 1/4 cup thinly sliced green onion; sauté briefly. Add 2 cups cooked brown or white rice and 2/3 cup thinly sliced, lightly steamed carrot pennies. Toss until heated through. Season to taste with salt, black pepper and a few drops of reduced-sodium soy sauce, if desired.

Makes 4 to 6 servings.

Per Serving (approx):
Calories 287
Carbohydrate 27 gm

Protein 19 gm
Sodium 639 mg

Fat 12 gm
Cholesterol 43 mg

Teriyaki Turkey

3 tablespoons brown sugar
3 tablespoons soy sauce
1 tablespoon lemon juice
1/4 teaspoon ground ginger
1 clove garlic, finely chopped
2 teaspoons cornstarch
1 can (20 ounces) pineapple
    chunks, juice reserved

1 pound turkey breast fillets
2 tablespoons oil
3 green onions, cut into
    1-inch pieces
1 red bell pepper, cut into
    1-inch pieces

In medium bowl combine brown sugar, soy sauce, lemon juice, ginger, garlic, cornstarch and 2 tablespoons of the reserved pineapple juice. Add turkey; let stand for at least 15 minutes. Drain; reserve marinade.

In large skillet warm oil until hot; add turkey, cover and cook for 8 to 10 minutes on each side. Add onions, bell pepper, pineapple chunks and reserved marinade. Cook for 2 minutes more or until turkey is no longer pink. Serve with rice.   Makes 4 servings.

Per Serving (approx):
| *Calories 342* | *Protein 26 gm* | *Fat 14 gm* |
| *Carbohydrate 29 gm* | *Sodium 825 mg* | *Cholesterol 61 mg* |

Turkey with Orange

2 turkey thighs or drumsticks
   (2 to 3 pounds)*
1/2 teaspoon paprika
1 medium onion, sliced
1/2 cup orange juice
   concentrate
1/3 cup water

2 tablespoons brown sugar
2 tablespoons chopped parsley
2 teaspoons soy sauce
1/2 teaspoon ground ginger
Orange twists, for garnish

Place turkey under broiler to brown. (If using only thighs, remove skin.) Transfer to Dutch oven or roasting pan; and sprinkle with paprika. Arrange onion slices over turkey. Combine juice concentrate, water, brown sugar, parsley, soy sauce and ginger. Pour over turkey and onion.

Cover and bake in pre-heated 400 degree oven for approximately 1 hour or until turkey is tender. Baste once or twice. Slice meat, coat with sauce and garnish with orange twists. Serve with rice or pasta.

Makes 4 servings.

*Note: Thighs may be boned before cooking.

Per Serving (approx):
Calories 152
Carbohydrate 11 gm

Protein 17 gm
Sodium 210 mg

Fat 5 gm
Cholesterol 56 mg

Turkey meat is extremely rich in riboflavin, niacin and calcium.

Thai Turkey and Mango Stir-Fry

1 1/4 pounds skinless and
  boneless turkey thighs
2 tablespoons reduced-sodium
  soy sauce
3 teaspoons rice wine
2 teaspoons cornstarch

4 teaspoons peanut oil
2 ripe mangoes, cut into
  1/4-inch slices
1/4 cup thinly sliced green
  onion
1 tablespoon grated fresh ginger

Slice turkey into thin strips. In shallow bowl combine 1 tablespoon of the soy sauce, 2 teaspoons of the rice wine and the cornstarch. Add turkey to mixture and toss to coat evenly. Let stand for 5 minutes.

Warm wok or large, heavy nonstick skillet over medium-high heat. Slowly add oil. Add turkey and stir-fry for 6 to 8 minutes or until cooked through. Add remaining 1 tablespoon soy sauce and 1 teaspoon rice wine. Stir-fry for 30 seconds. Add mango slices, green onion and ginger. Stir-fry for 2 to 3 minutes longer. Serve with hot rice. Makes 5 servings.

Per Serving (approx):
Calories 324
Carbohydrate 34 gm

Protein 26 gm
Sodium 337 mg

Fat 9 gm
Cholesterol 85 mg

Japanese-Style Turkey Steaks

1/2 teaspoon reduced-sodium
    chicken bouillon granules
2 tablespoons boiling water
2 tablespoons reduced-sodium
    soy sauce

2 tablespoons dry sherry
1 teaspoon ground ginger
1 garlic clove, crushed
1 pound turkey breast steaks,
    sliced 3/4 inch thick

In large shallow bowl, dissolve bouillon in boiling water. Add soy sauce, sherry, ginger, garlic and turkey. Refrigerate turkey mixture for 35 to 45 minutes.

Preheat grill for direct-heat cooking.* Drain marinade from turkey and discard. Grill turkey for 15 minutes or until turkey meat is no longer pink in center, turning every 5 minutes.   Makes 4 servings.

*Note: For information on direct-heat cooking, see page 284.

Per Serving (approx):
Calories 142   *Protein 27 gm*   *Fat 2 gm*
Carbohydrate 2 gm   *Sodium 381 mg*   *Cholesterol 70 mg*

Teriyaki Turkey Wings

2 pounds turkey wings
1 cup water
2/3 cup soy sauce
1/2 cup sherry

2 tablespoons brown sugar
2 tablespoons honey
1 teaspoon ground ginger
1/4 teaspoon garlic powder

Place turkey wings in casserole with water; cover and bake in 350 degree oven for 2 hours. Pour off liquid. Combine remaining ingredients and pour over turkey. Bake uncovered for 15 minutes; turn turkey over and bake for 15 minutes more. Serve turkey with sauce.

Makes 2 servings.

Per Serving (approx):
Calories 934   *Protein 92 gm*   *Fat 40 gm*
Carbohydrate 36 gm   *Sodium 943 mg*   *Cholesterol 256 mg*

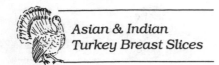
Firecracker Rolls

1 pound turkey breast slices
1 head bok choy
  (about 1 1/2 pounds)*
Peanut oil
2 tablespoons bottled
  Szechuan chile sauce or chile
  paste with garlic**

4 ounces sliced turkey ham
1/2 cup diagonally sliced
  green onion
1 red bell pepper, slivered

Pound turkey with mallet to flatten slightly; set aside.

Trim off green leafy parts from bok choy, leaving leaves whole. Slice up remaining bok choy crosswise; set aside. Add leafy bok choy to oil in hot skillet; cover and cook over medium-high heat for 2 minutes, shaking pan often to prevent sticking.

To make rolls, spread turkey slices with a little more than half the chile sauce, then top with turkey ham and leafy bok choy. Roll up meat into long rolls, starting from long side, and fasten rolls with picks. Coat rolls with remaining chile sauce.

To cook, sauté rolls in 2 tablespoons oil in skillet over medium-high heat, turning to brown all sides. Cook for 4 to 5 minutes or just until done. Remove picks and transfer rolls to platter; keep warm. Add a little oil to pan; heat pan and add reserved bok choy, green onion and red bell pepper. Stir-fry over high heat for 5 minutes or until tender-crisp. Spoon alongside meat, arranging grilled green onion as firecracker "fuses."

Makes 4 servings.

*Note: If bok choy is not available, use 8 leaves Swiss chard; stir-fry chard stems and 2 cups sliced celery.

**Note: This sauce is quite spicy. For a milder approach, substitute bottled American-style barbecue sauce.

Per Serving (approx):
Calories 276
Carbohydrate 4 gm

Protein 31 gm
Sodium 431 mg

Fat 15 gm
Cholesterol 77 mg

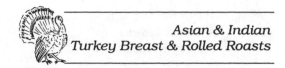

Oriental Turkey Breast Dinner

1/4 cup soy sauce
1 tablespoon honey
1 teaspoon sesame oil
1 teaspoon minced garlic
1 teaspoon minced fresh ginger
1 turkey half breast, boned and skinned (1 to 1 1/2 pounds)
4 small leeks, split lengthwise
4 ounces shiitake mushrooms, cut in halves

2 crookneck squash, quartered lengthwise
2 Japanese eggplant, quartered
1 red bell pepper, quartered
3 tablespoons white wine, chicken stock or water
Salt and pepper to taste
2 tablespoons chopped cilantro

Combine soy sauce, honey, sesame oil, garlic and ginger; brush over turkey breast, reserving some for vegetables. Let stand 1 hour, then remove breast from marinade and brown both sides of breast under broiler. Brown under broiler.

Place browned breast in center of double layer of heavy-duty foil about 18 inches square. Surround with vegetables. Brush vegetables with remaining marinade; spoon wine over breast. Season with salt and pepper, seal foil and bake in 350 degree oven for about 35 minutes. Sprinkle with cilantro and serve with rice.   Makes 4 servings.

Per Serving (approx):
Calories 397
Carbohydrate 81 gm

Protein 11 gm
Sodium 1167 mg

Fat 3 gm
Cholesterol 3 mg

Turkey Vegetable Tempura

This dish was actually invented by Spanish and Portuguese missionaries in Japan in the sixteenth century, and we brought it up to date using turkey.

1 pound turkey breast slices, cut in bite-sized pieces
1 cup cornstarch
2 eggs, lightly beaten
1 cup Japanese-flavored or plain bread crumbs

Oil, for deep-frying
3 cups assorted bite-sized pieces of broccoli, mushrooms, zucchini and green onions

Dip pieces of turkey in cornstarch, then in egg. Coat with bread crumbs. Deep-fry in oil at 375 degrees for 2 to 3 minutes. Repeat dipping procedure for vegetables, then cook for 1 minute or until tender-crisp. Serve with Ginger-Sherry Dipping Sauce.   Makes 4 servings.

GINGER-SHERRY DIPPING SAUCE:
Combine 1/4 cup each soy sauce and water, 2 tablespoons sherry, 1 tablespoon each grated fresh ginger and brown sugar and 1 minced green onion. Mix well.

Per Serving (approx):
Calories 770
Carbohydrate 69 gm

Protein 36 gm
Sodium 1346 mg

Fat 38 gm
Cholesterol 169 mg

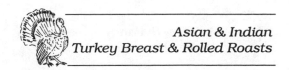
Turkey Yakitori

1/2 teaspoon reduced-sodium
    chicken bouillon granules
2 tablespoons boiling water
1 pound boneless turkey breast,
    cut into 1-inch cubes
2 tablespoons reduced-sodium
    soy sauce
2 tablespoons dry sherry or
    white wine

1 teaspoon ground ginger
1 clove garlic, pressed
3 green onions, cut into
    2-inch lengths
3/4 cup cubed green bell
    pepper

Dissolve bouillon granules in boiling water; mix in plastic bag with turkey, soy sauce, sherry, ginger and garlic. Prop bag in container so that all turkey is submerged. Allow to marinate for at least 4 hours in refrigerator.

Thread turkey onto skewers with green onion and bell pepper cubes. Grill over hot coals (or broil) 6 inches from heat, for 4 to 5 minutes on each side. Brush with remaining marinade while cooking. If desired, prepare additional marinade as dipping sauce. Do not use original marinade as dip when serving. Makes 4 servings.

Per Serving (approx):
Calories 143
Carbohydrate gm

Protein 27 gm
Sodium 350 mg

Fat 1 gm
Cholesterol 56 mg

Hunan Salad

Hunan cuisine's fiery flavors are captured in this zesty salad. No, we do not know of any way to make it milder. It is spicy!

2 turkey drumsticks
   (1 pound each)
2 ounces mung bean threads*
4 ounces snow peas, blanched

1 cup shredded Chinese cabbage
1/2 cup sliced cucumber
1/2 red bell pepper, sliced

Poach turkey in water to cover for 1 1/2 hours or until done and tender. Remove meat from bones; shred and chill.

Soak bean threads in enough cold water to cover for 15 minutes. Drain and plunge into boiling water for 3 minutes; drain and chill.

Toss all ingredients with Hunan Dressing.   **Makes 6 servings.**

HUNAN DRESSING:
Whisk 1/3 cup oil, 1/4 cup soy sauce, 1/4 cup white vinegar, 3 table-spoons peanut butter, 1 1/2 teaspoons chile paste, or 4 drops hot chile oil.

*Note: Bean threads are thin dry noodles made from mung bean flour; they may be found in Chinese markets or the Oriental food section of grocery stores.

Per Serving (approx):
Calories 346   *Protein 26 gm*   *Fat 24 gm*
Carbohydrate 6 gm   *Sodium 768 mg*   *Cholesterol 69 mg*

ITALIAN &
MEDITERRANEAN

Turkey Cacciatore

Chicken is the traditional meat for cacciatore, but we think you'll like this as well—possibly better.

1/2 cup thinly sliced onion	1/4 cup red wine
1/2 cup cubed green bell pepper	1 bay leaf
2 tablespoons margarine	2 teaspoons sugar
1/4 pound mushrooms, quartered	1/2 teaspoon dried basil
2 cloves garlic, minced	1/2 teaspoon dried thyme
1 can (8 ounces) stewed tomatoes	1/2 teaspoon dried oregano
	1/4 teaspoon salt
1 can (8 ounces) tomato sauce	4 turkey thighs (about 3 pounds)

In 3-quart saucepan over medium heat, sauté onion and bell pepper in margarine until onion is transparent and pepper is tender-crisp. Add mushrooms and garlic; cook for 2 to 3 minutes.

Stir in tomatoes, tomato sauce, wine, bay leaf, sugar, basil, thyme, oregano and salt. Bring to a boil. Add turkey thighs. Reduce heat to low; cover and cook for 1 to 1 1/2 hours or until turkey is tender and internal temperature of center of each turkey thigh reaches 180 to 185 degrees.

Serve over spaghetti, if desired.   Makes 4 to 6 servings.

Per Serving (approx):
Calories 297   *Protein 38 gm*   *Fat 11 gm*
Carbohydrate 10 gm   *Sodium 605 mg*   *Cholesterol 134 mg*

Only tom turkeys (males) gobble. Hen turkeys (females) make a clicking noise.

Italian Turkey

If you are interested in economy, this recipe calls for one turkey thigh to serve four people, which it does, very generously.

1 tablespoon corn oil
1 turkey thigh, boned and skinned,
   cut into 1-inch cubes
1 ripe tomato, peeled and cut into
   chunks
1 green bell pepper, thinly sliced
1 clove garlic, minced
2 tablespoons lemon juice

1 teaspoon dried basil or
   dried Italian seasoning
Salt and pepper to taste
2 teaspoons cornstarch dissolved in 3 tablespoons water
Cooked vermicelli
Grated Parmesan cheese
   (optional)

Heat oil in Dutch oven over high heat. Brown turkey thigh cubes. Reduce heat to low and add tomato, bell pepper, garlic, lemon juice, basil, salt and pepper. Cover and cook until meat is fork tender, about 45 minutes.

Stir cornstarch mixture into sauce and bring to a boil, stirring until sauce is thickened.

To serve, place turkey over cooked vermicelli and top each serving with 1 teaspoon Parmesan cheese, if desired.   Makes 4 servings.

Per Serving (approx):
Calories 268   *Protein 33 gm*   *Fat 12 gm*
Carbohydrate 5 gm   *Sodium 89 mg*   *Cholesterol 112 mg*

Sicilian Turkey Braciola

*In Sicily, cooking is often sweet and savory, tempered by refreshing fruits
and fruit ice desserts. Braciola is typically prepared with rolled flank steak.*

1 to 1 1/4 pounds ground turkey
3 teaspoons dried Italian
  seasoning, divided
2 packages (10 ounces each) frozen
  chopped spinach, thawed and
  squeezed dry
1 clove garlic, minced
1/2 teaspoon salt
1/4 teaspoon black pepper

1/2 cup raisins
3 hard-cooked eggs, sliced
1 tablespoon olive oil
3/4 cup chopped onion
1 can (28 ounces) crushed
  tomatoes
Salt and pepper to taste
1 tablespoon honey
1/2 teaspoon ground cinnamon

In medium bowl combine turkey with 1/2 teaspoon of the Italian seasoning. Place on 15-inch sheet of aluminum foil and spread to form rectangle approximately 8 by 10 inches.

In small bowl combine spinach, garlic, salt and pepper. Spread mixture
over turkey, leaving 1-inch border around sides. Scatter raisins on top.
Place eggs on short end of rectangle and roll up, jelly-roll style, pressing
ends together to seal in stuffing.

In large, deep skillet over medium heat, warm oil. Add onion and sauté
until translucent. Add tomatoes, remaining Italian seasoning and salt
and pepper to taste. Stir in honey and cinnamon. Carefully lift turkey
roll into skillet; spoon sauce over top. Reduce heat to medium-low; cover
and cook for 30 to 35 minutes or until turkey springs back to the touch.
Slice and serve with sauce.   Makes 4 to 6 servings.

Per Serving (approx):
Calories 325
Carbohydrate 28 gm

Protein 25 gm
Sodium 587 mg

Fat 12 gm
Cholesterol 175 mg

Turkey Parmigiana

2 egg whites
1 tablespoon skim milk or water
1/2 cup seasoned bread crumbs
2 tablespoons Parmesan cheese

1 pound turkey breast cutlets,
  1/4 inch thick
1 cup Italian spaghetti sauce
4 ounces part-skim mozzarella
  cheese, sliced

In shallow bowl beat egg whites with milk. In another shallow bowl, combine bread crumbs and Parmesan cheese.

Dip cutlets into egg mixture, then into bread crumb mixture. Arrange on greased 10- x 15- x 1-inch baking pan. Bake cutlets for 4 to 5 minutes in preheated 400 degree oven.

Pour spaghetti sauce evenly over cutlets. Top each cutlet with slice of mozzarella cheese. Bake for 4 to 5 minutes more to heat sauce and melt cheese.

Makes 4 servings.

Per Serving (approx):
Calories 301	*Protein 39 gm*	*Fat 8 gm*
Carbohydrate 15 gm	*Sodium 679 mg*	*Cholesterol 90 mg*

Creamy Turkey Piccata

1 pound turkey breast fillets
4 tablespoons butter
2 tablespoons flour
1 cup whipping cream or milk
1/2 cup white wine

1 tablespoon lemon juice
1/4 cup drained capers
Lemon slices and parsley sprigs,
  for garnish

In large skillet over medium heat, cook fillets in 2 tablespoons of the butter for 8 to 11 minutes on each side or until lightly browned and no longer pink in center. Remove from pan and keep warm.

Melt remaining butter in pan; stir in flour and whisk in cream. Simmer until sauce thickens slightly. Slowly stir in wine, lemon juice and capers; heat through. Serve sauce over fillets. Garnish with lemon slices and parsley.

Makes 4 servings.

Per Serving (approx):
Calories 339	*Protein 27 gm*	*Fat 20 gm*
Carbohydrate 7 gm	*Sodium 319 mg*	*Cholesterol 101 mg*

Country Parmigiana

No, we didn't convert this parmigiana recipe for you. This recipe came to us from Italy, where turkey is now widely used in place of veal and pork. Try it.

3 tablespoons milk
1 egg, lightly beaten
1/3 cup seasoned dry bread crumbs
1/3 cup grated Parmesan cheese
1 pound turkey breast slices

1 tomato, sliced
1 teaspoon crushed dried oregano
1 cup grated mozzarella cheese
Chopped parsley, for garnish

Whisk together milk and egg. On sheet of waxed paper, mix bread crumbs and Parmesan cheese. Dip turkey breast slices into egg mixture and then bread crumb mixture, coating both sides.

Place slices in single layer on greased shallow baking pan. In preheated 450 degree oven, bake for 8 to 10 minutes or until turkey is golden brown and no longer pink in center. Top turkey with tomato slices; sprinkle with oregano and mozzarella. Place under broiler until cheese bubbles. Garnish with parsley. Makes 4 servings.

Per Serving (approx):
Calories 331
Carbohydrate 8 gm

Protein 36 gm
Sodium 366 mg

Fat 17 gm
Cholesterol 144 mg

Turkey Consumption

Country	Pounds/Capita
U.K.	8.2
Ireland	8.8
Italy	10.4
Canada	10.4
France	12.3
United States	18.4
Israel	22.0

According to USDA 1990 data, the above countries consumed the most turkey.

Turkey Medallions Piccata

This is a classic Italian veal piccata. We changed only the meat, from veal to turkey.

1 pound turkey breast tenderloins, cut in 3/4-inch-thick medallions	1 teaspoon olive oil
	1 teaspoon margarine
Salt and pepper to taste	1 tablespoon lemon juice
1 large clove garlic, crushed	4 teaspoons drained capers

Lightly sprinkle one side of each medallion with salt and pepper.

In large nonstick skillet over medium-high heat, sauté turkey and garlic in oil and margarine for approximately 1 to 1 1/2 minutes per side, turning each medallion over when edges have turned from pink to white. Continue cooking medallions until meat thermometer reaches 170 to 175 degrees and centers of medallions are no longer pink.

Remove skillet from heat. Pour lemon juice over medallions and sprinkle capers over top; serve immediately.   Makes 4 servings.

Per Serving (approx):
Calories 150   *Protein 27 gm*   *Fat 4 gm*
Carbohydrate 1 gm   *Sodium 162 mg*   *Cholesterol 70 mg*

Turkey Perugia

This is another example of a great Italian veal dish being changed to turkey by the Italians. You'll see why when you prepare it.

1 1/2 tablespoons olive oil	1/2 cup reduced-sodium
1 small clove garlic, minced	chicken broth
1 teaspoon dried Italian	Juice and grated zest from 1
seasoning	small lemon
Salt and pepper to taste	1 tablespoon minced parsley
1 pound turkey breast tenderloins	2 cups hot cooked rice
1 1/2 cups thinly sliced fennel	Lemon wedges (optional)
3 tablespoons Marsala wine	Parsley sprigs (optional)

In small bowl combine 1 1/2 teaspoons of the olive oil, the minced garlic and seasonings. Brush mixture evenly on all sides of tenderloins.

In large nonstick skillet over medium-high heat, warm remaining 1 tablespoon oil. Add turkey and sauté until lightly browned. Remove turkey from skillet and set aside. Add fennel to skillet and sauté for 2 to 3 minutes. Remove fennel and set aside with turkey.

Add Marsala and broth to skillet; bring to a boil, scraping up browned bits from bottom of skillet. Return turkey and fennel to skillet; reduce heat to low. Sprinkle with lemon juice, lemon zest and minced parsley. Cover and simmer for 15 to 20 minutes or until turkey is cooked through.

Serve with rice and garnish with lemon wedges and parsley sprigs, if desired.   Makes 4 servings.

Per Serving (approx):
Calories 328
Carbohydrate 33 gm   *Protein 30 gm*   *Fat 7 gm*
                               Sodium 213 mg   *Cholesterol 70 mg*

Milano Turkey Roll with Tomato Basil Salsa

This recipe from Milan, Italy, was created originally with veal. Nowadays it's made with turkey.

6 boneless turkey breast slices
   (2 to 3 ounces each)
Salt and pepper to taste
2 cloves garlic, minced
1/2 cup chopped onion
1 each green and red bell
   pepper, chopped
3 tablespoons oil

Additional oil for brushing
   turkey
2 cups cooked rice
2/3 cup sliced ripe olives
3 tablespoons chopped fresh
   basil or 1 1/2 teaspoons dried
1 cup shredded Cheddar cheese

Pound turkey breast slices to 1/4 inch thick. Overlap to make large rectangle. Sprinkle with salt and pepper.

Sauté garlic, onion and bell peppers in the 3 tablespoons oil until soft. Combine with cooked rice, olives and basil. Spread rice mixture on turkey, leaving 1/2-inch border. Top with cheese. Roll up from long side; transfer to greased baking sheet. Brush with oil.

Bake in preheated 350 degree oven for 30 to 35 minutes. Let stand for 15 minutes before slicing. Serve warm or at room temperature with Tomato Basil Salsa.

TOMATO BASIL SALSA:
Combine 4 peeled, seeded and chopped tomatoes, 1/2 cup sliced green onion, 2 cloves garlic, minced, 3 tablespoons chopped fresh basil (or 1 1/2 teaspoons dried) and 1 1/2 tablespoons olive oil. Let stand for 1 hour for flavors to blend.

Makes 6 main-course servings, or 10 appetizer servings.

Per Main-Course Serving (approx) excluding Salsa:

Calories 339	*Protein 19 gm*	*Fat 18 gm*
Carbohydrate 24 gm	*Sodium 353 mg*	*Cholesterol 50 mg*

Florentine Turkey Bundles

The French call anything cooked with spinach "florentine," which is how this recipe got its name.

4 ounces mushrooms, thinly
  sliced
5 tablespoons olive oil
1/4 cup plus 2 tablespoons dry
  Marsala wine
3/4 cup whipping cream
1/4 cup shredded Swiss cheese
1/4 cup grated Parmesan cheese

1/4 cup ricotta cheese
1 package (10 ounces) frozen
  spinach, thawed and
  squeezed dry
Salt and pepper to taste
6 turkey breast cutlets
2 tablespoons unsalted butter

Sauté mushrooms in 2 tablespoons of the oil. Add 1/4 cup each Marsala and whipping cream. Simmer and reduce until thick. Mix in cheeses and spinach; season to taste with salt and pepper.

Pound each turkey cutlet until about 1/4 inch thick. Spread 1/4 cup stuffing over each, leaving 1/2-inch border. Roll up and tie securely with string. Sauté bundles in remaining olive oil until well browned. Add 1 tablespoon water; cover and cook over low heat for about 10 minutes or until cooked through.

Remove bundles from pan, slice and keep warm. Add remaining 1/2 cup cream and 2 tablespoons Marsala to pan, scraping up browned bits. Reduce until sauce coats spoon; swirl in butter and serve immediately with bundles. Makes 6 servings.

Per Serving (approx):
Calories 334
Carbohydrate 5 gm

Protein 7 gm
Sodium 212 mg

Fat 30 gm
Cholesterol 64 mg

Italian Stir-Fry

1 teaspoon cornstarch
1/2 teaspoon dried Italian seasoning
1/8 teaspoon salt
Dash of red pepper flakes
1/4 cup reduced-sodium chicken
   bouillon
1/4 cup white wine

1/2 pound turkey breast cutlets
   or slices, cut into 1/2-inch
   strips
1/4 cup green onion, thinly
   sliced
1 clove garlic, minced
1 1/2 teaspoons margarine

In small bowl combine cornstarch, Italian seasoning, salt, pepper flakes, bouillon and wine; set aside.

In medium nonstick skillet over medium-high heat, stir-fry turkey, onion and garlic in margarine for 2 minutes or until meat is no longer pink. Add bouillon mixture; cook and stir until sauce is thickened.

Serve over cooked spaghetti, if desired.   Makes 2 servings.

Per Serving (approx):
Calories 172
Carbohydrate 3 gm

Protein 27 gm
Sodium 261 mg

Fat 5 gm
Cholesterol 70 mg

By 1530, turkeys were being raised domestically in Italy, France and England. So when the Pilgrims and other early settlers arrived on the American shores, they were already familiar with eating turkey.

Florentine Turkey Roll

1 1/4 pounds ground turkey
1 small yellow onion,
   finely chopped
2 cloves garlic, minced
1 egg white
1/4 cup tomato juice
1/2 teaspoon dried basil
1/4 teaspoon cayenne pepper

1 package (10 ounces) frozen
   chopped spinach, thawed and
   squeezed dry
1 medium red bell pepper, cut
   into 1/2-inch-wide strips
1/2 cup grated part-skim mozzarella cheese
Fresh basil (optional)

In large bowl combine turkey, onion, garlic, egg white, juice, dried basil and cayenne. On 11- by 12-inch piece of waxed paper, pat turkey mixture into 10-inch square. Top mixture with spinach, bell pepper strips and cheese. Carefully lift waxed paper and roll up turkey mixture jelly-roll fashion. Seal edges.

On 2- x 10- x 15-inch jelly-roll pan, bake turkey roll, uncovered, at 350 degrees for 40 to 45 minutes or until meat thermometer registers 165 degrees in center of turkey roll.

Remove turkey roll from oven and let stand for 5 minutes before slicing. Place on serving platter and garnish with fresh basil, if desired.

Makes 6 servings.

Per Serving (approx):

Calories 181	*Protein 22 gm*	*Fat 9 gm*
Carbohydrate 4 gm	*Sodium 207 mg*	*Cholesterol 74 mg*

Turkey and Prosciutto Cordon Bleu

The classic French chicken Cordon Bleu is the mother of this recipe.

1 pound turkey breast cutlets,
   about 1/4 inch thick
2 tablespoons Dijon-style mustard
2 ounces prosciutto ham,
   very thinly sliced
2 ounces Gruyère, Jarlsberg
   or Samsoe cheese, sliced
   (low-fat Gruyère works well)

2 tablespoons chopped Italian
   parsley
1 tablespoon melted butter or
   olive oil
2 tablespoons freshly squeezed
   lemon juice
1 clove garlic, minced
Freshly ground black pepper
   to taste

Pound turkey slices lightly to flatten. Cut turkey into approximately 2-inch by 5-inch rectangles to make 16 pieces, allowing 4 turkey pieces per serving. Lay turkey flat on board and spread lightly with mustard. Cut prosciutto and cheese into 16 strips each. Lay slice of prosciutto and slice of cheese on top of each strip of turkey. Sprinkle with parsley. Roll up and thread bundles onto skewers, allowing 4 per skewer.

Mix together melted butter, lemon juice, garlic and pepper. Brush over turkey bundles. Place skewers on foil-lined rack in broiling pan.

Broil about 4 to 6 inches from heat until golden; turn and baste with butter mixture, broil the other side, allowing 4 to 5 minutes per side to cook through.   **Makes 4 servings.**

Per Serving (approx):
Calories 275   *Protein 32 gm*   *Fat 15 gm*
Carbohydrate 2 gm   *Sodium 477 mg*   *Cholesterol 89 mg*

Mediterranean Turkey and Eggplant Stir-Fry

1 pound ground turkey
1 cup thinly sliced onion
2 cloves garlic, minced
1 1/2 teaspoons crushed dried, oregano
1 teaspoon crushed dried mint
3/4 teaspoon salt
1/4 teaspoon black pepper
1 tablespoon olive oil

4 cups eggplant cut into 1/2-inch cubes
1 cup green bell pepper cut into 1/2-inch cubes
1 teaspoon sugar
1 medium tomato, peeled and cut into wedges
2 tablespoons crumbled feta cheese

In large nonstick skillet over medium-high heat, sauté turkey, onion, garlic, oregano, mint, salt and pepper in oil for 5 to 6 minutes or until meat is no longer pink. Remove turkey mixture from skillet and set aside.

In same skillet, sauté eggplant and bell pepper for 4 minutes or until vegetables are tender-crisp.

Combine turkey mixture with vegetable mixture. Stir in sugar and tomato. Cook mixture over medium-high heat for 4 to 5 minutes or until heated through. To serve, top turkey mixture with feta cheese.

Makes 4 to 6 servings.

Per Serving (approx):
Calories 257
Carbohydrate 13 gm

Protein 22 gm
Sodium 573 mg

Fat 13 gm
Cholesterol 87 mg

The early settlers brought domesticated turkeys from Europe and soon began cross breeding them with the larger wild turkeys they found here.

Scallopini #1

The name "scallopini" comes from the Italian word for a small square of veal. Turkepini?

1 turkey quarter breast
   (1 3/4 to 2 pounds) or
   equivalent turkey breast slices
1/4 cup flour
1 teaspoon salt
1/4 teaspoon paprika
1/8 teaspoon white pepper
2 tablespoons butter
2 tablespoons oil

6 ounces small mushrooms,
   halved (1 1/2 cups)
1/4 teaspoon minced garlic
3/4 cup dry white wine
1 tablespoon finely chopped
   parsley
1 1/2 teaspoons lemon juice
1/4 teaspoon crumbled dried
   Italian seasoning

Bone and skin turkey breast. Place meat in freezer for about 1 hour or until surface of meat is thoroughly chilled and slightly firm. Cut meat in 1/4-inch slices. Combine flour, salt, paprika and pepper; flour meat slices, shaking off excess.

Heat 1 tablespoon each butter and oil in large skillet. Add layer of meat and brown lightly on both sides. As meat is browned, remove and keep warm. Brown remaining turkey, adding remaining butter and oil as needed.

When all meat is browned, add mushrooms and garlic to skillet and sauté lightly. Return browned turkey to skillet. Combine wine, parsley, lemon juice and Italian seasoning. Pour over all and simmer rapidly for 5 to 10 minutes or until liquid is reduced and turkey is tender.

                     Makes about 6 servings.

Per Serving (approx):
Calories 336
Carbohydrate 6 gm

Protein 34 gm
Sodium 499 mg

Fat 18 gm
Cholesterol 92 mg

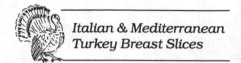

Scallopini #2

This is one of two different scallopini recipes in this cookbook. We've included both because scallopini is such a popular entree, and because turkey adapts so well to it.

4 tablespoons margarine
1/2 pound mushrooms,
   thinly sliced
1/4 cup flour
1/8 teaspoon black pepper

1 pound turkey breast slices or
   breast cutlets
1/4 cup dry sherry
1 tablespoon water
Chopped parsley, for garnish

Melt 2 tablespoons of the margarine in large skillet over medium heat. Add mushrooms and sauté until tender. Remove from pan.

Combine flour and pepper. Coat turkey with flour mixture, shaking off excess. Melt remaining margarine in skillet over medium-high heat; brown turkey on both sides, a few pieces at a time. Allow 1 to 2 minutes per side. Remove from pan.

Slowly add sherry and water to skillet, stirring until liquid is slightly thickened and smooth. Return turkey and mushrooms to pan until just heated through. Arrange on serving platter and garnish with chopped parsley.   Makes 4 servings.

Per Serving (approx):
Calories 253
Carbohydrate 8 gm

Protein 24 gm
Sodium 188 mg

Fat 12 gm
Cholesterol 55 mg

Turkey Shish Kabobs

Turkey is easy to cube and skewer with chunks of vegetables and fruit for the "meat on a stick" that is popular throughout the eastern Mediterranean area.

1 1/4 pounds boneless turkey thighs
3 tablespoons lemon juice
2 cloves garlic, minced
3 tablespoons fresh chopped oregano
   or 1 tablespoon dried
1 1/2 teaspoons fresh chopped basil
   or 2 teaspoons dried

1/4 teaspoon black pepper
1 small red bell pepper, cut
   into 2-inch cubes
1 small green bell pepper, cut
   into 2-inch cubes
1 medium sweet yellow onion,
   cut into 8 wedges

Cut turkey thighs into 2-inch pieces. In large bowl combine lemon juice, garlic and seasonings. Add turkey, bell peppers and onion; toss well to coat with marinade. Cover and refrigerate for 1 hour or longer, turning occasionally.

Prepare lightly greased outdoor grill for cooking. Thread meat and vegetables on skewers, alternating ingredients. Grill, uncovered, 5 to 6 inches over medium-hot coals for 30 to 40 minutes or until meat is cooked through and vegetables are tender, turning occasionally.

Makes 4 or 5 servings.

Per Serving (approx):
Calories 177
Carbohydrate 8 gm

Protein 24 gm
Sodium 68 mg

Fat 6 gm
Cholesterol 70 mg

> Turkey meat is one of the very lowest
> of all meats in caloric content.

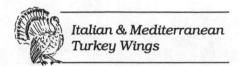

Moroccan Turkey Wings

Inexpensive turkey wings achieve elegance when immersed in this Moroccan marinade of vinegar, cumin, mace, sage and other exotic spices, and blended with dried apricots! The cuisine of the Casbah is yours with this exotic dish.

1/3 cup red wine vinegar	1/4 teaspoon ground mace
2 tablespoons olive oil	1 cup quartered dried apricots
3 cloves garlic, minced	Salt and pepper to taste
1 teaspoon each dried thyme, dried	3 pounds turkey wings
sage and ground ginger	1/4 cup firmly packed
1/2 teaspoon ground cumin	brown sugar
	1/2 cup Madeira wine

In 2-quart shallow ovenproof casserole, combine vinegar, oil, garlic, herbs and spices, apricots, salt and pepper. Add turkey wings and let marinate overnight.

Sprinkle brown sugar and Madeira wine into marinade, then cover and bake for 45 minutes at 350 degrees. Uncover and bake for 45 minutes more or until turkey is tender; turn wings several times during baking. Cut turkey wings in half and serve with rice, if desired.

Makes 4 or 5 servings.

Per Serving (approx):
Calories 783   *Protein 67 gm*   *Fat 37 gm*
Carbohydrate 35 gm   *Sodium 253 mg*   *Cholesterol 193 mg*

MEXICAN & SOUTHWESTERN

San Antonio Turkey Fajitas

Traditionally, these fajitas are served with a background of mariachi music coming from a flat-bottomed boat that is drifting by on the San Antonio River.

1 pound turkey breast cutlets
  or slices, cut into 1/2-inch
  strips
1/2 cup chopped cilantro
1 clove garlic, minced
1/2 teaspoon ground cumin
1/4 teaspoon chili powder
1/8 teaspoon reduced-sodium
  soy sauce
1/8 teaspoon Worcestershire
  sauce
2 teaspoons oil

1 red bell pepper, cut into slices
  1/8 inch by 2 inches
1 green bell pepper, cut into
  slices 1/8 inch by 2 inches
2 cups thinly sliced onion
  separated into rings
3 tablespoons lime juice
8 flour tortillas
Reduced-calorie sour cream
  (optional)
Guacamole (optional)
Pico de Gallo sauce or salsa
  (optional)

In 1-quart bowl combine turkey, cilantro, garlic, cumin, chili powder, soy sauce and Worcestershire sauce. Cover and refrigerate for 1 hour.

In large nonstick skillet over medium-high heat, stir-fry turkey mixture in 1 teaspoon of the oil for 4 minutes or until turkey is no longer pink. Remove from skillet and set aside.

Add remaining 1 teaspoon oil to skillet. Stir-fry bell peppers for 2 minutes or until slightly softened. Add onion; cook, stirring constantly, until vegetables are tender-crisp.

Return turkey strips to skillet. Pour lime juice over mixture and stir to combine. Remove from heat and serve immediately wrapped in flour tortillas. Garnish with sour cream, guacamole and Pico de Gallo sauce, if desired.

Makes 4 servings.

Per Serving (approx):
Calories 420
Carbohydrate 57 gm

Protein 35 gm
Sodium 509 mg

Fat 5 gm
Cholesterol 70 mg

Pavo Fajitas

1 tablespoon each Worcestershire
  sauce, soy sauce and vinegar
1 teaspoon chili powder
1 pound turkey breast slices,
  cut into 1-inch strips
1 clove garlic, finely chopped

1 tablespoon oil
1 medium onion, sliced
1 green bell pepper, sliced
Flour tortillas, avocado slices,
  sour cream and chopped
  cilantro

In medium bowl combine Worcestershire sauce, soy sauce, vinegar and chili powder. Add turkey; let marinate for 15 minutes. In medium skillet over medium-high heat, cook turkey in hot oil for 5 to 7 minutes or until turkey is no longer pink.

Remove turkey from skillet. Cook onion and bell pepper until tender-crisp. Return turkey to skillet; heat through. Serve with tortillas, avocado, sour cream and cilantro.   Makes 4 servings.

Per Serving (approx):
Calories 454	*Protein 34 gm*	*Fat 15 gm*
Carbohydrate 47 gm	*Sodium 595 mg*	*Cholesterol 61 mg*

Veracruz Turkey Slices

1 pound turkey breast slices
1 tablespoon oil
2 tomatoes, chopped
2 green onions, sliced
1 garlic clove, finely chopped
1 can (4 ounces) diced green chiles

1 teaspoon chopped cilantro
1/2 teaspoon dried crushed
  oregano leaves
Salt and pepper to taste
1 avocado, sliced

In large skillet over medium heat, cook turkey slices in hot oil for 4 to 6 minutes on each side or until turkey is no longer pink. Remove slices and keep warm.

In skillet simmer tomatoes, onions, garlic, chilies, cilantro, oregano, salt and pepper over medium-high heat for 7 minutes or until tomatoes soften and liquid evaporates; stir frequently. Spoon sauce over turkey slices. Garnish with avocado.   Makes 4 servings.

Per Serving (approx):
Calories 303	*Protein 26 gm*	*Fat 18 gm*
Carbohydrate 9 gm	*Sodium 490 mg*	*Cholesterol 61 mg*

Turkey Fajitas

1 cup thinly sliced onion
3 tablespoons oil
2 tablespoons lime juice
2 cloves garlic, minced
1/2 teaspoon dried oregano
1/2 teaspoon ground cumin
1/2 teaspoon chili powder

1 pound turkey breast cutlets,
  cut into strips
1/2 cup green or yellow bell pepper cut into strips
1/4 cup chopped cilantro or
  parsley
8 small flour tortillas, warmed
Sour cream (optional)

In shallow dish combine onion, 2 tablespoons of the oil, the lime juice,
garlic, oregano, cumin and chili powder. Add turkey; cover and let marinate for 1 hour.

In large skillet over medium-high heat, warm remaining oil. Add turkey
and marinade, bell pepper and cilantro. Sauté for 5 minutes, stirring
often, until turkey is no longer pink and vegetables are tender-crisp. To
serve, roll turkey mixture in warmed tortillas; garnish with sour cream,
if desired.   Makes 4 servings.

Per Serving (approx):
Calories 383
Carbohydrate 29 gm
Protein 31 gm
Sodium 363 mg
Fat 16 gm
Cholesterol 70 mg

The turkey is a native of Mexico, and
was introduced into Europe by the ex-
pedition of Cortez to the new world,
and called by his followers the 'American' or 'Mexican' peacock from its habit
of strutting.

Baked Chilies Rellenos

Mexico has been cooking with turkey for several thousand years, so they should know how to do it.

4 cans (4 ounces each) whole
   green chilies, drained, rinsed,
   seeds removed, slit on one
   side and opened flat
Nonstick vegetable cooking spray
1 package (4 ounces) reduced-
   fat Monterey jack cheese, cut
   into 1/2-inch strips
2 cups cooked turkey cut into
   1/2-inch strips (about 3/4 pound)

1/2 cup flour
1/2 teaspoon baking powder
Salt to taste
1/2 cup skim milk
3 eggs
2/3 cup shredded nonfat
   Cheddar cheese

Arrange chilies in 11- x 7 1/2- x 1 1/2-inch baking dish lightly coated with vegetable cooking spray. Fill each chile half with cheese and turkey. Fold over edges of chilies and place seamside down in dish.

In medium bowl combine flour, baking powder and salt. Whisk together milk and eggs. Slowly add egg mixture to flour mixture, beating until smooth. Pour over prepared chilies.

Bake at 450 degrees for 15 minutes. Turn off oven and remove casserole. Sprinkle cheddar cheese over top and return to hot oven for 1 minute to melt cheese. Serve immediately.   Makes 6 servings.

Per Serving (approx):
Calories 238
Carbohydrate 12 gm

Protein 30 gm
Sodium 434 mg

Fat 7 gm
Cholesterol 145 mg

Turkey Leg Tacos with Green Sauce

3 1/2 pounds turkey
   drumsticks (about 6)
1 medium onion, chopped
1 cup chopped celery with leaves
1 clove garlic, crushed

Salt to taste
1 teaspoon black pepper
18 corn tortillas
Sour cream, for accompaniment

In large soup pot, combine turkey drumsticks, onion, celery and garlic. Cover with water and add salt and pepper. Bring to a low boil; reduce heat to low and cover pot. Cook until drumsticks are fork tender, about 1 1/2 hours. Remove from heat and strain off broth. (Freeze broth for another use.)

When turkey is cool enough to handle, remove meat from bones. Discard bones and skin. Shred meat and set aside. Prepare Green Sauce.

Add turkey to Green Sauce. Heat through and add salt to taste.

To make tacos, wrap tortillas in foil and heat in oven. Spoon a little turkey mixture in middle of each soft, warm tortilla and fold over. Serve sour cream at the table. Allow 3 tacos per person.

Makes 6 servings.

GREEN SAUCE:
In blender or food processor, combine 2 cans (18 ounces each) Mexican green tomatoes (tomatillos), 3 or 4 fresh serrano chilies, seeded, and 1/3 cup well-packed cilantro leaves. Blend or process until smooth; set aside. In 12-inch skillet, heat 2 tablespoons corn oil; sauté 1 small diced onion with 2 large cloves minced garlic until onion is transparent. Pour in tomatillo mixture.

Per Serving (approx):
Calories 744	*Protein 62 gm*	*Fat 31 gm*
Carbohydrate 55 gm	*Sodium 354 mg*	*Cholesterol 165 mg*

Rio Grande Turkey

This is a super burrito!

2 pounds turkey thighs
1 can (8 ounces) tomato sauce
1 can (4 ounces) chopped green
  chilies
1/4 cup chopped onion
2 tablespoons chili powder

2 tablespoons Worcestershire
  sauce
1/4 teaspoon garlic powder
8 flour tortillas, warmed
Chopped lettuce
1/2 cup sour cream

Place turkey in skillet with tomato sauce, chilies, onion, chili powder, Worcestershire sauce and garlic powder. Bring to a boil; reduce heat, cover and simmer for 2 hours. Remove cover; cook for 15 minutes more.

Remove turkey from bones; shred, using 2 forks. Return turkey to tomato mixture and stir to combine. Spoon on tortilla with chopped lettuce; roll up to serve. Top with sour cream.   Makes 4 servings.

SLOW-COOKER METHOD:
Rinse turkey; remove skin. Place in slow cooker with tomato sauce, chilies, onion, chili powder, Worcestershire sauce and garlic powder. Cover. Cook on low setting for 10 hours. Remove turkey and continue cooking, uncovered, on high setting for 30 minutes more. Shred turkey and return to tomato mixture. Serve as above.

Per Serving (approx):
Calories 858
Carbohydrate 89 gm

Protein 65 gm
Sodium 1493 mg

Fat 27 gm
Cholesterol 151 mg

Empanadas Grande

These are traditionally made with tortillas, but this version uses pie crust, so if you wish, you can call them meat pies. Regardless of what you want to call them, make them.

1 pound ground turkey	1 teaspoon dried cumin
1 clove garlic, minced	1/2 teaspoon dried oregano
1 cup chopped onion	1/2 teaspoon red pepper flakes
1/2 cup chopped green bell pepper	1/8 teaspoon black pepper
1 tablespoon oil	1 package (15 ounces)
2 cups chopped tomatoes	refrigerated pie crusts
1 tablespoon dried parsley flakes	1 egg white, beaten
1 teaspoon dried cilantro	

In large skillet over medium-high heat, sauté turkey, garlic, onion and bell pepper in oil until turkey is no longer pink. Stir in tomato, parsley, cilantro, cumin, oregano, red pepper flakes and black pepper. Reduce heat to medium and cook for about 15 minutes or until most liquid is reduced, stirring occasionally.

Spray baking sheet with nonstick oil. Unfold one pie crust in center of baking sheet. Carefully spread half of turkey mixture to within 1 inch of edge of half of pie crust.

Brush pie crust edge with egg white. Encase meat by folding other half of pie crust over meat mixture. Using fork, press edges of crust together and pierce top of crust to make holes to allow steam to escape.

Repeat with remaining turkey mixture and pie crust.

Bake in preheated 400 degree oven for 20 to 25 minutes or until pastry is golden brown. To serve, cut each empanada into 4 wedges.

Makes 8 servings.

Per Serving (approx):
Calories 353   *Protein 13 gm*   *Fat 21 gm*
Carbohydrate 28 gm   *Sodium 374 mg*   *Cholesterol 38 mg*

Turkey in Salsa

Delicious! May be served over pasta or rice, or on a bed of chopped lettuce.

6 pounds turkey thighs
  (approximately 4)
1 onion, coarsely chopped
2 stalks celery, coarsely
  chopped
1/2 cup loosely packed parsley
2 dried red chilies
1 whole clove
1 onion, finely chopped
3 cloves garlic, minced
3 tablespoons oil
2 tablespoons chili powder

1 cup very finely ground
  almonds
1/2 cup very finely ground
  peanuts
1 can (4 ounces) chopped
  green chilies
1/4 cup chopped cilantro
Sour cream, shredded Monterey jack or Cheddar cheese,
  green salsa and shredded
  warm tortillas, for garnish

Place turkey, coarsely chopped onion and celery, parsley, dried chilies and clove in large pot; cover with water. Bring to a boil; reduce heat and simmer for about 1 hour or until tender. Remove turkey from stock; let cool. Remove meat from bones; shred in bite-sized pieces. Discard skin. Strain stock; reduce to 1 quart.

Sauté finely chopped onion and minced garlic in oil until soft; stir in chili powder, ground nuts and chopped chilies. Sauté for 1 minute more. Stir in stock; simmer until smooth and thickened. Add turkey and cilantro.

Serve with sour cream, shredded cheese, salsa and shredded warm tor-tillas.   Makes 6 to 8 servings.

Per Serving (approx) excluding garnish:
Calories 985   *Protein 103 gm*   *Fat 48 gm*
Carbohydrate 28 gm   *Sodium 886 mg*   *Cholesterol 279 mg*

Enchiladas Santa Fe Style

2 tablespoons oil
1/2 to 3/4 cup chopped onion
1 to 1 1/4 pounds ground turkey
1 teaspoon chili powder
1/2 teaspoon ground cumin
1/2 teaspoon salt

2 cans (10 ounces each) enchilada sauce (mild or hot to taste)
12 corn tortillas (6 inches)
1 cup shredded Monterey jack cheese
Sour cream or guacamole (optional)

In large skillet over medium heat, warm oil. Add onion and sauté for 5 minutes or until translucent. Add turkey, chili powder, cumin and salt; sauté for about 5 minutes or until meat is cooked through.

Transfer meat mixture to bowl and set aside. Into same skillet pour enchilada sauce; heat through.

Dip 4 tortillas in sauce to soften; place alongside eachother on lightly oiled or nonstick 12- x 14-inch jelly-roll pan and top evenly with half the turkey mixture. Dip 4 more tortillas into sauce and place on top of turkey; add another layer of turkey mixture. Dip remaining tortillas into sauce and place on top of turkey. Spoon a little sauce over each enchilada stack and sprinkle with cheese.

Bake enchiladas in preheated 375 degree oven for 20 minutes or until cheese is melted. To serve, top each enchilada stack with dollop of sour cream or guacamole, if desired.

Makes 4 to 6 servings.

Per Serving (approx):
Calories 425
Carbohydrate 32 gm

Protein 27 gm
Sodium 800 mg

Fat 21 gm
Cholesterol 86 mg

Tex-Mex Potato Boats

*This is one of those recipes that you can prepare a day or two in advance
and pop in the oven for 15 minutes when you're ready to serve. It might be a
good idea to double or triple this recipe and freeze the extras.*

2 potatoes, baked
1/2 pound ground turkey
1/2 cup chopped onion
1 clove garlic, minced
1 can (8 ounces) stewed
   tomatoes

1 teaspoon chili powder
1/4 teaspoon dried oregano
1/4 teaspoon ground cumin
1/4 teaspoon red pepper flakes
1/4 teaspoon salt
1/2 cup grated reduced-fat
   Cheddar cheese

Slice potatoes in half lengthwise. Scoop out center of potato to within
1/4 inch of potato skin. Reserve potato for other use.

In medium skillet over medium-high heat, combine turkey, onion and
garlic. Cook for 5 minutes or until turkey is no longer pink. Drain meat
juices if necessary. Add tomatoes, chili powder, oregano, cumin, red pepper flakes and salt. Cook for 15 minutes or until most liquid has evaporated.

Spoon turkey mixture into potato shells and sprinkle with cheese. Arrange on 9- x 13- x 2-inch jelly-roll pan and bake in 375 degree oven for
15 minutes or until cheese melts. Makes 4 servings.

Per Serving (approx):
Calories 209
Carbohydrate 20 gm
Protein 16 gm
Sodium 446 mg
Fat 7 gm
Cholesterol 51 mg

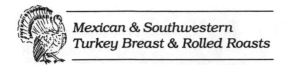
Turkey Molé

If you've never used chocolate with poultry before, you are in for a delightful surprise with this version of a traditional molé recipe.

1 turkey half breast (about 3 pounds)
3 quarts water
1 can (14 1/2 ounces) whole tomatoes
1/2 cup chopped onion
1/2 ounce unsweetened chocolate, melted
1/4 cup diced green chilies
1/4 cup cornmeal

1 tablespoon peanut butter
1 teaspoon chopped cilantro
1/2 teaspoon crushed red pepper flakes
1/4 teaspoon ground cinnamon
1/8 teaspoon ground cloves
1 clove garlic
Salt to taste
1/2 cup raisins

Poach turkey in water for 1 1/2 hours; drain and reserve 2 cups liquid. Blend remaining ingredients, except raisins, in blender for 30 seconds. Pour sauce over turkey; stir in raisins, cover and simmer for 20 minutes.

Makes 4 to 6 servings.

Per Serving (approx):
Calories 185
Carbohydrate 31 gm

Protein 5 gm
Sodium 339 mg

Fat 5 gm
Cholesterol 1 mg

It is quite reasonable to presume that the Mexican or southern turkey was the first introduced throughout Europe. Later, when the pilgrims settled here and found that the Indians were domesticating them and that they were numerous in the woods, they were no doubt used as a bird of feast, owing to their size and numbers. It was not until the Revolutionary War that the feast became national.

Spicy Lime and Cilantro Turkey Fajitas

The name of this recipe says it all!

1 tablespoon paprika
1/2 teaspoon onion salt
1/2 teaspoon garlic powder
1/2 teaspoon cayenne pepper
1/2 teaspoon fennel seeds
  1/2 teaspoon dried thyme

1/4 teaspoon white pepper
1 pound turkey breast tenderloins, butterflied
1 lime
4 pitas, cut in half, or 8 taco
  shells

In shallow, flat dish combine paprika, onion salt, garlic powder, cayenne pepper, fennel seeds, thyme and white pepper. Rub mixture over turkey; cover and refrigerate 1 hour. Prepare Sour Cream Sauce; refrigerate.

Prepare grill for direct-heat cooking. Grill turkey for 5 to 6 minutes or until meat thermometer registers 170 degrees in thickest part of tenderloin. Turn tenderloin after half of grilling time. Continue to grill. Remove to clean serving plate, and squeeze lime juice over tenderloins. Slice into 1/4-inch slices.

To serve, fill each pita half with turkey and top with Sour Cream Sauce. If desired, add shredded lettuce.   Makes 4 servings.

SOUR CREAM SAUCE:
In small bowl combine 1 cup fat-free sour cream, 1/4 thinly sliced green onion, 1/4 cup finely chopped cilantro, 1 can (4 ounces) green chilies, drained, 1 plum tomato, finely chopped, 1/2 teaspoon black pepper and 1/4 teaspoon cayenne pepper. Cover and refrigerate until ready to use.

Per Serving (approx):
Calories 371	*Protein 36 gm*	*Fat 3 gm*
Carbohydrate 46 gm	*Sodium 841 mg*	*Cholesterol 59 mg*

Tex-Mex Turkey Fillets

1 pound turkey breast
   fillets
1 tablespoon margarine
1/2 cup chopped green bell
   pepper
3/4 teaspoon chili powder

1 can (16 ounces) stewed
   tomatoes, chopped
1 can (4 ounces) sliced
   mushrooms, drained
3 green onions, thinly sliced
1 clove garlic, finely chopped

In large skillet over medium heat, cook turkey fillets in melted margarine for 8 to 11 minutes on each side or until turkey is no longer pink. Add remaining ingredients. Simmer, uncovered, for 5 to 7 minutes.

Makes 3 or 4 servings.

Per Serving (approx):
Calories 235
Carbohydrate 10 gm

Protein 26 gm
Sodium 376 mg

Fat 10 gm
Cholesterol 61 mg

Scientists recognize 5 subspecies within the United States. The Eastern Wild Turkey, *Meleagris gallipavos silvestris*, once extended from southern Maine and New Hampshire southward to northern Florida and westward to Eastern Texas and South Dakota.

Other subspecies include the Florida Turkey, the Rio Grande Turkey, Merrian's Turkey, and Gould's Turkey found only in the Southern tip of New Mexico. In addition, south of the border there are two other subspecies–Moore's Turkey and the Southern Mexican Turkey, *Meleagris gallopavo gallopavo*, the ancestor of our modern breeds.

Southwestern Turkey Hash

1 pound ground turkey
1 small onion, chopped
1 tablespoon oil
3 cups frozen potatoes O'Brien
Salt to taste

1/4 teaspoon black pepper
1 cup salsa
Sliced green onion (optional)
Sliced ripe olives (optional)

In large nonstick skillet over medium heat, sauté turkey and onion in oil for 5 to 6 minutes or until turkey is no longer pink.

Stir in potatoes, salt and pepper. Increase heat to medium-high and cook for 5 minutes, stirring occasionally. Stir in salsa. Continue cooking for 8 to 10 minutes or until potatoes are lightly browned, stirring occasionally. To serve, garnish with green onion and olives, if desired.

Makes 4 servings.

Per Serving (approx):
Calories 302
Carbohydrate 31 gm

Protein 24 gm
Sodium 467 mg

Fat 9 gm
Cholesterol 82 mg

Turkey Picadillo #1

Usually pork or beef are used to make this dish, but we think you'll like our turkey version.

2 tablespoons oil
1 to 1 1/4 pounds ground turkey
1 large onion, diced
1 green bell pepper, diced
1 clove garlic, minced
1 can (16 ounces) tomatoes,
   undrained

1/4 cup raisins
1/4 teaspoon ground cinnamon
1/4 cup slivered almonds,
   toasted
1/4 cup sliced black olives

In large skillet over medium-high heat, warm oil. Add turkey, onion, bell pepper and garlic. Cook, stirring frequently, until turkey turns light brown. Drain off fat.

Add tomatoes and then juice, raisins and cinnamon; stir. Bring to a boil; reduce heat to medium-low, cover and simmer for 10 minutes. Stir in almonds and olives and heat through.   Makes 5 servings.

Per Serving (approx):
Calories 319
Carbohydrate 20 gm

Protein 23 gm
Sodium 724 mg

Fat 18 gm
Cholesterol 65 mg

Turkey meat is lowest in cholesterol of all red meats and poultry.

Turkey Picadillo #2

This version is quite different from Turkey Picadillo #1.

1 pound ground turkey
1/2 cup chopped onion
1/4 cup chopped green bell pepper
2 cloves garlic, minced
1 tablespoon oil
1 teaspoon sugar
1/2 teaspoon ground cinnamon
1/2 teaspoon ground cumin

1/4 teaspoon ground cloves
1 can (14 1/2 ounces) stewed
   tomatoes
1 cup chopped Granny Smith
   apple
1/4 cup raisins
2 tablespoons thinly sliced
   pimiento stuffed olives

In large skillet over medium-high heat, sauté turkey, onion, bell pepper and garlic in oil until turkey is no longer pink.

Stir in remaining ingredients. Bring to a boil. Reduce heat, cover and simmer for 15 to 20 minutes.

Serve over rice and top with toasted almonds, if desired.

Makes 4 servings.

Per Serving (approx):
Calories 280
Carbohydrate 23 gm

Protein 22 gm
Sodium 471 mg

Fat 12 gm
Cholesterol 76 mg

Mexico City Turkey Breast

2 tablespoons flour
1 package (1 1/2 ounces) taco
   seasoning mix
1 1/4 to 2 pounds turkey breast,
   boned and skinned
3 tablespoons oil
1 cup chopped onion
3/4 cup diced green bell pepper

1 can (16 ounces) tomatoes
1 can (15 1/2 ounces) dark red
   kidney beans, drained
1/4 pound mushrooms,
   sliced
1 cup red wine
1 teaspoon sugar

In plastic bag combine flour and half of taco seasoning. Place turkey in bag and shake to coat. Remove turkey from the bag. Save the flour mixture. In large skillet over medium-high heat, sauté coated turkey in 2 tablespoons of the oil until lightly browned on all sides. Transfer turkey to 2-quart casserole.

Add remaining oil to skillet and sauté onion and bell pepper for 5 minutes. Add remaining flour mixture and taco seasoning.

Fold in tomatoes, beans, mushrooms, wine and sugar. Bring to a boil. Pour mixture over turkey breast in casserole. Cover and bake in preheated 350 degree oven for 40 to 45 minutes. Slice turkey breast and serve with sauce.   Makes 8 servings.

Per Serving (approx):
Calories 223
Carbohydrate 20 gm

Protein 21 gm
Sodium 649 mg

Fat 7 gm
Cholesterol 41 mg

CASSEROLES & MEAT LOAVES

Turkey and Asparagus Terrine

This old English recipe originally called for boiled tongue. Substituting turkey makes it a truly elegant dish.

1 pound ground turkey, minced
1/2 pound ham thickly sliced
  and diced
2 green onions, thinly sliced
1/3 cup dry white wine
1 egg, beaten

4 tablespoons cottage cheese or
  Greek yogurt
Pinch of ground allspice
Salt and pepper to taste
1/2 pound thin asparagus

Mix together all ingredients except asparagus. Line base of 1 1/2-pint loaf pan with foil. Cut asparagus to fit bottom of pan. Layer half of asparagus neatly in alternate directions. Spoon half of turkey mixture on top. Cover with remaining asparagus, then with remainder of turkey mixture. Smooth top. Cover with foil and place in roasting pan half filled with boiling water.

Cook at 325 degrees for about 1 hour. Terrine is cooked when mixture shrinks from sides of pan. Let cool, then turn out terrine. Slice.

Makes 4 servings.

Per Serving (approx):
Calories 310
Carbohydrate 11 gm

Protein 33 gm
Sodium 723 mg

Fat 13 gm
Cholesterol 155 mg

Although turkeys are native to the Americas, they were not domesticated here. In 1498 explorers from the Old World took turkeys from America to Spain. The domestication process began here. From Spain the turkey spread across Europe and was introduced into England between 1524 and 1541.

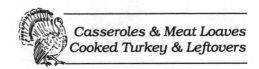

Rice-n-Turkey Casserole

2 cups cooked long-grain white
   or brown rice
2 cups cubed cooked turkey
2 medium zucchini, cut into
   1/4-inch rounds
3/4 cup shredded Monterey
   jack cheese

1 can (4 ounces) chopped green
   chilies, drained
2 medium tomatoes, halved
   lengthwise, then sliced
   crosswise

Prepare topping. Spread rice in greased 2-quart baking dish. Layer turkey, zucchini, cheese, chilies and tomatoes over rice. Spread topping over casserole. Sprinkle with cheese and bake at 350 degrees for 30 minutes.   Makes 6 servings.

TOPPING:
Combine 1 cup sour cream, 1/3 cup chopped onion, 1/2 teaspoon salt, 1/4 teaspoon dried oregano and black pepper to taste.

Per Serving (approx):
Calories 523	*Protein 27 gm*	*Fat 20 gm*
Carbohydrate 59 gm	*Sodium 679 mg*	*Cholesterol 76 mg*

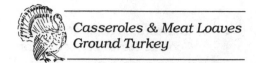

Meat Loaf Alaska

If you've ever had Baked Alaska (an ice cream loaf with a baked meringue frosting), you'll recognize this meat loaf with a mashed potato frosting as a similar concoction.

1 pound ground turkey	1/8 teaspoon black pepper
1 egg	1 teaspoon prepared horseradish
1/2 cup seasoned bread crumbs	1/2 teaspoon prepared mustard
1/4 cup water	4 servings instant mashed
1 tablespoon dried onion	potatoes
2 tablespoons catsup	1/2 cup grated cheese
1 tablespoon chopped green	
bell pepper	

Combine turkey, egg, bread crumbs, water, dried onion, catsup, bell pepper, black pepper, horseradish and mustard. Place in lightly greased 4 1/2- x 8 1/2- x 2 5/8-inch loaf pan, or shape in loaf form and place into lightly greased 1-inch baking dish.

Bake in preheated 350 degree oven for 45 to 60 minutes or until meat is no longer pink in center. Drain excess liquid. Prepare mashed potatoes and frost loaf with them. Sprinkle with cheese and return to oven. Bake for about 5 minutes or until cheese melts.   Makes 4 servings.

Per Serving (approx):
Calories 237
Carbohydrate 13 gm

Protein 24 gm
Sodium 303 mg

Fat 10 gm
Cholesterol 136 mg

Turkey and White Bean Casserole

2 turkey drumsticks (about
  2 3/4 pounds total)
1 1/4 cups water
1 cup chopped onion
1 bay leaf
Salt to taste
1/2 teaspoon dried thyme

2 cans (16 ounces each) white
  beans
1/4 cup tomato paste
4 smoky link sausages
  (6 ounces total), preferably
  made from turkey, halved

Place turkey drumsticks in large kettle with water, onion, bay leaf, salt and thyme. Bring to a boil. Cover tightly, reduce heat to low and simmer until meat is tender, about 1 1/2 to 1 3/4 hours. Let cool sufficiently to handle, then remove skin and bones, pulling meat off in chunks. Cut meat into 2-inch pieces. Boil down remaining cooking liquid to 3/4 cup.

Drain 1 can of beans and discard 1/2 cup liquid. Combine with the second can of beans and remaining liquid, reduced turkey cooking liquid and tomato paste; mix well. Add turkey chunks and halved sausages. Turn into 2 1/2-quart baking dish. Cover and bake in 350 degree oven for 45 minutes, uncovering during last 15 minutes.

Makes 6 servings.

Per Serving (approx):
Calories 404
Carbohydrate 44 gm

Protein 37 gm
Sodium 436 mg

Fat 9 gm
Cholesterol 69 mg

Mushroom-Stuffed Meat Loaf

1 pound ground turkey
1 egg
1/2 cup seasoned bread crumbs
1/4 cup water
1 tablespoon dried onion
2 tablespoons catsup

1 tablespoon chopped green bell
  pepper
1/8 teaspoon black pepper
1 teaspoon prepared horseradish
1/2 teaspoon prepared mustard

Prepare Mushroom Stuffing. Combine all meat loaf ingredients. Press half of meat mixture into lightly greased loaf pan. Top with 2 cups Mushroom Stuffing or your favorite vegetable stuffing, and spread remaining meat mixture over stuffing.

Bake in preheated 350 degree oven for 45 to 60 minutes or until meat is no longer pink in center.   Makes 4 servings.

MUSHROOM STUFFING:
In small skillet melt 1 tablespoon margarine over medium heat. Add 1/4 cup chopped onion and 1/4 pound sliced mushrooms; sauté for 2 minutes. Toss in 2 slices whole wheat bread (torn into cubes), 1 teaspoon dried parsley flakes, 1/4 teaspoon dried thyme and dash of salt and pepper. Stir constantly; cook until bread is lightly browned.

Per Serving (approx):
Calories 313
Carbohydrate 22 gm

Protein 26 gm
Sodium 510 mg

Fat 14 gm
Cholesterol 137 mg

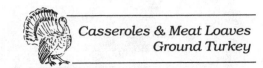
Turkey Noodle Dandy

You can make this casserole early in the day, then heat just before serving.

1 package (8 ounces) noodles
1 pound ground turkey
1 tablespoon butter
2 cans (8 ounces each) tomato sauce
1 cup cottage cheese

1/4 cup sour cream
1 package (8 ounces)
  cream cheese, softened
1/3 cup chopped green onion
2 tablespoons butter, melted

Cook noodles according to directions on package; drain. Meanwhile, sauté turkey in butter, stirring, until no longer pink. Stir in tomato sauce. Set aside.

In bowl combine cottage cheese, sour cream, cream cheese, and onion. In a lightly greased 2-quart casserole spread half the noodles; cover with cheese mixture, then with remaining noodles. Drizzle melted butter over all; top with turkey-tomato mixture. The casserole can be prepared ahead and refrigerated at this point.

If refrigerated, bake, uncovered, at 375 degrees for about 40 minutes. Or bake immediately after mixing at 375 degrees for 30 minutes.

Makes 6 servings.

Per Serving (approx):
Calories 378
Carbohydrate 8 gm

Protein 22 gm
Sodium 840 mg

Fat 28 gm
Cholesterol 121 mg

A Presidential Welcome

Q. Does the Federation do anything special to recognize Thanksgiving?

A. Since 1948 the National Turkey Federation has presented a live turkey and two dressed turkeys to the President of the United States.

Turkey Wings with Couscous Dressing

Inexpensive turkey wings served with couscous, the North African grain, results in an exotic dish worthy of becoming a favorite "new dish" in your home.

6 turkey wings
1 1/2 cups turkey or chicken
  broth
2 tablespoons butter
1 cup couscous
1/2 each red and green bell,
  pepper chopped

1/3 cup chopped onion
1 clove garlic, minced
2 tablespoons oil
1 egg, lightly beaten
Salt and pepper to taste
1/4 cup lemon juice
3 tablespoons honey

Fold turkey wings into triangles. Poach turkey wings in enough water to cover for 30 minutes. Drain the wings and reserve 1/2 cup liquid.

Bring broth and butter to a boil. Add couscous, cover and remove from heat; let stand for 5 minutes. Sauté bell peppers, onion and garlic in oil. Add to couscous with egg. Season to taste with salt and pepper.

Place turkey wings in baking dish; spoon couscous mixture into cavities. Mix lemon juice, honey and reserved poaching liquid; spoon over wings. Bake, covered, for 1 hour at 350 degrees, basting occasionally with pan juices. Uncover; bake for 15 minutes more. Makes 6 servings.

Per Serving (approx):
Calories 649
Carbohydrate 35 gm

Protein 55 gm
Sodium 593 mg

Fat 32 gm
Cholesterol 191 mg

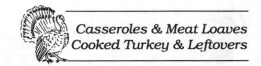
Turkey and Wild Rice Bake

This very simple recipe makes a very elegant dish. All you need is a can opener and an hour and twenty minutes. Or you may want to make it the previous day and warm it up before serving.

1 package (6 ounces) wild and white rice mix, uncooked

2 1/3 cups water

1 can (4 ounces) mushrooms, drained

1 can (14 ounces) whole artichoke hearts, quartered

1 jar (2 ounces) chopped pimiento, drained

2 cups cooked turkey, cubed

1 cup shredded Swiss cheese

In 2-quart casserole dish combine rice with seasoning packet, water, mushrooms, artichokes, pimiento and turkey. Cover and bake in preheated 350 degree oven for 1 hour and 15 minutes or until liquid is absorbed.

Top casserole with cheese and bake, uncovered, for 5 to 10 minutes or until cheese is melted and golden brown.   Makes 6 servings.

Per Serving (approx):
Calories 270
Carbohydrate 25 gm

Protein 24 gm
Sodium 572 mg

Fat 8 gm
Cholesterol 53 mg

Cashew-n-Cheese Cutlets

1/2 pound turkey breast cutlets
  or slices
1/8 teaspoon black pepper
2 ounces Swiss cheese, sliced
2 teaspoons seasoned bread
  crumbs

2 tablespoons white wine
  Worcestershire sauce
1 tablespoon coarsely
  chopped cashews

Lightly sprinkle cutlets with pepper. Place cheese slice on each cutlet. Roll up cutlet jelly-roll style to encase cheese. Carefully coat each cutlet roll in bread crumbs. In 14-ounce oval casserole dish, arrange cutlet rolls seam side down. Spoon Worcestershire sauce over cutlets. Bake in preheated 375 degree oven for 10 minutes.

Baste cutlets with pan drippings. Sprinkle cashews over top. Bake for 5 minutes or until turkey is no longer pink in center.   Makes 2 servings.

Per Serving (approx):
Calories 278
Carbohydrate 6 gm

Protein 36 gm
Sodium 343 mg

Fat 12 gm
Cholesterol 97 mg

Raising Turkeys

Modern turkey production methods have shortened the time it takes to bring turkeys to maturity. The hen usually takes 16 weeks and weighs 16—18 pounds when processed. This compares to the tom who takes 19 weeks to get to a market weight of 28—30 pounds.

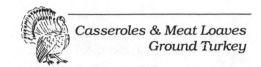

Individual Turkey Loaves with Corn Bread Stuffing

1 pound ground turkey
1/2 cup quick-cooking oats
1/4 cup water
1 teaspoon dried Italian seasoning
1 package (1 1/2 ounces) dried
   vegetable soup mix

3/4 cup corn bread stuffing mix
1/4 cup plus 2 tablespoons
   boiling water
Nonstick vegetable cooking spray

In medium bowl combine turkey, oats, water, Italian seasoning and soup mix.

In small bowl combine stuffing mix and boiling water; cover and set aside.

Coat 4 custard cups (6 ounces each) with vegetable cooking spray. In bottom of each cup, press 1/3 cup turkey mixture. Top with 3 tablespoons stuffing mixture. Press another 1/3 cup turkey mixture over stuffing, sealing all edges.

Place custard cups on baking sheet and bake in 350 degree oven for 30 minutes or until turkey is no longer pink in center.

To serve, loosen edges of loaves with knife and invert custard cups onto serving plate. If desired, serve with cranberry/orange relish.

Makes 4 servings.

Per Serving (approx):
Calories 304
Carbohydrate 27 gm

Protein 25 gm
Sodium 1027 mg

Fat 10 gm
Cholesterol 83 mg

Creamy Creole Turkey Bake

2/3 cup chopped onion
2/3 cup chopped celery
1/4 cup chopped green onion
1/3 cup chopped green bell pepper
1 clove garlic, minced
1 tablespoon margarine
1/4 pound mushrooms, sliced
4 ounces light cream cheese,
    softened

1 can (8 ounces) reduced-
    sodium stewed tomatoes,
    drained
1 1/2 teaspoons creole
    seasoning
4 ounces fettuccine, cooked
2 cups cooked turkey cut in
    1/2-inch cubes
1/4 cup grated Parmesan cheese

In medium nonstick skillet over medium-high heat, sauté onion, celery, green onion, bell pepper and garlic in margarine for 4 to 5 minutes or until vegetables are tender-crisp. Add mushrooms and sauté for 2 minutes. Remove from heat.

In medium bowl blend cream cheese, tomatoes and creole seasoning. Fold in vegetable mixture, fettuccine and turkey.

Pour mixture into 9-inch-square pan sprayed with vegetable cooking spray. Sprinkle cheese over top and bake at 325 degrees for 30 minutes or until bubbly.   Makes 4 servings.

Per Serving (approx):
Calories 380
Carbohydrate 32 gm

Protein 32 gm
Sodium 691 mg

Fat 14 gm
Cholesterol 100 mg

Ribbon Turkey Loaf

The green of the vegetables, the cream color of the cheese, and the pink of the meat, when cut across the loaf, gives you a ribbon that makes this meatloaf into an elegant pâté.

1 pound ground turkey	3 slices (1 ounce each) Swiss cheese
1/2 cup uncooked instant rice	1 package (10 ounces) frozen chopped spinach or broccoli, thawed and well drained
1 small onion, finely chopped	
1 egg, lightly beaten	
1 tablespoon instant beef bouillon	
1 teaspoon dried thyme	
1/2 teaspoon garlic powder	

Combine turkey, rice, onion, egg, bouillon and seasonings. Spoon half the mixture into lightly greased 9- x 5-inch loaf pan. Top with 1 slice of cheese, spinach, another slice of cheese and remaining turkey mixture. Bake in 350 degree oven for 40 minutes. Top with remaining slice of cheese. Bake 5 minutes more or until cheese melts.   Makes 6 servings.

Per Serving (approx):
Calories 270
Carbohydrate 19 gm

Protein 22 gm
Sodium 262 mg

Fat 11 gm
Cholesterol 103 mg

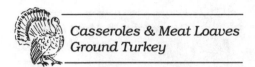
Sweet-n-Sour Barbecue Turkey Meatballs

1 pound ground turkey
1/2 cup unseasoned dry bread
   crumbs
2 tablespoons Worcestershire sauce
2 tablespoons oil

2/3 cup barbecue sauce
1/4 cup apricot jam
2 tablespoons each crushed
   pineapple and chopped green
   bell pepper

Combine turkey, bread crumbs and Worcestershire sauce. Shape into small meatballs, about 1 tablespoon of meat each. In large skillet heat oil. Cook meatballs, turning frequently, for 10 minutes. Combine remaining ingredients and pour over meatballs. Reduce heat to low and heat through.   Makes about 30 meatballs, 6 servings.

Per Serving (approx):
Calories 240   *Protein 15 gm*   *Fat 11 gm*
Carbohydrate 20 gm   *Sodium 367 mg*   *Cholesterol 55 mg*

Turkey Taco Bake

1 pound ground turkey
1/2 cup chopped onion
1 clove garlic, minced
1 tablespoon oil
1 package (1 1/2 ounces) taco
   seasoning mix

1 can (14 1/2 ounces) stewed
   tomatoes
1/3 cup skim milk
1 egg, beaten
1 package corn bread mix

In large skillet, sauté turkey, onion and garlic in oil until turkey is no longer pink. Stir in taco seasoning and tomatoes; reduce heat to low and cook until heated through. In medium bowl mix together milk and egg. Stir in corn bread mix until blended. Pour meat mixture into lightly greased 8-inch-square baking dish. Top with corn bread mixture. Bake in preheated 400 degree oven for 25 to 30 minutes or until corn bread is golden brown and toothpick comes out clean when inserted in center.

Makes 6 servings.

Per Serving (approx):
Calories 330   *Protein 20 gm*   *Fat 11 gm*
Carbohydrate 38 gm   *Sodium 1098 mg*   *Cholesterol 97 mg*

Swedish Turkey Meat Loaf

1 to 1 1/4 pounds ground turkey
1 cup pumpernickel bread crumbs
1 1/4 cups sour cream
1/2 cup chopped onion

1 tablespoon plus 1 teaspoon
   Worcestershire sauce
1/2 teaspoon salt
1/4 teaspoon black pepper
1/4 teaspoon ground allspice

In large bowl combine turkey with bread crumbs, 1 cup of the sour cream, the chopped onion, 1 tablespoon of the Worcestershire sauce, the salt, pepper and allspice. Pat mixture evenly into 9- x 5-inch loaf pan. Cover with foil and bake in preheated 350 degree oven 35 to 40 minutes or until loaf springs back to the touch and juices run clear when loaf is pierced. In small bowl combine remaining sour cream and Worcestershire sauce. Top meat loaf with mixture and place under broiler 6 to 8 inches from heat; broil for 1 to 4 minutes or until golden brown.

Makes 4 servings.

Per Serving (approx):
Calories 439	*Protein 30 gm*	*Fat 26 gm*
Carbohydrate 20 gm	*Sodium 615 mg*	*Cholesterol 132 mg*

Family Meat Loaf

1 pound ground turkey
1 egg
1/2 cup seasoned bread crumbs
1/4 cup water
1 tablespoon dried onion or
   1 medium onion, chopped

2 tablespoons catsup
1 tablespoon chopped green
   chopped green bell pepper
1/8 teaspoon black pepper
1 teaspoon prepared horseradish
1/2 teaspoon prepared mustard

Combine all ingredients; place in lightly greased 9- x 5- x 3-inch loaf pan, or shape in loaf form and place in lightly greased 1-quart baking dish. Bake in preheated 350 degree oven for 55 to 60 minutes or until meat is no longer pink in center of loaf. Unmold on platter; top with sliced tomatoes and garnish with parsley, if desired. Makes 4 servings.

Per Serving (approx):
Calories 263	*Protein 24 gm*	*Fat 12 gm*
Carbohydrate 14 gm	*Sodium 603 mg*	*Cholesterol 141 mg*

Spicy Turkey Meat Loaf

1 pound ground turkey
1 egg, lightly beaten
1 can (8 ounces) tomato sauce
1 small onion, chopped
1/2 cup crushed tortilla chips

1 package (1 1/2 ounces) taco
  seasoning mix
1 1/2 cups shredded lettuce
3/4 cup chopped tomato
3 tablespoons sour cream
2 tablespoons salsa

In medium bowl combine turkey, egg, tomato sauce, onion, tortilla chips and taco seasoning mix. Press turkey mixture into 9- x 5- x 3-inch loaf pan. Bake at 350 degrees for 50 minutes or until meat thermometer reaches 160 to 165 degrees and meat juices are no longer pink.

To serve, cut loaf into 6 equal slices and top each serving with lettuce, tomato, sour cream and salsa. Makes 6 servings.

Per Serving (approx):
Calories 198
Carbohydrate 12 gm

Protein 16 gm
Sodium 748 mg

Fat 10 gm
Cholesterol 93 mg

Great Meatballs

1 pound ground turkey
1 egg
1/2 cup seasoned bread crumbs
1/4 cup water
1 tablespoon dried onion

1 tablespoon chopped green
  bell pepper
1/8 teaspoon black pepper
2 tablespoons catsup

Combine all ingredients and mix thoroughly. Form about 1 tablespoon of mixture into each meatball. Arrange on lightly greased 10- x 15- x 1-inch baking pan. Bake in preheated 400 degree oven for 15 to 20 minutes or until meatballs are no longer pink in center.   Makes 6 servings.

Per Serving (approx):
Calories 180
Carbohydrate 9 gm

Protein 16 gm
Sodium 406 mg

Fat 9 gm
Cholesterol 99 mg

California Meat Loaf

1 to 1 1/4 pounds ground turkey
1/2 cup bread crumbs
1/2 teaspoon salt
1/2 teaspoon dried oregano
1/2 teaspoon dried basil
1/2 teaspoon black pepper
1 can (8 ounces) tomato sauce

6 slices onion
6 slices bacon, cooked crisp
6 slices tomato
1/2 cup sliced California black olives
1 cup shredded Monterey jack cheese

In large bowl combine turkey, bread crumbs, salt, oregano, basil, pepper and 3/4 cup of the tomato sauce.

Divide meat mixture into thirds; pat one-third into bottom of 8 1/2- x 4 1/2-inch loaf pan. Arrange 3 slices each of the onion, bacon and tomato over meat mixture; sprinkle with 1/4 cup of the olives and 1/3 cup of the cheese, then top with another one-third of meat mixture. Repeat layering, ending with meat. Spread with remaining tomato sauce and top with remaining 1/3 cup cheese.

Bake in preheated 375 degree oven for 45 to 50 minutes. Meat loaf is cooked through when it springs back to the touch and meat thermometer inserted in loaf registers 165 degrees.   Makes 4 to 6 servings.

Per Serving (approx):
Calories 395
Carbohydrate 33 gm

Protein 26 gm
Sodium 907 mg

Fat 18 gm
Cholesterol 79 mg

Top Producing Turkey States*			
1. North Carolina	61.0	6. Missouri	19.5
2. Minnesota	42.5	7. Indiana	14.8
3. Arkansas	23.0	8. Pennsylvania	8.6
4. California	23.0	9. Iowa	8.6
5. Virginia	21.0	10. South Carolina	6.1

In millions of turkeys
Based on estimated production in 1993

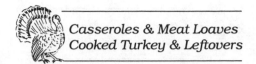

Turkey Pumpernickel Strata

Like the Turkey Pastrami and Cheese Strata on the next page, this dish is one to prepare a day or two in advance.

4 slices pumpernickel bread,
   cut into 1/2-inch cubes
1 cup cooked turkey cut into
   1/2-inch cubes
1 can (4 ounces) sliced
   mushrooms, drained
1 jar (2 ounces) chopped
   pimiento, drained

1 tablespoon dried onion
1 tablespoon dried chives
1 teaspoon garlic powder
1/4 teaspoon black pepper
1 cup grated reduced-fat
   Cheddar cheese
1 1/2 cups skim milk
4 eggs, lightly beaten

Reserve 1/2 cup bread cubes for topping. On ungreased 10- x 15- x 1-inch jelly-roll pan, bake remaining bread cubes at 400 degrees for 5 to 10 minutes or until bread is dry. Arrange cubes in bottom of 9-inch-square baking dish.

In medium bowl combine turkey, mushrooms, pimiento, onion, chives, garlic powder and black pepper. Spread turkey mixture over bread cube layer and top with cheese. Sprinkle reserved bread cubes over cheese.

In same bowl combine milk and eggs; pour over bread layer. Cover dish and refrigerate overnight. In preheated 325 degree oven, bake strata for 50 to 60 minutes or until knife inserted in center comes out clean. Allow strata to stand for 10 to 15 minutes before serving.   Makes 4 servings.

Per Serving (approx):
Calories 347
Carbohydrate 25 gm

Protein 31 gm
Sodium 862 mg

Fat 13 gm
Cholesterol 262 mg

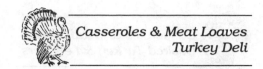
Turkey Pastrami and Cheese Strata

This is a wonderful dish for a crowd. You can assemble it the night before and bake it in the morning.

6 slices light rye bread,
  trimmed of all crusts*
1/2 pound turkey pastrami, cut in
  1/4-inch strips
6 slices white bread, trimmed
  of all crusts
6 eggs

3 cups milk
1 1/2 cups (about 6 ounces)
  grated Swiss cheese
1/8 teaspoon black pepper
1 teaspoon caraway seeds
  (optional)
1 teaspoon dry mustard

Generously grease 9- x 13-inch glass baking dish. Arrange rye bread slices on the bottom of the dish. Distribute turkey pastrami over bread slices. Top with white bread slices to make "sandwiches."

Beat eggs in large bowl. Add milk, cheese, pepper, caraway (if used) and dry mustard. Pour over sandwiches. Cover and refrigerate as long as overnight, as little as 1 hour. Bake, uncovered, in a 325 degree oven until puffed and golden, about 50 to 55 minutes.   Makes 6 servings.

*Note: If desired, 12 slices rye bread may be used instead of half rye and half white.

Per Serving (approx):
Calories 470
Carbohydrate 39 gm

Protein 31 gm
Sodium 914 mg

Fat 21 gm
Cholesterol 277 mg

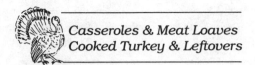

Turkey and Broccoli Skillet Soufflé

This dish takes a little extra effort but is well worth it.

4 eggs, separated
1/4 cup water
1/2 teaspoon cream of tartar
1 cup shredded Swiss cheese
1 tablespoon butter or margarine

1 cup finely chopped cooked
  broccoli
1 cup chopped cooked turkey
2 tablespoons chopped green
  onion
1 clove garlic, chopped

In large bowl with electric mixer at high speed, beat egg whites with water and cream of tartar until stiff peaks form. In small bowl with mixer at high speed, beat egg yolks until thick and lemon colored. Gently fold yolks into whites. Fold in 1/4 cup of the cheese.

In 10-inch ovenproof skillet over medium-high heat, melt butter. Stir in broccoli, turkey, green onion and garlic. Gently pour egg mixture into skillet; smooth top. Reduce heat to medium and cook for 5 minutes or until soufflé is lightly browned on bottom. Place skillet in preheated 350 degree oven and bake for 10 to 12 minutes or until puffed and golden. Sprinkle remaining cheese over soufflé and serve immediately.

Makes 4 servings.

Per Serving (approx):
Calories 272
Carbohydrate 3 gm

Protein 25 gm
Sodium 230 mg

Fat 17 gm
Cholesterol 265 mg

Turkey eggs, slightly larger than jumbo chicken eggs, occasionally may be purchased at health food stores or at farm markets. They are not a common retail item. Even though excellent for cooking and nutritious, they are expensive, costing abaout 75 cents per egg. The majority of turkey eggs are used to support turkey production.

Pumpkin Turkey Bake

This recipe solves the problem of what to do with Thanksgiving pumpkins.
You can stuff them and eat them.

1 pumpkin (4 1/2 to 5 pounds)
1 pound turkey thighs skinned,
   boned and cut into 1/2-inch
   cubes
1 tablespoon vegetable oil
1 cup coarsely chopped onion
3/4 cup thinly sliced celery
1/2 cup coarsely chopped green
   bell pepper

1 clove garlic, minced
1 package (8 ounces) frozen
   sugar snap peas, thawed
2 tablespoons brown sugar
1/8 teaspoon red pepper flakes
1/8 teaspoon ground cinnamon
1/4 cup turkey or chicken broth

Cut top from pumpkin; remove and set aside. With spoon scoop out seeds and discard.

Replace pumpkin top and place pumpkin in 8-inch-square baking pan. Bake in preheated 350 degree oven for for 50 to 60 minutes or until pumpkin feels slightly tender when squeezed (pumpkin should not be completely done at this point).

In large skillet over medium-high heat, sauté turkey in oil for 5 to 6 minutes or until lightly browned; remove from skillet and set aside. Add onion, celery, bell pepper and garlic to skillet; sauté for 2 minutes. Add peas and sauté mixture 1 additional minute. Stir in brown sugar, red pepper flakes, cinnamon and browned turkey.

Spoon turkey mixture into pumpkin; sprinkle with turkey broth. Replace pumpkin top and return to baking pan. Bake for 35 to 45 minutes or until pumpkin is tender and turkey cubes are done.

To serve, scoop out some of the pumpkin with turkey/vegetable mixture.
                               Makes 4 servings.

Per Serving (approx):
Calories 350   *Protein 29 gm*   *Fat 9 gm*
Carbohydrate 43 gm   *Sodium 122 mg*   *Cholesterol 85 mg*

Barbecue Meat Loaf

You can stay indoors and still have your barbecue with this dish.

6 tablespoons barbecue sauce
2 tablespoons water
2/3 cup rolled oats
   (old-fashioned or quick cooking)
1 large egg, lightly beaten
2 teaspoons chili powder, or to taste
2 teaspoons Worcestershire
   sauce
Salt to taste

1 to 1 1/4 pounds ground turkey
1/3 cup chopped red and/or
   green bell pepper
1/4 cup finely chopped onion
1/2 cup fresh or thawed frozen
   corn kernels
2 tablespoons drained canned
   chopped green chilies
Additional barbecue sauce or
   catsup (optional)

In large bowl combine 3 tablespoons of the barbecue sauce and the water. Add oats, egg, chili powder, Worcestershire sauce and salt; mix well. Add turkey, bell pepper, onion, corn and chilies; mix well. Pat into 9- x 5-inch loaf pan.

Bake in preheated 375 degree oven for 45 to 50 minutes; spread top of loaf with remaining 3 tablespoons barbecue sauce during last 10 minutes of cooking. Meat loaf is cooked through when it springs back to the touch and meat thermometer inserted in loaf registers 165 degrees.

Serve warm or cold, with additional barbecue sauce, if desired.

Makes 4 to 6 servings.

Per Serving (approx):
Calories 186
Carbohydrate 13 gm

Protein 17 gm
Sodium 253 mg

Fat 7 gm
Cholesterol 90 mg

POT PIES & PASTRIES

Turkey En Croute #1

Elegance is yours with this turkey tenderloin encased in a puff pastry with an oh-so-subtle sauce.

1 pound turkey breast
   tenderloins (2 pieces)
1 tablespoon butter

1 package (17 1/2 ounces)
   frozen puff pastry, thawed

Cook turkey in butter in skillet over medium-high heat for 5 minutes, turning to brown. Remove turkey and allow to cool slightly. Cut pastry in half; wrap each half around a tenderloin, gently stretching pastry to cover turkey.

Pinch edges of pastry together to seal. Decorate with additional pastry. Place seam side down on ungreased baking sheet. Bake in 375 degree oven for 25 to 30 minutes or until golden brown. Serve with sauce.

Makes 2 to 4 servings.

SAUCE:
In skillet used to brown turkey, combine 1 1/4 cups half-and-half, 1 tablespoon cornstarch, 1/2 teaspoon chopped dill weed, 1/8 teaspoon dried basil, 1/8 teaspoon black pepper and 1/8 teaspoon onion powder. Cook over medium heat, stirring constantly until thickened.

Per Serving (approx):
Calories 816
Carbohydrate 50 gm

Protein 35 gm
Sodium 699 mg

Fat 53 gm
Cholesterol 97 mg

Q. What breed of turkeys is most used by the industry?

A. All commercial turkeys produced today are the white broad breasted turkey breed. This breed was first used for commercial turkey production in the late 1950s. By the late 1960s, the majority of the industry used this turkey breed.

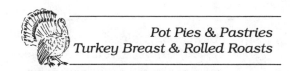
Turkey En Croute #2

So simple to make—so impressive to serve.

5 pound boneless turkey or
   boneless turkey breast
1 pound mushrooms, chopped
1/2 cup sliced green onion
2 cloves garlic, minced

1/4 cup butter, melted
2 tablespoons dry sherry
1/4 cup seasoned bread crumbs
2 eggs
Half of 17 1/4-ounce package
   frozen puff pastry, thawed

Roast turkey in preheated 350 degree oven until internal temperature registers 165 degrees, about 1 hour. Let cool slightly; remove netting.

Sauté mushrooms, onion and garlic in butter until soft. Stir in sherry, bread crumbs and 1 lightly beaten egg.

Cut turkey on diagonal into slices 1 inch thick, cutting only three-quarters of the way through meat. Fill space between slices with mushroom mixture.

Roll out pastry according to package directions. Place turkey cut side down in center of pastry; wrap pastry around turkey to cover completely, sealing edges with water. Place seam side down on baking sheet; brush remaining beaten egg over pastry. Prick surface with fork. Bake at 350 degrees until golden brown, about 1 hour. Let stand for 10 minutes. Slice to serve. Makes 10 to 12 servings.

Per Serving (approx):
Calories 495
Carbohydrate 12 gm

Protein 53 gm
Sodium 293 mg

Fat 26 gm
Cholesterol 178 mg

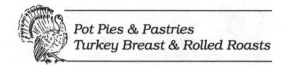

Turkey Pot Pies

You really should double this recipe and put the extra in your freezer. You may want to substitute prepared pie crust for pastry dough.

1 turkey quarter breast, (about 1 1/2 pounds)	1/4 teaspoon finely crumbled dried tarragon
1 teaspoon salt	1/8 teaspoon black pepper
1 cup sour cream	1 1/4 cups finely diced raw potato (2 small)
1 cup shredded sharp Cheddar cheese	1/3 cup chopped onion

Prepare pastry. To make 5 pies, divide dough in 10 wedges; shape each into small ball. Roll each out on lightly floured board to 6-inch circle. Fit 5 of the circles into 5 individual pie pans (5 inches diameter, 1 inch deep).

Remove bones and skin from turkey breast and cut turkey into 3/4-inch chunks. Sprinkle with 1/2 teaspoon of the salt. Place about 1/2 cup of chunks in each pan. In large bowl combine sour cream, cheese, tarragon and pepper. Mix in potato and onion. Spoon about 1/2 cup of this mixture over turkey in each pan. Moisten top edge of pastry and fit top pastries over pies. Fold edges under and press firmly together with fork; cut slits in top to allow steam to escape (decorative cutter may be used, if desired).

Bake in 350 degree oven for 1 hour or until pastry is nicely browned. Serve warm or cold.   Makes 5 servings.

PASTRY:
Mix 1/2 teaspoon salt with 3 cups sifted flour. Cut in 1 cup shortening until particles are size of peas. Sprinkle with about 1/2 cup cold milk; use just enough to make stiff dough. Shape into ball.

Per Serving (approx):
Calories 280
Carbohydrate 18 gm   *Protein 12 gm*   *Fat 18 gm*
                             Sodium 298 mg   *Cholesterol 30 mg*

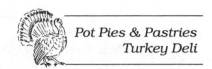

Torta Rustica

You see them often in gourmet delis—golden loaves of pastry stuffed with a savory filling. They're called "torta rustica," and with this recipe you can make them yourself.

2 loaves (1 pound each) frozen
   bread dough, thawed
2 each red and yellow bell peppers,
   halved and seeded
1 medium red onion, coarsely chopped
2 tablespoons olive oil
2 tablespoons drained capers
1/4 cup pitted and chopped
   oil-cured black olives
3 eggs, lightly beaten

4 tablespoons tomato paste
3 tablespoons chopped fresh
   basil or 1 tablespoon dried
1 teaspoon each dried thyme,
   sage and rosemary
8 ounces turkey salami slices
8 ounces turkey ham slices
1/2 pound fontina or
   mozzarella cheese, shredded
Additional oil, for brushing
   dough

Combine loaves of dough; let rise according to package directions until doubled.

Broil peppers, skin side up, until charred. Place in a plastic bag and seal for 5 minutes; peel off and discard skin; chop pepper.

In medium skillet sauté onion in oil until soft; add chopped peppers, capers and olives. Combine eggs, tomato paste and basil; stir into vegetable mixture.

To assemble torta, roll dough on floured surface into approximately 20-inch circle; sprinkle with thyme, sage and rosemary while rolling. Place in greased 10-inch-round pan, letting excess dough drape over sides. Layer half turkey salami and turkey ham slices on bottom and sides of dough; fill with egg mixture. Top with cheese and remaining turkey slices. Bring excess dough together in middle, leaving small vent for steam. Brush with additional oil and bake at 375 degrees for 50 to 55 minutes. Cut into wedges and serve warm or at room temperature.

Makes 10 to 12 servings.

Per Serving (approx):
Calories 191
Carbohydrate 8 gm

Protein 13 gm
Sodium 539 mg

Fat 12 gm
Cholesterol 94 mg

Savory Stuffing Pie

2 to 3 cups cooked bread stuffing
2 cups diced cooked turkey
2 cups cooked or canned
   corn kernels
2 cups shredded Cheddar cheese
1 cup whipping cream
1/2 cup thinly sliced green onion

1/2 cup diced red bell pepper
3 eggs, beaten
2 tablespoons flour
1 teaspoon salt
1/4 teaspoon black pepper
1/4 teaspoon hot pepper sauce

Lightly grease deep 9 1/2-inch pie plate. Press stuffing into bottom and up sides of pie plate to form shell. In medium bowl, combine remaining ingredients; mix well. Pour mixture into shell and bake in preheated 375 degree oven for 25 to 30 minutes or until heated through and golden.

Makes 6 servings.

Per Serving (approx):
Calories 530
Carbohydrate 28 gm

Protein 31 gm
Sodium 875 mg

Fat 33 gm
Cholesterol 236 mg

Mini Turkey Ham Quiche

1/3 cup diced turkey ham
1/4 cup reduced-calorie
   Cheddar cheese, shredded

1 frozen pie shell (6 inches)
1 egg, beaten
1/4 cup skim milk

Prepare pie shell according to package directions. Sprinkle ham and cheese over pie shell. In small bowl combine egg and milk; pour evenly into pie shell. Place on baking sheet and bake in preheated 350 degree oven for 20 to 25 minutes or until knife inserted in center comes out clean.

Makes 2 servings.

Per Serving (approx):
Calories 314
Carbohydrate 22 gm

Protein 14 gm
Sodium 575 mg

Fat 19 gm
Cholesterol 142 mg

California Turkey Puff

2 1/2 pounds turkey drumsticks
2/3 cup water
7 tablespoons butter
1/4 teaspoon each salt, dried thyme
   and dried dill weed
2/3 cup flour
3 eggs

2 carrots, thinly sliced
1 zucchini, sliced
1 green bell pepper, sliced
1 onion, sliced
1 cup sour cream
2 tablespoons Dijon-style
   mustard

Poach turkey drumsticks until tender, about 1 1/2 to 2 hours; let cool. Remove meat from bones and chop. Discard skin and bones.

Combine water, 5 tablespoons of the butter and the seasonings in 2-quart saucepan. Bring to a boil; add flour all at once. Remove from heat; beat with whisk until smooth. Beat in eggs one at a time until mixture is smooth and glossy. Spread in greased 9-inch pie plate. Bake at 400 degrees for 40 minutes. Turn off oven; leave popover in oven for 10 minutes, then remove.

Sauté vegetables in remaining 2 tablespoons butter; mix with turkey, sour cream and mustard. Spoon into popover. Bake at 350 degrees for 10 minutes or until heated through. Cut in wedges and serve.

Makes 6 servings.

Per Serving (approx):
Calories 597
Carbohydrate 20 gm

Protein 44 gm
Sodium 521 mg

Fat 38 gm
Cholesterol 270 mg

It was not only Californians who herded turkeys. In the 1700's turkeys raised near Suffolk were herded the 50 miles into London. Due to the severe weather, the turkeys were shod. That is, their feet were tied in cloth and covered with leather boots.

Cajun Skillet Pot Pie

World-famous Cajun cuisine traveled with French immigrants first to Acadia (now Nova Scotia) and then to Louisiana. Along the way, regional ingredients such as peppers and corn helped make these dishes unique.

2 cans (14 ounces) beef broth
2 turkey thighs (approximately 2 pounds)
Worcestershire sauce to taste
Hot pepper sauce to taste
3 tablespoons oil
5 tablespoons flour

2/3 cup chopped onion
1/2 cup chopped green bell pepper
1 package (10 ounces) frozen succotash, thawed
10 ready-to-bake refrigerated biscuits

In large saucepan over medium heat, bring beef broth to a boil. Add thighs, 1 tablespoon Worcestershire sauce and 1/2 teaspoon hot pepper sauce. Reduce heat to low; simmer thighs, uncovered, in broth mixture for 1 1/2 hours. Skim and discard foam.

Remove thighs to cutting board; discard skin and bones. Cut meat into pieces; reserve. Over high heat boil broth in saucepan until reduced to about 3 cups; reserve.

In 10-inch ovenproof skillet over medium heat, combine oil and flour. Cook for 5 to 6 minutes or until flour turns a deep reddish brown, stirring constantly. Stir in onion, bell pepper and succotash; gradually add broth and cook for 1 to 2 minutes or until sauce thickens, stirring constantly. Stir in turkey, adding Worcestershire and hot pepper sauce to taste.

Arrange biscuits on top of turkey mixture. Bake in preheated 400 degree oven for 10 minutes; reduce heat to 350 degrees and bake for 20 minutes longer or until biscuit topping is browned and filling is bubbly.

Makes 4 to 6 servings.

Per Serving (approx):
Calories 855
Carbohydrate 40 gm

Protein 90 gm
Sodium 1092 mg

Fat 37 gm
Cholesterol 257 mg

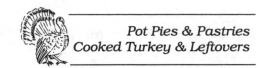

Mexican Shepherd's Pie

We have no idea where the title for this recipe came from, but we doubt that a shepherd made it. It is a delicious dish.

1/4 cup olive oil
3 tablespoons flour
1 cup chopped onions
1/2 cup chopped green or red
  bell pepper
1 garlic clove, minced
1 cup chicken broth
2 teaspoons chili powder
Salt to taste
1/2 teaspoon ground cumin
3 cups diced cooked turkey
2 cups shredded Monterey
  jack cheese

2 cups peeled, seeded and
  diced tomatoes
2 cups fresh corn kernels or
  1 package (10 ounces) frozen
  corn kernels, thawed
1 can (4 ounces) chopped mild
  green chilies
2 cups seasoned mashed
  potatoes
1 small pickled jalapeño
  pepper, chopped

In large skillet over medium-high heat, combine oil and flour. Cook for 5 to 6 minutes or until thickened and deep brown, stirring constantly. Add onion, bell pepper and garlic; sauté for 1 to 2 minutes. Gradually stir in broth. Continue cooking for 3 to 5 minutes or until sauce has thickened. Season with 1 1/2 teaspoons of the chili powder, the salt and cumin. Stir in diced turkey, cheese, tomatoes, corn and chilies.

In small bowl combine mashed potatoes with remaining 1/2 teaspoon chili powder and jalapeño. Transfer turkey mixture to 2-quart baking dish; spoon or pipe potato mixture on top. Bake in preheated 375 degree oven for 25 to 30 minutes or until golden and bubbly. Makes 6 servings.

Per Serving (approx):
Calories 517
Carbohydrate 37 gm

Protein 35 gm
Sodium 712 mg

Fat 25 gm
Cholesterol 88 mg

Sausage and Broccoli Quiche

2 tablespoons oil
1 pound turkey breakfast sausage
   patties
6 eggs
2 cups half-and-half
1/4 teaspoon salt
1/2 teaspoon black pepper

1/4 teaspoon ground nutmeg
2 unbaked 9-inch pie shells
2 cups shredded Swiss or
   Gruyère cheese
1 1/2 cups broccoli florets,
   cooked tender-crisp

In large skillet over medium-high heat, warm oil. Add sausage; cook for about 5 minutes or until firm and lightly browned, turning occasionally. Drain on paper towels and set aside.

In medium bowl combine eggs, half-and-half, salt, pepper and nutmeg; beat until well mixed.

Arrange sausage patties on bottom of pie shells. Equally divide cheese and broccoli between pie shells; divide egg mixture evenly over top. Bake in preheated 375 degree oven for 35 to 45 minutes or until set. Serve warm or at room temperature, cut into wedges. Makes 8 to 10 servings.

Recipe may be cut in half. If you're freezing extra quiche, thaw completely before use. To serve, cover loosely with foil and reheat in 350 degree oven for 15 minutes.

Per Serving (approx):
Calories 466
Carbohydrate 20 gm

Protein 21 gm
Sodium 610 mg

Fat 34 gm
Cholesterol 190 mg

> The incubation period to hatch a turkey egg is 28 days.

Sausage-Spinach Turnovers

For a special luncheon, these turnovers are ideal.

2 tablespoons olive oil
10 ounces turkey breakfast
  sausage links
1 tablespoon butter or
  margarine
1/4 cup chopped onion
1 package (10 ounces) frozen
  chopped spinach, thawed and
  well drained
1/2 teaspoon dried oregano

Salt to taste
Cayenne pepper to taste
1/3 cup shredded Swiss cheese
1/3 cup ricotta cheese
2 sheets frozen puff pastry,
  thawed, or pie pastry
  for 2-crust pie
1 egg
1 tablespoon water

In large skillet over medium-high heat, warm oil. Add sausage; cook for about 5 minutes or until firm and browned, turning occasionally. Remove from skillet; drain on paper towels and set aside.

Add butter and onion to skillet; sauté for 5 minutes or until onion is translucent. Stir in spinach, oregano, salt and cayenne. Remove from heat and let cool. Stir in Swiss cheese and ricotta until thoroughly combined.

On lightly floured surface with rolling pin, roll out each sheet of pastry to 10-inch square. Cut each sheet into 4 equal squares. On large baking sheet, place 6 squares. Top each with 2 sausage links; divide spinach mixture evenly over sausage. Fold opposite corners of pastry together to form triangles, crimping edges with fork.

In small bowl beat together egg and water; brush pastries with egg wash. Cut decorative shapes out of remaining 2 pastry squares and place on turnovers; brush decorations with egg wash. Bake in preheated 400 degree oven for 20 minutes or until golden brown. Serve warm.

Makes 6 servings.

Per Serving (approx):
Calories 213
Carbohydrate 6 gm

Protein 13 gm
Sodium 337 mg

Fat 15 gm
Cholesterol 72 mg

Italian Turkey Crust Pie

1 pound ground turkey or
  ground turkey breast
1/4 cup seasoned dry bread
  crumbs
1/4 cup milk
1 teaspoon garlic salt
1/2 teaspoon crushed dried
  oregano

1/4 teaspoon black pepper
1/2 cup tomato paste
1/2 cup sliced mushrooms
1/2 cup grated mozzarella
  cheese
2 tablespoons chopped green
  bell pepper
2 tablespoons sliced olives

In 9-inch pie plate, combine turkey, bread crumbs, milk, garlic salt, oregano and black pepper. Mix well.

Press mixture evenly over bottom and up sides of pie plate. Spread tomato paste evenly over turkey "crust." Top with mushrooms. Bake in preheated 350 degree oven for 25 minutes or until turkey is no longer pink. Sprinkle with cheese, bell pepper and olives. Bake an additional 10 minutes or until cheese is melted. Let cool for 5 minutes, then cut into wedges. Makes 6 servings.

Per Serving (approx):
Calories 181
Carbohydrate 8 gm

Protein 17 gm
Sodium 191 mg

Fat 9 gm
Cholesterol 64 mg

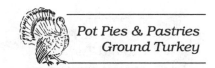

Super Turkey Burger Pie

Actually, this is a pie in which the turkey is the top and bottom crust, and the stuffing is the filling. It's perfect for an after-the-game meal. Prepare it a day or two ahead and refrigerate, then warm it up just before serving.

2 pounds ground turkey	3 tablespoons chopped parsley
2 eggs or 1/2 cup egg substitute	2 tablespoons chili sauce
1/4 cup skim milk	Salt to taste
1/4 cup bread crumbs	Dash of black pepper

In large bowl combine turkey, eggs, milk, bread crumbs, parsley, chili sauce, salt and pepper. On 2- x 10- x 15-inch jelly-roll pan, shape half of turkey mixture into 7-inch-diameter patty. On 10- by 11-inch piece of waxed paper, shape remaining turkey mixture into 8-inch-diameter patty.

Prepare stuffing and glaze. Spoon stuffing over 7-inch circle of turkey mixture to within 1/2 inch of edge. Carefully lift waxed paper and place 8-inch turkey patty over stuffing. Remove waxed paper. Press turkey mixture edges together to seal. Bake at 350 degrees for 60 to 70 minutes or until 165 degrees is reached on meat thermometer. Spread glaze over burger during last 10 minutes of baking.   Makes 8 servings.

VEGETABLE AND BREAD STUFFING:
In 10-inch skillet over medium-high heat, sauté 1 cup shredded potato, 1/2 cup shredded carrot, 1/2 cup zucchini and 1/4 cup chopped onion in 2 tablespoons margarine for 4 to 5 minutes or until vegetables are tender. In medium bowl combine vegetable mixture, 1 egg or 1/4 cup egg substitute, 1 tablespoon bread crumbs and 1/2 cup shredded mozzarella cheese.

GLAZE:
In small bowl combine 1/4 cup catsup, 2 tablespoons brown sugar and 1 teaspoon dry mustard.

Per Serving (approx):

Calories 295	*Protein 26 gm*	*Fat 15 gm*
Carbohydrate 14 gm	*Sodium 310 mg*	*Cholesterol 168 mg*

Spicy Spanakopita

We've added ground turkey to the traditional Greek cheese and spinach pie, to bring a whole new dimension to turkey and to your home with this recipe.

1 1/2 pounds ground turkey
2 tablespoons butter
2 pounds fresh spinach,
   steamed and drained, or 2
   packages (10 ounces each) frozen
   spinach, thawed and well drained
4 ounces feta cheese, crumbled

1/2 cup chopped walnuts
1/2 teaspoon each black pepper
   and ground allspice
1 egg
8 to 10 phyllo leaves, folded
   lengthwise
1/2 cup butter, melted

Brown turkey in the 2 tablespoons butter; combine with spinach, cheese, walnuts, seasonings and egg.

In greased 10-inch pie plate, lay first folded phyllo leaf across plate so both ends extend over edge. Brush with melted butter. Working quickly, fan remaining leaves around plate, brushing each with melted butter, so entire bottom of plate is covered. Keep unused leaves covered. Spoon filling onto phyllo leaves in pan. Fold edges over and add more leaves to cover top. Brush with butter. Bake at 350 degrees for 40 to 45 minutes or until golden brown.								Makes 8 servings.

Per Serving (approx):
Calories 431
Carbohydrate 19 gm

Protein 23 gm
Sodium 547 mg

Fat 29 gm
Cholesterol 140 mg

Turkey Lurky Pie

This very, very British dish was made for centuries with beef. This is one of their recipes which they converted to turkey.

4 tablespoons margarine or
  butter
1 tablespoon oil
1 onion, chopped
1 pound ground turkey
1/2 pound carrots,
  coarsely chopped

2 teaspoons tomato puree
1 teaspoon flour
2 tablespoons water
Pinch of dried thyme (optional)
Salt and pepper to taste
2 pounds potatoes, peeled and
  cut into 1/8-inch slices

Heat 1 tablespoon of the margarine and the oil in a pan. Lightly brown onion and turkey.

Add carrots and tomato puree. Sprinkle in flour and mix well. Add water, thyme and seasoning. Remove from heat and spoon into casserole (gratin) dish. Layer potatoes over top, overlapping. Sprinkle with salt and additional pepper, and dot with remaining margarine. Cover with foil.

Bake at 375 degrees for 45 to 50 minutes or until potatoes are almost cooked. Remove foil. Increase heat to 450 degrees and bake for 15 minutes more or until potatoes are golden brown and crisp on surface. Serve with green vegetable or salad.
          Makes 4 servings.

Per Serving (approx):
Calories 587
Carbohydrate 66 gm

Protein 27 gm
Sodium 371 mg

Fat 24 gm
Cholesterol 82 mg

The largest turkey ever raised was in Petersborough, England by Leacraft Turkeys, Ltd. He weighed in at 86 pounds!

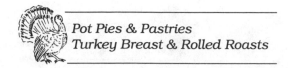

Lattice-Crust Turkey Pot Pies

2 cans (13 3/4 ounces each)
   reduced-sodium chicken broth
1 cup water
1 skinless, boneless turkey breast
   (about 1 1/2 pounds)
5 tablespoons light margarine
1 package (10 ounces) frozen pearl
   onions, thawed
1/2 teaspoon sugar
1/4 cup flour
2 1/2 cups low-fat milk

1/2 teaspoon dried marjoram
Salt and pepper to taste
10 ounces frozen petite peas,
   thawed
2 cups carrots in matchstick
   pieces
1 prepared pie crust pastry or
   1 frozen unbaked pie crust,
   thawed
1 egg beaten with 1 tablespoon
   water

In Dutch oven over high heat, bring chicken broth and water to a boil. Add turkey and more water to cover, if necessary. Reduce heat to low; simmer, uncovered, for about 25 minutes per pound or until turkey is cooked through. If time allows, refrigerate turkey to cool in broth.

Remove turkey from broth and cut into cubes; set aside. Skim and discard fat from broth. Strain broth, reserving 1 cup for sauce; reserve remainder for another use.

In large saucepan over medium-high heat, melt 1 tablespoon of the margarine. Add onions and sugar; reduce heat to medium and sauté for 5 minutes. Remove onions; stir remaining margarine and flour into saucepan. Cook for 1 to 2 minutes or until mixture is bubbling and slightly golden, stirring constantly.

Whisk in milk and reserved 1 cup chicken broth; cook until thickened, stirring constantly. Season with marjoram, salt and pepper. Stir in cubed turkey, cooked onions, peas and carrots; remove from heat.

Divide turkey mixture among six 2-cup baking dishes or ramekins. With pastry wheel or knife, cut pie pastry into strips. Brush rim of each ramekin lightly with egg wash.

Arrange pastry strips decoratively on top of turkey mixture, pressing onto rim of dish. Bake pies in preheated 400 degree oven for 10 minutes. Reduce temperature to 350 degrees and bake for 25 minutes longer or until crusts are golden and turkey mixture is bubbly. Makes 6 servings.

Per Serving (approx):
Calories 446

Protein 36 gm

Fat 16 gm

Carbohydrate 39 gm

Sodium 808 mg

Cholesterol 113 mg

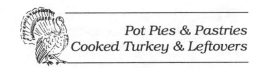
Country-Style Turkey Pie

A classic!

1/4 cup butter or margarine
1/3 cup sifted flour
3 cups milk
1 tablespoon chicken seasoned
   stock base
Salt to taste
1/2 teaspoon Worcestershire
   sauce
2 tablespoons dry sherry
3 drops hot pepper sauce

2 cups diced cooked turkey
   meat
1 1/2 cups sliced mushrooms
1 cup cooked chopped carrot
1 can (8 ounces) small whole
   onions, drained
1 tablespoon melted butter,
   for pastry
1 tablespoon grated Parmesan
   cheese

Prepare Herb Pastry. Melt butter in saucepan; blend in flour. Stir in milk slowly; add chicken base, salt and Worcestershire sauce. Cook, stirring, until sauce boils and thickens. Stir in sherry and hot pepper sauce. Add turkey, mushrooms, carrot, and drained onions; heat through.

Turn into 1 1/2-quart baking dish. Place Herb Pastry over dish, fluting edge of pastry against rim. Bake in 400 degree oven for about 20 minutes or until pastry is almost done. Brush top with melted butter and sprinkle with cheese. Bake for 10 minutes longer or until nicely browned.

Makes 6 servings.

HERB PASTRY:
Combine 1 1/2 cups sifted flour, 3/4 teaspoon salt and 1/4 teaspoon dried poultry seasoning. Cut in 1/2 cup shortening until particles are about size of peas. Sprinkle with about 1/3 cup cold milk, using just enough to make dough hold together. Roll pastry to fit top of baking dish. Cut out steam vents in pie crust.

Per Serving (approx):
Calories 593
Carbohydrate 42 gm

Protein 24 gm
Sodium 535 mg

Fat 36 gm
Cholesterol 81 mg

Bacon and Vegetable Bread

1/2 cup margarine, melted
1/3 cup grated Parmesan cheese
3 packages (10 ounces each) flaky
  refrigerated biscuits,
  quartered
Nonstick vegetable cooking spray

12 ounces turkey bacon,
  cooked and crumbled
1/2 cup chopped green bell
  pepper
1/2 cup chopped onion

In small bowl combine margarine and cheese. Roll biscuit quarters in mixture. In bottom of bundt pan sprayed with vegetable cooking spray, layer one-third of the biscuits. Sprinkle with half the bacon, bell pepper and onion. Repeat layers, ending with layer of biscuits.

Bake at 350 degrees for 25 to 30 minutes or until bread is golden brown. Makes 20 slices.

Per Slice (approx):
Calories 238
Carbohydrate 20 gm

Protein 7 gm
Sodium 872 mg

Fat 15 gm
Cholesterol 19 mg

Talking Back

Q Are turkeys really dumb?

A Turkeys are not dumb. Ask any hunter who has gone after wild turkey! However, the domesticated bird is far less cunning and more docile, probably because food, water, and shelter are provided.

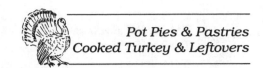
Turkey Quiche in Potato Shells

4 large potatoes, baked and cooled
1/4 cup margarine, melted
1 pound cooked turkey breast,
  cut into 1/2-inch cubes
5 large eggs, beaten
2 ounces cream cheese, softened
1/4 cup finely chopped
  green onion
1/4 cup finely chopped
  red bell pepper
Salt and pepper to taste
1/2 cup sour cream (optional)
1 cup shredded Cheddar
  cheese, (optional)

Slice potatoes in half lengthwise. With spoon remove center of potato to within 1/4 inch of potato skin. Save removed potato for another use. Place potato shells on 2- x 10- x 15-inch jelly-roll pan. Brush inside of each potato shell with margarine.

In large bowl combine turkey, eggs, cream cheese, onion, bell pepper, salt and pepper. Divide turkey mixture evenly among potato shells. Bake at 400 degrees for 15 to 20 minutes or until mixture is puffed and knife inserted in center of mixture comes out clean. Serve with sour cream and cheese, if desired. Makes 8 servings.

Per Serving (approx):
Calories 325
Carbohydrate 25 gm
Protein 24 gm
Sodium 224 mg
Fat 14 gm
Cholesterol 184 mg

Italian Turkey Sausage Roll

1 pound turkey sausage,
   crumbled
2 cloves garlic, minced
1/2 green or red bell pepper,
   chopped
1/2 red onion, chopped
Olive oil, as needed
1 can (14 1/2 ounces) stewed
   tomatoes, drained

1 cup grated Monterey jack
   cheese
1/4 cup chopped fresh basil
   or 1 tablespoon dried
1 teaspoon dried Italian
   seasoning
2 tablespoons grated
Parmesan
   cheese

Sauté sausage, garlic, bell pepper and onion in oil until sausage is browned. Add tomatoes. Add chopped zucchini or mushrooms, if desired. Simmer for 10 minutes. Let cool.

On lightly floured surface, roll out dough to 14- by 18-inch rectangle. Top with sausage filling and sprinkle with jack cheese, herbs and Parmesan. With long side of rectangle nearest you, carefully roll up into log. Pinch seams. Place on greased baking sheet. Brush with olive oil. Bake in preheated 400 degree oven for 30 to 35 minutes. Let cool for at least 15 minutes before slicing.   Makes 18 to 20 slices.

YEASTED DOUGH:
Dissolve 1 package dry yeast in 1/2 cup warm water (105 to 115 degrees). Add 2 tablespoons olive oil, 1 cup warm water, 4 cups flour and 1 teaspoon salt. Stir and mix with fork. Knead on lightly floured surface until smooth and elastic, about 5 minutes. Form into ball. Put into oiled bowl, turning to coat all surfaces with oil. Cover and let rise in warm place until doubled, about 45 minutes.

Per Slice (approx):
Calories 168
Carbohydrate 21 gm

Protein 8 gm
Sodium 316 mg

Fat 6 gm
Cholesterol 18 mg

SAUTÉ & STIR-FRY

Turkey Framboise

This sample of nouvelle cuisine takes just minutes to prepare, and its elegant flavor is impressive. Keep this recipe in mind for a special meal when you have little time to cook and are ready for a culinary triumph.

4 turkey fillets
   (about 1 1/4 pounds)
Salt and pepper to taste
3 tablespoons butter
2 tablespoons raspberry liqueur

1/2 cup whipping cream
1 tablespoon raspberry jam
1/3 cup fresh or frozen
   raspberries

Season turkey with salt and pepper to taste. Heat butter in skillet and sauté turkey for 4 minutes per side. Add raspberry liqueur; cook for 2 minutes more. Remove turkey and keep warm. Add cream and jam to skillet; cook until thickened, about 5 minutes. Add raspberries and heat through. Pour over turkey fillets and serve immediately.

Makes 4 servings.

Per Serving (approx):
Calories 197
Carbohydrate 9 gm

Protein 1 gm
Sodium 197 mg

Fat 16 gm
Cholesterol 50 mg

Poached Turkey Normande

2 turkey breast tenderloins
1/2 cup chopped onion
1/2 cup sliced celery
3 peppercorns
1/2 teaspoon salt

2/3 cup diced apple
1/3 cup orange juice
3 tablespoons jellied
   cranberry sauce
4 teaspoons orange marmalade

Place tenderloins, onion, celery, peppercorns and salt in large skillet. Pour in enough boiling water to cover turkey. Place lid on skillet and poach tenderloins over low heat for about 30 minutes or until done. Remove tenderloins from liquid.

In small saucepan over medium heat, combine apple, orange juice, cranberry sauce and orange marmalade. Cook until sauce is hot and apple pieces are tender but hold their shape. Spoon over tenderloins.

Makes 4 servings.

Per Serving (approx):
Calories 198
Carbohydrate 17 gm

Protein 27 gm
Sodium 364 mg

Fat 2 gm
Cholesterol 70 mg

Glazed Turkey Steaks
with Apricot Nut Pilaf

No, this is not a California recipe. It came to us from England, where nouvelle cuisine has become widespread.

2 tablespoons olive oil
1 onion, chopped
1/2 cup chopped dried apricots
3 tablespoons pine nuts
1/4 teaspoon ground turmeric
1/2 pound long-grain rice
2 cups vegetable stock
Salt and pepper to taste
2 teaspoons chopped fresh rosemary

1 clove garlic, crushed
4 turkey breast steaks
    (approximately 4 ounces each)
Grated zest and juice of
    1 large orange
1 teaspoon honey
2 teaspoons cornmeal
2 tablespoons water

Heat 1 tablespoon of the oil in saucepan. Stir in onion, apricots, pine nuts, turmeric and rice. Cook quickly for 1 to 2 minutes. Pour in vegetable stock, salt and pepper. Bring to a boil, stirring occasionally. Cover and cook gently for 20 minutes or until all stock has been absorbed.

Meanwhile, put remaining oil in frying pan. Add rosemary, garlic and turkey steaks. Fry quickly to brown on all sides. Add orange zest, juice and honey. Cover and cook for 5 minutes.

Blend cornmeal with water. Stir into liquid in frying pan. Bring to a boil and cook for 1 minute. Serve with pilaf, garnished with orange segments and fresh rosemary, if desired.   Makes 4 servings.

Per Serving (approx):
Calories 570
Carbohydrate 86 gm

Protein 14 gm
Sodium 1047 mg

Fat 19 gm
Cholesterol 12 mg

Turkey Fricassee with Dumplings

This dish combines a time-honored cooking method with all of the flavor reminiscent of American Sunday dinners on a farm—nourishing, delicious, comforting and warming.

2 pounds turkey wings, each
    cut into 2 or 3 pieces
2 tablespoons butter or
    margarine
2 tablespoons oil
1/3 cup finely chopped onion
8 medium mushrooms, sliced
1 can (10 3/4 ounces) cream of
    chicken soup

1/2 cup dry white wine
1/2 teaspoon dried thyme
1/4 cup whipping cream
2 cups buttermilk baking mix
2 teaspoons dried parsley
    flakes
2/3 cup milk

In a Dutch oven melt butter with oil. Sauté wings until browned; remove. In the same pan sauté onion and mushrooms until onion is soft and transparent Stir in soup, wine and thyme.

Return wings to pot. Cover and cook over low heat for 1 1/2 hours or until wings are tender. Stir in cream. Mix together baking mix, parsley flakes and milk with fork. Drop by spoonfuls onto turkey mixture that is at a slow boil. Cook for 10 minutes. Cover; cook for an additional 10 minutes.   Makes 4 to 6 servings.

Per Serving (approx):
Calories 721
Carbohydrate 42 gm

Protein 42 gm
Sodium 1251 mg

Fat 41 gm
Cholesterol 141 mg

French Turkey Fillets

Yes, you can have elegant entrees that are low in calories, fat and cholesterol.

1 pound skinless, boneless
   turkey breast fillets
Salt and pepper to taste
1 tablespoon oil

2 tablespoons light margarine
3 tablespoons minced shallot
   or green onion
1 cup white wine

Season fillets with salt and pepper. In a large nonstick skillet over medium-high heat, warm oil. Add fillets and cook for 2 minutes on each side or until lightly browned. Reduce heat to medium-low; cook for 2 to 3 minutes longer on each side or until cooked through. Remove fillets and set aside; keep warm.

Heat 1 tablespoon of the margarine in skillet until melted. Add shallots and sauté for 1 minute. Stir in wine. Increase heat to medium-high; boil wine for 1 to 2 minutes or until it reduces to thick, syrupy sauce. Remove skillet from heat and swirl in remaining margarine. To serve, pour sauce over turkey fillets. Makes 4 servings.

Per Serving (approx):
Calories 214
Carbohydrate 2 gm

Protein 28 gm
Sodium 126 mg

Fat 7 gm
Cholesterol 70 mg

Spicy Breakfast Sausage

1 pound ground turkey
1 egg or 2 egg whites,
   lightly beaten
1/3 cup dry bread crumbs
2 green onions, minced
1 clove garlic, minced

1/2 teaspoon crushed fennel seed
1/2 teaspoon each dried thyme
   and ground cumin
1 pinch each red pepper flakes,
   salt and ground nutmeg
1 tablespoon oil

Mix together all ingredients except oil. Form into 8 patties. Brown patties in hot oil for 4 to 5 minutes on each side. Makes 8 servings.

Per Serving (approx):
Calories 122
Carbohydrate 4 gm

Protein 12 gm
Sodium 137 mg

Fat 7 gm
Cholesterol 68 mg

Spicy Cajun Hash

2 tablespoons oil
1 to 1 1/4 pounds ground turkey
2 tablespoons butter or
   margarine
2 tablespoons flour
1 cup chopped onion
1/2 cup chopped bell pepper
1 cup chicken broth

1 1/2 tablespoons
   Worcestershire sauce
1 package (10 ounces) frozen
   corn kernels, thawed
2 cups diced cooked potato
Salt and pepper to taste
Hot pepper sauce to taste
Hot biscuits (optional)

In large skillet over medium heat, warm oil. Add turkey; sauté for 10 minutes, stirring frequently, until cooked through. Remove turkey and set aside. Add butter and flour to skillet. Cook for 4 to 5 minutes or until mixture is browned, stirring constantly. Add onion and bell pepper. Cook for 5 minutes or until vegetables are tender, stirring often. Stir in chicken broth and Worcestershire sauce; cook until thickened, stirring constantly. Add cooked turkey, corn and potato; cook for 2 to 3 minutes longer or until heated through. Season with salt, pepper and hot pepper sauce. Serve over biscuits, if desired. Makes 4 to 6 servings.

Per Serving (approx):
Calories 330
Carbohydrate 26 gm

Protein 20 gm
Sodium 444 mg

Fat 16 gm
Cholesterol 79 mg

Homemade Turkey Sausage

1 pound ground turkey
1/2 teaspoon fennel seed
1 teaspoon Italian seasoning

1 1/2 teaspoons onion powder
1/4 teaspoon ground or rubbed
   sage

Combine all ingredients well to blend flavors. Shape into 6 patties and fry in nonstick skillet coated with nonstick vegetable cooking spray until lightly browned and cooked through, 5 to 6 minutes per side.

Makes 6 servings.

Per Serving (approx):
Calories 126
Carbohydrate .5 gm

Protein 14 gm
Sodium 63 mg

Fat 7 gm
Cholesterol 46 mg

Morning Sausage and Apples

Granny Smith apples are particularly good in this dish.

1 pound turkey breakfast sausage
1/2 cup firmly packed brown sugar
1/2 cup whipping cream

1/2 teaspoon ground cinnamon
2 apples, cut into wedges
4 frozen waffles, toasted

Cut turkey into 8 patties. Place in nonstick skillet and cook over medium heat for 10 minutes, turning occasionally. Add sugar, cream, cinnamon and apples.

Cook for 5 minutes more, stirring constantly until thickened. Serve over hot waffles. Makes 4 servings.

Per Serving (approx):
Calories 452
Carbohydrate 44 gm

Protein 20 gm
Sodium 708 mg

Fat 22 gm
Cholesterol 92 mg

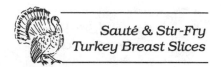

Turkey Mornay

1 pound turkey breast slices
  (approximately 8 slices)
2 eggs, beaten
2/3 cup fine dry bread crumbs
4 tablespoons oil

2 packages (3 ounces each)
  cream cheese
4 slices (3/4 ounce each)
  processed Swiss cheese
1/3 cup milk
2 tablespoons dry white wine

Dip turkey in egg; coat with bread crumbs. Heat 2 tablespoons of the oil in skillet over medium-high heat. Add half the turkey. Cook for 3 minutes; turn and cook for 2 minutes more. Place turkey on platter; cover to keep warm. Repeat with remaining oil and turkey.

Meanwhile, combine cheeses and milk in saucepan. Warm over low heat, stirring until cheeses melt and mixture is smooth. Stir in wine. Serve over turkey. Makes 4 servings.

Per Serving (approx):
Calories 597
Carbohydrate 15 gm

Protein 41 gm
Sodium 641 mg

Fat 41 gm
Cholesterol 237 mg

Turkey Slices with Green Peppercorn Sauce

1 1/4 pounds thin slices of
  turkey breast
Salt and pepper to taste
2 tablespoons each oil and butter

1 cup dry white wine
3 green onions, minced
1 tablespoon Dijon-style mustard
1 tablespoon green peppercorns

Season turkey slices and sauté in hot oil and butter for 2 minutes on each side; remove and keep warm. Add white wine, onions, mustard and peppercorns to pan and simmer for 5 minutes. Serve over turkey slices. Makes 6 servings.

Per Serving (approx):
Calories 239
Carbohydrate 1 gm

Protein 21 gm
Sodium 210 mg

Fat 14 gm
Cholesterol 61 mg

Turkey Steaks Kiev

This delicious entree comes from Kiev, where this classic recipe was born.
Now it is world famous. We have adapted it using turkey, with wonderful
results. See for yourself.

1/2 stick (1/4 cup) butter or margarine, chilled	1 egg
8 turkey breast steaks or slices (about 1 pound total)	1 teaspoon salt
	1/8 teaspoon black pepper
	3/4 cup fine dry bread crumbs
1/4 cup finely chopped parsley	Oil, for frying

Cut stick of butter into 8 pieces; chill in freezer. Meanwhile, place each
turkey steak between 2 sheets of waxed paper and pound to about 1/8
inch thickness.

Place 1 piece of butter and 1 teaspoon parsley on each pounded steak.
Fold sides to seal in butter, then roll up, securing each roll with wooden
pick. Beat egg slightly. Mix together salt, pepper and bread crumbs.

One at a time, dip rolled turkey steaks in egg, then in crumb mixture to
coat well. Place steaks in refrigerator for at least 1 hour or until thoroughly chilled.

When ready to cook, heat 1/2 inch oil in skillet to 350 degrees. Fry
rolled turkey steaks for 5 to 7 minutes or until tender and golden brown,
turning once. Drain well and serve hot.   Makes 4 servings.

Per Serving (approx):
Calories 442   *Protein 4 gm*   *Fat 41 gm*
Carbohydrate 14 gm   *Sodium 860 mg*   *Cholesterol 85 mg*

Turkey Veronique

We have enjoyed Chicken Veronique, Veal Veronique and now Turkey Veronique (with cream sauce)—a very special entree.

1 1/2 tablespoons cornstarch
Salt and pepper to taste
1 pound turkey breast tenderloins
2 to 3 tablespoons butter or
   margarine

1/3 cup finely chopped shallot
1/2 cup white wine
1 1/2 cups seedless green
   and/or red grapes
1/2 cup half-and-half

On waxed paper, combine 1 tablespoon of the cornstarch, the salt and pepper. Dust tenderloins with mixture.

In large skillet over medium heat, melt 2 tablespoons of the butter. Sauté tenderloins for about 4 minutes on each side or until golden brown. Remove tenderloins from skillet; cover to keep warm.

In same skillet cook shallot in drippings for 2 to 3 minutes or until soft, adding remaining butter if needed. Stir in wine, scraping up browned bits; bring to a boil. Add tenderloins; reduce heat to low, cover and simmer for 10 to 15 minutes. Add grapes; cook for 1 minute or until heated through.

In cup stir remaining cornstarch into half-and-half until well blended. Increase heat to medium; stir cornstarch mixture into liquid in skillet and cook until thickened, stirring constantly. Serve sauce over tenderloins.

Makes 4 servings.

Per Serving (approx):
Calories 297
Carbohydrate 17 gm

Protein 28 gm
Sodium 166 mg

Fat 13 gm
Cholesterol 101 mg

Champagne-Sauced Turkey

This sophisticated dish is best for a small dinner party because it needs some last-minute attention.

4 turkey breast tenderloins
  (approximately 1 1/4 pounds total)
2 shallots, chopped
1 1/2 cups sliced mushrooms
1/4 cup butter

2 cups Champagne
2 cups whipping cream
Salt and pepper to taste
8 ounces angel hair pasta,
  cooked and drained

Sauté turkey, shallots and mushrooms in butter until turkey is browned. Add Champagne; cover and simmer until turkey is cooked through, about 10 minutes. Remove turkey to plate; cover and keep warm. With slotted spoon, remove mushrooms and shallots to another plate.

In the same pan over high heat simmer Champagne until reduced by about half. Stir in cream and simmer until slightly thickened, about 10 to 15 minutes. Return mushrooms to pan and stir. Season with salt and pepper.

Slice turkey neatly against grain. Serve over pasta with Champagne sauce.

Makes 4 to 6 servings.

Per Serving (approx):
Calories 595
Carbohydrate 25 gm

Protein 30 gm
Sodium 251 mg

Fat 41 gm
Cholesterol 215 mg

> To meet market demand for turkeys during the holiday season, the industry "sets" more eggs during April, May and June.

Turkey Steak Diane

4 tablespoons margarine
1 pound turkey breast steaks
3 tablespoons chopped green
   onion
2 tablespoons dry sherry

2 tablespoons Worcestershire
   sauce
2 teaspoons finely chopped
   parsley

Melt 1 tablespoon of the margarine in skillet over medium heat. When margarine begins to bubble, add turkey. Cook for 3 minutes; turn. Reduce heat to medium low. Cover; cook for 5 minutes more or until juices run clear.

Meanwhile, melt another tablespoon margarine in small saucepan over medium heat. Add green onion; cook and stir for 2 to 3 minutes. Add sherry and Worcestershire sauce; cook for 2 minutes more to reduce sauce. Stir in remaining 2 tablespoons margarine. Serve sauce immediately over turkey steaks. Sprinkle with parsley.　　Makes 4 servings.

Per Serving (approx):
Calories 268　　　　*Protein 25 gm*　　　*Fat 18 gm*
Carbohydrate 1 gm　*Sodium 202 mg*　　*Cholesterol 61 mg*

Basic Turkey Schnitzel

Our personal favorite variation is Champignon Schnitzel.

6 turkey breast cutlets
Salt and pepper to taste
1/2 cup flour
2 tablespoons each butter and
  oil

1/4 cup butter
1/4 cup lemon juice
2 tablespoons chopped parsley

Flatten turkey cutlets to l/4 inch thickness by pounding between 2 sheets of plastic wrap. Salt and pepper cutlets. Dip one side in flour.

Meanwhile, heat the 2 tablespoons butter and 2 tablespoons oil in skillet. Sauté cutlets for 3 minutes on each side. Remove to warmed platter.

Add the 1/4 cup butter, lemon juice and parsley to skillet. Bring to a boil. Cook to reduce slightly, then pour over cutlets.   Makes 6 servings.

SCHNITZEL A LA HOLSTEIN: Garnish basic schnitzel with egg fried in butter and topped with crisscrossed flat anchovies. Serve with capers and chopped onion.

CHAMPIGNON SCHNITZEL: Sauté sliced mushrooms in butter; add whipping cream to make sauce and serve basic schnitzel smothered in this rich sauce.

Per Serving (approx) for basic schnitzel:
Calories 211
Carbohydrate 5 gm

Protein 6 gm
Sodium 194 mg

Fat 17 gm
Cholesterol 43 mg

California Turkey Schnitzel

When you start with turkey cutlets and use your imagination, a whole new world of "veal" cookery is open to you—at a very small price!

6 turkey breast cutlets
2 eggs, lightly beaten
1 cup dry bread crumbs or
   1/2 cup crumbs and
1/2 cup grated Parmesan cheese*

2 tablespoons each butter and
   oil
1/4 cup butter
1/4 cup lemon juice
2 tablespoons chopped parsley

Flatten turkey cutlets to 1/4 inch thickness by pounding between 2 sheets of plastic wrap. Dip in egg, then in bread crumbs. Refrigerate for 15 minutes.

Heat the butter and oil; sauté cutlets for 3 minutes on each side; remove to warmed platter. Add the 1/4 cup butter, lemon juice, and parsley to skillet; bring to a boil. Cook to reduce slightly; pour over cutlets. Serve with noodles or spaetzle. Makes 6 servings.

*Note: Salt and pepper may be needed if cheese is omitted.

Per Serving (approx):
Calories 263
Carbohydrate 13 gm

Protein 9 gm
Sodium 272 mg

Fat 19 gm
Cholesterol 114 mg

Turkey Drives

In the late 1800s, there was a concentration of turkey growers in the area known as Round Valley near Covelo (parallel with Legget and Orland in Northern California). The flocks ranged in size from 100—500 birds. When the poults were big enough to forage well, the owners brought the broods together. The journey involved traversing Ham's Pass, going through Stony Creek Valley, and ended in West Sacramento. Those in charge of the drive were usually a few adult males; they were accompanied by some boys, dogs, and a supply wagon. It took the group 75—100 days to make the 250 mile trip. Once at West Sacramento, the turkeys were either sold to customers in the capital city or placed on river boats and sent to San Francisco.

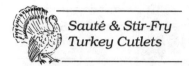

Schnitzel Florentine

6 turkey breast cutlets
1/2 cup flour
Salt and pepper to taste
2 tablespoons each butter and
   oil

1 1/2 pounds spinach, cooked
   and well drained
2 tablespoons grated Parmesan
   cheese

Flatten turkey cutlets to 1/4 inch thickness by pounding between 2 sheets of plastic wrap. Dip in flour. Salt and pepper each side.

Heat butter and oil in skillet. Sauté turkey for 3 minutes on each side. Prepare Hollandaise Sauce.

Arrange schnitzel on mound of freshly boiled and drained spinach. Top with Hollandaise Sauce. Sprinkle with Parmesan cheese and heat in oven to brown slightly. Serve with noodles, if desired.

Makes 6 servings.

HOLLANDAISE SAUCE:
Melt 1/2 cup butter over hot water in top of double broiler. Remove from heat and let cool. Blend 4 beaten egg yolks into butter. Add 1/3 cup boiling water slowly, stirring constantly. Cook over hot water, stirring constantly until thickened. Remove from heat. Stir in 3 tablespoons lemon juice, 1/4 teaspoon salt and dash of cayenne.   Makes about 1 cup.

Per Serving (approx):
Calories 359
Carbohydrate 13 gm

Protein 12 gm
Sodium 502 mg

Fat 29 gm
Cholesterol 202 mg

Peppered Turkey Medallions with Chutney Sauce

1/2 to 1 tablespoon mixed
   peppercorns
1 pound turkey breast tenderloins,
   cut into 3/4-inch medallions
1 teaspoon margarine
2 teaspoons olive oil

2 tablespoons minced green
   onion
1/4 cup reduced-sodium
   chicken bouillon
2 tablespoons brandy
1/4 cup chutney

Crush peppercorns in spice grinder, food processor or mortar with pestle. Pat peppercorns on both sides of turkey medallions. Refrigerate for 30 minutes.

In large nonstick skillet over medium heat, sauté medallions in margarine and 1 teaspoon of the oil for 4 to 5 minutes per side or until no longer pink in center. Remove medallions from pan and keep warm.

Add remaining teaspoon of oil to skillet and sauté onion for 30 seconds. Add bouillon and cook for 45 seconds to reduce liquid. Stir in brandy and cook for 1 to 2 minutes. Reduce heat to low and blend in chutney.

To serve, pour chutney sauce over medallions.   Makes 4 servings.

Per Serving (approx):
Calories 218
Carbohydrate 11 gm

Protein 28 gm
Sodium 142 mg

Fat 4 gm
Cholesterol 70 mg

Turkey Viennese

1 teaspoon paprika
1/8 teaspoon white pepper
1 1/2 pounds turkey thighs,
  skinned, boned and
  cut into 1/4-inch strips
2 tablespoons margarine
1 1/2 cups finely chopped onion

1 clove garlic, minced
1 bay leaf
1/3 cup reduced-sodium
  chicken bouillon
1/4 cup tomato sauce
1/4 cup imitation sour cream
1/2 teaspoon sugar

In small bowl mix paprika and pepper; sprinkle over turkey strips to coat.

In 3-quart saucepan over medium-high heat, sauté turkey strips in 1 tablespoon of the margarine until lightly browned; remove from pan and set aside.

In same saucepan sauté onion and garlic in remaining margarine. Cook and stir until onion begins to brown. Add bay leaf, bouillon and tomato sauce; bring to a boil. Reduce heat to medium and simmer for about 5 minutes; stir to prevent mixture from sticking to pan.

Add turkey to sauce, cover and reduce heat to low. Simmer 12 minutes or until turkey is tender. Fold sour cream and sugar into mixture; heat through. Serve with egg noodles, if desired.   Make 4 servings.

Per Serving (approx):
Calories 254
Carbohydrate 8 gm

Protein 24 gm
Sodium 271 mg

Fat 14 gm
Cholesterol 85 mg

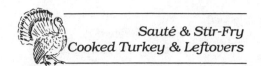

Spicy Orange Turkey

12 ounces cooked turkey breast
1/2 cup water
3 tablespoons orange juice
   concentrate
1 tablespoon lemon juice
1 teaspoon chili powder

1/2 teaspoon onion powder
4 teaspoons cornstarch
1 medium green bell pepper, cut
   into 1-inch chunks
1 large orange, peeled and
   sliced crosswise

Cut turkey into 1/8-inch slices; set aside. Combine water, orange juice concentrate, lemon juice, seasonings and cornstarch in skillet. Cook over medium heat, stirring constantly until thickened.

Layer turkey, bell pepper and orange slices in skillet. Bring to a boil; reduce heat, cover and simmer for 6 to 8 minutes.

To serve, place orange slices and bell pepper around edge of platter; place turkey in center. Stir sauce; pour small amount over turkey. Pass remaining sauce.   Makes 4 servings.

Per Serving (approx):
Calories 148
Carbohydrate 13 gm

Protein 19 gm
Sodium 43 mg

Fat 5 gm
Cholesterol 46 mg

Turkey Medallions with Cumberland Sauce

Cumberland sauce, of English origin, is customarily served with baked ham, but we think you'll like it with turkey as much as we do.

1/2 cup red or black currant
   jelly
3 tablespoons port wine
1 1/2 teaspoons Dijon mustard
4 teaspoons lemon juice
Dash of cayenne pepper
2 teaspoons margarine

2 teaspoons cornstarch
4 teaspoons cold water
2 turkey breast tenderloins
Salt and pepper to taste
2 tablespoons olive oil
1 tablespoon margarine

In small saucepan over medium-high heat, combine jelly, port wine, mustard, lemon juice, cayenne pepper and the 2 teaspoons margarine until jelly is melted.

In small bowl combine cornstarch and water. Stir into jelly mixture. Bring sauce to a boil and cook until thickened. Reduce heat and keep warm.

Cut tenderloins into medallion-shaped slices (about 3/4 inch thick). Season to taste with salt and pepper. In large skillet over medium-high heat, sauté medallions in the olive oil and 1 tablespoon margarine for about 2 1/2 minutes per side or until no longer pink in thickest part.

Spoon thin layer of sauce on each plate; arrange medallions over sauce. Garnish with sour cream, if desired. Makes 4 servings.

Per Serving (approx):
Calories 347   *Protein 27 gm*   *Fat 13 gm*
Carbohydrate 29 gm   *Sodium 144 mg*   *Cholesterol 70 mg*

Turkey Lemon Cutlets

This is a personal favorite of one of the editors of this cookbook. Besides the great taste, it is low in fat, calories and sodium. We serve it with steamed rice and slices of fruit, such as mango and pineapple.

2 tablespoons flour
1/4 teaspoon salt
1/4 teaspoon black pepper
8 turkey breast cutlets
2 tablespoons margarine

1/2 cup white wine
6 thin slices lemon
1/4 cup chopped parsley
1/4 cup chopped fresh basil

In shallow plate combine flour, salt and pepper. Dip turkey cutlets lightly in flour mixture to coat each side.

In large nonstick skillet over medium-high heat, sauté turkey in margarine for 1 to 2 minutes per side or until turkey is no longer pink in center. Remove turkey from skillet and keep warm.

In same skillet add wine, lemon slices, parsley and basil. On medium-high heat cook for 3 to 4 minutes or until sauce is slightly thickened, stirring occasionally. Return turkey to skillet; reduce heat, cover and heat for 1 to 2 minutes.   Makes 8 servings.

Per Serving (approx):
Calories 64
Carbohydrate 6 gm

Protein 1 gm
Sodium 109 mg

Fat 3 gm
Cholesterol 90 mg

Gypsy Cutlets

This started out as a Magyar (Hungarian) gypsy dish made with chicken. We made a few changes that we think you'll like.

1 pound skinless turkey breast
   cutlets, thinly sliced
2 teaspoons paprika
Salt and pepper to taste
1 1/2 tablespoons oil
1/2 cup thinly sliced onion

1 can (14 1/2 ounces) Cajun-
   or Mexican-style stewed
   tomatoes, including juice
1/4 cup sour cream substitute
   or low-fat sour cream

Season cutlets on both sides with paprika, salt and pepper. In large non-stick skillet over medium-high heat, warm oil. Add cutlets and brown for 1 minute on each side. Remove and set aside.

To same skillet add onion and sauté for 1 minute or until slightly softened. Add tomatoes and their liquid. Cook for 5 minutes or until sauce thickens, stirring often. Stir in sour cream substitute until well mixed.

Reduce heat to medium-low. Return cutlets and any juices to skillet and simmer for 1 to 2 minutes or until turkey is just cooked through. To serve, spoon sauce over turkey.   **Makes 4 servings.**

Per Serving (approx):
Calories 207   *Protein 30 gm*   *Fat 6 gm*
Carbohydrate 7 gm   *Sodium 479 mg*   *Cholesterol 70 mg*

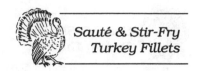

Turkey Fillets in Mustard Cream Sauce

This is one of four recipes in this book that came to us from the British Turkey Federation. We think you'll like it as much as we do.

2 tablespoons butter	1 cup dry white wine
1 tablespoon olive oil	1/3 cup light stock
4 skinless turkey fillets	1/3 cup half-and-half
(approximately 4 ounces each)	2 tablespoons Dijon mustard
1 small onion, finely	Salt and pepper to taste
chopped	

Heat butter and oil in large, deep frying pan. Add turkey fillets and cook on both sides until light brown. Add onion and cook for 2 more minutes. Pour wine and stock over fillets; cover and simmer for 15 to 20 minutes or until tender.

Remove turkey fillets from pan and keep warm. Boil liquid until reduced by half. Remove from heat, stir in half-and-half and mustard, then heat gently without boiling. Season to taste.

Strain sauce and pour over turkey. Serve with fresh vegetables, if desired.   Makes 4 servings.

Per Serving (approx):
Calories 357   *Protein 29 gm*   *Fat 22 gm*
Carbohydrate 3 gm   *Sodium 429 mg*   *Cholesterol 109 mg*

Skillet-Simmered Turkey Thighs

3 turkey thighs
(about 1 1/2 pounds each)
2 tablespoons oil
1 tablespoon margarine
1 can (10 3/4 ounces)
condensed chicken broth
1 cup chopped fresh
mushrooms
3 tablespoons instant minced
onion

1/2 cup dry white wine
Salt to taste
1 teaspoon dry mustard
1 teaspoon paprika
1/4 teaspoon dried basil
1/4 teaspoon dried sage
1/8 teaspoon black pepper
3 tablespoons cornstarch
3 tablespoons water

Brown turkey thighs in heavy skillet or Dutch oven in heated oil and margarine.

Combine broth, mushrooms, onion, wine, salt, mustard, paprika, basil, sage and pepper. Pour over browned turkey pieces and bring to a boil. Reduce heat, cover and simmer for about 2 hours or until meat is tender.

Remove turkey to serving dish, cut in serving portions and keep hot. Skim off and discard any fat from cooking liquid. Mix cornstarch with water and stir into liquid in pan. Cook, stirring, until sauce boils and thickens. Serve over turkey.   Makes 6 servings.

Per Serving (approx):
Calories 885
Carbohydrate 7 gm

Protein 127 gm
Sodium 661 mg

Fat 38 gm
Cholesterol 381 mg

Turkey Jardiniere

1 pound turkey breast slices
1 teaspoon lemon pepper
2 medium carrots, cut into
   3-inch julienne strips

1 small zucchini, cut into
   3-inch julienne strips
1 small onion, chopped
1 cup water

Pound turkey between pieces of plastic wrap. Sprinkle turkey with lemon pepper; set aside.

Combine vegetables and water in saucepan. Bring to a boil; reduce heat, cover and simmer for 5 minutes or until tender-crisp.

Remove vegetables, reserving liquid in pan. Place vegetables on turkey. Roll up and secure with toothpicks. Cook turkey rolls in butter in skillet over medium heat for 15 minutes, turning frequently until evenly browned. Prepare sauce and serve over turkey. Makes 4 servings.

WINE-LEMON SAUCE:
To 2/3 cup reserved liquid from vegetables, add 2 tablespoons white wine, 1 1/2 teaspoons cornstarch, 1 teaspoon lemon juice and 1/4 teaspoon grated lemon zest. Cook over medium heat, stirring constantly until thickened.

Per Serving (approx):
Calories 195
Carbohydrate 6 gm

Protein 28 gm
Sodium 309 mg

Fat 6 gm
Cholesterol 70 mg

Southern Fried Turkey with Gravy

2 pounds turkey wings	1 egg, beaten
1/2 cup flour	1 cup oil
1/2 teaspoon salt	1 cup milk
1 teaspoon black pepper	

Cut turkey at joint to separate middle wing portion from wing drumette. Combine flour, salt and pepper in shallow dish. Reserve 1 tablespoon flour mixture for gravy. Coat turkey with egg, then with flour mixture.

Fry turkey in hot oil in skillet over medium-high heat for about 10 minutes, turning to brown evenly. Reduce heat to low. Cover and simmer for 1 hour.

Remove cover; increase heat to medium-high. Cook for 10 minutes more, turning occasionally to crisp. Place turkey on platter.

Make gravy by pouring all but 1 tablespoon oil out of skillet. Stir in reserved flour mixture. Cook and stir for 1 minute. Gradually add milk. Cook and stir over medium until thickened. Serve with turkey.

Makes 4 servings.

Per Serving (approx):
Calories 965
Carbohydrate 15 gm

Protein 49 gm
Sodium 437 mg

Fat 78 gm
Cholesterol 160 mg

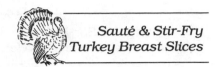

Turkey Creole

3 tablespoons butter
1 pound turkey breast slices
1 green bell pepper, cut into chunks
2 stalks celery, sliced
1 medium onion, cut into wedges
2 tomatoes, cut into chunks

1 can (15 ounces) tomato sauce
1/4 teaspoon each dried thyme,
  black pepper, paprika
  and garlic powder
1/8 teaspoon cayenne pepper

Melt 1 tablespoon of the butter in skillet. When butter begins to brown, add half the turkey. Cook for 3 minutes; turn and cook for 2 minutes more. Place turkey on platter; cover to keep warm. Repeat with 1 more tablespoon butter and remaining turkey.

In same skillet melt remaining 1 tablespoon butter over medium heat. Add bell pepper, celery and onion. Cook for 3 minutes or until vegetables are tender-crisp, stirring frequently. Stir in tomatoes, tomato sauce and seasonings. Bring to a boil; reduce heat and simmer for 15 minutes. Serve over turkey and rice. Makes 4 servings.

Per Serving (approx):
Calories 510
Carbohydrate 62 gm

Protein 36 gm
Sodium 1191 mg

Fat 13 gm
Cholesterol 86 mg

Technical advances in turkey genetics, production and processing have created a turkey which produces a pound of meat, using a smaller amount of feed, in less time than most other domestic meat-producing animals.

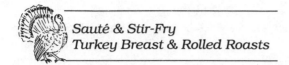
Almond-Crusted Turkey Steaks

1 turkey half breast
   (about 2 pounds)
1/2 cup raw almonds
1/4 cup grated Parmesan
   cheese
1/4 teaspoon dried basil

1/4 teaspoon paprika
Salt to taste
3 tablespoons each butter and
   oil, divided
1/2 cup white wine
2 teaspoons lemon juice

Remove skin from turkey and cut meat in half-inch slices parallel to top of breast. Place slices between sheets of waxed paper and pound to about 1/4 inch thickness.

Grind or grate almonds. Mix with cheese, basil, paprika and salt on sheet of waxed paper. Dip turkey slices, one at a time, into mixture, coating both sides.

Heat 1 tablespoon each butter and oil in 10-inch skillet. Add turkey slices to cover bottom of skillet; brown over medium heat, turning once. Cook each slice for about 4 minutes.

Remove turkey to heated serving platter. Add remaining butter and oil, and cook remaining turkey. Add wine and lemon juice to skillet and boil rapidly until very slightly thickened. Spoon over steaks.

Makes 4 to 6 servings.

Per Serving (approx):
Calories 648
Carbohydrate 4 gm

Protein 55 gm
Sodium 307 mg

Fat 43 gm
Cholesterol 151 mg

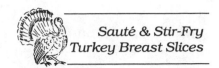

Turkey Slices Orangerie

Visions of duck a l'orange come to mind with this easy recipe for breast of turkey slices and a few simple ingredients. This dish takes just twenty minutes to prepare but is a classic in its own right.

1 to 1 1/4 pounds turkey breast slices	3/4 cup chicken broth
Salt and pepper to taste	1/3 cup sherry
1/3 cup flour	2 tablespoons orange marmalade
3 tablespoons butter	1/4 cup whipping cream
1 onion, chopped	

Dredge turkey slices in seasoned flour. Brown turkey in butter in skillet over medium-high heat. Add onion, chicken broth and sherry to skillet. Cover and simmer for 15 minutes. Remove turkey from pan; set aside and keep warm.

Add orange marmalade and cream to pan juices; simmer for about 5 minutes or until thickened. Serve sauce over turkey slices.

Makes 4 servings.

Per Serving (approx):
Calories 388   *Protein 27 gm*   *Fat 19 gm*
Carbohydrate 21 gm   *Sodium 518 mg*   *Cholesterol 98 mg*

Turkey and Broccoli Stir-Fry

1 pound turkey breast cutlets,
  cut into 1/2-inch strips
1 tablespoon dry white wine
  or sherry
2 tablespoons reduced-sodium
  soy sauce
1 cup reduced-sodium
  chicken bouillon
1 tablespoon cornstarch

6 tablespoons slivered almonds
3 tablespoons oil
1/3 cup thinly sliced green
  onion
2 cloves garlic, minced
1 pound broccoli, cut
  into 1-inch pieces
1/2 pound mushrooms,
  sliced

In medium bowl combine turkey, wine and 1 tablespoon of the soy sauce.
Set aside.

In small bowl, combine bouillon, remaining soy sauce and cornstarch.
Set aside.

In wok or large skillet over medium-high heat, stir-fry almonds in 2 tablespoons of the oil, stirring to coat. Add turkey with marinade and stir-fry
until turkey loses pink color and almonds are lightly browned. Remove
from pan.

Add remaining oil to pan and stir-fry onion, garlic and broccoli until
vegetables are tender-crisp. Add mushrooms and stir-fry for an additional minute. Fold in turkey and almonds. Add bouillon mixture and
cook and stir until thickened.   Makes 6 servings.

Per Serving (approx):
Calories 246   *Protein 23 gm*   *Fat 13 gm*
Carbohydrate 10 gm   *Sodium 286 mg*   *Cholesterol 47 mg*

POT ROASTS & STEWS

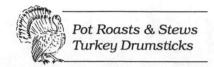

Drumsticks with Sauerkraut

In this main dish that serves four, it's the oven that does most of the work.

3 1/2 cups sauerkraut
1 apple, peeled, cored and sliced
1 medium onion, chopped
Brown sugar to taste
4 turkey drumsticks
   (about 3 pounds total)

Melted butter or margarine
Salt and pepper to taste
1/4 cup catsup
1 tablespoon Worcestershire
   sauce
Sweet potato or banana squash
   chunks (optional)

Drain sauerkraut and spread over bottom of large casserole or baking pan big enough to accommodate drumsticks. Mix in apple and onion. Taste; if too sour to suit you, add sprinkling of brown sugar.

Arrange drumsticks on top, pushing them down into mixture. Brush tops with butter and sprinkle with salt and pepper. Stir catsup and Worcestershire sauce together and spread over each drumstick. Cover pan with lid or foil.

Bake at 325 degrees for 1 hour. Uncover long enough to dot drumsticks with a little more butter, if necessary. Replace lid and bake for about 45 minutes longer or until meat is fork tender.

During last hour of baking, sweet potatoes or pieces of banana squash can be added to the casserole as it bakes, if you wish. Dinner, then, might be drumsticks and kraut, sweet potatoes or squash.

Makes 4 servings.

Per Serving (approx):
Calories 630
Carbohydrate 25 gm

Protein 71 gm
Sodium 1770 mg

Fat 27 gm
Cholesterol 215 mg

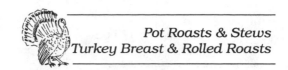

Cape Cod Turkey Roast

1 turkey breast (1 1/2 to 2 pounds)
2 cans (14 ounces each)
  chicken broth
1 bay leaf
1/2 teaspoon dried summer savory

2 medium onions, quartered
2 carrots, quartered
1/2 pound new potatoes, halved
1 cup fresh or frozen broccoli
  florets or

Place roast, broth and seasonings in 4-quart Dutch oven. Cover and simmer for 1 1/2 to 2 1/2 hours or until turkey is no longer pink and meat thermometer reaches 180 degrees. Add onions, carrots and potatoes; cook for 20 minutes more. Add broccoli; cook for 10 minutes. Slice roast; serve with vegetables and broth.　　　Makes 4 to 6 servings.

Per Serving (approx):
Calories 102
Carbohydrate 19 gm

Protein 4 gm
Sodium 823 mg

Fat 1 gm
Cholesterol 2 mg

Cranberry Turkey Roast

2 tablespoons flour
1/4 teaspoon black pepper
1 boneless turkey breast
2 tablespoons oil
1/4 cup chopped onion

1 1/2 cups fresh cranberries
  or canned whole berry
  cranberry sauce
1/2 cup orange juice
3 tablespoons sugar, or to taste*
1 teaspoon grated orange zest

On waxed paper combine flour and pepper. Coat turkey breast with flour mixture. In Dutch oven over medium heat, warm oil. Brown roast in oil until golden. Remove and set aside; pour off all but 1 tablespoon oil. In remaining oil over medium heat, cook onion for 3 minutes, stirring frequently. Add cranberries, orange juice, sugar and orange zest; bring to a boil. Cook for 2 to 3 minutes. Return turkey to Dutch oven and cover with cranberry mixture. Reduce heat to low, cover and simmer, turning turkey once or twice, for 30 to 40 minutes.　　　Makes 6 servings.

*Note: If using canned cranberry sauce, sugar may be omitted.

Per Serving (approx):
Calories 229
Carbohydrate 15 gm

Protein 27 gm
Sodium 163 mg

Fat 6 gm
Cholesterol 70 mg

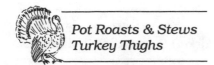

Dutch Oven Pot Roast

2 pounds turkey thighs,
  skin removed
2 small onions, quartered
1 tablespoon oil
1/2 cup reduced-sodium
  chicken bouillon
2 cloves garlic, minced
1/4 teaspoon salt
1/2 teaspoon dried basil
1/2 teaspoon black pepper

1/4 teaspoon dried thyme
4 small potatoes, peeled and
  cut in half
4 small carrots, cut into chunks
1/2 pound cabbage, cut into
  wedges
1 tablespoon cornstarch
1/4 cup cold water
2 tablespoons chopped parsley

In 5-quart Dutch oven over medium-high heat, brown turkey thighs and onions for 4 to 5 minutes in oil, turning thighs after 3 minutes. Add bouillon, garlic, salt, basil, pepper and thyme. Bring to a boil, reduce heat to low, cover and cook for 30 minutes or until turkey is tender.

Remove thighs from pan; add potatoes and carrots. Place turkey thighs over vegetables. Return mixture to a boil; reduce heat to low, cover and cook for 15 minutes or until vegetables are tender. Add cabbage; cover and cook for 8 to 10 minutes or until cabbage is fork tender.

Remove turkey and vegetables to platter. Keep warm. In small bowl combine cornstarch and water; stir into hot pan juices and cook for 1 minute over medium heat or until mixture is thickened.

To serve, pour sauce over turkey and vegetables. Garnish witn parsley.

Makes 4 servings.

Per Serving (approx):
Calories 339
Carbohydrate 34 gm

Protein 30 gm
Sodium 340 mg

Fat 9 gm
Cholesterol 97 mg

Italian Turkey with Vegetables

2 pounds turkey drumsticks
1 can (14 1/2 ounces) stewed
   tomatoes
1 teaspoon dried Italian seasoning
1/8 teaspoon garlic powder

1 package (16 ounces) frozen
   vegetable blend of your choice
2 tablespoons cornstarch
2 tablespoons grated Parmesan
   cheese

Rinse turkey and place in Dutch oven. Add tomatoes, herbs and garlic. Cover and bake in 350 degree oven for 1 1/2 hours. Add vegetables and re-cover. Bake for 30 minutes more. Remove pot from oven; remove turkey and keep warm. Blend a small amount of cooking liquid with cornstarch to form paste. Add to Dutch oven. Cook over medium heat, stirring constantly, until thickened. Serve with turkey; sprinkle with cheese.

Makes 4 servings.

Per Serving (approx):
Calories 453   *Protein 50 gm*   *Fat 17 gm*
Carbohydrate 26 gm   *Sodium 482 mg*   *Cholesterol 137 mg*

Pot Roast with Olives

3 pounds turkey drumsticks
   (2 or 3 drumsticks)
1/4 cup flour
2 tablespoons oil
2 large cloves garlic, thinly sliced
1 green bell pepper, chopped

2 medium onions, cut into
   wedges
1/2 cup minced parsley
2 cups dry white wine
1/2 cup sliced stuffed Spanish
   olives

Dip drumsticks into water; coat thickly with flour and brown in oil in Dutch oven. Drain off excess oil. Arrange garlic, bell pepper, onion and parsley around drumsticks. Pour in wine, cover and bring to a boil. Simmer for 2 to 2 1/4 hours until very tender, turning once or twice for even cooking. Add 1/2 to 1 cup water if necessary. Add olives during last 15 minutes. Separate meat from bones and serve with cooking liquid.

Makes 4 servings.

Per Serving (approx):
Calories 724   *Protein 70 gm*   *Fat 33 gm*
Carbohydrate 19 gm   *Sodium 624 mg*   *Cholesterol 202 mg*

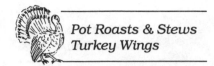

Garden Fresh Turkey Skillet Dinner

Versatile turkey wings are joined by garden fresh vegetables in this very simple recipe. If you don't like zucchini, use some other vegetable!

4 turkey wings
  (about 3/4 pound each)
2 tablespoons butter or margarine
1 tablespoon oil
1 medium onion, thinly sliced
1 large clove garlic, minced
2 large ripe tomatoes, coarsely
  chopped (about 2 cups)

1/4 cup chopped parsley
2 teaspoons chopped fresh
  tarragon or 1/2 teaspoon
  dried, crushed
Salt and pepper to taste
2 medium zucchini, each cut
  into 8 chunks

Using sharp knife cut each turkey wing into 2 pieces at elbow joint. Rinse and pat dry. Melt butter with oil in large skillet. Sauté turkey wings until golden on all sides; remove from skillet. Lightly sauté onion and garlic. Add tomatoes, parsley and tarragon, stirring to combine. Bring to a boil.

Return turkey wings to skillet. Sprinkle with salt and pepper. Reduce heat, cover and simmer for 1 to 1 1/4 hours or until turkey is tender. Add zucchini and continue cooking, covered, for 20 minutes or until zucchini is tender. Makes 4 servings.

Per Serving (approx):
Calories 535   *Protein 51 gm*   *Fat 32 gm*
Carbohydrate 10 gm   *Sodium 280 mg*   *Cholesterol 161 mg*

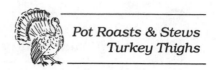

Country Pot Roast

2 turkey thighs (2 to 3 1/2
  pounds total)*
Salt and pepper to taste
1/2 cup finely chopped onion
2 cloves garlic, minced
1/2 teaspoon crumbled dried basil
1/4 teaspoon dried thyme
1 cup chicken or turkey broth

3 medium potatoes,
  peeled and halved
6 medium carrots,
  cut into chunks
1 tablespoon cornstarch
1/4 cup cold water
2 tablespoons chopped parsley

Rinse turkey and pat dry. Place skin side up in nonstick Dutch oven. Salt and pepper to taste. Bake in pre-heated 450 degree oven for 25 minutes or until skin is crisp. Drain and discard any fat.

Add onion, garlic, basil, thyme and broth to pot. Cover and simmer over low heat (or bake at 375 degrees) until turkey is nearly tender, about 1/2 hour. Add potatoes and carrots. Cover and cook until vegetables are tender, about 20 minutes.

Remove turkey and vegetables to platter and keep warm. Skim any fat from pan juices and discard. Mix cornstarch and cold water and stir into simmering pan juices. Cook, stirring, until sauce is thickened. Garnish with parsley.   Makes 4 servings.

*Note: Thighs may be boned before cooking.

Per Serving (approx):
Calories 143
Carbohydrate 8 gm

Protein 18 gm
Sodium 57 mg

Fat 5 gm
Cholesterol 56 mg

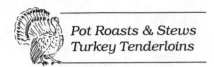

Poached Turkey Tenderloins

Make this recipe on a weekend and serve it when you have little time to cook. It stores nicely in the refrigerator for two days.

2 turkey breast tenderloins
   (1 1/4 to 1 1/2 pounds total)
1/2 cup chopped celery
   with leaves
1/4 cup sliced green onion

3 tablespoons chopped fresh
   tarragon or 1 teaspoon dried,
   crushed
1/4 teaspoon salt
1/4 teaspoon white pepper
3/4 cup white wine

In large skillet arrange tenderloins in single layer. Add celery, onion, tarragon, salt, pepper and wine. Add water to just cover tenderloins.

Cover skillet and simmer mixture over low heat for 40 minutes or until tenderloins are done. Remove tenderloins and keep warm. Increase heat under pan and reduce poaching liquid to about 1 cup. Serve over tenderloins, or store reserved poaching liquid, covered, in refrigerator.

Makes 4 servings.

Per Serving (approx):
Calories 180
Carbohydrate 0 gm

Protein 37 gm
Sodium 197 mg

Fat 2 gm
Cholesterol 97 mg

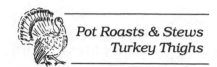

Garlic Slow-Cooker Turkey

1 1/4 pounds skinless,
   boneless turkey thighs
Salt and pepper to taste
1 tablespoon olive oil

1 head garlic, separated,
   and cloves peeled
1/2 cup dry white wine
1/2 cup reduced-sodium
   chicken broth

Season turkey lightly with salt and generously with pepper. In large skillet over medium-high heat, warm oil. Add thighs and brown for about 10 minutes.

Place turkey in slow cooker and add remaining ingredients. Cook on medium to high setting for 2 1/2 to 3 1/2 hours. Remove garlic cloves from pot. Crush and return to juices if desired. Serve juices over meat.

Makes 5 servings.

Per Serving (approx):
Calories 188
Carbohydrate 5 gm

Protein 24 gm
Sodium 165 mg

Fat 7 gm
Cholesterol 85 mg

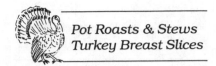

Turkey Creole with Mushrooms

We wanted a Creole recipe with a low cholesterol count, so we used turkey. We think you'll be as pleased as we were with the results.

1 teaspoon corn oil	1 green bell pepper, diced
1/4 pound mushrooms, sliced	1 can (16 ounces) chopped
4 tablespoons dry white wine	stewed tomatoes
1 onion, minced	1 pound boneless turkey breast
1 clove garlic, minced	slices, cutlets or tenderloin
1 small bay leaf	steaks, 1/4 to 1/2 inch thick

Preheat oil in nonstick skillet over high heat. Add mushrooms and cook until browned. Stir in remaining ingredients except turkey. Simmer, uncovered, for 5 to 6 minutes. Remove bay leaf.

Arrange turkey in single layer in shallow baking dish. Spoon sauce over top. Bake turkey, uncovered, in preheated 375 degree oven for about 15 minutes, basting occasionally. For cutlets that are thinner, cook less time.   Makes 4 servings.

Per Serving (approx):
Calories 297
Carbohydrate 11 gm

Protein 40 gm
Sodium 223 mg

Fat 8 gm
Cholesterol 56 mg

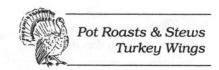

Oven-Barbecued Turkey Wings

So-very-inexpensive turkey wings become gourmet fare in this recipe.

4 turkey wings (about 3 pounds)
1/2 teaspoon smoke salt
2 tablespoons oil
1 can (15 ounces) tomato sauce
1/4 cup vinegar

1 teaspoon chili powder
1/4 teaspoon black pepper
1/8 teaspoon garlic powder
1 can (8 ounces) pineapple
    slices (liquid reserved)

Sprinkle turkey wings with smoke salt. Brown slowly on all sides in heated oil. Pour off and discard any fat in pan.

Combine tomato sauce, vinegar, chili powder, pepper, garlic powder and 1/4 cup syrup drained from pineapple slices. Pour over browned wings and bring to a boil.

Cover pan and bake at 350 degrees for about 1 1/4 hours, basting once or twice. Uncover, and skim off and discard any fat on sauce. Top each wing with pineapple slice. Bake, uncovered, for 15 minutes longer.

Makes 4 large servings.

Per Serving (approx):
Calories 667
Carbohydrate 17 gm

Protein 67 gm
Sodium 1131 mg

Fat 37 gm
Cholesterol 193 mg

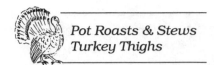

Turkey Navarin

The original French recipe calls for lamb. We use turkey thighs. Just as good? No, we think it is better.

1 3/4 pounds boneless
   turkey thighs
2 tablespoons oil
Black pepper to taste
2 tablespoons flour
1/4 teaspoon sugar
2 1/2 cups beef broth
1/2 cup white wine
1 tablespoon tomato paste
1 clove garlic, minced

1 or 2 sprigs fresh rosemary or
   1/4 teaspoon dried
1 or 2 sprigs fresh thyme or
   1/4 teaspoon dried
6 to 8 small potatoes,
   scrubbed but unpeeled
16 pearl onions, peeled
12 baby carrots, peeled
1 1/2 cups fresh or frozen peas
Salt and pepper to taste
1 tablespoon chopped parsley

Cut turkey into 1 1/2-inch cubes. In large skillet over medium-high heat, warm oil. Add turkey; sprinkle with pepper to taste. Cook for 6 to 8 minutes or until browned on all sides, turning occasionally.

Remove turkey from skillet and set aside. Reduce heat to medium; stir flour and sugar into drippings in pan. Cook for 2 to 3 minutes or until flour is a rich amber color, stirring constantly. Add beef broth, wine, tomato paste and garlic. Stir well, scraping bottom of pan to incorporate browned bits. Return turkey and any juices to pan. Tie herb sprigs together with kitchen string and add to skillet, or stir in dried herbs. Reduce heat to low; cover partially and simmer for 15 minutes.

Cut potatoes in halves or quarters: stir into pan with onions and carrots. Continue simmering, partially covered, for 20 minutes. Add peas and simmer for 6 to 8 minutes longer or until turkey and vegetables are tender. To serve, season with salt and pepper to taste and sprinkle with minced parsley. Makes 4 servings.

Per Serving (approx):
Calories 880   *Protein 56 gm*   *Fat 18 gm*
Carbohydrate 98 gm   *Sodium 763 mg*   *Cholesterol 112 mg*

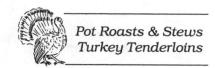

Light and Easy Turkey Tenderloin

1/2 cup carrot, julienne sliced
  to 1/4 inch
1 turkey breast tenderloin
  (approximately 1/2 pound)
2 green onions, sliced
2 slices red or green bell pepper

1/8 teaspoon garlic powder
1/8 teaspoon dried rosemary
1/8 teaspoon salt
Dash of black pepper
1 tablespoon white wine

On 12- by 16-inch foil rectangle, place carrots and top with tenderloin. Arrange onions and bell pepper slices over tenderloin. Sprinkle with garlic powder, rosemary, salt and black pepper.

Fold up edges of foil to form bowl shape. Pour wine over ingredients. Bring 2 opposite sides of foil together above food; fold edges over and down to lock fold. Fold short ends up and over.

Place foil bundle on small baking sheet and bake in preheated 400 degree oven for 20 to 25 minutes or until meat reaches 170 degrees. Check for doneness by opening foil bundle carefully to insert meat thermometer in thickest part of meat.   Makes 2 servings.

Per Serving (approx):
Calories 150	*Protein 27 gm*	*Fat 2 gm*
Carbohydrate 5 gm	*Sodium 226 mg*	*Cholesterol 70 mg*

The breast meat of roasted turkeys ranks higher in protein than any of the other cooked meats.

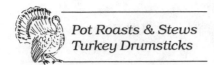

Drumstick Dinner

4 turkey drumsticks
2 tablespoons oil
1 tablespoon butter
1 medium onion, sliced
1 can (16 ounces) stewed
   tomatoes
3 cubes chicken bouillon
1/2 teaspoon garlic salt
1/2 teaspoon dried oregano

1/2 teaspoon crumbled
   dried basil
8 small or 4 large potatoes
2 or 3 zucchini, sliced
   3/4 inch thick
1 tablespoon cornstarch
2 tablespoons warm water
2 tablespoons chopped parsley

Brown drumsticks on all sides in oil and butter in skillet. Remove to large baking pan and top with onion slices. In same skillet heat tomatoes with bouillon cubes and seasonings. Pour over drumsticks. Cover pan with foil, crimping to edge of pan. Bake for 2 hours at 325 degrees or until almost tender, basting once or twice.

Meanwhile, boil potatoes; slip off skins. Tuck potatoes and zucchini in and around meat and spoon liquid over them. Cover and bake for 30 minutes longer. Mix cornstarch and water and stir into hot sauce. Bake for 5 to 10 minutes to thicken slightly. Sprinkle with chopped parsley.

Makes 4 servings.

Per Serving (approx):
Calories 987   *Protein 79 gm*   *Fat 35 gm*
Carbohydrate 90 gm   *Sodium 1411 mg*   *Cholesterol 216 mg*

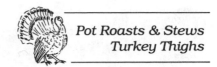

Aprés Ski Turkey Stew

1 1/2 pounds turkey thighs, boned, skinned and cut into 1-inch cubes
1 tablespoon oil
1 cup peeled tomato, cut into chunks
1 cup green bell pepper, thinly sliced
1 clove garlic, minced

2 tablespoons lemon juice
1 teaspoon dried Italian seasoning or 1/2 teaspoon dried basil and 1/2 teaspoon dried oregano
Salt and pepper to taste
2 1/2 teaspoons cornstarch
3 tablespoons cold water

In 3-quart saucepan over medium-high heat, sauté turkey in oil on all sides.

Add tomato, bell pepper, garlic, lemon juice, seasonings, salt and pepper. Cover, reduce heat to low, and simmer for about 12 minutes or until turkey is fork tender.

In small bowl mix cornstarch and cold water. Stir into hot turkey mixture and cook until thickened.

Serve over noodles, if desired. Makes 4 servings.

Per Serving (approx):
Calories 190
Carbohydrate 5 gm

Protein 23 gm
Sodium 100 mg

Fat 8 gm
Cholesterol 85 mg

Tenderness depends on the age of the bird when processed. All birds marketed at retail are classified and labeled as "Young Turkey." The proper cooking method will yield a moist, juicy, turkey.

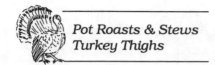

Hungarian Goulash

Americans have taken goulash and made it their own but often omit sauerkraut and sour cream, two of the most important ingredients in this famous Hungarian stew. Here it is—the original.

1 1/4 pounds boneless turkey
   thighs
2 tablespoons oil
3/4 cup chopped onion
4 teaspoons paprika
1 can (14 ounces) reduced-sodium
   chicken broth
2 tablespoons tomato paste

1 can (8 ounces) sauerkraut,
   drained
1/4 teaspoon caraway seeds
Salt and pepper to taste
1/2 cup sour cream
Buttered noodles
Chopped parsley (optional)

Trim thighs and cut into 2-inch pieces. In Dutch oven over medium heat, warm oil. Add turkey, in batches if necessary to avoid crowding; cook for 6 to 8 minutes or until well browned on all sides. Remove turkey and set aside.

Stir onion into pan; sauté for about 2 minutes or until softened. Add paprika and stir well. Stir in broth, tomato paste, sauerkraut and caraway seeds. Add salt and pepper to taste.

Toss turkey with sauerkraut. Cover pan partially with lid and reduce heat to very low; simmer for 40 to 50 minutes or until turkey is tender, stirring occasionally. Just before serving, stir in sour cream; do not boil.

Serve on bed of buttered noodles and sprinkle with parsley, if desired.

                                              Makes 4 servings.

Per Serving (approx):
Calories 425
Carbohydrate 23 gm

Protein 34 gm
Sodium 603 mg

Fat 22 gm
Cholesterol 117 mg

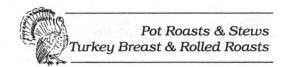

Herb-Sauced Turkey and Vegetables

This elegant one-dish meal is for company or for your family.

2 quarts turkey or chicken broth
1 turkey breast (2 1/2 pounds)
1 onion, chopped
1 cup chopped fresh basil
10 sprigs parsley
3/4 teaspoon dried thyme
1 pound new potatoes,
  quartered
1 pound pearl onions, peeled

2 bunches baby carrots,
  trimmed
3/4 pound green beans,
  trimmed and strings removed
4 tablespoons butter
2 tablespoons flour
1/3 cup each Dijon-style
  mustard and whipping cream
Salt and pepper to taste

Bring broth to a boil. Add turkey breast, onion, basil, parsley and thyme. Reduce heat; cover and simmer for 1 1/2 to 2 hours. Add potatoes and pearl onions during last 20 minutes. Add baby carrots and green beans during last 10 minutes. Drain turkey and vegetables; reserve broth. Remove skin from turkey. Slice turkey and arrange with vegetables on platter; keep warm.

Melt butter in saucepan; whisk in flour. Cook for 5 minutes. Add 2 cups reserved broth. Cook for 5 minutes, stirring constantly until thickened. Reduce heat; add mustard and cream. Season with salt and pepper. Serve turkey with vegetables and sauce.   Makes 6 servings.

Per Serving (approx):
Calories 571
Carbohydrate 38 gm

Protein 49 gm
Sodium 671 mg

Fat 25 gm
Cholesterol 134 mg

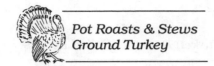
Turkey Tortilla Stew

1 1/2 pounds ground turkey
1 medium onion, finely chopped
2 cloves garlic, minced
2 teaspoons oil
2 1/2 cups water
1 can (16 ounces) no-salt-
　added tomatoes
1 can (15 ounces) pinto beans in
　chili sauce, undrained

1 can (10 ounces) reduced-
　sodium tomato soup
1 cup whole corn kernels
1 can (4 ounces) green chilies,
　chopped
1/4 teaspoon black pepper
12 corn tortillas (6 inch), cut
　into 1/4-inch strips
2 tablespoons oil

In large Dutch oven over medium-high heat, sauté turkey, onion and garlic in oil for 5 minutes or until turkey is no longer pink. Add water, tomatoes, beans, soup, corn, chilies and black pepper. Heat until mixture is bubbly; reduce heat to low and simmer for 30 minutes.

In large skillet over medium-high heat, sauté tortilla strips in the 2 tablespoons oil for 30 seconds or until lightly browned and crisp. Drain on paper towels. Add tortilla strips to turkey stew just before serving to let them soften.   Makes 6 servings.

Per Serving (approx):
Calories 497
Carbohydrate 55 gm

Protein 31 gm
Sodium 761 mg

Fat 17 gm
Cholesterol 82 mg

PASTAS & GRAINS

Meatballs in a Pasta Crown

The ring mold makes an "everyday" meal into a special occasion.

1 pound ground turkey
1 cup finely chopped onion
1 clove garlic, minced
3 tablespoons dried parsley flakes
1/2 cup seasoned bread crumbs
1/4 cup grated Parmesan cheese
Salt and pepper to taste

1 tablespoon oil
3 cups spaghetti sauce
8 ounces thin spaghetti
1/2 teaspoon dried Italian
   seasoning
1/2 cup grated mozzarella
   cheese

In medium bowl combine turkey, onion, garlic, 1 tablespoon of the parsley, the bread crumbs, Parmesan cheese, salt and pepper. Shape mixture into 12 meatballs.

In large skillet over medium-high heat, sauté meatballs in oil. Reduce heat to medium-low, cover skillet and cook for 6 to 8 minutes or until meatballs are no longer pink in center.

In large saucepan over low heat, warm spaghetti sauce. Prepare spaghetti according to package directions. Drain; do not rinse. Return spaghetti to cooking pan. Stir in remaining parsley, Italian seasoning and mozzarella cheese.

Arrange meatballs in bottom of lightly greased ring mold. Top with spaghetti, pressing firmly to mold spaghetti around meatballs. Allow mold to stand for 1 to 2 minutes. Invert mold onto large platter. Spoon spaghetti sauce into center of pasta crown.   Makes 6 servings.

Per Serving (approx):
Calories 501
Carbohydrate 58 gm

Protein 26 gm
Sodium 1030 mg

Fat 19 gm
Cholesterol 59 mg

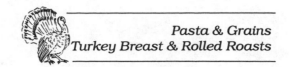

Turkey with Wild Rice

1 box (6 3/4 ounces) instant
    long-grain and wild rice mix
2 tablespoons slivered
    almonds

3 1/4 cups water
1 turkey breast (2 pounds)
1 box (10 ounces) frozen
    chopped broccoli, thawed

Combine seasoning packet from rice, almonds and 1 cup of the water in 3-quart casserole. Add turkey. Bake in 325 degree oven for 1 1/2 hours. Stir in the remaining 2 1/4 cups hot water, rice and broccoli. Bake for 30 minutes or to internal temperature of 170 degrees. Let stand for 10 minutes before slicing. Wrap and refrigerate any remaining turkey and rice.   Makes 4 servings.

Per Serving (approx):
Calories 515
Carbohydrate 41 gm

Protein 52 gm
Sodium 120 mg

Fat 16 gm
Cholesterol 122 mg

Per Capita Consumption of Turkey*

Year	Pounds	Year	Pounds
1974	8.7	1985	11.6
1975	8.3	1986	12.9
1976	8.9	1987	14.7
1977	8.8	1988	15.7
1978	8.7	1989	16.6
1979	9.3	1990	17.6
1980	10.3	1991	18.0
1981	10.6	1992	18.0
1982	10.6	1993	18.1**
1983	11.0	1994	18.2**
1984	11.0		

*Statistical series revised by USDA in 1992 to reflect inspected turkeys consumed
**Estimated by NTF

Versatile Turkey Sauce

This sauce is good with pasta, noodles or rice. Add basil and oregano for Italian-style turkey spaghetti sauce, or add cumin and kidney beans for chili con turkey.

1 pound ground turkey
1 medium onion, chopped
1/2 medium green bell pepper, chopped
1/4 cup sliced celery
1 can (14 1/2 ounces) stewed tomatoes

1 can (12 ounces) tomato juice
1 can (6 ounces) tomato paste
1 tablespoon Worcestershire sauce
1/2 teaspoon salt
1/4 teaspoon garlic powder

Place turkey and fresh vegetables in large skillet. Cook over medium heat for 10 minutes, stirring and separating turkey as it cooks. Add remaining ingredients. Bring to a boil; reduce heat and simmer for 5 minutes, stirring occasionally. Serve over pasta or rice.

Makes 6 servings.

Per Serving (approx):
Calories 185
Carbohydrate 16 gm

Protein 16 gm
Sodium 666 mg

Fat 6 gm
Cholesterol 55 mg

Turkey Tetrazzini

Don't pass up this recipe. Sure, it takes some time and effort, but it's well worth it.

1 large turkey thigh
   (about 2 pounds) or
   2 small turkey thighs
   (about 1 pound each)
3/4 cup water
1 cube chicken bouillon
8 ounces medium noodles
   (about 4 cups cooked)
1/3 cup finely chopped
   onion
1/4 cup butter
1/4 cup flour

1 can (13 ounces) evaporated
   milk
1 can (4 ounces) sliced
   mushrooms, undrained
1/2 teaspoon salt
Dash each of ground nutmeg
   and black pepper
1/4 cup dry sherry
1 cup grated Swiss cheese
1/2 cup sliced almonds
1 cup buttered soft bread
   crumbs

Place turkey thigh in large pot with water and bouillon cube. Cover tightly and cook for 1 to 1 1/2 hours or until meat is tender. Let cool sufficiently to handle. Remove skin and bone; cut meat into bite-sized chunks. Measure cooking liquid (should be about 1 cup); add water if necessary to make this amount.

Cook noodles in boiling salted water according to package directions. Meanwhile, prepare sauce. Sauté onion lightly in butter. Blend in flour. Slowly stir in milk, the 1 cup cooking liquid and mushrooms. Cook, stirring, until sauce boils and thickens. Stir in salt, nutmeg, pepper and sherry. Drain noodles.

Place half the noodles in 2 1/2-quart baking dish. Add half the turkey, half the sauce and half the cheese. Sprinkle with 1/4 cup almond slices. Repeat layers, topping with buttered crumbs. Bake at 350 degrees for about 20 to 30 minutes or until hot and lightly browned on top.

Makes 6 servings.

Per Serving (approx):
Calories 731
Carbohydrate 54 gm

Protein 51 gm
Sodium 594 mg

Fat 33 gm
Cholesterol 185 mg

Spanish Rice with Turkey Sausage

1 pound turkey sausage links
1 cup chopped onion
1 red bell pepper, chopped
1 red bell pepper, chopped
1 can (14 1/2 ounces) no-salt-
   added stewed tomatoes

1 small can tomato sauce
1 1/4 cups water
1 cup uncooked white rice
1/4 teaspoon black pepper

Spray large skillet with nonstick cooking spray. Warm over medium-high heat for about 30 seconds. Add turkey breakfast sausage. Cook for 12 to 15 minutes or until lightly browned and no longer pink in center, turning occasionally. Remove from skillet and keep warm. Drain skillet.

Add onion and bell pepper to skillet. Cook, stirring, for 5 to 7 minutes or until vegetables are tender-crisp. Sir in stewed tomatoes, tomato sauce, 1 1/4 cups water, rice and black pepper. Heat until mixture just begins to boil.

Reduce heat to low. Cook, covered, for 15 to 20 minutes or until rice is tender and liquid is absorbed, stirring twice. Add sausage and stir gently. Cook until thoroughly heated.   Makes 6 servings.

Per Serving (approx):
Calories 193
Carbohydrate 19 gm

Protein 13 gm
Sodium 362 mg

Fat 7 gm
Cholesterol 40 mg

A male turkey is a "tom," a female is a "hen," a baby is a "poult" and a large group of turkeys is a "flock."

Smoked Turkey Risotto

Tired of pasta? Try this turkey risotto. Although risotto is really just another rice dish, it has its own unique character. The rice absorbs the broth a little at a time, until each grain is plump and creamy yet firm to the bite.

1/2 cup chopped onion
1 tablespoon oil
4 tablespoons unsalted butter
2 cups Arborio rice
6 to 7 cups chicken or turkey
   stock

1/2 pound smoked turkey
   breast, cut into strips
2 cups chopped green apple
1/3 cup grated Parmesan cheese
3 tablespoons whipping cream
2 tablespoons chopped fresh
   basil or parsley

In heavy pot sauté onion in oil and 2 tablespoons of the butter until soft. Stir in rice, coating well with cooking fat. Heat stock to boiling. Begin adding stock in 1/2- to 3/4-cup increments, stirring continuously.* Allow all stock to be absorbed each time before adding more.

When rice is nearly cooked (about 20 minutes), stir in turkey and apple. When all stock has been added and rice is cooked to al dente stage (about 30 minutes), remove pan from heat. Stir in cheese, cream, basil and remaining 2 tablespoons butter. Serve immediately. Do not reheat.

Makes 6 servings.

*Note: Regulate heat so that liquid is absorbed steadily, neither too fast nor too slow.

Per Serving (approx):
Calories 450
Carbohydrate 61 gm

Protein 16 gm
Sodium 1160 mg

Fat 16 gm
Cholesterol 43 mg

Manicotti

So easy to make!

2 cups finely chopped cooked turkey
15 ounces ricotta cheese
1 egg, lightly beaten
1 package (10 ounces) frozen chopped
   spinach, thawed and well
   drained
1/4 cup grated Parmesan cheese

1/2 teaspoon ground nutmeg
3 cups marinara or
   spaghetti sauce
8 ounces manicotti shells,
   cooked
1/2 to 3/4 cup shredded
   mozzarella cheese

In medium bowl combine turkey, ricotta, egg, spinach, Parmesan and nutmeg. Into 9- x 12-inch baking pan, spoon thin layer of marinara sauce.

Fill manicotti shells with turkey mixture and arrange over sauce. Pour remaining sauce on top; sprinkle with mozzarella.

Bake for 25 to 30 minutes or until hot and bubbly.

Makes 4 to 6 servings.

Per Serving (approx):

Calories 505	*Protein 34 gm*	*Fat 21 gm*
Carbohydrate 45 gm	*Sodium 1033 mg*	*Cholesterol 117 mg*

Stuffed Turkey-Rice Roll

*If you want an easy, inexpensive and elegant main course for entertaining,
this is it.*

2/3 cup long-grain white rice	2 green or red bell peppers,
1/4 teaspoon salt	chopped
1 1/3 cups boiling water	2 to 3 tablespoons olive oil
6 turkey breast cutlets	1/2 cup sliced ripe olives
Salt and pepper to taste	3 tablespoons chopped fresh
2 cloves garlic, minced	basil or 1 1/2 teaspoons dried
4 green onions, sliced	1 cup shredded Cheddar cheese

Stir rice and salt into boiling water; reduce heat and simmer, covered,
for 20 minutes.

Pound turkey cutlets to 1/4 inch thick. On work surface overlap cutlets
to make large rectangle; sprinkle with salt and pepper.

Sauté garlic, green onions and bell pepper in 2 tablespoons olive oil;
combine with cooked rice, olives and basil. Spoon rice mixture onto cutlets, leaving half-inch border. Sprinkle with cheese. Roll up from long
side. Brush with 1 tablespoon olive oil and bake at 350 degrees for 30 to
35 minutes. Allow to rest for 15 minutes before slicing. Serve warm or
at room temperature with Fresh Tomato Salsa.   Makes 6 servings.

FRESH TOMATO SALSA:
Combine 4 tomatoes, peeled, seeded and chopped, 3 tablespoons chopped
fresh basil or 1 1/2 teaspoons dried, 4 green onions, chopped, 1 clove
garlic, minced, and 1 tablespoon olive oil. Let stand for about 1 hour for
flavors to blend.

Per Serving (approx):
Calories 238   *Protein 6 gm*   *Fat 15 gm*
Carbohydrate 21 gm   *Sodium 398 mg*   *Cholesterol 20 mg*

Stuffed Pasta Shells Italiano

This is a good make-ahead recipe.

1 pound ground turkey
1 cup minced onion
1 cup grated peeled eggplant
2 cloves garlic, minced
1 tablespoon oil
1 can (28 ounces) tomatoes
1 can (8 ounces) tomato sauce
1 cup red wine or water

1 teaspoon each garlic salt,
   dried oregano and dried basil
1/2 teaspoon each dried
   tarragon and crushed red
   pepper flakes
1 package (12 ounces) jumbo
   pasta shells
1/2 cup grated Parmesan cheese
3/4 cup grated mozzarella cheese

Brown turkey, onion, eggplant and garlic in hot oil; do not burn. Set aside. Simmer tomatoes, tomato sauce, wine and seasonings for 15 minutes. Cook pasta shells until done but still firm; drain.

Combine turkey mixture and Parmesan cheese with half of tomato sauce mixture. Use to stuff shells*; place in 9- x 13-inch pan. Spoon remaining sauce over each and top with mozzarella cheese. Bake at 350 degrees for 30 minutes.   **Makes 8 to 10 servings.**

*Note: If shells are stuffed ahead of time and refrigerated, do not add sauce or grated cheese until just before baking, and increase cooking time by 8 to 10 minutes.

Per Serving (approx):
Calories 362
Carbohydrate 42 gm

Protein 22 gm
Sodium 450 mg

Fat 9 gm
Cholesterol 54 mg

Pesto Meatballs with Zucchini and Pasta

This is about as Italian as you can get with a pasta.

1 1/2 cups packed fresh basil
   leaves
1 1/2 pounds ground turkey
1 cup freshly grated
   Parmesan cheese
1 cup soft white bread crumbs
3 large cloves garlic, minced
1 egg, lightly beaten
1/4 teaspoon each salt and
   pepper

2 tablespoons olive oil
1 1/4 cups chicken or turkey
   broth
1 to 1 1/2 pounds fine egg
   noodles (2 to 3 ounces
   per person)
3 cups thinly sliced zucchini
8 sprigs basil, for garnish
Additional Parmesan cheese,
   for topping

Put basil leaves in food processor or blender and chop fine. Transfer to mixing bowl with turkey, 3/4 cup Parmesan cheese, bread crumbs, garlic, egg, salt and pepper. Mix ingredients with fork; do not mix with hands or meat becomes tough. Shape into balls (about the size of large walnut) with your hands.

Heat 1 tablespoon of the olive oil in 12-inch nonstick skillet; brown half the meatballs on all sides. Remove from pan with slotted spoon and repeat browning with remaining oil and meatballs. Return first batch of meatballs to skillet, pour in broth and bring to a boil. Reduce heat and simmer for 12 minutes.

Place noodles in boiling water and cook according to package directions. At the same time, add zucchini to meatballs and cook until tender-crisp; do not overcook. Serve meatballs and zucchini over cooked pasta in warmed shallow bowls. Garnish with sprigs of basil and pass remaining Parmesan cheese at the table.   Makes 8 servings.

Per Serving (approx):
Calories 319
Carbohydrate 23 gm

Protein 25 gm
Sodium 655 mg

Fat 15 gm
Cholesterol 110 mg

Cannellini Sauté

Smoked turkey breast sautéed with a medley of vegetables makes a quick and delicious one-dish meal.

1 1/2 to 2 pounds smoked
  turkey breast
1 clove garlic, minced
1 medium onion, chopped
1/2 green bell pepper, chopped
2 tablespoons olive oil
1/2 medium head red cabbage,
  thinly sliced
1 medium head Chinese cabbage,
  thinly sliced

2 tablespoons chopped fresh
  rosemary or 3/4 teaspoon
  dried
2/3 cup chicken stock
2 tablespoons red wine
1 can (28 ounces) plum
  tomatoes, drained and
  chopped
2 cans (15 ounces each)
  cannellini beans, drained
Salt and pepper to taste

Cut turkey breast into 1-inch cubes. In large skillet sauté garlic, onion and bell pepper in oil until soft, about 2 minutes. Add turkey cubes, cabbages and rosemary; sauté for 3 minutes. Add chicken stock, red wine, tomatoes, beans, salt and pepper; simmer for 5 minutes. Serve with pasta or rice in cabbage leaf cups, if desired.   Makes 8 servings.

Per Serving (approx):
Calories 334
Carbohydrate 31 gm

Protein 32 gm
Sodium 1640 mg

Fat 8 gm
Cholesterol 45 mg

Trattoria Eggplant Turkey Rolls

1 eggplant (1 1/4 pounds)
1/4 cup olive oil
2 tablespoons minced garlic
1/2 teaspoon dried basil
1/2 teaspoon dried oregano
6 to 8 ounces smoked or cooked
   turkey breast, thinly sliced

1 1/2 cups no-salt-added
   spaghetti sauce
6 ounces sliced Monterey jack
   cheese
4 servings hot pasta

Cut eggplant lengthwise into 1/2-inch-thick slices. Lay slices in single layer in lightly greased, shallow baking pans. Brush with half the olive oil. Sprinkle with half the garlic and herbs. Broil 2 inches from heat for 4 to 5 minutes or until cooked. Turn slices, brush with remaining oil and sprinkle with remaining garlic and herbs. Broil until done.

Top eggplant with turkey and roll up with meat inside. Place in baking dish, pour spaghetti sauce over and top with cheese. Bake uncovered at 425 degrees for 25 to 30 minutes or until hot and bubbly. Serve with hot pasta.
                                                              Makes 4 servings.

Per Serving (approx):
Calories 540   *Protein 26 gm*   *Fat 33 gm*
Carbohydrate 35 gm   *Sodium 868 mg*   *Cholesterol 78 mg*

J. A. Brillalt-Savarin, in his book *The Physiology of Taste*, published in 1791, called the turkey "one of the most beautiful presents which the New World has made to the Old."

Turkey Fillets with Champagne-Mushroom Sauce

For a truly special and easy-to-make entree, serve this champagne and mushroom-sauced breast of turkey over your favorite pasta.

4 turkey fillets (approximately 1 1/4 pounds)
3 tablespoons butter
3 shallots, chopped
2 cups Champagne
2 cups whipping cream

6 ounces assorted mushrooms, sliced*
2 tablespoons each capers and chopped chives
Salt and pepper to taste
8 ounces pasta, cooked and drained

Brown turkey fillets in butter for 3 to 4 minutes on each side. Add shallots and Champagne; cover and simmer for 10 minutes. Uncover; remove fillets and keep warm.

Increase heat to high and let Champagne reduce by half. Add remaining ingredients except pasta; simmer for 10 to 15 minutes or until slightly thickened. Slice fillets; serve on bed of pasta with sauce.

Makes 4 to 6 servings.

*Note: Any combination of wild or domestic mushrooms may be used.

Per Serving (approx):
Calories 594
Carbohydrate 41 gm

Protein 16 gm
Sodium 337 mg

Fat 41 gm
Cholesterol 181 mg

Turkey Sausage Ragout on Pasta

Here is a very different and interesting use of sausage.

2 cloves garlic, finely chopped
1 carrot, sliced
1 medium onion, chopped
1 green bell pepper, chopped
2 tablespoons oil
1/4 cup dry white wine (optional)

1 teaspoon dried basil
1 jar (14 ounces) spaghetti
  sauce
1/4 cup chopped parsley
Hot cooked pasta

Prepare Turkey Sausage.* In large skillet, cook sausage, garlic, carrot, onion and bell pepper in hot oil until sausage is no longer pink, about 5 minutes, stirring occasionally. Stir in remaining ingredients except parsley and pasta. Cover and simmer for 15 minutes, stirring occasionally. Stir in parsley. Serve over hot cooked pasta.   Makes 4 servings.

*Note: Or purchase 1 pound prepared turkey sausage.

TURKEY SAUSAGE:
Combine 1 pound ground turkey, 1 egg or 2 egg whites, lightly beaten, 1/3 cup dry bread crumbs, 2 green onions, minced, 1 clove garlic, minced, 1/2 teaspoon crushed fennel seed, 1/2 teaspoon each dried thyme and ground cumin, and 1 pinch each of red pepper flakes, salt and ground nutmeg.

Per Serving (approx):
Calories 345   *Protein 19 gm*   *Fat 21 gm*
Carbohydrate 19 gm   *Sodium 961 mg*   *Cholesterol 61 mg*

Peppercorn Turkey over Spinach Noodles

1 tablespoon crushed green
  peppercorns
4 turkey tenderloins
  (approximately 6 ounces each)
1 Granny Smith or tart apple,
  unpeeled, cored and thinly
  sliced
2 tablespoons margarine
1/4 cup sliced green onion
1 clove garlic, minced

1/2 cup sliced mushrooms
1 teaspoon crumbled dried
  rosemary
1/2 teaspoon celery seeds
1 tablespoon cornstarch
1/2 cup dry white wine or sherry
1/2 cup chicken broth
1 pound spinach noodles,
  prepared according to
  package directions

Press peppercorns into each side of turkey tenderloins; set aside.

In 12-inch nonstick skillet over medium-high heat, cook apples in 1 table-spoon of the margarine for 2 to 3 minutes or until tender-crisp. Remove apples from skillet; set aside.

In same skillet add turkey and remaining 1 tablespoon margarine and cook for 4 to 5 minutes on each side; remove tenderloins. Add onion, garlic, mushrooms, rosemary and celery seeds to skillet. Reduce heat and sauté for 2 to 3 minutes.

In small bowl dissolve cornstarch in wine and broth; add to vegetable mixture in skillet. Bring mixture to a boil, stirring constantly. Return tenderloins to skillet; reduce heat and simmer for 5 minutes or until sauce is slightly thickened.

To serve, slice turkey into medallions. Arrange noodles on 6 plates; top with apples and turkey and spoon vegetable mixture over top.

Makes 6 servings.

Per Serving (approx):
Calories 367
Carbohydrate 61 gm

Protein 11 gm
Sodium 185 mg

Fat 7 gm
Cholesterol 72 mg

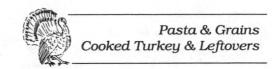
Spaghetti Pie

This is quite easy to make—and well worth the effort.

6 ounces spaghetti, cooked according to package instructions and drained
1 egg white, lightly beaten
1/3 cup grated Parmesan cheese
2 1/2 tablespoons margarine, melted
1 cup chopped onion
1 clove garlic, minced

1 package (10 ounces) frozen mixed vegetables, thawed
2 tablespoons flour
1 teaspoon dried poultry seasoning
1/8 teaspoon black pepper
1 1/2 cups skim milk
2 cups cubed cooked turkey

In medium bowl combine spaghetti, egg white, cheese and 1 tablespoon of the margarine. Press pasta mixture over bottom and up sides of well-greased 9-inch pie plate. Grease 10- by 12-inch piece of aluminum foil. Press foil, greased side down, next to pasta shell. Bake in preheated 350 degree oven for 25 to 30 minutes or until pasta shell is set and slightly browned on edges.

In medium saucepan over medium-high heat, sauté onion and garlic in remaining margarine for 2 to 3 minutes or until onion is translucent. Fold in vegetables and cook for 1 minute. Sprinkle flour, poultry seasoning and pepper over mixture, stirring to combine. Remove pan from heat.

Slowly pour milk over vegetable mixture, stirring constantly. Return saucepan to medium heat; cook and stir until mixture is thickened. Add turkey, reduce heat to medium-low and simmer for 5 minutes or until heated through. Pour mixture into cooked pasta shell.

To serve, cut spaghetti pie into 6 wedges.   Makes 6 servings.

Per Serving (approx):
Calories 325
Carbohydrate 35 gm

Protein 24 gm
Sodium 238 mg

Fat 9 gm
Cholesterol 41 mg

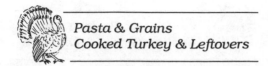
Tetrazzini Pasta Supper

This very elegant entree takes just a few minutes to make, thanks to its use of turkey leftovers.

6 quarts salted water
16 ounces tubular pasta, such as ziti or penne
2 tablespoons butter or margarine
3 green onions, minced
2 cloves garlic, minced
1 pound fresh shiitake mushrooms, stems removed and caps sliced, or fresh domestic mushrooms, sliced

3 tablespoons dry sherry
1/2 teaspoon dried tarragon
Salt and pepper to taste
2 to 3 cups coarsely chopped cooked turkey
1/2 cups part-skim ricotta cheese
3/4 cup freshly grated Parmesan cheese

In large saucepan over high heat, bring water to a boil. Cook pasta according to package directions until tender. Scoop out and reserve 1 cup cooking water from pasta. Drain pasta and place in large serving bowl.

Meanwhile, in large skillet over low heat, melt butter. Add onions and garlic; cook for about 1 minute or until tender, stirring constantly. Increase heat to high; add mushrooms, sherry, tarragon and 1/4 teaspoon each salt and pepper. Cook for about 5 minutes or until liquid is evaporated and mushrooms are browned, stirring constantly. Add turkey; cook for 1 minute longer or until heated through.

To serve, pour warm turkey mixture over hot pasta. Add ricotta and Parmesan cheeses with about 1/3 cup reserved hot cooking water. Toss and add additional cooking water, if necessary, to make creamy sauce. Season with additional salt and pepper; serve immediately.

Makes 6 servings.

Per Serving (approx):
Calories 704
Carbohydrate 99 gm

Protein 41 gm
Sodium 425 mg

Fat 16 gm
Cholesterol 130 mg

ROASTING BREASTS
& ROLLED ROASTS

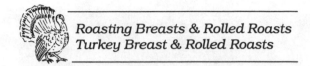

Turkey Della Robbia

The ring of fruit around the turkey half breast on the platter makes a spectacular dish, with very little special effort on your part.

1 turkey half breast (1 1/2 pounds)	2 nectarines or peaches
Oil, as needed	4 plums
Salt and pepper to taste	2 tablespoons sugar
1/3 cup peach or apricot preserves	2 tablespoons grated lemon zest
	1 tablespoon lemon juice
	1 pound seedless grapes

Place turkey bone side down on rack in roasting pan. Brush with oil and sprinkle with salt and pepper. Roast at 450 degrees for 20 minutes. Spoon preserves over turkey, cover pan with foil and reduce oven heat to 350 degrees. Roast for 45 minutes longer or until thermometer registers 170 degrees.

When roast is nearly done, quarter nectarines and plums and combine in large saucepan with sugar, lemon zest and lemon juice. Cook, stirring gently, for 5 minutes or until juices collect and fruit is tender but not mushy. Add grapes and heat through.

To serve, transfer turkey to serving platter. Lift fruit from juice with slotted spoon and place in ring around turkey. For sauce, pour pan drippings into cup. Remove fat on top, then combine with juice from fruit. Serve as sauce with turkey.   Makes 4 servings.

Per Serving (approx):
Calories 577   *Protein 46 gm*   *Fat 17 gm*
Carbohydrate 59 gm   *Sodium 211 mg*   *Cholesterol 130 mg*

Pineapple-Mustard-Glazed Turkey Breast

1 turkey half breast, bone in
  (2 1/2 pounds)
1/3 cup pineapple preserves

1 teaspoon lemon juice
2 teaspoons Dijon-style
  mustard

Prepare grill for indirect-heat cooking. Place turkey, skin side up, on rack over drip pan. Cover and grill turkey breast for 1 to 1 1/4 hours, or until meat thermometer inserted in thickest portion of breast registers 170 degrees.

In small bowl combine preserves, lemon juice and mustard. Brush glaze on breast 1/2 hour before end of grilling time. At end of cooking time, remove turkey breast from grill and let stand for 15 minutes. To serve, slice breast and arrange on platter.   Makes 6 servings.

Per Serving (approx):
Calories 295   *Protein 37 gm*   *Fat 10 gm*
Carbohydrate 13 gm   *Sodium 134 mg*   *Cholesterol 96 mg*

Indirect-Heat Cooking

"Indirect" grilling over a drip pan with hot coals on the outside is recommended for whole birds and large turkey parts such as the whole breast. This slower cooking method allows time for the meat to cook through to the center without burning on the outside.

Spread one layer of charcoal in an outdoor grill; pile charcoal in the center to form a pyramid. Light and let burn to white-coal, slow-heat stage, about one-half hour. Divide glowing coals in half, arranging along both sides of grill, leaving the center open. Place foil drip pan in the center of the grill. Place the turkey on a rack over a drip pan. Cover the grill, either with its own top or with a "tent" of heavy-duty aluminum foil. (If using foil, punch four vent holes in the center and seal edges, leaving four to six openings around the rim of the grill.)

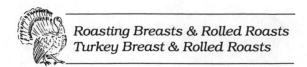

Turkey Breasts Verde

1 turkey breast (2 to 4 pounds)
1 cup extravirgin olive oil
1/4 teaspoon black pepper
Juice of 1 lemon
2 cloves garlic

3 cups chopped fresh basil
   and/or parsley
3 tablespoons grated Parmesan
   cheese
2 tablespoons pine nuts

Rub turkey with 1/2 cup of the olive oil and sprinkle with black pepper. Place turkey in baking dish. Cover and bake in preheated 350 degree oven for 45 minutes or until lightly browned.

Meanwhile, combine lemon juice, remaining olive oil, garlic, basil and cheese in electric blender and blend until smooth. Serve turkey covered with this sauce. Sprinkle with pine nuts.   Makes 4 servings.

Per Serving (approx):
Calories 716
Carbohydrate 6 gm

Protein 28 gm
Sodium 142 mg

Fat 65 gm
Cholesterol 65 mg

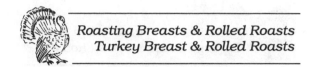
Roast Turkey Breast
with Spiced Cherry Sauce

This delicious entree is low in calories, sodium and cholesterol.

1 turkey breast, bone in (4 to 6 pounds)	2 tablespoons vinegar
1 can (16 ounces) dark pitted cherries, drained, juice reserved	1/8 teaspoon ground cloves
	1/2 teaspoon ground cinnamon
	1 1/2 tablespoons cornstarch
1/4 cup sugar	2 tablespoons brandy (optional)

Wipe turkey with damp paper towel. Place breast on rack in shallow roasting pan. Place in preheated 325 degree oven and roast for 1 1/2 to 2 1/4 hours or until meat thermometer inserted into thickest part, not touching bone, registers 170 degrees.

While breast is roasting, in small saucepan combine all but 3 tablespoons cherry juice, sugar, vinegar, cloves and cinnamon. Bring to a boil; reduce heat and cook for 10 minutes. Mix reserved cherry juice with cornstarch. Stir into hot liquid, stirring constantly until thickened. Add cherries and heat through. Stir in brandy, if desired.

Remove turkey breast from oven and allow to stand for 10 to 15 minutes. Remove skin from breast and slice breast. Serve 2 tablespoons warm sauce over each serving of breast. Makes 16 servings.

Per Serving (approx):
Calories 144	*Protein 27 gm*	*Fat 1 gm*
Carbohydrate 32 gm	*Sodium 45 mg*	*Cholesterol 56 mg*

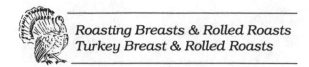
Turkey Breast with Southwestern Corn Bread Dressing

5 cups coarsely crumbled corn bread
4 English muffins,
  coarsely crumbled
3 mild green chilies, roasted,
  peeled, seeded and chopped
1 red bell pepper, roasted, peeled,
  seeded and chopped
3/4 cup pine nuts, toasted
1 tablespoon chopped cilantro
1 tablespoon chopped parsley
1 1/2 teaspoons chopped
  fresh basil
1 1/2 teaspoons chopped
  fresh thyme
1 1/2 teaspoons chopped
  fresh oregano
1 pound bulk turkey sausage
3 cups chopped celery
1 cup chopped onion
2 to 4 tablespoons turkey broth
  or water, or as needed
1 turkey breast (5 to 6 pounds),
  bone in
2 tablespoons chopped garlic
1/2 cup chopped cilantro

In large bowl combine corn bread, muffins, chilies, bell pepper, pine nuts, cilantro, parsley, basil, thyme and oregano.

In large skillet over medium-high heat, sauté sausage, celery and onion for 8 to 10 minutes or until sausage is no longer pink and vegetables are tender. Combine mixture with corn bread mixture. Add broth if mixture is too dry. Set aside.

Loosen skin on both sides of turkey breast, being careful not to tear skin and leaving it connected at breast bone. Spread 1 tablespoon garlic under loosened skin over each breast half. Repeat procedure with 1/4 cup cilantro on each side.

Place turkey breast in lightly greased 13- x 9- x 2-inch roasting pan. Spoon half of stuffing mixture under breast cavity. Spoon remaining stuffing into lightly greased 2-quart casserole; set aside.

Roast turkey breast, uncovered, for 2 to 2 1/2 hours or until meat thermometer registers 170 degrees in deepest portion of breast. Bake remaining stuffing, uncovered, along with turkey breast during last 45 minutes.   Makes 12 servings.

Per Serving (approx):
Calories 422   *Protein 45 gm*   *Fat 16 gm*
Carbohydrate 26 gm   *Sodium 677 mg*   *Cholesterol 128 mg*

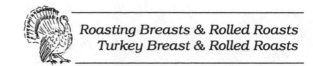
Rolled Turkey Breast
with Fruit Sauce

1 turkey breast, boned and
   butterflied (approximately
   3 pounds)

Salt and pepper to taste
1/4 cup chopped dried apricots
1/4 cup cranberry relish

Season turkey breast with salt and pepper. Spread dried fruit and cranberry relish over surface of breast. Roll up and tie. Roast in 450 degree oven for approximately 40 to 45 minutes. Slice and serve with Fruit Sauce.

Make 10 servings.

FRUIT SAUCE:
In large heavy saucepan, carmelize 1/4 cup sugar. Add 1/2 cup raspberry vinegar, 1 cup orange juice and 1/2 cup Riesling wine. Reduce to thick and syrupy consistency. Add 2 cups turkey stock; bring to a boil and reduce consistency of sauce.

Per Serving (approx):
Calories 248
Carbohydrate 11 gm

Protein 30 gm
Sodium 391 mg

Fat 8 gm
Cholesterol 73 mg

The new broad-breasted turkeys are so tender they require only about half as long roasting as those in our grandmother's day.

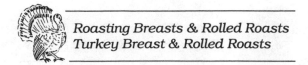

Foil-Baked Turkey Roast
with Raspberry Sauce

1 turkey breast (1 1/2 to 2 pounds)
1 tablespoon margarine, cut
  into small pieces

1/4 teaspoon each dried dill
  weed, crushed dried basil
  and black pepper

Place turkey on sheet of aluminum foil. Top with margarine. Sprinkle with seasonings. Bring edges of foil together up and over meat and fold over twice. Fold edges in twice to seal. Place packet in shallow pan.

Bake in 350 degree oven for about 1 1/2 to 2 hours or until turkey is no longer pink in center and meat thermometer reaches 180 degrees. Open foil carefully. Slice meat and serve with juices or Raspberry Sauce.

Makes 4 to 6 servings.

RASPBERRY SAUCE:
In small saucepan over medium heat, combine 1/4 cup butter, 1/2 cup raspberry or currant jelly, 1/4 cup red wine, 2 tablespoons lemon juice, 2 tablespoons cider vinegar, and 2 teaspoons prepared mustard. Bring to a boil; cook for 3 minutes. Reduce heat to low and add 1 tablespoon cornstarch dissolved in 1 tablespoon cold water; stir until thickened.

Per Serving (approx):
Calories 349
Carbohydrate 25 gm

Protein 24 gm
Sodium 185 mg

Fat 16 gm
Cholesterol 81 mg

Golden Delicious Turkey Roast

1 turkey breast (1 1/2 to 2 pounds)
1 cup unsweetened apple cider
  or apple juice
2 tablespoons soy sauce

2 tablespoons cornstarch
  dissolved in 2 tablespoons
  cold water

Place turkey, cider and soy sauce in roasting pan; cover tightly with foil. Roast at 325 degrees for 1 1/2 to 2 hours or until meat thermometer reaches 180 degrees and turkey is no longer pink in center.

Pour liquid from pan into small saucepan; stir in cornstarch mixture. Bring to a boil; simmer until sauce begins to thicken. Serve turkey with sauce. **Makes 4 to 6 servings.**

Per Serving (approx):
Calories 183
Carbohydrate 6 gm

Protein 25 gm
Sodium 1117 mg

Fat 7 gm
Cholesterol 60 mg

Herb-Roasted Turkey and Potatoes

1 turkey breast (1 1/2 pounds)
1 clove garlic, thinly sliced
4 red potatoes
3/4 teaspoon onion salt

3/4 teaspoon dried oregano
2 tablespoons margarine,
  melted
Paprika

Make cuts in surface of turkey and insert garlic slices. Place turkey, skin side up, in 9- x 9-inch pan. Quarter potatoes and place around roast. Combine onion salt and oregano. Sprinkle roast with two-thirds of the onion-oregano mixture. Drizzle margarine over potatoes and sprinkle with remaining onion-oregano mixture and paprika. Bake in 350 degree oven for 1 1/2 hours or to internal temperature of 170 degrees. **Makes 4 servings.**

Per Serving (approx):
Calories 339
Carbohydrate 33 gm

Protein 28 gm
Sodium 115 mg

Fat 11 gm
Cholesterol 61 mg

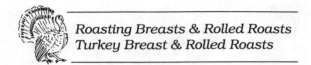

Pineapple Minted Turkey Breast

Salt to taste
1 turkey breast (4 to 6
   pounds), bone in, skin removed
1 can (20 ounces) pineapple chunks
   in natural juice

1/2 cup pineapple or apple
   juice
1 1/2 tablespoons cornstarch
2 teaspoons dried mint

Salt breast to taste and place on rack in shallow roasting pan; cover with aluminum foil. Place in preheated 325 degree oven and roast for 1 1/2 to 2 1/4 hours or until meat thermometer registers 170 degrees when inserted into thickest part, not touching bone.

During roasting time, drain pineapple chunks; set aside. To juice add additional pineapple or apple juice to measure 1 1/2 cups. In medium saucepan stir together cornstarch, mint and salt. Gradually stir in juice until smooth. Stirring constantly, bring to a boil over medium heat and boil for 1 minute. Remove from heat. Remove 1/2 cup of mixture for glaze. Stir pineapple chunks into remaining mixture for sauce; keep warm.

Remove turkey breast from oven 45 minutes before done. Brush with glaze. Return to oven, uncovered, and continue roasting, brushing frequently with glaze until breast tests done.

Remove turkey breast from oven and allow to stand for 10 to 15 minutes before slicing. Heat sauce and serve 1 1/2 tablespoons over each serving of sliced turkey.   Makes 16 servings.

Per Serving (approx):
Calories 143	*Protein 26 gm*	*Fat 1 gm*
Carbohydrate 20 gm	*Sodium 76 mg*	*Cholesterol 56 mg*

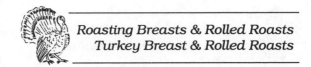

Half Turkey Breast, Southwest Style

This self-basting turkey (the stuffing does the basting) is very reminiscent of the Southwest.

1 turkey half breast (approximately
   1 1/2 pounds)
3 slices bacon, chopped
2 cloves garlic, minced
1/3 cup minced onion
1 teaspoon dried basil
1/2 teaspoon dried thyme

1 bay leaf, crushed
1/3 cup butter, melted
2 cloves garlic, minced
3 red or green bell peppers,
   quartered
3 leeks, halved

Guide knife-sharpening steel through thickest part of breast. Combine bacon, garlic, onion and herbs; pack into hole created by knife steel.* Brush with combined butter and garlic; grill in covered barbecue for about 1 hour and 20 minutes, basting occasionally. After 1 hour, place pepper quarters and leeks on grill, basting and turning until done. Or roast turkey breast in 350 degree oven for about 1 1/2 hours, basting with garlic butter. Place peppers and leeks around breast for last 30 minutes. Makes 4 to 6 servings.

*Note: If knife-sharpening steel is unavailable, lift skin and pack seasoning under skin.

Per Serving (approx):
Calories 267
Carbohydrate 19 gm

Protein 5 gm
Sodium 275 mg

Fat 19 gm
Cholesterol 48 mg

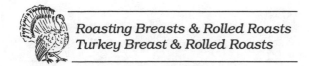

Stuffed Turkey Breast
with Pesto Sauce

1 turkey breast (4 to 6 pounds), boned
   and butterflied

Prepare stuffing, Marmalade Glaze and Pesto Sauce. Spoon stuffing over each breast. Bring sides together to encase stuffing; fasten with skewers. In 11- x 9- x 1-inch roasting pan, place breast skewered side down on meat rack. Bake in preheated 350 degree oven for 2 to 2 1/2 hours or until breast meat reaches 170 to 175 degrees. Brush with glaze 2 or 3 times during last 30 minutes of baking. To serve, slice turkey breast across roll and offer Pesto Sauce with each serving, if desired.

Makes 16 servings.

STUFFING:

In large skillet over medium-high heat, sauté 1 pound turkey sausage and 1/4 cup chopped onion, stirring to break up meat, until meat is no longer pink and onion is translucent. Drain and set aside. In large bowl combine 1 can (8 ounces) mushroom stems and pieces, drained, 2 1/2 cups French bread cut into 1/2-inch cubes, 1/4 cup pine nuts, toasted, 1 egg, 1/8 teaspoon cayenne pepper and 2 tablespoons Pesto Sauce. Add sausage mixture and stir to combine.   Makes 3 cups.

GLAZE:

In small bowl combine 1/4 cup marmalade, 1 tablespoon margarine, melted and 1/4 teaspoon ginger. Use as a basting sauce for turkey breast.

Makes 1/4 cup.

PESTO SAUCE:

In electric blender container (or food processor bowl fitted with metal blade) combine 2/3 cup olive or oil, 2 cups tightly packed parsley, 1/2 cup grated Parmesan cheese, 2 cloves garlic, 4 teaspoons dried basil, 1 tablespoon capers and 1/8 teaspoon black pepper. Blend or process for 30 seconds or until mixture is smooth. Place in covered container and refrigerate. May be kept up to 1 week.   Makes 1 cup.

Per Serving (approx) excluding additional Pesto Sauce:

Calories 323	*Protein 40 gm*	*Fat 15 gm*
Carbohydrate 6 gm	*Sodium 296 mg*	*Cholesterol 121 mg*

Cranapple Roasted Turkey Breast I

Here's a delicious turkey and dressing idea for a small holiday gathering.

1 onion, chopped
2 ribs celery with leaves, chopped
1 green apple, cored and chopped
6 tablespoons butter
1 cup chopped fresh
   cranberries
1 cup reduced-sodium turkey or
   chicken broth

5 slices rye bread, torn into
   small pieces
1 egg, lightly beaten
Salt and pepper to taste
1 turkey breast, bone in
   (about 3 pounds)
1/4 cup apple brandy

Sauté onion, celery and apple in 4 tablespoons of the butter until tender-crisp, about 3 minutes. Add cranberries, broth, bread pieces, egg, salt and pepper. Mix gently; mound on greased baking sheet.

Place turkey breast, skin side up, over dressing. Melt remaining 2 tablespoons butter with apple brandy. Baste turkey breast with butter mixture.

Roast in preheated 350 degree oven, basting occasionally, until meat thermometer inserted in thickest part of breast registers 170 degrees, about 1 hour and 15 minutes. Makes 6 servings.

Per Serving (approx):
Calories 579	*Protein 47 gm*	*Fat 25 gm*
Carbohydrate 35 gm	*Sodium 634 mg*	*Cholesterol 169 mg*

The Voyage of Turkey

When Neil Armstrong and Edwin Aldrin sat down to eat their first meal on the moon, their food packets contained roasted turkey and all the trimmings.

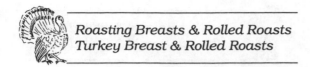
Cranapple Roasted Turkey Breast II

Like version "I," this is perfect for a small holiday dinner.

1 turkey breast (2 pounds)
1 cup apple juice
Salt and pepper to taste
2 cups fresh or canned whole
  cranberries
1 apple, chopped

1/4 cup sugar
1 tablespoon cornstarch
  dissolved in 1 tablespoon
  cold water
1/4 cup strawberry jam

Place turkey in 9- x 9-inch baking pan. Pour apple juice over turkey; season with salt and pepper. Bake in preheated 350 degree oven, basting occasionally, for 1 hour and 15 minutes.

Combine cranberries, apple and sugar. Place around turkey. Bake for 15 to 30 minutes longer or until turkey is no longer pink and meat thermometer registers 170 degrees. (Total cooking time is 20 to 25 minutes per pound.) Remove roast to platter; keep warm.

Stir cornstarch mixture and jam into cranberry mixture in pan. Heat for 5 minutes longer or until sauce thickens and fruit is soft. Serve fruit sauce over sliced turkey.   Makes 6 to 8 servings.

Per Serving (approx):
Calories 260
Carbohydrate 25 gm

Protein 25 gm
Sodium 100 mg

Fat 7 gm
Cholesterol 61 mg

Repeated History

President Lincoln proclaimed Thanksgiving a national holiday in 1863, in response to a campaign organized by magazine editor Sara Josepha Hale.

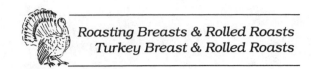
Cranberry Turkey

1 turkey half breast (approximately   Salt and pepper to taste
   4 pounds)

Season turkey with salt and pepper. Place in open roasting pan. Bake in 325 degree oven for 1 1/2 hours.

Prepare sauce. Spoon some over turkey. Bake for about 30 minutes more or to internal temperature of 170 degrees. Let turkey stand for 10 minutes before slicing. Meanwhile, heat remaining sauce; serve with turkey.

Makes 8 servings.

SAUCE:
Combine 1 can (16 ounces) whole berry cranberry sauce, 1/4 teaspoon ground cloves and 1/2 cup firmly packed brown sugar.

Per Serving (approx):
Calories 386
Carbohydrate 29 gm

Protein 54 gm
Sodium 135 mg

Fat 6 gm
Cholesterol 125 mg

Feathers, Feathers, and More Feathers

It's estimated that turkeys have approximately 3,500 feathers at maturity. • The bulk of turkey feathers are disposed of; however, some feathers may be used for special purposes. • For instance, dyed feathers are used to make American Indian costumes or as quills for pens. • The costume that "Big Bird" wears on "Sesame Street" is rumored to be made of turkey feathers. • Turkey feather down has been used to make pillows. • And recently turkey and chicken feathers have been found to be effective in absorbing oil spills at sea.

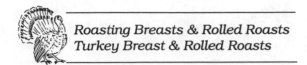

Easy Baked Turkey Breasts

1 turkey breast (2 to 4 pounds)
1/2 cup extravirgin olive oil
4 large potatoes, peeled and
   cut into eighths
1 cup coarsely chopped
   tomato

1/2 teaspoon black pepper
1 teaspoon dried oregano
6 large mushrooms, sliced
1 tablespoon chopped parsley

Preheat oven to 350 degrees. Place turkey in oven-proof casserole. Add olive oil, potatoes, tomatoes, pepper, oregano and mushrooms. Bake, uncovered, for 1 hour. Baste with sauce from casserole every 20 minutes. Remove from oven and sprinkle with parsley.   Makes 4 servings.

Per Serving (approx):
Calories 778
Carbohydrate 83 gm

Protein 34 gm
Sodium 83 mg

Fat 34 gm
Cholesterol 61 mg

ROASTING WHOLE & HALF TURKEYS

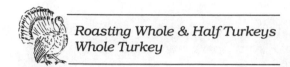

Roast Turkey with Peanut Sauce

Don't let the peanut butter in the ingredients stop you from making this version of "satay," a traditional Indonesian dish.

1 turkey (about 10 pounds)
2 lemons
Garlic salt and black pepper
  to taste

1/4 cup butter, melted
12 carrots, cut in
  pieces
2 onions, sliced

Preheat oven to 400 degrees. Pierce rinds of lemons and place inside turkey cavity; truss bird. Sprinkle turkey with garlic salt and pepper; place on rack in roasting pan. Reduce oven to 325 degrees; place turkey in oven. Baste with melted butter throughout cooking. If skin gets too dark, cover lightly with foil tent.

Cook turkey for 15 to 20 minutes per pound or until meat thermometer inserted into breast measures 175 degrees. Put carrots and onions around turkey during last 30 minutes of cooking; stir occasionally.

Slice turkey. Serve with carrots, onions and Peanut Sauce.

                           Makes 12 to 14 servings.

THAI PEANUT SAUCE:
Heat 2 tablespoons vegetable oil. Sauté 1 onion, chopped and 2 cloves garlic, minced. Reduce heat; add 1 tablespoon brown sugar. Cook for 3 minutes. Add 1 can (14 1/2 ounces) chicken broth and 1 cup creamy peanut butter. Cook and stir until smooth. Remove from heat; stir in 3 tablespoons soy sauce and 1 to 2 tablespoons red pepper flakes.

Per Serving (approx):
Calories 858
Carbohydrate 19 gm

Protein 91 gm
Sodium 740 mg

Fat 46 gm
Cholesterol 256 mg

> Turkeys today are available as boneless roasts, halves, quarters, or cut-up parts; also as precooked rolls.

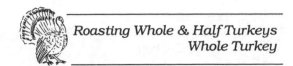
Roast Turkey with Giblet Stuffing and Gravy

For a traditional festive occasion, this classic recipe—turkey with a giblet stuffing and gravy—is quite simple to make.

1 turkey (12 to 14 pounds),
  with giblets
1 onion, quartered
2 stalks celery, chopped

Packaged seasoned stuffing
  mix (enough for 12- to
  14-pound turkey)
Salt and pepper to taste
5 tablespoons flour

Remove giblets from turkey. Place giblets in medium saucepan with onion and celery. Add water to cover. Bring to a boil; reduce heat, cover and simmer for 45 minutes to 1 hour or until giblets are done. Let cool enough to handle; remove giblets and chop, reserving cooking liquid for gravy. Prepare seasoned stuffing mix according to package directions, adding chopped giblets.

Rub salt and pepper into turkey neck and body cavities. Lightly spoon stuffing into neck cavity; close with skewer. Fill body cavity. Secure drumsticks lightly with string. Roast uncovered on roasting rack in 325 degree oven for 20 to 22 minutes per pound or to internal temperature of 175 to 180 degrees. Because of variations in turkeys, begin checking for doneness about one hour ahead. Any extra stuffing may be baked in covered casserole along with turkey during last hour of roasting. Uncover stuffing during final 10 minutes of cooking. Remove turkey to platter and let stand for at least 20 minutes before carving.

Meanwhile, make gravy by pouring off all but 6 tablespoons drippings from roasting pan. Over low heat, stir in flour until thickened. Let flour cook for about 30 seconds or until bubbly. Measure reserved giblet cooking liquid; add water to make 2 1/2 cups. Add to roasting pan, stirring until smooth.   Makes 10 to 12 servings.

Per Serving (approx):
Calories 735
Carbohydrate 10 gm

Protein 98 gm
Sodium 400 mg

Fat 34 gm
Cholesterol 282 mg

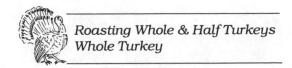
Port-Sauced Turkey

We're not sure whether this recipe originated in Spain or in England, but it is an exciting change of pace for roast turkey.

1 orange, unpeeled
1 turkey (10 to 12 pounds)
Salt and pepper to taste
1/2 cup butter, melted
1 large onion, cut in wedges
3/4 pound white boiling
   potatoes, quartered
1/2 cup sliced mushrooms

1/2 cup sliced leeks
3 carrots, cut in 2-inch chunks
1/4 cup flour
1/4 cup balsamic vinegar*
   or malt vinegar
1 1/2 cups ruby Port wine
4 cups chicken broth

Pierce rind of orange in several places with fork and place in cavity of turkey. Salt and pepper outside of turkey; place in deep roasting pan. Baste with 1/4 cup of the butter. Roast in 350 degree oven.

Meanwhile, sauté onion, potatoes, mushrooms, leeks and carrots in remaining 1/4 cup butter for 3 minutes. Sprinkle flour over vegetables and stir in. Add remaining ingredients and bring to a boil.

After turkey has roasted for 45 minutes, spoon vegetables and liquid over turkey, making sure vegetables are well covered with liquid. Continue cooking for about 1 1/2 hours longer or until meat thermometer placed in the thickest part of breast registers 175 degrees. Serve with braised vegetables and some of braising liquid.* Makes 8 to 10 servings.

*Note: Remaining braising liquid makes an excellent soup base.

Per Serving (approx):
Calories 1150
Carbohydrate 21 gm

Protein 129 gm
Sodium 1219 mg

Fat 56 gm
Cholesterol 399 mg

> "For turkey braised, the Lord be praised"—from a 19th Century Guide to Food Preparation.

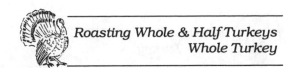
Roast Turkey with Oyster Stuffing

It was probably the Pilgrims who came up with the idea of stuffing turkey with oysters . . . and a very good idea it was, and still is.

1 turkey (12 to 14 pounds)   Salt and pepper to taste

Prepare Oyster Stuffing. Rub salt and pepper into neck and body cavities. Lightly spoon Oyster Stuffing into neck cavity; close with skewer. Fill body cavity. Secure drumsticks lightly with string. Roast uncovered on roasting rack in 325 degree oven for 20 to 22 minutes per pound or to internal temperature of 170 to 180 degrees, thick part of drumstick feels soft when pressed with thumb and forefinger, or when drumstick moves easily. Any remaining stuffing may be baked, in covered casserole, along with turkey during last hour of roasting. Uncover dressing during final 10 minutes of cooking. Let turkey stand for at least 20 minutes before carving.   Makes 12 servings.

OYSTER STUFFING:

Dry 1 loaf (1 pound) white bread slices overnight in open air, or on rack in 250 degree oven for 1 to 1 1/4 hours.

In skillet sauté 2 cups finely chopped celery and 2 cups finely chopped onion in 3/4 cup butter or margarine until tender. Warm 1/2 cup milk over low heat in small saucepan. Tear bread into 1/2-inch pieces, making about 11 cups; place in large mixing bowl. Sprinkle warm milk over bread and toss lightly. Add onion mixture and 3 containers (8 ounces each) fresh or frozen oysters, drained* to bread; toss to mix well. Sprinkle with 1 teaspoon lemon juice, 1/4 teaspoon ground nutmeg, 3/4 teaspoon dried poultry seasoning, 1/4 teaspoon salt and 1/4 teaspoon pepper; mix thoroughly.

*Note: If desired, canned oysters may be substituted.

Per Serving (approx):
Calories 918   *Protein 97 gm*   *Fat 46 gm*
Carbohydrate 30 gm   *Sodium 833 mg*   *Cholesterol 339 mg*

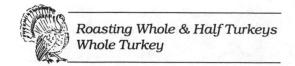
Turkey Southwest Style with Sage Corn Bread Stuffing and Chile Gravy

1 turkey (12 to 14 pounds)　　　　1/2 teaspoon dried sage
1/4 cup butter

Prepare Sage Corn Bread Stuffing. Spoon stuffing into turkey cavity and truss. Melt butter and add sage; brush over turkey.

Roast at 325 degrees for 3 to 3 1/2 hours or until meat thermometer registers 170 to 180 degrees, thick part of drumstick feels soft when pressed with thumb and forefinger, or when drumstick moves easily. Let stand for 20 minutes before carving; reserve drippings for Chile Gravy.

Makes 10 to 12 servings.

SAGE CORN BREAD STUFFING:
Sauté 1 cup chopped onion and 3/4 cup chopped celery in 1/4 cup butter until soft. Combine with 3 cups corn bread stuffing mix, 1 cup chicken broth, 1 cup corn kernels (fresh, frozen or canned), 1/4 cup diced green chilies, 1/2 cup chopped walnuts, toasted, 1 egg, lightly beaten, 1 teaspoon dried sage, salt and pepper to taste.

CHILE GRAVY:
Pour fat and drippings into 4-cup measure. Skim off and reserve 1/3 cup fat. Discard remaining fat, reserving drippings. Add enough broth to drippings to measure 4 cups. Melt fat in saucepan; stir in 1/2 cup flour until smooth. Cook for 2 minutes, stirring. Gradually add broth, 1/4 diced green chilies, 1 teaspoon dried sage and dash of pepper. Bring to a boil. Reduce heat; simmer, covered, until thickened slightly, for about 5 minutes.

Per Serving (approx):
Calories 917	*Protein 105 gm*	*Fat 49 gm*
Carbohydrate 14 gm	*Sodium 791 mg*	*Cholesterol 341 mg*

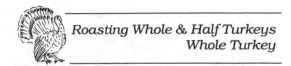
Roast Turkey with Dried Fruit Stuffing

Make it a Scandinavian Christmas with this very different recipe.

1 turkey (10 to 12 pounds)   Salt and pepper to taste

Rub salt and pepper into turkey neck and body cavities. Secure drumsticks lightly with string. Insert meat thermometer into center of thigh next to body, but not touching bone. Roast uncovered on roasting rack in 325 degree oven for 20 to 22 minutes per pound. Turkey is done when meat thermometer registers 170 to 180 degrees, thick part of drumstick feels soft when pressed with thumb and forefinger, or when drumstick moves easily.

Prepare Dried Fruit Stuffing. When turkey is done, remove from oven and let stand for 20 to 30 minutes before carving. Meanwhile, increase oven temperature to 350 degrees. Add hot water to baking pans with ramekins to depth of 1/4 to 1/2 inch. Cover pans with aluminum foil. Bake stuffing for 20 minutes; uncover and bake for an additional 10 minutes. To serve, carve turkey. Run spatula around inside of each ramekin; turn out individual servings of stuffing.   Makes 12 servings.

DRIED FRUIT STUFFING:
Bake 16 slices white bread in single layers on baking sheets for 25 mintues, turning once. Set aside; cool. Cut cooled bread into 1/4-inch pieces. Sauté 1 large onion, finely minced and 1 cup finely minced celery in 1/2 cup butter or margarine. Combine with 2 cups finely minced and peeled apple, 3 cups finely chopped pitted prunes and bread in large mixing bowl. Combine 1 can (14 1/2 ounces) chicken broth and 1/3 cup orange juice; add to bread mixture, tossing lightly to moisten thoroughly. Place in 12 greased ramekins, 3 1/2 inches each. Place ramekins in 2 baking pans, 9 x 13 inches each.*

*Note: If desired, stuffing may be baked instead 9- x 13-inch baking pan. Cover baking pan with aluminum foil and bake for 30 minutes at 350 degrees.

Per Serving (approx):
Calories 910   *Protein 89 gm*   *Fat 39 gm*
Carbohydrate 51 gm   *Sodium 725 mg*   *Cholesterol 267 mg*

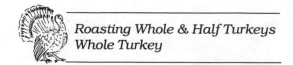

Butterflied Chile-Buttered Turkey

1 turkey (10 to 12 pounds)

Spread turkey as flat as possible (have butcher saw through backbone). Arrange skin side up on rack in baking pan. Prepare Chile Butter.

Roast turkey at 325 degrees for 2 1/2 to 3 hours, basting every 20 minutes with Chile Butter.   Makes 8 servings.

CHILE BUTTER:
Combine 3/4 cup butter, 2 cloves garlic, minced, 1 small green chile, seeds removed, minced, 1 teaspoon dried coriander or 1 tablespoon chopped cilantro, and 1 teaspoon ground cumin.

Per Serving (approx):
Calories 1064   *Protein 127 gm*   *Fat 61 gm*
Carbohydrate 2 gm   *Sodium 483 mg*   *Cholesterol 415 mg*

Turkey in an Oven-Roasting Bag

If you want to serve this turkey with stuffing, we suggest that you bake your stuffing separately. We have not had great success with stuffed poultry of any kind in an oven-roasting bag.

2 tablespoons flour   Salt and pepper to taste (optional)
1 turkey (8 to 12 pounds)

Place flour in oven-roasting bag and shake. Season turkey with salt and pepper, if desired. Place turkey in bag; place bag in baking dish.

Close bag with tie and make six 1/2-inch slits in top of bag. Cook in preheated 350 degree oven for 2 to 2 1/2 hours. Let stand for 20 minutes. Slice and serve with your favorite sauce.   Makes 8 to 12 servings.

Per Serving (approx):
Calories 603   *Protein 84 gm*   *Fat 29 gm*
Carbohydrate 1 gm   *Sodium 236 mg*   *Cholesterol 245 mg*

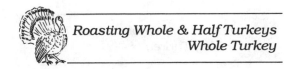
Roast Turkey Athena

Here is a very interesting alternative to a bread stuffing, compliments of Greece.

1 turkey (12 to 15 pounds)
Salt and pepper to taste
1 onion halved
2 sprigs parsley plus
   more for garnish
1/4 cup olive oil

2 tablespoons lemon juice
1/2 teaspoon dried basil,
   finely crushed
Poached peach and pear halves,
   for garnish

Season inside cavity of turkey with salt and pepper, and tuck in onion and 2 parsley sprigs. Fasten neck skin to back; truss and tie wings and drumsticks to bird. Place turkey, breast side up, on rack in shallow pan. Combine oil, lemon juice and basil. Brush over skin of turkey. Insert meat thermometer so bulb is in center of inside thigh muscle or thickest part of breast (do not allow to touch bone).

Roast, uncovered, in 325 degree oven, for about 4 1/2 to 5 hours for unstuffed turkey (about 170 to 180 degrees on meat thermometer). Baste occasionally with pan drippings. Make Bulgur Wheat Stuffing. When ready to serve, garnish turkey with peach and pear halves and parsley. Serve Bulgur Wheat Stuffing separately.   Makes 10 servings.

BULGUR WHEAT STUFFING:
Cook 1 cup chopped onion and 1 cup sliced celery in 1/2 cup butter or margarine just until vegetables begin to soften. Stir in 2 cups uncooked bulgar wheat, 1/2 teaspoon salt, 1/4 teaspoon herb seasoned pepper and 1/2 teaspoon dried poultry seasoning. Add 2 cans (10 3/4 ounces each) condensed chicken broth, 1 cup water and 1 tablespoon lemon juice. Cover and bring to a boil. Reduce heat and simmer for 15 to 20 minutes or just until vegetables are tender and liquid is absorbed. Stir in 1 cup small wedges ripe olives and 1/4 cup finely chopped parsley.

Per Serving (approx):
| *Calories 1129* | *Protein 115 gm* | *Fat 55 gm* |
| *Carbohydrate 44 gm* | *Sodium 1055 mg* | *Cholesterol 338 mg* |

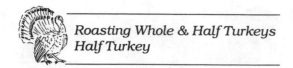
Maple-Glazed Turkey
with Apple-Pecan Stuffing

This came to us from maple syrup country. It has an interesting, subtle sweet flavor.

1 half turkey (5 to 6 pounds)
Salt and pepper to taste
4 tablespoons butter or margarine, melted

1/3 cup maple or maple-flavored syrup
1/3 cup dark corn syrup

Rinse turkey; drain and pat dry. Rub salt and pepper into neck and body cavities. Tie leg to tail with string. Lay wing flat over white meat and tie string around breast to hold wing down. Skewer skin to meat along cut edges to prevent shrinking. Place turkey on rack in shallow roasting pan, skin side up. Brush skin with 2 tablespoons of the melted butter. Insert meat thermometer into inside thigh muscle, not touching bone. Roast in 325 degree oven for 2 to 2 1/2 hours or to an internal temperature of 170 to 180 degrees.

Meanwhile, combine the remaining 2 tablespoons melted butter with the maple and corn syrups. Brush over turkey during last hour of roasting, basting several times to use all of glaze.

When turkey is done, remove from oven and let stand for 20 to 30 minutes before carving. Meanwhile, cover stuffing casserole and bake for 25 to 30 minutes at 325 degrees. Uncover during last 5 to 10 minutes of baking.   Makes 6 servings.

APPLE-PECAN STUFFING:
Tear 8 slices soft white bread into small, 1/4-inch pieces to make 6 cups. Sauté 1 small onion, chopped, and 1/2 cup chopped celery with leaves in 1/4 cup melted butter or margarine. Combine onion mixture with bread, 1 large apple, peeled, cored and chopped, and 1/2 cup pecans. Beat together 1/2 cup turkey or chicken stock, 1 egg, 3/4 teaspoon dried sage, 1/2 teaspoon salt and 1/8 teaspoon pepper. Slowly add to bread mixture, tossing lightly to mix well. Add additional stock if more moist dressing is desired. Place in greased 2-quart casserole.

Per Serving (approx):
Calories 1000   *Protein 83 gm*   *Fat 51 gm*
Carbohydrate 52 gm   *Sodium 755 mg*   *Cholesterol 304 mg*

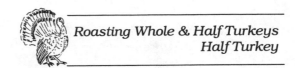
Turkey a la Jamaica

This is a mild version of Caribbean cooking. Want it closer to the original? Add your favorite chili sauce and/or chile peppers.

2 tablespoons dried onion
3 teaspoons ground thyme
2 teaspoons each onion powder
  and sugar
1 teaspoon ground allspice
1 teaspoon black pepper

1/2 teaspoon cayenne pepper
1/4 teaspoon each ground
  nutmeg and ground cinnamon
1 half turkey
1 cup water

In small bowl combine seasonings. Rub on top and bottom and under edges of skin of turkey. Place turkey on rack in baking dish, skin side up. Add water to dish. Cover with foil. Cook for 60 minutes. Remove foil and cook for 45 to 60 minutes more. Let stand for 20 minutes before slicing. Makes 12 servings.

Per Serving (approx):
Calories 309
Carbohydrate 2 gm

Protein 42 gm
Sodium 103 mg

Fat 15 gm
Cholesterol 123 mg

Handle with Care

- Do not leave turkey at room temperature.

- Refrigerate turkey at 40 degrees F. or below

- Cook ground or boneless turkey to a minimum internal temperature of 160 degrees F.

- Cook bone-in turkey to a minimum internal temperature of 170 degrees F.

- Cook whole turkey to an internal temperature of 180 degrees F. in inner thigh.

- Cool food rapidly. Store in small, shallow containers.

- Keep hands, utensils and work areas clean.

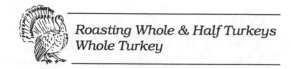
Roast Turkey with Jalapeño Corn Bread Stuffing

1 turkey (10 to 12 pounds),
  with giblets

1 cube chicken bouillon
2 1/2 cups water

Remove giblets from turkey. Rinse giblets and place, with chicken bouillon cube, in saucepan with water. Bring to a boil; cover and simmer until tender, about 1 hour. Set giblets aside for later use in gravies or soups. Reserve broth; let cool. Prepare Jalapeño Corn Bread Stuffing.

Lightly spoon stuffing into neck cavity; close with skewer. Fill body cavity. Secure drumsticks lightly with string. Roast uncovered on roasting rack in 325 degree oven for 20 to 22 minutes per pound or to internal temperature of 170 to 180 degrees.

Remaining stuffing may be baked, in covered 1 1/2-quart casserole dish, along with turkey during last hour of roasting. Uncover stuffing during final 10 minutes of cooking. Let turkey stand for at least 20 minutes before carving.   Makes 10 to 12 servings.

JALAPEÑO CORN BREAD STUFFING:
To make corn bread, combine 1 1/3 cups cornmeal, 2/3 cup flour, 2 tablespoons sugar and 1 tablespoon baking powder in medium bowl. Beat 1 egg with 1 cup milk; add to dry ingredients, mixing just until moistened. Stir in 1/4 cup melted butter or margarine. Pour batter into greased 8-inch-square baking pan. Bake at 425 degrees for 20 to 25 minutes, or until golden. Remove from oven and cool.

Make stuffing by crumbling corn bread into a large bowl. Add 6 cups dry bread cubes. Sauté 1 pound turkey sausage with 1 cup chopped onion and 1 1/2 cups chopped celery in skillet until sausage loses red color and is crumbly. Drain off all but 1/4 cup fat from sausage in skillet. Add 1 teaspoon salt, 1 teaspoon dried poultry seasoning and 1/4 cup chopped, seeded jalapeño peppers to sausage. Combine sausage mixture with bread mixture, tossing to mix well. Beat together 1 cup reserved broth from cooking giblets with 2 eggs; add to stuffing. (Add additional reserved giblet broth if desired for a more moist stuffing.)

Per Serving (approx):
Calories 859
Carbohydrate 44 gm

Protein 88 gm
Sodium 1213 mg

Fat 36 gm
Cholesterol 303 mg

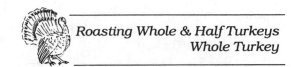

Maple-Basted Roast Turkey with New England Stuffing

1 turkey (10 to 16 pounds),
  with giblets
1 1/2 teaspoons dried poultry
  seasoning
Salt and pepper to taste

1/2 cup light maple syrup
1/2 to 1 cup reduced-sodium
  chicken broth
5 tablespoons flour
1/2 cup cranberry juice

Remove giblets from cavity of turkey; set aside for another use. Season turkey with poultry seasoning, salt and pepper.

Truss turkey and place in large roasting pan. Roast turkey in preheated 325 degree oven, allowing 14 to 18 minutes per pound (3 to 4 hours), until juices run clear (larger birds need less cooking time per pound). Baste with maple syrup during last hour. While turkey is roasting, prepare New England Stuffing. Place in oven with turkey for last 30 minutes of cooking time. Remove cooked turkey to serving platter; skim off and discard all fat from pan juices.

To prepare gravy, pour degreased pan juices into heatproof measuring cup and add enough chicken broth to measure 5 cups. Return juices to roasting pan and stir to incorporate any browned bits. In measuring cup stir flour into cranberry juice to dissolve; whisk into juices into roasting pan. Place over medium heat and cook for 5 to 10 minutes or until gravy thickens, stirring constantly. Season gravy to taste with salt and pepper. To serve, carve turkey, discarding skin. Spoon gravy over slices and accompany with stuffing.   Makes 12 to 18 servings.

NEW ENGLAND STUFFING:
Cube 10 slices dried bread into large bowl. In large skillet over medium-low heat, melt 1/4 cup low-fat margarine. Add 1 cup chopped onion, 1/2 cup chopped celery and 1 teaspoon dried poultry seasoning. Sauté for 8 to 10 minutes until vegetables are softened. Add vegetables and 1/2 cup dried cranberries, cherries or mixed fruit bits to bread cubes; toss to combine. Stir in 1 1/2 cups reduced-sodium chicken broth and season with salt and pepper to taste. Transfer to greased baking dish.

Per Serving (approx) including stuffing and gravy:

Calories 425	*Protein 59 gm*	*Fat 11 gm*
Carbohydrate 18 gm	*Sodium 390 mg*	*Cholesterol 150 mg*

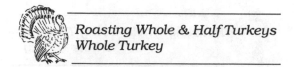

Southwest Turkey Roast

1 turkey (12 to 14 pounds)

Prepare Southwestern Rice Stuffing and Orange Glaze.

Spoon stuffing into turkey cavity and truss. Roast for 20 minutes per pound at 325 degrees (or use Grill Method, below), basting with Orange Glaze. Cover with foil if skin gets too dark. Let stand for 20 to 30 minutes before carving. Serve with stuffing.   Makes 12 to 14 servings.

SOUTHWESTERN RICE STUFFING:
Stir 1 1/2 cups long-grain rice, 1 tablespoon butter and 1/4 teaspoon salt into 3 cups boiling water; reduce heat and simmer, covered, for 20 minutes. Sauté 3 cloves garlic, minced, 3 medium red or green bell peppers, chopped, 1 large red onion, chopped, 5 jalapeño chilies, seeded and finely chopped, and 3 ears corn, kernels cut off cob, or 1 package (10 ounces) frozen whole kernel corn, thawed, in 3 tablespoons olive oil; combine with rice and 1/4 cup chopped cilantro or 2 teaspoons dried coriander and 1/4 teaspoon chili powder.

ORANGE GLAZE:
Sauté 2 cloves garlic, chopped, in 1/4 cup melted butter until soft. Add 1/2 cup orange marmalade and 1/2 teaspoon ground cumin. Heat through.

GRILL METHOD:
Do not stuff turkey. Roast in covered grill, using indirect method,* for 10 to 15 minutes per pound to 180 to 185 degrees internal temperature at thigh. Bake stuffing in uncovered casserole at 375 degrees for 30 to 35 minutes, moistening occasionally with juices caught in drip pan.

*Note: For information on indirect-heat cooking, see page 255.

Per Serving (approx) including glaze:
Calories 796	*Protein 85 gm*	*Fat 37 gm*
Carbohydrate 30 gm	*Sodium 439 mg*	*Cholesterol 258 mg*

BARBECUING & GRILLING

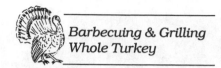

Turkey Grill

Marinate a butterflied whole turkey in fruit juices and wine for a delectable dinner party main course.

1 quart each cranberry juice
   and orange juice
1 bottle Sauvignon Blanc
   (reserve 1/4 cup for glaze)
2 teaspoons each chopped
   fresh rosemary and thyme
   or 1 teaspoon each dried

1 cup chopped onion
Salt and pepper to taste
1 turkey, butterflied
   (about 12 pounds)

Combine all ingredients except turkey. Place turkey in marinade for 2 hours; turn turkey halfway through. Place turkey on grill with cover, breast side up, and cook for approximately 15 to 20 minutes per pound. (Internal temperature should be 170 degrees). Brush with Rosemary-Wine Glaze last 15 minutes of cooking time.　　Makes 8 to 10 servings.

ROSEMARY-WINE GLAZE:
Blend together 3/4 cup honey, 1/4 cup each Sauvignon Blanc and lemon juice, and 1 tablespoon chopped fresh rosemary.

Per Serving (approx):
Calories 1225
Carbohydrate 59 gm

Protein 128 gm
Sodium 499 mg

Fat 44 gm
Cholesterol 368 mg

Direct-Heat Cooking

Remove top grill rack; open all vents. Mound 40 to 50 briquettes in center of lower grill rack or bottom of grill; ignite briquettes. When coals become ash gray (about 20 to 40 minutes), spread them evenly over lower grill rack or bottom of grill. Lightly grease top grill rack and reposition it over hot coals; place turkey on grill rack.

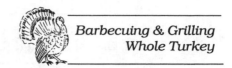

Southwestern Butterflied Turkey with Roasted Garlic

Never grilled a whole turkey? One good way is to split it down the back and lay it flat. Makes the grilling quick and easy.

1 turkey (10 to 12 pounds)	1 teaspoon red pepper flakes
3/4 cup butter, melted	1 teaspoon ground cumin
2 tablespoons chopped cilantro or	Salt to taste
1 teaspoon dried coriander	

Ask butcher to saw turkey through backbone, leaving breast attached. Spread turkey flat. Prepare medium-hot charcoal fire. When coals are gray, arrange around perimeter of barbecue. Put turkey on grill, skin side up. Combine butter, cilantro, pepper flakes, cumin and salt. Baste turkey with seasoned butter. Cover, leaving vents partly open, and grill for about 2 hours, adding fresh briquettes as needed. Baste every 20 minutes. About 1 hour before turkey is done, prepare Roasted Garlic and corn. Serve turkey with Roasted Garlic and Grilled Corn, squeezing cloves of garlic over turkey as you eat. **Makes 10 servings.**

ROASTED GARLIC:
Select 8 to 10 medium heads garlic. Cut across top of each to expose cloves; do not peel. Place each on sheet of aluminum foil; drizzle with olive oil. Sprinkle with chopped herbs, if desired. Close foil packets and place around turkey about 1 hour before turkey is done.

GRILLED CORN WITH SAVORY BUTTER:
To grill corn in husk, peel back husk and remove silk. Pull husk back up and tie with string. Soak corn in water for 15 minutes. Grill for 15 to 20 minutes, turning occasionally. Serve with melted butter flavored with minced fresh herbs (1 tablespoon per 1/2 cup butter) or spices (2 teaspoons chili powder to 1/2 cup butter, for example).

Per Serving (approx) excluding garlic and corn:

Calories 1056	*Protein 126 gm*	*Fat 61 gm*
Carbohydrate 0 gm	*Sodium 530 mg*	*Cholesterol 415 mg*

Sonoma Turkey Barbecue

Some of the best wines and some of the best turkeys share a common heritage: Sonoma County, California. Everyone knows that Sonoma County produces premium wines, but, unknown to most, Sonoma County is also home to the largest turkey breeding operation in the world. The Nicholas Turkey Breeding Farms ships more than 300 million turkey eggs each year to growers in Europe, Asia and throughout the United States. You'll enjoy this classic Sonoma County turkey barbecue.

1/3 cup tomato paste
1/2 cup White Zinfandel
1/2 cup each chopped red
   onion and cilantro
2 teaspoons each chili powder
   and cumin

Salt and pepper to taste
1 half breast turkey
   (2 to 3 pounds)
1 to 2 tablespoons oil

Mix together tomato paste, wine, onion, cilantro, chili powder, cumin, salt and pepper. Rub turkey breast with oil.

Grill in covered barbecue, using indirect method,* for 10 to 15 minutes per pound to 170 degrees internal temperature. Brush with some sauce during last 1/2 hour of cooking time. Thin remaining sauce to desired consistency, bring to a boil and serve with sliced turkey.

Makes 4 to 6 servings.

*Note: For information on indirect-heat cooking, see page 255.

Per Serving (approx):
Calories 484	*Protein 63 gm*	*Fat 21 gm*
Carbohydrate 7 gm	*Sodium 249 mg*	*Cholesterol 153 mg*

Thai Turkey Kabobs

Thailand and California are joined in this recipe with the blending of Asian ingredients with wine.

1 1/2 pounds turkey breast fillets
   or tenderloins
1 cup Chardonnay wine
1/3 cup soy sauce

1 tablespoon minced fresh ginger
   or 1 teaspoon ground
3 cloves garlic, minced

Cut turkey into 1-inch cubes. Combine wine, soy sauce, ginger and garlic. Pour over turkey and let marinate for 2 hours in refrigerator. Remove turkey; reserve 1/2 cup marinade and prepare Thai Peanut Sauce.

Thread turkey on skewers. Brush with half the sauce. Grill over medium coals for 10 to 15 minutes or until done; turn frequently. Heat remaining sauce thoroughly, thinning with Chardonnay if necessary, and serve with turkey kabobs. Makes 6 servings.

THAI PEANUT SAUCE #2:
Sauté 1/2 cup chopped onion in 1 tablespoon each sesame oil and vegetable oil until soft. Add 1/2 cup reserved marinade, 1/3 cup peanut butter, 2 tablespoons each brown sugar and catsup, 1/2 teaspoon ground coriander and dash of red pepper flakes. Whisk together.

Per Serving (approx):
Calories 342
Carbohydrate 11 gm

Protein 31 gm
Sodium 1042 mg

Fat 16 gm
Cholesterol 69 mg

Roman-Style Grilled Turkey Breast

2 tablespoons lemon juice
2 tablespoons olive oil
2 tablespoons minced fresh
   oregano or 2 teaspoons dried
2 to 3 cloves garlic, minced

1 teaspoon red pepper flakes
1 teaspoon black pepper
1 teaspoon salt
1 turkey breast (4 to 6 pounds)

Prepare covered grill for indirect-heat cooking.* When coals are hot, arrange in double layer around drip pan, with 8 to 10 unlit coals at outer edge of fire. Add 1 cup water to drip pan and open all vents.

In small bowl combine lemon juice, 1 tablespoon of the oil, oregano, garlic, red pepper flakes, 3/4 teaspoon of the black pepper and 1/2 teaspoon of the salt.

Working from broad "neck end" of breast, carefully run fingers under skin to loosen. Leave skin attached at base of breast to hold in seasonings. Spread combined seasonings under skin and rub into flesh. Rub outside of skin with remaining oil and sprinkle with remaining salt and black pepper.

Place turkey breast on grill over drip pan; cover and grill for 15 to 30 minutes per pound or until meat thermometer inserted in thickest part of breast registers 170 to 175 degrees. Turn breast every 30 minutes to brown evenly; let stand for 10 minutes before carving.

Makes 8 to 10 servings.

*Note: For information on indirect-heat cooking, see page 255.

Per Serving (approx):
Calories 374
Carbohydrate 1 gm

Protein 82 gm
Sodium 377 mg

Fat 5 gm
Cholesterol 226 mg

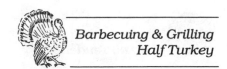

Teriyaki Turkey Luau

Hawaii is in your own backyard with this luau recipe, the aromas from which will probably bring out grass skirts and ukuleles.

1 half turkey (5 to 6 pounds)	2 tablespoons honey
Salt to taste	1 tablespoon soy sauce
4 sweet potatoes	3 tablespoons lime juice
Oil	Dash of ground ginger
2 tablespoons butter or margarine	4 slices pineapple, canned or fresh
2 tablespoons dark brown sugar, firmly packed	

Skewer turkey skin to meat along cut edges to prevent shrinking during roasting. Rub cavity lightly with salt. Tie leg to tail with string. Lay wing flat over white meat and tie string around breast end to hold wing down.

Prepare grill for indirect-heat cooking.* Slowly cook turkey for about 20 minutes per pound or until meat thermometer inserted in thickest part of breast registers 170 to 175 degrees. Add more charcoal as needed to maintain heat (about every 30 minutes).

Meanwhile, scrub sweet potatoes; pat dry, then prick each with fork and brush with vegetable oil. Wrap each in a square of aluminum foil, over-lapping ends. Bake along with turkey, turning occasionally during final hour of cooking.

For basting sauce, melt butter in small saucepan. Add brown sugar, honey, soy sauce, lime juice and ginger, stirring to combine. Heat through. Brush on turkey during last hour of roasting.

When turkey is done, remove from grill and let stand for 20 minutes before carving. Continue cooking potatoes. Grill pineapple slices, brushing with remaining sauce and turning once. Carve turkey. Serve with sweet potatoes and pineapple slices.   Makes 4 generous servings.

*Note: For information on indirect-heat cooking, see page 255.

Per Serving (approx):
Calories 1072	*Protein 114 gm*	*Fat 48 gm*
Carbohydrate 46 gm	*Sodium 710 mg*	*Cholesterol 325 mg*

Mesquite-Grilled Turkey

1 cup mesquite chips
2 pounds turkey breast
  tenderloins or fillets

Black pepper to taste
Salsas, for accompaniment

In small bowl cover mesquite chips with water and allow to stand for 2 hours. Preheat charcoal grill for direct-heat cooking.* Drain water from mesquite chips and add chips to hot coals.

Sprinkle tenderloins with pepper and grill for 15 to 20 minutes or until turkey is no longer pink in center and registers 170 degrees on meat thermometer. Turn turkey halfway through grilling time. Allow to stand 10 minutes before serving.

To serve, slice turkey into 1/2-inch-thick medallions and arrange on serving plate. Top with choice of salsas.   Makes 8 servings.

*Note: For information on direct-heat cooking, see page 284.

Per Serving (approx) using tenderloins:
Calories 129	*Protein 27 gm*	*Fat 2 gm*
Carbohydrate 0 gm	*Sodium 76 mg*	*Cholesterol 70 mg*

Turkey a l'Orange

1 pound turkey breast
   tenderloins
1 tablespoon brown sugar
2 teaspoons cornstarch

1/2 cup orange juice
1 1/2 teaspoons lemon juice
1 teaspoon butter
1 tablespoon brandy (optional)

Place turkey on broiler pan. Move oven rack so top of turkey is 5 inches from heat. Broil 10 minutes; turn. Broil for 10 minutes on each side.*

Meanwhile, combine sugar and cornstarch in saucepan; add juices and butter. Cook over medium heat, stirring constantly until thickened. Serve over turkey.   Makes 2 to 4 servings.

TO FLAME:
Heat brandy in small pan over low heat until it begins to sizzle along sides of pan when tilted. Remove from heat. Using long match, light brandy; pour over turkey and sauce.

MICROWAVE METHOD:
Place turkey in glass baking dish; cover with plastic wrap, turning back corner to vent. Microwave on high for 4 minutes. Turn turkey over. Cover. Microwave on high for 2 to 5 minutes more or until no longer pink. Combine sugar, cornstarch, juices, butter and brandy (if used) in 2-cup glass measure. Microwave on high for 2 minutes, stirring halfway through cooking.

*Note: Recipe is written for large (2 per package) turkey breast tenderloins. Decrease total cooking time to 10 minutes if small (3 or 4 per package) tenderloins are used.

Per Serving (approx):
Calories 178
Carbohydrate 5 gm

Protein 27 gm
Sodium 74 mg

Fat 6 gm
Cholesterol 72 mg

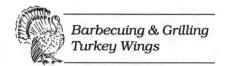
Zesty Grilled Turkey Wings

For a delicious, economical barbecue, this dish scores high.

4 turkey wings
3 cans beer or
   4 cups chicken broth
1/2 teaspoon salt
1/2 teaspoon black pepper
1 can (16 ounces) Italian-style
   tomatoes, drained
1/2 cup each cider vinegar,
   beef broth and melted butter

1/2 cup chopped onion
2 tablespoons each
   Worcestershire sauce
   and brown sugar
1/2 teaspoon each curry
   powder and chili powder

Simmer turkey wings in beer, salt and pepper for 30 minutes. Place all remaining ingredients in blender or food processor; blend to make sauce. In pan, cook sauce for 20 minutes over medium heat or until slightly thickened. Grill wings, basting liberally with sauce, for about 30 minutes.* Serve any remaining sauce with wings.   Makes 4 servings.

*Note: Wings can be baked in 350 degree oven, for 1 hour, basting with sauce occasionally.

Per Serving (approx):
Calories 771
Carbohydrate 22 gm

Protein 51 gm
Sodium 682 mg

Fat 46 gm
Cholesterol 207 mg

Pineapple and Turkey on Skewers

1 pound turkey steaks
1 can (16 ounces) pineapple
   chunks with juice
2 tablespoons regular or
   reduced-calorie Italian
   salad dressing

1 tablespoon soy sauce or
   Worcestershire sauce
1/4 teaspoon ground cinnamon
   or apple pie spice
Salt and pepper to taste

Cut turkey into 1 1/2-inch cubes. Thread on skewers, alternating with pineapple. Reserve pineapple juice. Brush turkey with salad dressing. Broil or barbecue 3 inches from heat source, turning frequently, for approximately 15 minutes. Meanwhile, combine reserved pineapple juice, soy sauce and spice in small saucepan. Simmer, uncovered, to thicken glaze. Spoon over turkey just before serving.   Makes 4 servings.

Per Serving (approx):
Calories 300
Carbohydrate 25 gm

Protein 38 gm
Sodium 330 mg

Fat 5 gm
Cholesterol 25 mg

Mustard-Topped Turkey Steaks

1 pound turkey steaks
2 teaspoons vegetable oil
2 tablespoons reduced-calorie
   mayonnaise
1 tablespoon white wine

1 1/2 tablespoons bread
   crumbs
1 1/2 teaspoons Dijon-style
   mustard
1/4 teaspoon sugar

Preheat broiler. Brush turkey steaks with oil on both sides. In small bowl combine remaining ingredients; set aside. Place turkey on boiler rack. Broil 5 to 6 inches from heat for 5 minutes on each side. Spread mustard mixture over turkey; broil for 1 1/2 to 2 minutes longer or until topping is hot and golden brown. Slice to serve.   Makes 4 servings.

Per Serving (approx):
Calories 183
Carbohydrate 3 gm

Protein 27 gm
Sodium 247 mg

Fat 6 gm
Cholesterol 73 mg

Island Grilled Turkey Breast

1 half breast turkey
  (approximately 4 pounds)

Place foil drip pan on bottom of kettle grill surrounded by hot coals. Place turkey on rack over drip pan. Cover. Cook for 2 to 2 1/2 hours or to internal temperature of 170 degrees. (Add coals during cooking to maintain heat.) Meanwhile, combine Island Sauce ingredients. Brush turkey with sauce frequently during last 30 minutes of grilling.

Makes 8 servings.

ISLAND SAUCE:
Combine 1/4 cup butter, melted, 1/3 cup honey, 1 tablespoon Dijon mustard, 1 teaspoon curry powder and 1/4 teaspoon garlic powder.

Per Serving (approx):
Calories 371	*Protein 55 gm*	*Fat 12 gm*
Carbohydrate 12 gm	*Sodium 223 mg*	*Cholesterol 141 mg*

Glazed Sesame Turkey

1 turkey breast (2 to 3 pounds)   1 teaspoon sesame seeds

Prepare grill for indirect-heat cooking.* Put foil drip pan on bottom of kettle grill surrounded by hot coals. Place turkey on rack over drip pan. Cover. Cook for 1 hour. (Add coals during cooking to maintain heat.) Prepare Orange-Apricot Sauce. Brush turkey with sauce and sprinkle with sesame seeds. Cook for 30 minutes more to internal temperature of 170 degrees. Serve with remaining sauce.   Makes 2 to 4 servings.

ORANGE-APRICOT SAUCE:
Combine 1 cup orange marmalade, 1/2 cup apricot nectar, 1 tablespoon soy sauce and 1 tablespoon cornstarch. Cook, stirring frequently, until thickened.

*Note: For information on indirect-heat cooking, see page 255.

Per Serving (approx):
Calories 518	*Protein 53 gm*	*Fat 6 gm*
Carbohydrate 63 gm	*Sodium 381 mg*	*Cholesterol 120 mg*

Midsummer Turkey Kabobs

3 ears corn, cut into 1-inch
  slices
2 medium zucchini, cut into
  3/4-inch pieces
2 red bell peppers, cut into
  1-inch cubes

2 turkey tenderloins
  (approximately 1 pound),
  cut into 1-inch cubes
1/3 cup reduced-calorie
  Italian salad dressing

In medium saucepan over high heat, parboil corn for about 1 to 2 minutes. Remove from water and plunge into cold water.

In large bowl place corn, zucchini, peppers, turkey and dressing. Cover and refrigerate for 1 to 2 hours.

Drain turkey and vegetables, discarding marinade. Alternately thread turkey cubes and vegetables on eight 9-inch skewers, leaving 1/2-inch space between turkey and vegetables.

On charcoal grill, cook kabobs for 18 to 20 minutes total, brushing with additional dressing. Turn skewers after first 10 minutes.

Makes 4 servings.

Per Serving (approx):
Calories 218
Carbohydrate 18 gm

Protein 30 gm
Sodium 381 mg

Fat 4 gm
Cholesterol 70 mg

Chutney-Curry Grill

It took us 3 years to get the recipe for the best-ever chutney that makes up the glaze. It comes from Partner/Chef Danny at Ella's, a thirty-seven seat restaurant in San Francisco.

2 teaspoons chopped fresh mint
1 teaspoon each black pepper
  and minced garlic

Salt to taste
2 cups plain yogurt
4 to 6 turkey thighs

Combine mint, pepper, garlic and salt with yogurt; mix well. Brush over turkey; let stand in refrigerator for 2 hours. Grill over medium-hot coals to 170 degrees internal temperature, about 45 minutes. Turn and baste with glaze during last 15 minutes of grilling.　　Makes 4 to 6 servings.

GLAZE:
Mix together 1 cup chutney, 1/2 cup Gewürztraminer wine and 2 teaspoons curry powder.

CHUTNEY:
Bring 1 package (1 pound) brown sugar and 1 1/2 cups cider vinegar to a boil. Add 3 cups peeled green apples cut into little cubes and return to a boil. Add 1 lemon, very thinly sliced, 2 cloves garlic, minced, 3/4 cup diced red bell pepper, 1 cup diced onion, 1 1/2 cups raisins, 1 teaspoon salt and 2 teaspoons cayenne pepper. Boil until thick, stirring consistently.

Per Serving (approx):
Calories 590
Carbohydrate 46 gm

Protein 252 gm
Sodium 867 mg

Fat 64 gm
Cholesterol 200 mg

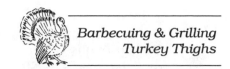

Lemony Barbecued Turkey Thighs

Economical turkey thighs become a delicious treat with this unusual recipe using lemon and white wine.

4 small turkey thighs (1/2 to 3/4 pound each) or 2 large turkey thighs (1 to 1 1/2 pounds each) 1/4 cup oil	1/2 teaspoon black pepper 1 teaspoon crushed dried rosemary 2 tablespoons vinegar 2 tablespoons soy sauce 2 tablespoons lemon juice

Combine oil, wine, pepper, rosemary, vinegar, soy sauce and lemon juice in heavy plastic bag. Add turkey thighs; close bag securely. Refrigerate for 6 to 8 hours or overnight, turning occasionally. Remove thighs from marinade, reserving marinade.

Grill thighs, uncovered, over single layer of slow coals approximately 1 to 1 1/2 hours or until tender and cooked through, turning once and adding more charcoal as needed to maintain temperature. Pour reserved marinade into small saucepan and heat on grill along with thighs, basting thighs with marinade every 15 minutes. Drizzle remaining heated marinade over thighs before serving.   Makes 4 servings.

Per Serving (approx):
Calories 577   *Protein 69 gm*   *Fat 30 gm*
Carbohydrate 2 gm   *Sodium 809 mg*   *Cholesterol 210 mg*

Bigger, Better, Best

Improvements in genetics, feed and management practices have made domesticated turkeys more efficient at converting feed to protein than turkeys found in the wild. About 2.8 pounds of feed are required for every pound of weight gain.

Domesticated turkeys are also bred to have more breast meat, meatier thighs and white feathers. Greater efficiency has lowered cost to consumers making turkey an excellent food value.

Mixed Turkey Grill
with Two-Alarm Barbecue Sauce

Select a variety of turkey sausages—Polish style, smoked, and Italian style—
to make this a truly "mixed" grill.

1 bottle (12 ounces) chili sauce
2 cups catsup
1 can (15 ounces) thick tomato
  sauce
1/2 cup firmly packed
  brown sugar
3 tablespoons chili powder
2 tablespoons Worcestershire
  sauce

2 tablespoons lemon juice
1 tablespoon ground coriander
3 cloves garlic, minced
Approximately 3 pounds
  turkey thighs
Olive oil
2 pounds assorted turkey
  sausages

Whisk together chili sauce, catsup, tomato sauce, brown sugar, chili
powder, Worcestershire sauce, lemon juice, coriander and garlic.

Prepare medium-hot charcoal fire. Brush turkey thighs with olive oil.
Grill sausages and thighs until sausages are cooked through and thighs
register 175 degrees on meat thermometer. Baste thighs with barbecue
sauce during final 15 minutes of cooking.   Makes 10 to 12 servings.

Per Serving (approx):
Calories 360
Carbohydrate 21 gm

Protein 35 gm
Sodium 1120 mg

Fat 15 gm
Cholesterol 110 mg

Turkey Kabobs

1 pound turkey breast fillets,
  cut into 1-inch-wide strips
1/2 pound sliced turkey bacon,
  slices halved
1 red bell pepper, cut into
  2-inch squares

1/3 cup lemon juice
1/3 cup honey
2 tablespoons soy sauce
1/4 teaspoon black pepper
1 clove garlic, minced
1 teaspoon cornstarch

Thread turkey, bacon slices and bell pepper onto wooden skewers. In shallow dish combine lemon juice, honey, soy sauce, black pepper and garlic. Add prepared skewers; marinate for at least 15 minutes. Reserve marinade at room temperature.

Grill or broil skewers about 5 minutes on each side or until turkey and bacon are cooked through. To make dipping sauce, stir cornstarch into marinade; heat until sauce boils and thickens slightly.

Makes 14 to 18 kabobs, 4 to 6 servings.

Per Serving (approx):
Calories 257
Carbohydrate 19 gm

Protein 23 gm
Sodium 868 mg

Fat 10 gm
Cholesterol 70 mg

Fear of Flying

Domesticated turkeys cannot fly. Wild turkeys can fly for short distances up to 55 miles per hour and can run 25 miles per hour.

Oriental Turkey Fillets

1 pound turkey breast fillets
1/4 cup peanut oil
1/4 cup soy sauce

2 cloves garlic, minced
2 tablespoons grated fresh ginger
Salt and pepper to taste

Place fillets in shallow baking dish. In small bowl whisk together oil, soy sauce, garlic, ginger, salt and pepper. Pour over fillets, turning to coat well. Cover and refrigerate for 1 hour or longer.

Prepare grill for direct-heat cooking.* Remove fillets from marinade; discard marinade. Grill, uncovered, 6 inches over medium-hot coals, for 3 to 5 minutes on each side or until cooked through.

Makes 2 or 3 servings.

*Note: For information on direct-heat cooking, see page 284.

Per Serving (approx):
| *Calories 293* | *Protein 26 gm* | *Fat 20 gm* |
| *Carbohydrate 2 gm* | *Sodium 1175 mg* | *Cholesterol 61 mg* |

Peppery Turkey Fillets

1 pound turkey breast fillets
1/4 cup Worcestershire sauce
1 tablespoon Dijon mustard

1 tablespoon oil
2 teaspoons cracked black
  pepper

Place fillets in shallow baking dish. In small bowl combine Worcestershire, mustard and oil. Pour over fillets, turning to coat well. Cover and refrigerate for 1 hour or longer.

Prepare grill for direct-heat cooking.* Remove fillets from marinade; sprinkle with pepper to taste. Grill, uncovered, 5 to 6 inches over medium-hot coals for 3 to 5 minutes on each side or until cooked through.

Makes 2 to 3 servings.

*Note: For information on direct-heat cooking, see page 284.

Per Serving (approx):
| *Calories 185* | *Protein 27 gm* | *Fat 8 gm* |
| *Carbohydrate 1 gm* | *Sodium 192 mg* | *Cholesterol 69 mg* |

Turkey Zanzibar

1 pound turkey breast
   tenderloins
1 tablespoon oil
1 teaspoon curry powder

1/2 teaspoon ground cumin
Salt and pepper to taste
1/2 small lemon or lime
Mango chutney (optional)

Brush tenderloins on both sides with oil and rub with seasonings. Squeeze lemon over turkey; set aside.

Prepare grill for direct-heat cooking* or preheat broiler. Grill or broil tenderloins 5 to 6 inches from heat source for 5 to 8 minutes on each side or until cooked through. Serve with mango chutney (if desired) and Cool Cucumber Salad.   Makes 4 servings.

COOL CUCUMBER SALAD:
In medium size bowl combine 1 cup plain low-fat yogurt, 2 tablespoons thinly sliced green onion, 1 tablespoon vegetable oil, 1 tablespoon lemon or lime juice and 1 tablespoon minced parsley. Stir in 1 teaspoon honey or sugar; season to taste with salt, black pepper and paprika. Add 1 1/2 cups thinly sliced cucumber and toss gently. Serve on lettuce leaves.

*Note: For information on direct-heat cooking, see page 284.

Per Serving (approx) (excluding salad):
Calories 161
Carbohydrate 1 gm

Protein 28 gm
Sodium 57 mg

Fat 4 gm
Cholesterol 70 mg

Fruited Turkey Kabobs

1 pound turkey breast tenderloins
1 green bell pepper

1 orange
1/4 fresh pineapple

Cut turkey into 1-inch cubes. Combine marinade ingredients in large bowl; add turkey and let stand for 15 minutes. Cut bell pepper, orange and pineapple each into 8 chunks. leaving rind on pineapple and orange. Alternate with turkey on skewers.

Grill 4 inches from hot coals for about 20 minutes, turning frequently. Bring remaining marinade to a boil. Serve with rice and marinade on the side. Boil the marinade before you serve it.   Makes 4 servings.

MARINADE:
Combine 1/2 cup lemon juice, 1/2 cup oil, 3/4 teaspoon dried oregano, 1/8 teaspoon black pepper and 1/8 teaspoon garlic powder.

Per Serving (approx):
Calories 620
Carbohydrate 51 gm

Protein 30 gm
Sodium 65 mg

Fat 33 gm
Cholesterol 69 mg

Hot-n-Spicy Barbecued Drumsticks

These drumsticks are definitely different! Their piquant and spicy glaze will truly wake up your taste buds.

4 large turkey drumsticks
   (about 1 1/2 pounds each) or
   8 small turkey drumsticks
   (about 3/4 pound each)
1 can (8 ounces) tomato sauce
Juice of 1 lemon

4 large cloves garlic, crushed
2 tablespoons sugar
1 teaspoon chili powder
Salt and pepper to taste
1 teaspoon Worcestershire sauce
1/4 teaspoon hot pepper sauce

Wrap each drumstick in heavy-duty aluminum foil, leaving room for steam expansion and keeping dull side of foil out. Grill over single layer of slow coals, 1 hour for large drumsticks and 45 minutes for small drumsticks, turning every 15 minutes and adding additional charcoal as needed to maintain temperature.

Meanwhile, prepare barbecue sauce by combining tomato sauce, lemon juice, garlic, sugar, chili powder, salt, pepper, Worcestershire sauce and hot pepper sauce in small bowl.

Remove aluminum foil from drumsticks and continue grilling for an additional 30 minutes over slow coals, basting twice on each side with sauce and turning drumsticks after 15 minutes.   Makes 8 servings.

Per Serving (approx):
Calories 273
Carbohydrate 6 gm

Protein 35 gm
Sodium 270 mg

Fat 12 gm
Cholesterol 104 mg

Grilled Turkey Breast
with Cherry Sauce

1 turkey breast, bone in
   (approximately 5 pounds)
1 can (21 ounces) cherry pie
   filling

2 tablespoons soy sauce
2 tablespoons cooking sherry
1/2 teaspoon ground ginger
1/2 teaspoon ground allspice

Preheat grill for indirect-heat cooking.*

Place turkey, skin side up, on grill rack over drip pan. Cover grill and cook for 60 to 90 minutes or until meat thermometer inserted in thickest portion of turkey breast registers 170 degrees.

In small saucepan over low heat, combine cherry filling, soy sauce, sherry, ginger and allspice. Simmer for 5 minutes to blend flavors. In blender container puree 1/2 cup sauce. Brush pureed sauce over turkey breast during last 10 minutes of grilling time.

Remove turkey breast from grill and let stand for 15 minutes. To serve, slice breast, arrange slices on platter and top with remaining warm sauce.

Makes 10 to 12 servings.

*Note: For information on indirect-heat cooking, see page 255.

Per Serving (approx):
Calories 234
Carbohydrate 18 gm

Protein 31 gm
Sodium 274 mg

Fat 4 gm
Cholesterol 71 mg

Herbed Turkey
and Vegetable Kabobs

2 turkey tenderloins
   (approximately 1 1/2 pounds)
1 medium onion
12 mushrooms, 1 1/2 inches
   in diameter
1 large green bell pepper
3 medium zucchini
12 cherry tomatoes

1 cup margarine
1/4 cup chopped parsley
1 teaspoon dried thyme
1 teaspoon dried marjoram
1/2 teaspoon salt
1/8 teaspoon black pepper
1 teaspoon lemon juice
1 small clove garlic

To make kabobs use 12 metal skewers about 9 inches each. Cut each turkey tenderloin in half lengthwise; cut each half into 6 chunks, for total of 24 chunks. Quarter onion; separate pieces. Cut stems of mushrooms even with caps. Cut bell pepper into 12 chunks. Cut each zucchini into 1-inch chunks, to make total of 18 chunks.

To build turkey-zucchini kabobs, use 4 turkey chunks and 3 zucchini chunks for each of 6 skewers. Alternate turkey and zucchini chunks, beginning and ending with turkey.

To build vegetable kabobs, arrange as follows: 1 mushroom, 1 bell pepper chunk, 1 onion piece, 1 cherry tomato, 1 bell pepper chunk, 1 onion piece, 1 cherry tomato and 1 mushroom.

Prepare herbed butter by melting margarine in small saucepan; remove from heat. Stir in parsley, thyme, marjoram, salt, pepper and lemon juice; add garlic clove.

Prepare grill for direct-heat cooking.* Place turkey-zucchini kabobs over hot, glowing coals; baste with herbed butter. Cook for 10 minutes; turn and baste again. Add vegetable kabobs to grill and baste; cook an additional 10 minutes or until turkey and vegetables are done as desired.

Makes 6 servings.

*Note: For information on direct-heat cooking, see page 284.

Per Serving (approx):
Calories 322
Carbohydrate 8 gm

Protein 3 gm
Sodium 562 mg

Fat 31 gm
Cholesterol 320 mg

Herb Grilled Turkey and "Sweets"

3 to 4 tablespoons olive oil
1/4 cup white wine
2 tablespoons
   Worcestershire sauce
1 tablespoon honey
1 teaspoon salt
1 teaspoon crushed dried rosemary

1/2 teaspoon dried thyme
1/4 teaspoon black pepper
1 clove garlic, minced
1 boneless turkey breast
   (approximately 1 1/2 pounds)
4 small sweet potatoes,
   scrubbed and cut in half
   lengthwise

In shallow baking dish combine oil, wine, Worcestershire sauce, honey, salt, rosemary, thyme, pepper and garlic. Mix well, reserving 2 tablespoons. Add turkey to herb marinade, coating both sides. Cover and let marinate in refrigerator for 3 hours or overnight.

Prepare coals in covered grill at least 30 minutes before grilling, placing grill 6 to 8 inches above coals. Reserving marinade, place turkey on grill over medium-hot coals. Cover and grill for 20 to 30 minutes per pound, brushing often with marinade and turning several times.

Meanwhile, brush cut sides of potatoes with reserved 2 tablespoons marinade. Place potatoes at edge of grill around roast and cook for 30 to 40 minutes; turn several times and brush with marinade. To serve, slice turkey and accompany with potatoes.   Makes 6 servings.

Per Serving (approx):
Calories 306   *Protein 28 gm*   *Fat 10 gm*
Carbohydrate 25 gm   *Sodium 497 mg*   *Cholesterol 70 mg*

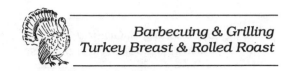

Turkey Breast Dijon

This tender, boneless white meat should be sliced on an angle and served like London Broil.

1 boneless turkey breast
   (1 1/2 pounds)
1/2 cup Dijon mustard
6 tablespoons chopped green onion
2 tablespoons soy sauce

4 tablespoons fresh lemon juice
1/2 teaspoon cayenne pepper
   (optional)
4 tablespoons oil

Place turkey breast in wide shallow bowl. In small bowl combine remaining ingredients except oil; whisk in oil. Pour half of mixture over turkey, cover and refrigerate for 1 hour or longer. Reserve remaining mixture for basting.

Prepare covered grill for indirect-heat cooking.* When coals are hot, arrange in double layer around drip pan. Remove breast from marinade, discard marinade, and place turkey on grill over drip pan. Open all vents, cover and grill over medium-hot coals for 20 minutes per pound or until cooked through, turning and basting 2 or 3 times with reserved marinade.   Makes 4 to 6 servings.

*Note: For information on indirect-heat cooking, see page 255.

Per Serving (approx):
Calories 272
Carbohydrate 3 gm

Protein 26 gm
Sodium 897 mg

Fat 17 gm
Cholesterol 61 mg

Cajun Grilled Turkey

To convert Cajun Grilled Turkey to a "smoked" recipe, add water-soaked aromatic wood chips or herbs to the coals while cooking.

1 turkey half breast (2 to 3 pounds)
2 tablespoons oil
1 tablespoon Worcestershire sauce
1 large clove garlic, minced
1 teaspoon dried Italian seasoning

1 teaspoon paprika
1/2 teaspoon cayenne pepper
1/2 teaspoon black pepper
1/4 teaspoon salt

Prepare covered grill for indirect-heat cooking.* Place turkey in shallow roasting pan. In small bowl combine remaining ingredients. Carefully loosen skin from breast to form pocket. Rub half seasoning mixture under skin and remainder over outside of breast. Cover and refrigerate until coals are ready.

Bank hot coals in double layer around drip pan with 6 to 8 unlit coals at outer edge of fire. Add 1 cup water to drip pan. Open all vents on grill. Place turkey on grill, skin side down, 5 to 6 inches over drip pan. Grill, covered, for 20 to 30 minutes per pound or until meat thermometer inserted in the thickest part of breast registers 170 to 175 degrees. Turn 3 times during cooking.   Makes 4 to 6 servings.

*Note: For information on indirect-heat cooking, see page 255.

Per Serving (approx):
Calories 257
Carbohydrate 1 gm

Protein 30 gm
Sodium 176 mg

Fat 15 gm
Cholesterol 87 mg

Hawaiian Turkey Fillets

1/4 cup soy sauce
1/4 cup pineapple juice
1 tablespoon brown sugar
1/4 teaspoon ground ginger
1 clove garlic, finely chopped

1/8 teaspoon cayenne pepper
  (optional)
1 pound turkey fillets
1/2 teaspoon cornstarch
Fresh pineapple wedges

In medium bowl or plastic food bag, combine soy sauce, pineapple juice, brown sugar, ginger, garlic and cayenne (if used). Add turkey; let marinate for several hours or overnight in refrigerator.

Remove turkey from marinade; reserve marinade. Grill or broil turkey for about 4 to 6 minutes on each side or until turkey is no longer pink.

In small saucepan mix cornstarch with reserved marinade. Cook, stirring occasionally, until sauce boils and slightly thickens. Serve sauce with turkey. Garnish with pineapple.   Makes 3 to 4 servings.

Per Serving (approx):
Calories 176
Carbohydrate 6 gm

Protein 28 gm
Sodium 1093 mg

Fat 5 gm
Cholesterol 69 mg

Tenderloins with Plum Sauce

1 pound turkey breast tenderloins
1 can (16 ounces) purple plums
1/2 cup apple juice

4 teaspoons cornstarch
1/4 teaspoon ground allspice

Place turkey on broiler pan. Move oven rack so top of turkey is 5 inches from heat. Broil 10 minutes; turn. Broil for 10 minutes on each side. Meanwhile, drain plums, reserving syrup. Combine syrup, apple juice and cornstarch in saucepan. Cook over medium heat, stirring constantly until thickened. Meanwhile, pit and coarsely chop plums. Add plums and allspice to sauce. Cook for 1 minute more. Serve over turkey.

Makes 4 servings.

MICROWAVE METHOD:
Place turkey in glass baking dish. Cover with plastic wrap, turning back cover to vent. Microwave on high for 4 minutes. Turn turkey over. Cover. Microwave on high for 5 minutes or until no longer pink. Combine plum syrup, apple juice and cornstarch in 2-cup glass measure. Microwave on high for 3 to 4 minutes, stirring once every minute. Meanwhile, pit and coarsely chop plums. Add plums and allspice to sauce. Microwave on high for 1 minute. Serve over turkey.

Per Serving (approx):
Calories 225	*Protein 28 gm*	*Fat 5 gm*
Carbohydrate 21 gm	*Sodium 65 mg*	*Cholesterol 69 mg*

Tangy Turkey Tenders

1 1/2 cups lemon-lime soda
1/4 cup soy sauce
1/4 cup oil
1 teaspoon horseradish powder

1 teaspoon garlic powder
1 pound turkey breast
    tenderloins, butterflied

In plastic bag combine soda, soy sauce, oil, horseradish powder and garlic powder. Add turkey. Seal bag and refrigerate for at least 2 hours or overnight. Preheat grill for direct-heat cooking.* Remove turkey from plastic bag; discard marinade. Grill turkey 5 to 6 minutes per side or until meat is no longer pink in center.

Makes 4 servings.

*Note: For information on direct-heat cooking, see page 284.

Per Serving (approx) excluding roll:
Calories 157	*Protein 27 gm*	*Fat 4 gm*
Carbohydrate 2 gm	*Sodium 242 mg*	*Cholesterol 70 mg*

Midwestern Turkey Barbecue

2 pounds turkey thighs or drumsticks

Wrap turkey in heavy-duty foil. Cook for 45 minutes in covered kettle grill 4 inches from medium-hot coals; turn. Cook for 45 minutes more. (Add coals during cooking to maintain heat.)

Meanwhile, prepare Midwest Sauce. Remove turkey from foil. Brush with sauce and grill 10 minutes more, turning occasionally. Serve with remaining sauce.   Makes 4 servings.

OVEN METHOD: Place turkey in casserole or Dutch oven; add 1 cup water. Cover. Bake in 350 degree oven for 2 hours. Pour off liquid; increase oven temperature to 400 degrees. Combine sauce ingredients and pour over turkey. Bake uncovered for 30 minutes more.

MIDWEST SAUCE:
In saucepan combine 1/4 cup catsup, 3 tablespoons chili sauce, 1 tablespoon brown sugar, 1 tablespoon chopped onion, 2 teaspoons butter, 2 teaspoons Worcestershire sauce, 2 teaspoons prepared mustard, 1/2 teaspoon celery seed, 1/4 teaspoon garlic powder, and dash of hot pepper sauce. Bring to a boil; reduce heat and simmer for 10 minutes.

Per Serving (approx):
Calories 332   *Protein 46 gm*   *Fat 13 gm*
Carbohydrate 7 gm   *Sodium 369 mg*   *Cholesterol 145 mg*

Turkey Normande

2 pounds turkey drumsticks

Rinse turkey; pat dry. Wrap each drumstick in heavy-duty foil. Cook for 45 minutes in covered kettle grill, 4 inches from medium-hot coals; turn. Cook for 45 minutes more. (Add coals during cooking to maintain heat.)

Meanwhile, prepare sauce. Remove turkey from foil. Brush with sauce and grill for 10 minutes more, turning occasionally. Heat remaining sauce and serve with turkey.   Makes 4 to 6 servings.

TO MAKE AHEAD:
Rinse turkey; pat dry. Place in skillet with 1 cup water. Bring to a boil; reduce heat, cover and simmer for 2 hours. Pour off liquid. Cover and refrigerate.

Before serving, grill turkey 4 inches from medium-hot coals for 30 minutes, turning occasionally. Brush with Normande Sauce and grill for 10 minutes more.

NORMANDE SAUCE:
Combine 1 cup apple butter and 2 tablespoons soy sauce.

Per Serving (approx):
Calories 319
Carbohydrate 25 gm

Protein 30 gm
Sodium 425 mg

Fat 11 gm
Cholesterol 90 mg

MICROWAVE COOKING

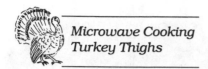

Turkey Bourguignon

Beef Bourguignon is one of France's most traditional dishes. It comes from the Burgundy region and has many variations. This version makes two thoroughly modern substitutions: turkey for health, microwaving for speed.

3 slices bacon, diced
1 medium onion, thinly sliced
3 tablespoons flour
12 small white onions, peeled
1/2 teaspoon dried thyme
3/4 cup Burgundy or other dry
   red wine

1/4 cup hot water
1 bay leaf
1 3/4 pounds turkey thighs,
   skin removed
1 cup sliced mushrooms

In 3-quart microwave-safe utensil, place bacon; cover with paper towel. Microwave on high for 3 to 4 minutes or until crisp, stirring twice. Stir in onion, flour, white onions, thyme, wine and water; add bay leaf.

Place thighs, smooth side down, on top of mixture; cover with plastic wrap. Microwave on high for 5 minutes. Reduce power to medium-high; microwave for 30 minutes, turning thighs halfway through cooking time and adding mushrooms during last 5 minutes. Let stand, covered, for 10 minutes.   Makes 2 or 3 servings.

Per Serving (approx):
Calories 580
Carbohydrate 37 gm

Protein 60 gm
Sodium 287 mg

Fat 17 gm
Cholesterol 170 mg

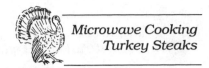
Turkey Cordon Bleu

1/4 cup butter
1 pound turkey breast steaks
1 1/2 cups seasoned croutons, crushed
1/4 teaspoon paprika

2 slices (1 ounce each) turkey ham
2 slices (1 ounce each) Swiss cheese
4 teaspoons Dijon mustard

Place butter in glass baking dish. Microwave on high for 45 to 60 seconds.

Pound turkey between pieces of plastic wrap to uniform thickness. Combine crumbs and paprika. Dip turkey in melted butter, then in crumb mixture. Place 1/2 slice turkey ham and 1/2 slice cheese on each turkey steak; spread each with 1 teaspoon mustard. Roll up and secure with toothpicks.

Arrange rolls in circle in glass baking dish. Cover with waxed paper and microwave on high for 5 minutes. Rearrange uncooked portions toward outer edge of dish. Microwave on high for 5 to 7 minutes more. Remove toothpicks before serving.   Makes 4 servings.

Per Serving (approx):
Calories 485
Carbohydrate 26 gm

Protein 39 gm
Sodium 950 mg

Fat 25 gm
Cholesterol 121 mg

Tom Turkey at Work

Q. How many poults can one Tom turkey father?

A. A Tom turkey can produce as many as 1500 poults during a hen's 6-month production cycle.

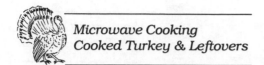
Fettuccine Alfredo Plus

If you're too busy to go to Rome and have fettuccine at Alfredo's, make this at home, put some opera on the stereo and enjoy!

3 tablespoons butter or
  margarine
2 tablespoons flour
1 1/2 cups milk
1 cup grated Parmesan cheese

1 cup sliced mushrooms
1 medium onion, sliced
1 cup diced cooked turkey
8 ounces fettuccine, cooked
1/4 cup sliced almonds

In 4-cup glass measure, place 2 tablespoons of the butter. Microwave on high for 40 seconds. Blend in flour until smooth; gradually stir in milk. Microwave on high for 3 1/2 to 4 1/2 minutes, stirring every minute until thick and bubbly. Add Parmesan cheese; stir to blend. Cover with plastic wrap and set aside.

In 2-quart microwave-safe utensil, combine remaining butter, mushrooms and onion. Cover with plastic wrap; microwave on high for 4 minutes, stirring twice. Add turkey and re-cover with plastic wrap; microwave for 2 minutes. Stir in cheese sauce and pour over pasta, tossing to combine. Serve sprinkled with almonds.   Makes 4 servings.

Per Serving (approx):
Calories 474
Carbohydrate 29 gm

Protein 30 gm
Sodium 720 mg

Fat 27 gm
Cholesterol 301 mg

Turkey Manicotti

1 pound ground turkey
1/2 cup finely chopped onion
1 teaspoon garlic powder
1/2 teaspoon dried Italian seasoning
1/4 teaspoon black pepper
1 1/2 cups cottage cheese
1 package (10 ounces) frozen chopped
  spinach, thawed and squeezed dry

1/2 cup grated Parmesan cheese
1 cup plain yogurt
1/4 cup egg substitute or 1 egg
1 tablespoon dried parsley flakes
12 manicotti shells, uncooked
4 cups spaghetti sauce
1 1/2 cups grated mozzarella
  cheese

In 1-quart microwave-safe dish, combine turkey, onion, garlic powder, Italian seasoning and pepper. Microwave on high for 4 to 5 minutes or until no longer pink, breaking up turkey halfway through cooking time.

In large bowl combine cottage cheese, spinach, Parmesan cheese, yogurt, egg substitute, parsley and turkey mixture. Stuff uncooked manicotti shells with turkey mixture. In bottom of 9- x 13-inch microwave-safe baking dish, spoon 2 cups of the spaghetti sauce. Layer manicotti shells over sauce. Top manicotti shells with remaining turkey mixture and spaghetti sauce. Cover baking dish with vented plastic wrap. Microwave on high for 10 minutes, turning dish halfway through microwave time. Microwave on medium-high for 17 minutes, turning dish halfway through microwave time.

Uncover dish and sprinkle mozzarella cheese over manicotti during last 3 minutes of microwave time. Let stand for 15 minutes before serving.

Makes 6 servings.

Per Serving (approx):
Calories 457
Carbohydrate 25 gm

Protein 36 gm
Sodium 1654 mg

Fat 24 gm
Cholesterol 96 mg

Turkey Crust Pie

Here is another way to use stuffing as a pie shell.

1 pound ground turkey
1/4 cup seasoned dry bread
   crumbs
1/4 cup milk
1 teaspoon garlic salt
1/2 teaspoon crushed dried
   oregano
1/4 teaspoon black pepper

1/2 cup tomato paste
1/2 cup sliced mushrooms
1/2 cup grated mozzarella
   cheese
2 tablespoons chopped
   green bell pepper
2 tablespoons sliced olives

In 9-inch microwave-safe pie plate, combine turkey, bread crumbs, milk, garlic, oregano and black pepper. Mix well. Press mixture evenly over bottom and up sides of pie plate. Cover with waxed paper. Microwave on high for 3 minutes. Rotate plate a half turn; microwave for 1 to 3 minutes more or until turkey is no longer pink.

Carefully drain any excess juices. Spread tomato paste evenly over turkey "crust." Top with mushrooms, cheese, bell pepper and olives. Cover, and microwave on high for 1 1/2 minutes or until cheese is melted. Let stand for 5 minutes. Cut into wedges.   Makes 6 servings.

Per Serving (approx):
Calories 181
Carbohydrate 8 gm

Protein 17 gm
Sodium 191 mg

Fat 9 gm
Cholesterol 64 mg

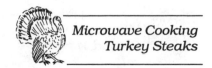

Turkey Marengo

Legend has it that Napoleon Bonaparte's chef invented Chicken Marengo in 1800 to celebrate the Battle of Marengo. We thought it was time for an update, so we used turkey instead of chicken and a microwave oven instead of a campfire.

1 pound turkey steaks	1 clove garlic, minced
1 can (8 ounces) tomatoes, cut up, juice reserved	3/4 teaspoon dried Italian seasoning
1 cup sliced mushrooms	1/2 tablespoon cornstarch
1 small onion, chopped	2 tablespoons cold water
1/4 cup dry red wine	

Cut turkey steaks in half and place in 10- x 7-inch microwave-safe dish. In medium bowl combine tomatoes with their juice, mushrooms, onion, wine, garlic and Italian seasoning. Pour over turkey. Cover with plastic wrap; microwave on medium-high for 20 minutes. Halfway through cooking time, rearrange turkey, moving parts at center of dish to outside; re-cover and complete cooking. Remove turkey to serving plate; cover with aluminum foil and let stand for 5 minutes.

Combine cornstarch and water; slowly stir into tomato mixture. Microwave on high for 2 minutes or until thickened and bubbly. Serve turkey topped with sauce.

Makes 4 servings.

Per Serving (approx):
Calories 156   *Protein 28 gm*   *Fat 2 gm*
Carbohydrate 6 gm   *Sodium 153 mg*   *Cholesterol 70 mg*

> The larger the turkey the more meat there is in proportion to bone. Large turkeys are a better buy.

Turkey Tacos

1 pound ground turkey
2 tablespoons dried onion
1 tablespoon chili powder
1 teaspoon paprika
1/2 teaspoon ground cumin
1/2 teaspoon dried oregano
Salt to taste
1/4 teaspoon garlic powder

1/8 teaspoon black pepper
10 taco shells
1 to 2 tomatoes, chopped
2 to 3 cups shredded lettuce
2/3 cup grated Cheddar cheese
Taco sauce, sour cream, guac-
    amole, chopped or sliced
    olives and chopped onions

In 1-quart microwave-safe container, combine turkey, onion, chili powder, paprika, cumin, oregano, salt, garlic powder and pepper. Cover and microwave on high for 5 to 6 minutes or until meat is no longer pink, stirring 1 or 2 times during cooking. Spoon into taco shells; top each taco evenly with tomato, lettuce, cheese, and other toppings, if desired.

Makes 5 servings.

Per Serving (approx):
Calories 320
Carbohydrate 20 gm
Protein 23 gm
Sodium 276 mg
Fat 17 gm
Cholesterol 82 mg

Nacho Special

1 to 1 1/4 pounds ground turkey
1 package taco seasoning mix
1/4 cup water
2 ounces shredded mild
    Monterey jack cheese
1 can (16 ounces) refried beans
2 tablespoons chopped green chilies

2 cups shredded or chopped
    lettuce
3 to 4 tomatoes, chopped
1 package (8 ounces) unsalted
    tortilla chips
1 cup prepared guacamole
1/2 cup sour cream

Place turkey in microwave-safe casserole; cover with waxed paper. Microwave on high for 4 minutes, stirring after 2 minutes. Stir in seasoning mix and water. Microwave on high for 2 minutes. In shallow microwave-safe baking dish, combine meat mixture and cheese; shape into rings. Spoon beans on top and sprinkle with chilies; cover with waxed paper and microwave on medium-high for 2 to 3 minutes. Around meat mixture, arrange shredded lettuce. Top with tomatoes and tortilla chips. Mound guacamole in center; top with sour cream.   Makes 8 servings.

Per Serving (approx):
Calories 440
Carbohydrate 37 gm
Protein 22 gm
Sodium 824 mg
Fat 24 gm
Cholesterol 53 mg

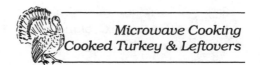

Turkey Chili with Black Beans

For full blending of flavors, make this dish one day prior to serving.

1 cup chopped onion
1 red bell pepper, cut in
　1/4-inch cubes
2 cloves garlic, minced
2 jalapeño peppers, seeded
　and minced
1 can (28 ounces) tomatoes,
　coarsely chopped, liquid reserved
1 tablespoon chili powder
1 1/2 teaspoons ground
　cumin
1 1/2 teaspoons ground
　coriander

1/2 teaspoon dried oregano
1/2 teaspoon dried marjoram
1/4 teaspoon red pepper flakes
1/4 teaspoon ground cinnamon
1 can (16 ounces) black beans,
　rinsed and drained
2 cups cooked turkey
　cut in 1/2-inch cubes
1/2 cup coarsely chopped
　cilantro
4 tablespoons shredded
　reduced-fat Cheddar cheese

In 3-quart microwave-safe dish, combine onion, bell pepper, garlic, jalapeño peppers and tomatoes. Stir in chili powder, cumin, coriander, oregano, marjoram, red pepper flakes and cinnamon. Cover dish. Microwave on high for 10 minutes; stir halfway through. Stir in beans and turkey; re-cover dish. Microwave on high for 4 minutes; stir in cilantro. To serve, ladle into bowls and garnish with cheese.

Makes 4 to 6 servings.

Per Serving (approx):
Calories 278
Carbohydrate 26 gm

Protein 30 gm
Sodium 632 mg

Fat 6 gm
Cholesterol 60 mg

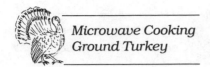
Meatball Rigatoni

1 to 1 1/4 pounds ground
   turkey
3/4 cup finely chopped onion
1/2 cup seasoned dry bread
   crumbs
1/4 cup grated Parmesan cheese,
   plus more for sprinkling

1 can (6 ounces) tomato paste
1 teaspoon dried Italian
   seasoning
1 jar (30 ounces) chunky vegetable spaghetti sauce
8 ounces small rigatoni,
   cooked and drained

In medium bowl mix turkey, onion, bread crumbs, the 1/4 cup grated Parmesan, 3 tablespoons of the tomato paste and the Italian seasoning. Shape mixture into 12 meatballs.

In 10-inch microwave-safe pie plate, arrange meatballs in circle; cover with waxed paper. Microwave on high for 6 minutes. Rearrange and turn meatballs. Re-cover and microwave on high for 4 to 6 minutes longer.

Meanwhile, in medium bowl combine spaghetti sauce and remaining tomato paste; add cooked meatballs. Discard juices from pie plate. Place rigatoni in plate; spoon in meatballs and sauce to combine. Cover with waxed paper. Microwave on high for 5 minutes or until sauce is bubbly. Sprinkle with additional Parmesan; cover and let stand for 5 minutes before serving.   Makes 4 to 6 servings.

Per Serving (approx):
Calories 405
Carbohydrate 46 gm

Protein 22 gm
Sodium 929 mg

Fat 15 gm
Cholesterol 71 mg

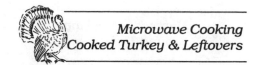

Divine Cheddar Divan

If you prefer, use broccoli in place of the asparagus.

2 tablespoons butter or
  margarine
2 tablespoons flour
1 cup milk
2 teaspoons Dijon mustard
1/8 teaspoon cayenne pepper,
  or to taste

8 slices cooked turkey
2 cups asparagus spears,
  partially cooked
1/2 cup shredded sharp
  Cheddar cheese

In 4-cup glass measure, place butter; microwave on high for 40 seconds. Stir in flour; gradually stir in milk. Microwave on high for 3 to 4 minutes, stirring every minute until thick. Stir in mustard and cayenne.

In shallow 2 1/2-quart microwave-safe utensil, place turkey. Arrange asparagus on top with tips to center. Pour sauce over top; cover with waxed paper. Microwave on medium for 7 to 8 minutes; sprinkle cheese over top. Microwave on medium for 2 to 3 minutes more. Allow to stand, covered, for 5 minutes before serving.   Makes 4 servings.

Per Serving (approx):
Calories 247
Carbohydrate 7 gm

Protein 23 gm
Sodium 258 mg

Fat 14 gm
Cholesterol 76 mg

Easy Microwave Turkey Lasagne

1 pound ground turkey
1 clove garlic, chopped
1 cup chopped onion
1 can (14 1/2 ounces) tomatoes,
   chopped, liquid reserved
1 can (6 ounces) tomato paste

2 1/2 teaspoons dried Italian
   seasoning or dried oregano
8 uncooked lasagna noodles
1 container (12 ounces) low-fat
   cottage cheese
2 cups (8 ounces), shredded
   part-skim mozzarella cheese

In 2-quart, microwave-safe casserole, combine ground turkey, garlic and onion; cover. Microwave on high for 5 minutes, stirring halfway through cooking time. Stir in tomatoes, including juice, tomato paste and seasoning. Microwave, uncovered, on high for 5 minutes.

Lightly grease 2-quart oblong microwave-safe casserole. Spoon one-third of sauce (about 1 1/3 cups) over bottom of dish. Top with 4 lasagna noodles, breaking noodles to fit. Spoon cottage cheese over noodles. Sprinkle mozzarella over top of cottage cheese. Spoon one-third more sauce over cheese; top with remaining noodles. Spoon remaining sauce over noodles and cover with vented plastic wrap.

Place several layers of paper toweling in bottom of microwave oven to absorb any spills. Microwave on high for 5 minutes. Reduce power to medium; microwave for 20 to 25 minutes or until noodles are tender.

Makes 8 servings.

Per Serving (approx):
Calories 325
Carbohydrate 29 gm

Protein 27 gm
Sodium 616 mg

Fat 11 gm
Cholesterol 56 mg

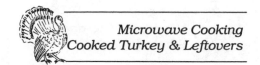

Easy Elegant Cream Soup with Tarragon

This soup, a salad and a dessert are a perfect combination for a luncheon party.

3 tablespoons butter or
  margarine
1/4 cup minced shallot
  or green onion
1/3 cup flour
3 cans (13 3/4 ounces each)
  chicken broth or about 5 cups
  homemade turkey broth

2 cups finely diced cooked
  turkey
1 cup whipping cream
1 tablespoon minced fresh
  tarragon or basil
Salt and pepper to taste

In 3-quart microwave-safe utensil, place butter. Microwave on high for 1 minute. Add shallot; microwave on high for 2 to 3 minutes, stirring once. Blend in flour; gradually add broth, stirring to blend. Cover with plastic wrap; microwave on high for 10 minutes, stirring every 2 minutes. Stir in turkey and cream. Microwave on medium-high for 5 minutes, stirring twice. Stir in tarragon and season with salt and pepper to taste. Makes 6 servings.

Per Serving (approx):
Calories 320
Carbohydrate 9 gm

Protein 18 gm
Sodium 236 mg

Fat 24 gm
Cholesterol 90 mg

The Whole Turkey

1 turkey (10 pounds)
8 tablespoons butter, softened
1 teaspoon paprika
1 medium onion, diced
1 medium carrot, diced
1 medium rib celery, diced

1 1/4 teaspoons dried poultry
  seasoning
2 cups homemade turkey
  stock
3 tablespoons flour
Salt and freshly ground pepper
  to taste

Rub turkey with 5 tablespoons of the butter, and sprinkle with paprika. In bowl combine onion, carrot, celery and poultry seasoning. Place in body cavity. Or use your favorite stuffing in place of the vegetables. Tie drumsticks together with string. Place turkey, breast side down, on microwave-proof rack and roasting pan. Tent pan with waxed paper.

Estimate entire cooking time at 1 1/2 to 2 hours, allowing 10 to 11 minutes per pound in 700-watt oven, more or less if yours is larger or smaller. Microwave on high for 10 minutes. Reduce setting to medium and continue cooking for 30 minutes, or to halfway point of estimated cooking time. Turn turkey breast side up. Pour off accumulated juices and reserve. Continue cooking on medium, covered with waxed paper, until entire time is up, about 45 minutes. Remove turkey from oven, cover with foil and let stand for 20 minutes. Turkey is done when meat thermometer inserted in thickest part of thigh, not touching bone, reaches 180 degrees.

To make gravy, combine cooking juices in 1-quart microwave-proof bowl and let stand for 5 minutes. Skim off clear yellow fat. Add enough stock to measure 2 1/2 cups. Microwave on high until boiling, 3 minutes.

In 1-quart microwave-proof bowl, microwave remaining butter on high until melted. Whisk in flour and microwave on high until light brown, about 2 minutes. Whisk in hot cooking liquid and microwave on high until thickened, about 2 minutes. Season with salt and pepper to taste.

                          Makes 8 to 12 servings.

Per Serving (approx):
Calories 703   *Protein 85 gm*   *Fat 37 gm*
Carbohydrate 7 gm   *Sodium 593 mg*   *Cholesterol 266 mg*

Layered Meat Loaf Ring

A very attractive presentation!

3/4 pound mushrooms
1 to 1 1/4 pounds ground turkey
2 slices bread, torn into small pieces
1/4 cup catsup
1 egg, lightly beaten

1/2 teaspoon salt
1/4 teaspoon black pepper
4 green onions, chopped
1 can (8 ounces) tomato sauce
1 teaspoon Worcestershire sauce

Set aside 10 whole mushrooms; finely chop remaining mushrooms. In large bowl combine chopped mushrooms, turkey, bread, catsup, egg, salt and pepper; mix to blend.

In center of 9-inch microwave-safe pie plate, place inverted 6-ounce custard cup. Pack half of meat mixture in pie plate, forming circle around cup. Cut 5 remaining mushrooms lengthwise in half; place on top of meat mixture. Spoon chopped green onions over mushrooms and meat; top with remaining meat mixture.

Pat meat loaf and press edges firmly to seal; cover with waxed paper. Microwave on high for 5 minutes; reduce power to medium and microwave 20 minutes longer. Let stand, covered, for 5 minutes.

Slice remaining 5 mushrooms and place in 2-cup glass measure. Stir in tomato sauce and Worcestershire sauce. Microwave on high for minutes, stirring once.

To serve, place meat loaf on serving plate, remove custard cup and spoon sauce around top.   Makes 4 to 6 servings.

Per Serving (approx):
Calories 184
Carbohydrate 13 gm

Protein 17 gm
Sodium 672 mg

Fat 7 gm
Cholesterol 91 mg

Holiday Strata

2 cups chopped cooked turkey
2 packages (8 ounces each) frozen
  hash brown potatoes, thawed
2 cups shredded Cheddar cheese
1 cup chopped onion
1 cup chopped red and green
  bell pepper

4 eggs
3/4 cup milk
1 clove garlic, crushed
1/2 teaspoon salt
White pepper to taste

In greased shallow 2 1/2-quart microwave-safe baking dish, layer half each of turkey, hash browns, cheese, onion and bell pepper. Repeat layers.

In 4-cup glass measure, beat together eggs, milk, garlic, salt and white pepper. Microwave on medium for 3 to 5 minutes or until mixture begins to cook around edges; stir 3 or 4 times during cooking.

Pour egg mixture over layered ingredients; cover lightly with plastic wrap. Microwave on medium for 15 to 20 minutes, rotating dish once. Allow to stand, covered, for 5 minutes. Serve hot.   Makes 6 to 8 servings.

Per Serving (approx):
Calories 282
Carbohydrate 14 gm

Protein 23 gm
Sodium 329 mg

Fat 15 gm
Cholesterol 166 mg

Turkey Favored for Holiday Table

In 1991, about 300 million turkeys were raised. We "guesstimate" that 45 million of those turkeys were eaten at Thanksgiving, 23 million at Christmas and 19 million at Easter.

Persian Pita Turkey

This is a truly exciting, exotic dish!

1 tablespoon olive oil
1 red onion, sliced into thin
    rings
1 pound turkey breast tenderloins,
    sliced and cut into thin strips
1/2 teaspoon ground cumin
Salt and pepper to taste
1/8 teaspoon ground cinnamon
1/2 cup dried apricot halves,
    each snipped in half

1/4 cup golden raisins
1 small head escarole, torn
    into pieces and divided
1 can (16 ounces) garbanzo
beans,
    drained and rinsed
6 whole wheat pita breads,
    each cut in half
1/2 cup plain low-fat yogurt
    (optional)

In 3-quart microwave-safe dish, combine olive oil and onion slices; cover with plastic wrap. Microwave on high for 2 minutes, stirring once. Add turkey, cumin, salt, pepper and cinnamon. Stir to combine.

Arrange mixture to form ring against sides of dish. Cover and microwave on medium-high for 3 minutes, stirring twice. Stir in apricots and raisins. Cover and microwave on medium-high for 2 minutes. Add half the escarole and all the garbanzo beans. Cover and microwave on high for 1 1/2 minutes. Let stand, covered, for 5 minutes.

To serve, line pitas with remaining escarole and fill with hot turkey mixture. Top with yogurt, if desired.   Makes 4 servings.

Per Serving (approx):
Calories 575	*Protein 42 gm*	*Fat 8 gm*
Carbohydrate 86 gm	*Sodium 770 mg*	*Cholesterol 70 mg*

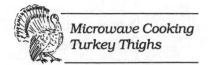
Sweet-n-Sour Turkey

Sweet and sour pork is a staple on the menus of most Chinese restaurants.
We've re-created it with turkey, and speeded things up by cooking it in a
microwave oven.

1 medium onion, chopped	1/4 cup lemon or lime juice
1/2 cup chopped celery	2 tablespoons cider vinegar
2 teaspoons water	1 1/2 pounds boneless turkey
1 cup chili sauce	thighs, cut into 1-inch chunks
1/2 cup firmly packed brown	1 tablespoon cornstarch
sugar	1 tablespoon water

In 4-cup glass measure, combine onion, celery and the two teaspoons water. Cover with plastic wrap; microwave on high for 3 minutes. Add chili sauce, brown sugar, lemon juice and vinegar; stir. Cover and microwave on high for 5 minutes.

In 3-quart microwave-safe casserole, place turkey; pour hot sauce over top. Cover with plastic wrap; microwave on high for 17 minutes, stirring 3 times.

In cup, mix cornstarch and the 1 tablespoon water. Stir into turkey mixture; re-cover and microwave on high for 5 minutes or until sauce is thick. Let stand, covered, for 5 minutes.   Makes 6 servings.

Per Serving (approx):
Calories 246   *Protein 20 gm*   *Fat 4 gm*
Carbohydrate 32 gm   *Sodium 701 mg*   *Cholesterol 71 mg*

Sweet and Sour Meatballs

1 pound ground turkey
1 egg
1/2 cup seasoned bread crumbs
1/2 cup water
1 tablespoon dried onion

1 tablespoon green bell peppers,
  chopped
1/8 teaspoon black pepper
2 tablespoons catsup

Combine all ingredients and mix thoroughly. Shape into 1 1/2-inch meatballs. Prepare Sweet and Sour Sauce.

Add meatballs to Sweet and Sour Sauce. Cover and microwave on high for 6 to 7 minutes or until meatballs are no longer pink inside. Gently stir in pineapple chunks. Microwave, uncovered, on high for 2 minutes.

Makes 6 servings.

SWEET AND SOUR SAUCE:
Combine 1/2 cup brown sugar and 3 tablespoons cornstarch in deep 2-quart microwave-safe casserole dish. Stir in juice from 1 can (20 ounces) pineapple chunks (chunks reserved), 6 tablespoons water, 3 tablespoons vinegar, and 1 tablespoon soy sauce. Microwave on high for 5 minutes, stirring twice. Stir in 1 large green bell pepper, chopped.

Per Serving (approx):
Calories 326
Carbohydrate 46 gm

Protein 17 gm
Sodium 585 mg

Fat 9 gm
Cholesterol 99 mg

Medically Oriented

Q. Are turkeys fed hormones or drugs?

A. No. Turkeys are not fed hormones. They are federally banned for used in poultry. For treatment of disease or illness, drugs are used at therapeutic levels under FDA regulations.

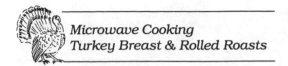

Turkey Breast a la King

4 tablespoons butter or margarine
1/4 teaspoon paprika
1 boneless turkey breast
  (approximately 1 1/2 pounds)
4 tablespoons flour
10 can (10 3/4 ounces) chicken broth

1/4 cup chopped green bell
  pepper
2 tablespoons chopped pimiento
1 cup sliced mushrooms
1/4 teaspoon salt
Dash black pepper

Place 1 tablespoon of the butter in 1-cup glass measure; microwave on high for 20 seconds or until melted. Blend in paprika. Place turkey breast skin side down on microwave-safe roasting rack or utensil. Cover with loose tent of waxed paper. Estimate total cooking time based on 10 minutes per pound; divide time in half. Microwave on high for 5 minutes. Reduce power to medium-high and microwave for remainder of first half of time.

Turn breast over and brush with butter and paprika mixture. Re-cover turkey roast with waxed paper. Microwave on medium-high for remaining time. Remove breast to platter; cover with aluminum foil and let stand for 10 minutes.

In 4-cup glass measure, place remaining butter. Microwave on high for 45 seconds or until melted. Blend in flour, then slowly add chicken broth. Microwave on high for 3 minutes, stirring twice. Add bell pepper, pimiento and mushrooms; continue to microwave for 2 to 4 minutes longer, stirring twice. Sauce should be thick and peppers tender. Stir in salt and pepper. Slice turkey and serve with sauce. Makes 6 servings.

Per Serving (approx):
Calories 237
Carbohydrate 5 gm

Protein 30 gm
Sodium 564 mg

Fat 10 gm
Cholesterol 92 mg

Golden Breaded Turkey Tenderloins

Some folks call this Wienerschnitzel.

1 egg, beaten
2 tablespoons butter or
   margarine, melted
1 1/2 teaspoons curry powder
1 cup buttery cracker crumbs
   (about 25 crackers)

1 pound turkey breast
   tenderloins, each cut into
   6 to 8 chunks
Chutney

In small bowl, combine egg and butter. On waxed paper blend curry powder and cracker crumbs. Dip turkey into egg mixture and then into crumbs. On microwave-safe roasting dish, arrange tenderloins with thicker parts toward outside. Cover with waxed paper. Reserve remaining crumbs.

Microwave on medium-high for 12 minutes per pound. Halfway through cooking, turn tenderloins and sprinkle with remaining crumbs. Cover with double thickness of paper towels. Cook, removing paper towels during last 2 minutes. Let stand, uncovered, for 5 minutes. Serve with chutney.

Makes 4 servings.

Per Serving (approx):
Calories 311   *Protein 30 gm*   *Fat 15 gm*
Carbohydrate 15 gm   *Sodium 338 mg*   *Cholesterol 139 mg*

Pasta Pie

8 ounces spaghetti, cooked
  and drained
1/4 cup grated Parmesan cheese
1 tablespoon butter or margarine
1 pound sweet or hot Italian
  turkey sausage
1/2 cup chopped onion
1 bell pepper, chopped

1 can (15 ounces) herbed
  tomato sauce
1 clove garlic, minced
1 tablespoon chopped parsley
1/2 teaspoon dried basil
1/2 teaspoon dried oregano
4 ounces shredded mozzarella
  cheese

In 10-inch microwave-safe pie plate, place spaghetti. Add Parmesan cheese and butter; toss until evenly coated. Arrange pasta on bottom and up sides of plate to form pasta crust; cover with aluminum foil and set aside.

In 2 1/4-quart microwave-safe utensil, arrange sausage; cover with waxed paper. Microwave on high for 4 minutes. Cut sausage into thin slices. Stir in onion and bell pepper; cover with waxed paper and microwave on high for 3 to 4 minutes, stirring twice. Drain off pan juices. Stir tomato sauce, garlic, parsley, basil and oregano into meat mixture; pour into pasta shell.

Sprinkle mozzarella cheese in circle over sauce. Microwave, uncovered, on high for 1 to 2 minutes or until cheese is melted. Cover with foil and let stand for 5 minutes.   Makes 4 to 6 servings.

Per Serving (approx):
Calories 266
Carbohydrate 19 gm

Protein 16 gm
Sodium 1096 mg

Fat 14 gm
Cholesterol 60 mg

SANDWICHES, BURGERS, HOAGIES & SLOPPY JOES

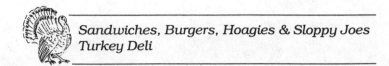

Muffaletta

This Sicilian sandwich is the perfect solution for feeding eight or more and you can make it the day before.

1 jar (5 ounces) pimiento stuffed olives, chopped

1 can (3 1/4 ounces) pitted black olives, chopped

2 tablespoons olive oil

3 tablespoons minced parsley

1 tablespoon drained capers

1 1/2 teaspoons minced garlic

1/2 teaspoon dried oregano

1 loaf (1 pound) round Italian or French bread

1/2 pound turkey salami slices

4 ounces provolone cheese, thinly sliced

In medium bowl combine olives, oil, parsley, capers, garlic and oregano.

With serrated bread knife slice bread in half lengthwise. Hollow out each bread half, leaving 3/4 inch outside shell. Reserve removed bread for another use.

Over bottom half of bread shell, spread half the olive mixture. Evenly arrange 4 ounces turkey salami over olive mixture. Top with cheese and remaining turkey salami.

In top half of bread shell, spread remaining olive mixture. Invert top bread shell over bottom bread half and press down firmly. Wrap muffaletta in foil. Refrigerate overnight.

To serve, cut muffaletta into 8 wedges.   Makes 8 servings.

Per Serving (approx):
Calories 248
Carbohydrate 18 gm

Protein 11 gm
Sodium 1008 mg

Fat 15 gm
Cholesterol 22 mg

Barbecue on a Bun

Here's another "prepare-a-day-ahead" recipe to feed a hungry crowd. This dish may be made in a slow cooker.

2 cups tomato-vegetable juice
1 cup diet cola
1 tablespoon prepared mustard
1 tablespoon bottled hot sauce
1 tablespoon Worcestershire
   sauce

2 cups shredded cooked
   turkey breast
8 hamburger buns
Coleslaw (optional)

In large saucepan over high heat, bring vegetable juice to a boil. Reduce heat to low and simmer juice down to half. Stir in cola, mustard, hot sauce and Worcestershire sauce; simmer for 2 to 3 minutes to combine well. Add turkey to sauce mixture and simmer for 15 minutes.

To serve, spoon approximately 1/3 cup turkey barbecue on bottom half of each bun, top with coleslaw (if desired) and remaining bun halves.

Makes 8 servings.

Per Serving (approx):
Calories 190
Carbohydrate 24 gm

Protein 14 gm
Sodium 475 mg

Fat 4 gm
Cholesterol 29 mg

Tortilla Flats

4 flour tortillas (9 inch)
1 pound ground turkey
1 egg white
1/3 cup tomato sauce
4 green onions, chopped
1/4 pound mushrooms,
   very thinly sliced
2 cloves garlic, minced
1/2 teaspoon ground allspice
1/2 teaspoon crumbled dried oregano

1/4 teaspoon freshly ground
   black pepper
12 soft sun-dried tomato halves,
   cut in strips and soaked in
   small amount of water
3/4 cup grated Monterey jack
   cheese
3 tablespoons shelled
   pistachio nuts

Lay out tortillas in single layer on 2 baking sheets. In bowl mix together ground turkey, egg white, tomato sauce, green onions, mushrooms, garlic, allspice, oregano, pepper and tomato strips. Pat mixture over surface of the tortillas, allowing 1/2-inch border around edge. Sprinkle with grated cheese and nuts.

Bake in 425 degree oven for 10 to 12 minutes or until tortillas are golden brown on edges and meat is cooked through.   Makes 4 servings.

Per Serving (approx):
Calories 545
Carbohydrate 46 gm

Protein 38 gm
Sodium 624 mg

Fat 23 gm
Cholesterol 154 mg

Apple-Cinnamon Sausage Sandwich

Perfect for breakfast, lunch or brunch.

1 pound turkey breakfast sausage	8 English muffins, split and toasted
1 apple, cored and cut into 8 rings	1/3 cup apple jelly
2 tablespoons water	1/2 cup plain yogurt
	1/8 teaspoon ground cinnamon

Shape turkey breakfast sausage into eight 3-inch patties. Place in non-stick or lightly greased skillet. Cook over medium heat for 8 minutes, turning occasionally. Remove patties and set aside.

Place apple rings and water in same skillet. Cover; reduce heat to medium-low and cook for 3 minutes. Place sausage on apples. Cover; cook for 3 minutes more or until apples are tender.

Assemble sandwich as follows: muffin half, apple jelly, yogurt, sprinkle of cinnamon, apple ring, sausage patty, muffin half.   Makes 8 servings.

Per Serving (approx):
Calories 191
Carbohydrate 24 gm

Protein 10 gm
Sodium 409 mg

Fat 6 gm
Cholesterol 32 mg

Voted #1

Q. What is the most popular form of turkey eaten?

A. American households consume turkey more often as a sandwich than any other way, with sandwiches accounting for 44% of all turkey consumption. Low fat, convenient products like ground turkey, sausage, bacon and various turkey parts are increasingly popular.

Turkey Dinner Sandwiches

Lunch or dinner in less than twenty minutes.

1/4 cup flour
1/4 teaspoon dried poultry
  seasoning
1/8 teaspoon salt
1 pound turkey breast slices
  (4 to 6 slices)
3 tablespoons oil
8 ounces cream cheese,
  softened

1/3 cup chopped walnuts
1 tablespoon honey
4 to 6 slices multigrain bread,
  toasted
Lettuce
1/2 to 3/4 cup whole berry
  cranberry sauce

On sheet of waxed paper combine flour, poultry seasoning and salt. Dip turkey slices into mixture, coating both sides.

In large skillet over medium heat, cook turkey slices in hot oil for 4 to 6 minutes on each side or until turkey is no longer pink.

Meanwhile, in small bowl combine cream cheese, walnuts and honey. Spread half of toasted bread slices with 2 tablespoons cream cheese mixture; top with lettuce, turkey slice, 2 tablespoons cranberry sauce and toasted bread slice. Makes 4 to 6 servings.

Per Serving (approx):
Calories 485
Carbohydrate 32 gm

Protein 23 gm
Sodium 350 mg

Fat 29 gm
Cholesterol 83 mg

Turkey Bruschetta

This Italian open-faced sandwich was traditionally made with veal cutlet. Ours is made with turkey cutlet. They even like it in Italy.

1 pound turkey breast cutlets, thinly sliced
Salt and pepper to taste
2 tablespoons olive oil
1 tablespoon dried Italian seasoning
1 to 2 cloves garlic, minced

1 small loaf Italian bread, cut in 3/4-inch-thick slices
4 ripe Italian plum tomatoes, sliced
1/2 cup shredded part-skim mozzarella cheese
6 to 8 sprigs fresh basil and/or marjoram sprigs (optional)

Preheat broiler. Sprinkle cutlets with salt and pepper; place on broiling pan. Broil 3 to 5 inches from heat source for 1 1/2 to 2 minutes per side or until cooked through.

Meanwhile, in small bowl combine oil, Italian seasoning and garlic. Brush on bread and place in broiling pan with turkey. Toast lightly on both sides. Top bread with cutlets and tomato slices; sprinkle with mozzarella.

Place under broiler just until cheese melts. Garnish with herb sprigs, if desired, and serve immediately.   Makes 4 servings.

Per Serving (approx):
Calories 395
Carbohydrate 36 gm

Protein 36 gm
Sodium 490 mg

Fat 11 gm
Cholesterol 79 mg

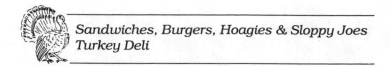

Fiesta Pinwheel Sandwiches

If these large Armenian bread rounds are not available, you can make miniature sandwiches by using pita bread instead.

1 pound cream cheese, softened
1/4 cup chopped parsley
2 rounds soft or hard Armenian
   cracker bread

1/2 pound sliced cooked
   turkey breast
1/4 pound turkey pastrami
   or turkey ham slices

Combine cream cheese and parsley. Set aside.

To soften hard bread, wet both sides thoroughly; cover with towel and let stand for 10 minutes. Meanwhile, prepare Fiesta Filling. Spread cream cheese mixture and filling over bread and top each with remaining ingredients.

Roll up into log, wrap with plastic wrap and chill for at least 1 hour before slicing. Slices may be secured with toothpicks.

Makes 4 to 6 servings.

FIESTA FILLING:
Combine 1 tomato, minced, 1/2 cup chopped green bell pepper, 1/2 red onion, minced, and alfalfa sprouts or chopped fresh spinach.

Per Serving (approx):
Calories 407	*Protein 22 gm*	*Fat 30 gm*
Carbohydrate 10 gm	*Sodium 521 mg*	*Cholesterol 122 mg*

Curried Pinwheel Sandwiches

1 pound cream cheese, softened
2 teaspoons curry powder
1 tablespoon chopped fresh mint
1/4 cup chopped parsley

2 rounds soft or hard Armenian
    cracker bread
1/2 pound sliced cooked turkey

Combine cream cheese, curry powder, mint and parsley. Set aside.

To soften hard bread, wet both sides thoroughly; cover with towel and let rest for 10 minutes. Meanwhile, prepare Indian Curry Filling. Spread cream cheese mixture and filling over bread, and top with turkey.

Roll up into log, wrap with plastic wrap and chill for at least 1 hour before slicing. Slices may be secured with toothpicks.

Makes 4 to 6 servings.

INDIAN CURRY FILLING:
Combine 1/2 cup diced almonds, toasted, 4 green onions, chopped, and 1 cup currants.

Per Serving (approx):
Calories 456
Carbohydrate 15 gm

Protein 21 gm
Sodium 325 mg

Fat 35 gm
Cholesterol 112 mg

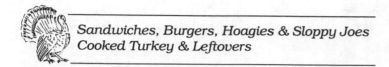

Pita Pockets

1/2 cup plain low-fat yogurt
1 tablespoon honey
1 tablespoon lemon juice
1 teaspoon curry powder
1/8 teaspoon black pepper
2 cups diced cooked turkey
1/2 cup diced bell pepper

1/2 cup diced celery
1/2 cup thinly sliced green
  onion
1/4 cup raisins
6 individual whole wheat pita
  breads, lightly toasted
1 cup sprouts (bean, alfalfa or
  radish)

n medium bowl, combine yogurt, honey, lemon juice, curry and black pepper. Add turkey, bell pepper, celery, green onion and raisins; toss to mix well. To serve, split pitas. Divide salad mixture among pitas; top with sprouts.   Makes 4 to 6 servings.

Per Serving (approx):
Calories 308
Carbohydrate 46 gm

Protein 23 gm
Sodium 292 mg

Fat 4 gm
Cholesterol 37 mg

Open-Faced Sandwiches Olé

1 1/2 to 2 cups coarsely
  chopped cooked turkey
1/2 cup prepared salsa
  or to taste
2 French rolls, split

4 thin slices Monterey jack
  cheese
Ripe avocado slices and/or
  pickled jalapeño pepper
  slices (optional)

Preheat broiler. In medium bowl combine turkey and salsa. Remove soft inside from rolls, leaving crusty "shells"; spoon in turkey mixture and top with cheese.

Broil sandwiches about 6 inches from heat source for 3 minutes or until cheese is melted and lightly browned. To serve, top sandwiches with avocado and/or jalapeno, if desired.   Makes 2 to 4 servings.

Per Serving (approx):
Calories 180
Carbohydrate 12 gm

Protein 18 gm
Sodium 246 mg

Fat 7 gm
Cholesterol 40 mg

Oven-Baked
Monte Cristo Sandwiches

8 slices firm-textured white
    sandwich bread
1 tablespoon Dijon mustard
8 slices cooked turkey
8 thin slices Swiss cheese
    (about 6 ounces)

1 tablespoon butter or
    margarine
1 tablespoon oil
3 eggs
3/4 cup milk
1/8 teaspoon black pepper

Spread bread slices with mustard. On each of 4 slices, layer 2 slices each turkey and Swiss cheese; top with remaining bread.

On 15 1/2- x 10 1/2-inch jelly-roll pan, combine butter and oil. Heat in preheated 400 degree oven for 3 minutes or until butter melts. Tilt pan to coat with butter mixture; pour excess into small bowl.

In shallow bowl beat eggs with milk and pepper. Dip sandwiches in egg mixture; place on hot jelly-roll pan. Drizzle remaining butter over tops of sandwiches.

Bake for 20 minutes or until golden brown, turning halfway through cooking time. Drain sandwiches on paper towels. Slice diagonally and serve immediately.
                                      Makes 4 servings.

Per Serving (approx):
Calories 394
Carbohydrate 32 gm

Protein 28 gm
Sodium 522 mg

Fat 17 gm
Cholesterol 215 mg

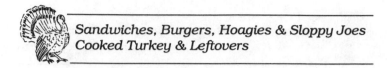

Tarragon Turkey Pitas

2 cups cooked turkey breast
   cut in 1/2-inch dice
1/2 cup low-fat lemon yogurt
1 tablespoon reduced-calorie
   mayonnaise

1/4 teaspoon finely crushed
   dried tarragon
1/2 cup green grapes, halved
4 mini whole wheat pitas
4 lettuce leaves

In medium bowl combine yogurt, mayonnaise and tarragon. Fold in turkey and grapes; cover and refrigerate for at least 1 hour.

Trim tops from pita pockets. Line inside of pitas with lettuce. Carefully fill pitas with turkey mixture. Makes 4 servings.

Per Serving (approx):
Calories 216   *Protein 19 gm*   *Fat 4 gm*
Carbohydrate 27 gm   *Sodium 771 mg*   *Cholesterol 26 mg*

Turkey Pistachio Sandwich

1/2 cup plain yogurt
1/4 cup chopped salted
   pistachio nuts
1 teaspoon dried dill weed

4 lettuce leaves
8 slices whole wheat bread
8 ounces cooked turkey
   breast, sliced

In small bowl combine yogurt, pistachio nuts and dill. Cover and refrigerate for at least 1 hour or overnight to allow flavors to blend.

To serve, arrange a lettuce leaf on a bread slice and top lettuce leaf with 2 ounces turkey. Spoon 2 tablespoons yogurt mixture over turkey and top with another bread slice. Turkey mixture will keep up to 4 days in refrigerator. Makes 4 servings.

Per serving (approx):
Calories 265   *Protein 25 gm*   *Fat 7 gm*
Carbohydrate 26 gm   *Sodium 303 gm*   *Cholesterol 42 mg*

Turkey Burger Plus

1 pound ground turkey
1 1/2 cups seasoned
   bread crumbs
1/3 cup finely chopped onion
1 egg, beaten

1 teaspoon soy sauce
1 teaspoon Worcestershire sauce
1/2 teaspoon garlic powder
1/4 teaspoon dry mustard
4 burger buns, toasted

In large bowl combine turkey, bread crumbs, onion, egg, soy sauce, Worcestershire sauce, garlic powder and mustard. Shape mixture into 4 patties, each 1/2 inch thick. On lightly greased broiling pan about 6 inches from heat, broil burgers for 3 to 4 minutes per side or until no longer pink in center. Serve burgers on buns.   Makes 4 servings.

Per Serving (approx):
Calories 378
Carbohydrate 33 gm

Protein 28 gm
Sodium 807 mg

Fat 14 gm
Cholesterol 144 mg

South of the Border Burgers

1 pound ground turkey
1 teaspoon chili powder
1/2 teaspoon instant chicken
   bouillon

4 ounces shredded Cheddar
   cheese
4 sesame sandwich buns
6 ounces guacamole

Combine turkey, chili powder and bouillon. Shape into 4 burgers. Cook in nonstick skillet over medium heat for 12 to 15 minutes, turning occasionally. Top each burger with 1/4 cup cheese. Cover. Remove from heat and let stand for 2 minutes or until cheese melts. Meanwhile, spread buns with guacamole. Serve burgers in buns.   Makes 4 servings.

Per Serving (approx):
Calories 466
Carbohydrate 24 gm

Protein 32 gm
Sodium 570 mg

Fat 27 gm
Cholesterol 117 mg

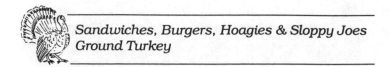

Pita Burgers

Pita burgers adapt popular pita pocket breads to a Mediterranean-style burger flavored with herbs of the Middle East.

1 to 1 1/4 pounds ground turkey	1/4 teaspoon cayenne pepper
2 cloves garlic, minced	6 pita breads, opened and
2 teaspoons paprika	lightly grilled
1 teaspoon ground cumin	3 plum tomatoes, thinly sliced
1 teaspoon ground allspice	1 small cucumber, thinly sliced
1/2 teaspoon salt	

Prepare lightly greased grill for cooking. In medium bowl combine turkey, garlic and seasonings. Form mixture into 6 patties. Grill, uncovered, 5 to 6 inches over medium-hot coals for 4 to 5 minutes on each side or until burgers are cooked through and spring back when touched.

Meanwhile, prepare Yogurt Sauce. Serve burgers in pita pockets topped with Yogurt Sauce, tomatoes and cucumbers.   Makes 4 to 6 servings.

YOGURT SAUCE:
In a small bowl combine 1 cup plain yogurt, 1 tablespoon minced parsley, 2 teaspoons minced cilantro (optional), and 1 1/2 teaspoons minced fresh mint or 1/2 teaspoon dried mint. Season with salt and pepper to taste.

Per Serving (approx):
Calories 252
Carbohydrate 26 gm

Protein 20 gm
Sodium 564 mg

Fat 8 gm
Cholesterol 60 mg

He-Man Burgers

1 to 1 1/4 pounds
  ground turkey
1/2 cup chopped green onion
1/4 to 1/3 cup prepared shrimp
  cocktail sauce

Salt and pepper to taste
4 or 5 pumpernickel or onion
  rolls split and lightly toasted
1/3 cup prepared horseradish
  sauce or sour cream

Prepare grill or preheat broiler. In medium bowl combine turkey, green onion, cocktail sauce, salt and pepper. Form into 4 or 5 burgers. Grill or broil for 4 to 6 minutes on each side or until burgers are cooked through and spring back to the touch. Spread cut side of rolls with horseradish sauce. Place burgers on lower half of rolls. Top with other half of rolls.

Makes 4 to 5 servings.

Per Serving (approx):
Calories 241
Carbohydrate 22 gm

Protein 19 gm
Sodium 481 mg

Fat 9 gm
Cholesterol 68 mg

Taco Burgers

1 pound ground turkey
1/4 cup spicy taco sauce
Salt to taste
4 slices (1 ounce each)
  reduced-fat Monterey jack cheese

4 hamburger buns
4 tablespoons guacamole
  (optional)

Remove grill rack from charcoal grill. Prepare grill for direct-heat cooking. In medium bowl combine ground turkey, taco sauce and salt. Shape into 4 burgers about 1/2 inch thick. Grease cold grill rack and position over hot coals. Grill turkey burgers for 5 to 6 minutes per side. Top each burger with slice of cheese during last minute of grilling time. To serve, place each turkey burger on bottom half of bun and top with 1 tablespoon guacamole, if desired. Place top half of bun on burger.

Makes 4 servings.

Per Serving (approx):
Calories 395
Carbohydrate 23 gm

Protein 32 gm
Sodium 541 mg

Fat 19 gm
Cholesterol 80 mg

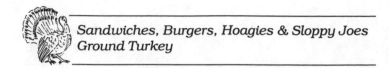

Teriyaki Turkey Burgers

Try adding Italian salad dressing and seasoned bread crumbs to ground turkey for an Italian burger. Or add taco sauce to ground turkey topped with Monterey jack cheese and guacamole dip for a taste of Mexico.

1 pound ground turkey	1 tablespoon sesame seeds,
1/2 cup finely chopped	toasted
water chestnuts	1/4 cup plum preserves
1/4 teaspoon black pepper	4 hamburger buns
2 tablespoons teriyaki sauce	

In large bowl combine turkey, water chestnuts, pepper, teriyaki sauce and 2 teaspoons of the sesame seeds. Evenly divide turkey mixture into 4 burgers, each approximately 1/2 inch thick.

On broiling pan 3 to 4 inches from heat, broil burgers for 3 to 4 minutes per side or until turkey is no longer pink in center.

In small saucepan over low heat, combine preserves and remaining 1 teaspoon sesame seeds. Heat until preserves are melted.

To serve, place a burger on bottom half of each bun, drizzle sauce over each burger and top each with other half of bun.   Makes 4 servings.

Per Serving (approx):
Calories 369

Protein 25 gm

Fat 12 gm

Carbohydrate 40 gm

Sodium 814 mg

Cholesterol 85 mg

Oriental Burgers

If you're looking for a really different flavor in a burger, try this recipe. The burgers are a bit spicy, but you can tone that down by reducing the amount of Chinese chile paste.

1 to 1 1/4 pounds ground turkey
2 to 3 tablespoons Chinese
 plum sauce*
3 green onions, chopped
1 tablespoon chopped fresh ginger

1 1/2 teaspoons Chinese chile
 paste with garlic*
1/2 teaspoon salt
4 or 5 hamburger rolls, split
 and lightly toasted

Prepare grill or preheat broiler. In medium bowl combine all ingredients but rolls. Form into 4 or 5 burgers.

Grill or broil for 4 to 6 minutes on each side until burgers are cooked through and spring back to the touch. Serve burgers warm on toasted rolls.   Makes 4 or 5 servings.

*Note: Available in the Oriental food section of your grocery store.

Per Serving (approx):
Calories 254   *Protein 20 gm*   *Fat 9 gm*
Carbohydrate 24 gm   *Sodium 535 mg*   *Cholesterol 68 mg*

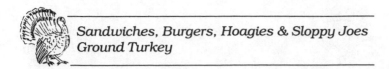

Turkey Burgers al Greco

1 pound ground turkey
1 1/2 cups seasoned
  bread crumbs
1/2 cup finely chopped onion
1 egg, beaten
1 teaspoon soy sauce
1 teaspoon Worcestershire sauce
1/2 teaspoon garlic powder

1/4 teaspoon dry mustard
4 mini pitas
6 tablespoons crumbled
  feta cheese
1 cup chopped tomato
1/2 cup thinly sliced cucumber
1/2 cup thinly sliced onion

In large bowl combine turkey, bread crumbs, onion, egg, soy sauce, Worcestershire sauce, garlic powder and mustard. Shape mixture into 4 patties, each 1/2 inch thick. On lightly greased broiling pan about 6 inches from heat, broil burgers for 3 to 4 minutes per side or until no longer pink in center.

To open pitas, cut off tops; insert burgers. Evenly sprinkle cheese, tomato, cucumber and onion into each pita.   Makes 4 servings.

Per Serving (approx):
Calories 339
Carbohydrate 16 gm

Protein 27 gm
Sodium 621 mg

Fat 18 gm
Cholesterol 175 mg

Turkish Burgers

This recipe takes the burger out of its "fast food" class and makes it a gourmet entree.

1 pound ground turkey	1/8 teaspoon ground nutmeg
1 egg, lightly beaten	2 2/3 tablespoons sour cream
1/2 cup plain bread crumbs	4 hamburger buns
4 pimiento-stuffed olives, chopped	8 slices cucumber
1 tablespoon minced parsley	4 tablespoons crumbled feta
1 clove garlic, minced	cheese
1/4 teaspoon ground cinnamon	

Preheat charcoal grill for direct-heat cooking.

In medium bowl combine turkey, egg, bread crumbs, olives, parsley, garlic, cinnamon and nutmeg. Evenly divide turkey mixture into 4 burgers, approximately 3 1/2 inches in diameter.

Grill burgers 5 to 6 minutes per side or meat is no longer pink.

To serve, spread 2 teaspoons sour cream on each bottom half of bun. Place turkey burger on each bun, top each with 2 cucumber slices, 1 tablespoon feta cheese and remaining half of bun.   Makes 4 servings.

Per Serving (approx):
Calories 439	*Protein 30 gm*	*Fat 17 gm*
Carbohydrate 42 gm	*Sodium 584 mg*	*Cholesterol 149 mg*

Mexican Turkey Burgers

1 pound ground turkey
1 1/2 cups seasoned bread crumbs
1/2 cup finely chopped onion
1 egg, beaten
1 teaspoon soy sauce
1 teaspoon Worcestershire sauce

1/2 teaspoon garlic powder
1/4 teaspoon dry mustard
4 burger buns, toasted
1 avocado, sliced (optional)
4 ounces Monterey jack cheese

In large bowl combine turkey, bread crumbs, onion, egg, soy sauce, Worcestershire sauce, garlic powder and mustard. Shape mixture into 4 patties, each 1/2 inch thick. On lightly greased broiling pan about 6 inches from heat, broil burgers for 3 to 4 minutes per side or until no longer pink in center.

Just before serving, top each burger with cheese; heat until cheese melts. Serve burgers on buns topped with sauce and, if desired, avocado.

Makes 4 servings.

SAUCE:
In small bowl combine 1/2 cup sour cream substitute, 1/4 cup chunky salsa and 1/2 teaspoon chopped cilantro.

Per Serving (approx):
Calories 548
Carbohydrate 37 gm

Protein 35 gm
Sodium 1079 mg

Fat 29 gm
Cholesterol 168 mg

For several decades after 1810 the turkey persisted in considerable numbers, especially at and beyond the frontier. However, the animal's behavior proved to be its undoing. Many of its habits which led to its successful domestication in Mexico by the Indians also contributed to its demise as a wild species.

Creamy Mushroom Turkey Burgers

1 pound ground turkey
1 1/2 cups seasoned bread crumbs
1/2 cup finely chopped onion
1 egg, beaten
1 teaspoon soy sauce
1 teaspoon Worcestershire sauce
1/2 teaspoon garlic powder
1/4 teaspoon dry mustard
1/2 pound mushrooms,
    thinly sliced

1/4 teaspoon dried thyme
2 tablespoons margarine
2 tablespoons brandy
1/2 teaspoon garlic powder
Salt to taste
1/8 teaspoon pepper
1 cup plain low-fat yogurt
4 burger buns, toasted

In large bowl combine turkey, bread crumbs, onions, egg, soy sauce, Worcestershire sauce, garlic powder and mustard. Shape mixture into 4 patties, each 1/2 inch thick. On lightly greased broiling pan about 6 inches from heat, broil burgers for 3 to 4 minutes per side, or until no longer pink in center.

While burgers are cooking, in medium skillet over medium-high heat, sauté mushrooms and thyme in margarine for 1 to 2 minutes. Add brandy, garlic powder, salt and pepper; cook for 1 minute. Stir in yogurt and heat until warm.

Serve burgers on buns topped with mushroom mixture.

Makes 4 servings.

Per Serving (approx):
Calories 361
Carbohydrate 19 gm

Protein 29 gm
Sodium 674 mg

Fat 19 gm
Cholesterol 145 mg

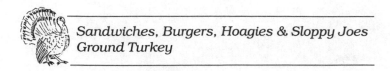
Tarragon-Mustard Burgers

1 to 1 1/4 pounds ground turkey
2 tablespoons tomato paste
1 1/2 teaspoons minced fresh
   tarragon or 1/2 teaspoon dried
Salt and pepper to taste

4 or 5 slices tomato
2 or 3 English muffins, split and
   lightly toasted
Sprigs of fresh tarragon
   (optional)

Prepare grill or preheat broiler. In medium bowl combine turkey, tomato paste, tarragon, salt and pepper. Form into 4 or 5 burgers and grill or broil for 4 to 6 minutes on each side or until burgers are cooked through and spring back to the touch.

Prepare Tarragon-Mustard Sauce. Place slice of tomato and burger on top of each English muffin half. Top with warm Tarragon-Mustard Sauce. Garnish with sprigs of fresh tarragon, if desired. Makes 4 or 5 servings.

TARRAGON-MUSTARD SAUCE:
In top of double boiler set over hot water, blend 1 1/2 tablespoons butter or margarine and 1 1/2 tablespoons Dijon mustard. Remove from heat; add 1 tablespoon tarragon vinegar. Stir in 1/4 cup reduced-fat sour cream and 1 teaspoon minced fresh tarragon or 1/4 teaspoon dried. Season with salt, black pepper and cayenne pepper to taste.

Per Serving (approx):
Calories 263
Carbohydrate 18 gm

Protein 20 gm
Sodium 477 mg

Fat 12 gm
Cholesterol 77 mg

Giant Stuffed Turkey Burger

You can also make this under your broiler or in an oven.

1 pound ground turkey
1/4 cup quick rolled oats
1 egg
1/2 teaspoon garlic powder
Dash of black pepper
1/2 cup chopped onion
1/4 cup drained dill pickle relish

2 tablespoons catsup
2 teaspoons prepared mustard
2 slices (1 ounce each) reduced-fat, low-sodium American cheese, cut into 4 equal strips
Lettuce (optional)
Tomato slices (optional)

Preheat grill for direct-heat cooking.*

In medium bowl combine turkey, oats, egg, garlic powder and pepper. Divide turkey mixture in half. On 2 pieces (each 10 by 11 inches) waxed paper, shape each half of turkey mixture into 6-inch-diameter circle. Sprinkle onion and relish over one circle of turkey mixture, leaving 1/2-inch border around outside edges; top with catsup and mustard. Arrange cheese strips, spoke fashion, over catsup and mustard. Carefully place remaining turkey mixture circle on top of cheese. Remove top layer of waxed paper from turkey mixture. Press turkey mixture edges together to seal.

Lightly grease cold grill rack and position over hot coals. Invert giant turkey burger onto grill rack; remove waxed paper. Grill burger for 8 minutes per side or until internal temperature of 165 degrees is reached on meat thermometer. To turn giant burger, slide flat baking sheet under burger and invert onto another flat cookie sheet, then carefully slide burger back onto grill rack. To serve, cut burger into fourths. Serve with lettuce and tomato slices, if desired.   Makes 4 servings.

Note: For more information on direct-heat cooking, see page 284.

Per Serving (approx):
Calories 269
Carbohydrate 8 gm

Protein 27 gm
Sodium 559 mg

Fat 14 gm
Cholesterol 133 mg

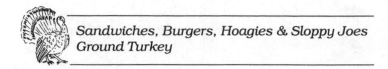

Reuben Turkey Burgers

This is an adaptation of the famous sandwich made at Reuben's restaurant in New York City.

1 pound ground turkey	1/4 teaspoon dry mustard
1 1/2 cups bread crumbs	4 slices Swiss cheese
1/2 cup finely chopped onion	(1 ounce each)
1 egg, beaten	4 burger buns, toasted
1 teaspoon soy sauce	4 tablespoons rinsed and
1 teaspoon Worcestershire sauce	drained sauerkraut
1/2 teaspoon garlic powder	4 tablespoons Russian dressing

In large bowl combine turkey, bread crumbs, onion, egg, soy sauce, Worcestershire sauce, garlic powder and mustard. Shape mixture into 4 patties, each 1/2 inch thick.

On lightly greased broiling pan about 6 inches from heat, broil burgers for 3 to 4 minutes per side or until no longer pink in center.

During last 2 to 3 minutes of cooking, top each burger with cheese; heat until cheese melts. Place burgers on buns and top with 1 tablespoon sauerkraut and Russian dressing. Heat if desired.   Makes 4 servings.

Per Serving (approx):
Calories 563	*Protein 38 gm*	*Fat 30 gm*
Carbohydrate 37 gm	*Sodium 1111 mg*	*Cholesterol 170 mg*

Norwegian Burgers

1/2 cup sour cream
1 teaspoon prepared horseradish
1/3 cup diced cucumber
1/4 teaspoon ground nutmeg
1 pound ground turkey
1/3 cup chopped mushrooms
1/3 cup chopped green onion,
  including some green tops

1/3 cup crumbled cooked bacon
1/2 teaspoon black pepper
Oil, for brushing on grill rack
8 slices pumpernickel bread,
  buttered on one side
4 slices Jarlsberg cheese
8 thin slices of large tomato

Prepare a medium-hot fire for direct-heat cooking. In small bowl combine sour cream, horseradish, cucumber and nutmeg. Set aside. In large bowl combine turkey, mushrooms, onion, bacon and pepper. Divide mixture into 4 equal portions and shape into patties the same size as pumpernickel slices.

Place patties on oiled grill and cook for 8 minutes. Turn and cook for 7 minutes longer or until done to your preference. During last few minutes of cooking, place bread slices, buttered side down, on outer edges of grill to toast lightly. During last minute or so of cooking, place cheese slice on each patty.

Spread sour cream mixture on toasted side of each bread slice. Place patties on bread slices. Arrange 2 slices tomato, overlapping, on top of each patty. Top with remaining bread slices. Slice in half on diagonal to serve.   Makes 4 servings.

Per Serving (approx):
Calories 588   *Protein 38 gm*   *Fat 26 gm*
Carbohydrate 49 gm   *Sodium 611 mg*   *Cholesterol 130 mg*

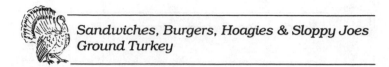
Stuffing Burgers

You can call these Thanksgiving burgers, if you like, because they taste just like a Thanksgiving turkey.

3 tablespoons butter or
  margarine
1/4 cup chopped celery
1/4 cup chopped onion
3/4 cup seasoned dry stuffing
  mix
1/4 cup chicken broth or water,
  boiling

Salt and pepper to taste
1/4 teaspoon dried sage or
  dried poultry seasoning
1 to 1 1/4 pounds ground
  turkey
1/4 cup chopped parsley
Cranberry relish (optional)

In large skillet over medium heat, melt 2 tablespoons of the butter. Add celery and onion; sauté for 5 minutes or until softened. Add stuffing, broth, salt, pepper and sage; mix well. Let mixture cool completely.

In large bowl combine turkey, stuffing mixture and parsley. Form into 4 or 5 burgers. Add remaining butter to skillet and melt over medium-high heat. Add burgers; brown for 1 minute on each side. Reduce heat to medium-low and cook for 4 to 5 minutes on each side or until burgers are cooked through and spring back to the touch. Serve with cranberry relish, if desired. **Makes 4 or 5 servings.**

Per Serving (approx):
Calories 211
Carbohydrate 5 gm

Protein 17 gm
Sodium 293 mg

Fat 14 gm
Cholesterol 85 mg

> Some historians claim that the English colonists of Jamestown, Virginia, celebrated the first Thanksgiving with a traditional, ancient harvest home festival, a sort of homecoming weekend, several years before the Pilgrims.

Roumanian Turkey Burgers

1 pound ground turkey
1 or 2 cloves garlic, crushed
1/2 teaspoon dried thyme
1/2 teaspoon salt

1/4 teaspoon ground allspice
1/4 teaspoon ground cloves
1/4 teaspoon black pepper
4 burger buns, toasted

In a large bowl combine turkey, garlic, thyme, salt, allspice, cloves and pepper. Shape mixture into 4 patties, each 1/2 inch thick. On lightly greased broiling pan, broil burgers for 3 to 4 minute per side or until no longer pink in center. Serve burgers on buns.   Makes 4 servings.

Per Serving (approx):
Calories 299
Carbohydrate 22 gm

Protein 24 gm
Sodium 567 mg

Fat 12 gm
Cholesterol 74 mg

Bavarian Turkey Burgers

1 pound ground turkey
1 1/2 tablespoons prepared
  horseradish
1 1/2 teaspoons Dijon mustard

1 1/2 teaspoons paprika
1/4 teaspoon black pepper
1/8 teaspoon salt
4 burger buns, toasted

In large bowl, combine turkey, horseradish, mustard, paprika, pepper and salt. Shape mixture into 4 patties, each 1/2 inch thick. On lightly greased broiling pan about 6 inches from heat, broil burgers for 3 to 4 minutes per side or until no longer pink in center. Serve burgers on buns.   Makes 4 servings.

Per Serving (approx):
Calories 303
Carbohydrate 23 gm

Protein 24 gm
Sodium 347 mg

Fat 13 gm
Cholesterol 74 mg

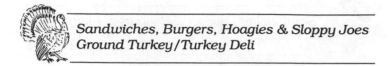
Meatball Parmigiana Hoagie

1 pound ground turkey
1 cup dry bread crumbs
1/3 cup chopped parsley
1 teaspoon dried Italian
  seasoning
1 egg

3 tablespoons grated
  Parmesan cheese
1 jar (14 ounces) spaghetti sauce
6 French rolls
1/2 cup grated mozzarella
  cheese

Combine turkey, bread crumbs, parsley, Italian seasoning, egg and Parmesan. Mix well, then let stand for 5 minutes. Form into 1-inch meatballs; place in lightly greased baking dish 13 x 9 x 2 inches. Cover and bake in preheated 350 degree oven for about 15 minutes or until meatballs are no longer pink. Stir in spaghetti sauce; heat for 10 minutes longer. Spoon meatball mixture onto sliced rolls; sprinkle with grated mozzarella cheese. **Makes 6 servings.**

Per Serving (approx):
Calories 363
Carbohydrate 38 gm

Protein 24 gm
Sodium 945 mg

Fat 13 gm
Cholesterol 101 mg

Turkey Hoagies for a Crowd

2 tablespoons oil
2 teaspoons red wine vinegar
1/2 teaspoon dried oregano
1 loaf (1 pound) French bread
2 cups shredded lettuce
1 large tomato, thinly sliced

1 medium onion, thinly sliced
  and separated into rings
3/4 to 1 pound varied
  turkey deli slices
1 package (8 ounces)
  provolone cheese, sliced

In small bowl combine oil, vinegar and oregano; set aside. Cut bread in half lengthwise and arrange lettuce, tomato and onion over bottom half. Drizzle oil and vinegar mixture over vegetables. Top with turkey and cheese slices. Cover with remaining bread half. To serve, cut hoagie into 8 slices. **Makes 8 servings.**

Per Serving (approx):
Calories 371
Carbohydrate 34 gm

Protein 20 gm
Sodium 923 mg

Fat 17 gm
Cholesterol 40 mg

Turkey Joe #1

1 pound ground turkey
2 tablespoons oil
1 1/2 cups chopped onion
1 1/2 cups chopped celery
Dash of black pepper
1/2 cup chopped green bell
   pepper

1 can (10 1/2 ounces)
   condensed tomato soup
1 tablespoon barbecue sauce
   (optional)
1 teaspoon salt
12 buns, toasted and buttered

Brown turkey in oil. Stir in chopped vegetables and cook just until tender. Add black pepper, bell pepper, soup, barbecue sauce (if used) and salt. Simmer for 30 minutes. Serve in buns.   Makes 12 servings.

Per Serving (approx):
Calories 224
Carbohydrate 27 gm

Protein 11 gm
Sodium 632 mg

Fat 8 gm
Cholesterol 30 mg

Turkey Joe #2

1 pound ground turkey
1 medium onion, chopped
2 tablespoons oil

1 cup barbecue sauce
1 tablespoon sweet pickle relish
6 hamburger buns

Cook turkey and onion in skillet in hot oil over medium heat for 8 to 10 minutes or until turkey is no longer pink, stirring and separating turkey as it cooks. Stir in barbecue sauce and relish. Cook for 2 to 3 minutes more. Serve in buns.   Makes 6 servings.

Per Serving (approx):
Calories 275
Carbohydrate 30 gm

Protein 18 gm
Sodium 615 mg

Fat 9 gm
Cholesterol 57 mg

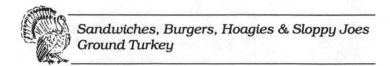

Really Rapid Pizza

Two favorite foods, pizza and turkey, team up in this quick and easy recipe, which takes just 30 minutes to prepare.

1 package (8 ounces) refrigerated crescent rolls	1 can (6 ounces) pizza sauce
1 1/2 tablespoons oil	4 ounces sliced mozzarella or Monterey jack cheese
1 to 1 1/4 pounds ground turkey	2 tablespoons grated Parmesan cheese
Salt to taste	
1 teaspoon crumbled dried basil	

Unroll and separate rolls. Arrange together in lightly greased 11-inch pizza pan to form crust; pinch seams together well. Brush with 1 1/2 teaspoons of the oil. Bake on lowest rack of hot oven at 425 degrees for 8 to 10 minutes or until edges brown lightly.

Meanwhile, heat remaining tablespoon oil in skillet. Add turkey and brown lightly, stirring to break up into chunks. Season with salt and basil. When crust is about half baked, remove from oven and spread with 2 tablespoons pizza sauce. Top with turkey and spoon on remaining sauce. Cover with sliced cheese and sprinkle with grated Parmesan. Return to oven and bake for about 20 minutes longer or until cheese is melted and edges are well browned. Let stand for 3 to 4 minutes, then cut into wedges to serve.   Makes 4 to 6 servings.

Per Serving (approx):
Calories 497   *Protein 33 gm*   *Fat 24 gm*
Carbohydrate 38 gm   *Sodium 1060 mg*   *Cholesterol 109 mg*

Breakfast Pizza

This is a great crowd pleaser, particularly with the younger set.

1 pound turkey breakfast sausage
1 package (8 ounces)
   refrigerated crescent rolls
1 cup frozen hash brown
   potatoes, thawed
1 cup reduced-fat Cheddar
   cheese, shredded

5 medium eggs, beaten
1/4 cup milk
1/2 teaspoon salt
1/4 teaspoon black pepper
2 tablespoons grated Parmesan
   cheese

In medium skillet over medium heat, sauté sausage for 6 to 10 minutes or until no longer pink.

Unroll crescent rolls and separate dough. In 12-inch round pizza pan, arrange crescent rolls with points toward center. Press rolls over bottom and up sides of pan to form pizza crust, sealing perforations. Top crust with sausage, potatoes and Cheddar cheese.

In small bowl combine eggs, milk, salt and pepper. Pour egg mixture very slowly over sausage and potato mixture. Top with Parmesan cheese. Bake for 25 minutes in preheated 375 degree oven.

To serve, slice pizza into 8 wedges.   Makes 8 servings.

Per Serving (approx):
Calories 328
Carbohydrate 18 gm

Protein 20 gm
Sodium 704 mg

Fat 18 gm
Cholesterol 205 mg

Greek Pizza

1 package (10 ounces) refrigerated
   pizza dough
2 tablespoons olive oil
2 teaspoons garlic powder
1 teaspoon dried tarragon
1 teaspoon crushed dried rosemary
1 pound ground turkey
1/2 cup chopped onion

2 ounces feta cheese, crumbled
1 1/4 cups grated Monterey
   jack cheese with jalapeño
   peppers
1/2 cup sliced black olives
2 tablespoons chopped fresh
   chives

In 12-inch pizza pan, press dough to fit. Brush dough with oil and sprinkle with garlic powder, tarragon and rosemary. Bake dough at 400 degrees for 8 to 10 minutes or until lightly browned. Remove pizza crust from oven.

In large nonstick skillet over medium heat, sauté turkey and onion for 5 to 6 minutes or until turkey is no longer pink.

Evenly spread turkey mixture over pizza crust. Sprinkle feta and Monterey jack cheeses, olives and chives over turkey. Bake at 400 degrees for 10 to 15 minutes or until cheese is melted.

To serve, cut pizza into 8 slices. Makes 8 servings.

Per Serving (approx):
Calories 300
Carbohydrate 23 gm

Protein 15 gm
Sodium 478 mg

Fat 16 gm
Cholesterol 63 mg

MORE STUFFINGS
& SAUCES

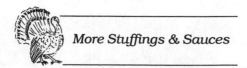

California-Style Stuffing I

1 cup chopped onion
1 cup chopped celery
1 cup chopped peeled
  tart apple
3/4 cup butter or margarine
1 1/2 cups broth or water

2 packages (6 ounces each)
  regular seasoned stuffing
  mix or seasoned
  corn bread stuffing mix
1/4 cup finely chopped
  parsley

Sauté onion, celery and apple in butter for about 10 minutes. Combine with broth. Add stuffing mix and parsley and mix well. Turn into buttered 2-quart casserole. Cover and place in 325 degree oven.

Bake for 45 minutes, removing cover during last 10 minutes of baking to crisp top. **Makes 10 servings.**

Per Serving (approx):
Calories 237
Carbohydrate 24 gm

Protein 4 gm
Sodium 730 mg

Fat 14 gm
Cholesterol 35 mg

California-Style Stuffing II

1 pound turkey sausage
1/4 cup chopped onion
1 can (8 ounces) mushroom
  stems and pieces, drained
2 1/2 cups French bread cut
  in 1/2-inch cubes

1/4 cup pine nuts, toasted
1 egg
1/8 teaspoon cayenne pepper
2 tablespoons Pesto Sauce
  (see page 264)

In large skillet over medium-high heat, sauté sausage and onion, stirring to break up meat, until meat is no longer pink and onion is translucent. Drain and set aside. In large bowl combine sausage mixture, mushrooms, bread, nuts, egg, cayenne pepper and Pesto Sauce.

Makes 6 to 8 servings.

Per Serving (approx):
Calories 215
Carbohydrate 20 gm

Protein 13 gm
Sodium 458 mg

Fat 9 gm
Cholesterol 58 mg

Green Onion and Corn Bread Stuffing

1 can (10 1/2 ounces) condensed
  French onion soup
1 soup can of water
1/4 cup margarine
1 cup celery cut into 1/4-inch
  cubes

1 cup thinly sliced green onion
1 to 1/2 teaspoons dried
  poultry seasoning
2 packages (8 ounces each)
  corn bread stuffing mix

In 5-quart saucepan combine soup, water, margarine, celery, onion and poultry seasoning. Bring to a boil and remove from heat.

Stir in corn bread stuffing mix. Bake mixture in 1 1/2-quart casserole coated with nonstick vegetable cooking spray. Bake, covered, at 350 degrees for 45 minutes or until set.   Makes 12 servings.

Per Serving (approx):
Calories 200   *Protein 5 gm*   *Fat 6 gm*
Carbohydrate 32 gm   *Sodium 683 mg*   *Cholesterol 0 mg*

We find in the Tamil language of India, a word "toka"–peacock, the primitive meaning of which refers to a train or trailing skirt. This word adopted into the Hebrew language becomes "tukki" and by a slight change of the genius of the English language becomes what we are looking for, "turkey."

Other sources say that the American Indian name for the bird was "firkee" and still others think the present name "turkey" came from the alarm call of the bird, "turc, turc, turc."

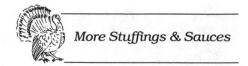

Cranberry Fruit Stuffing

3 cups herb-seasoned stuffing
  mix
2 cups chopped mixed dried fruit
1 cup chopped celery
2/3 cup chopped onion
1 cup whole cranberry sauce

1/2 teaspoon dried sage
1/2 teaspoon dried thyme
1 1/2 cups turkey broth or
  reduced-sodium chicken
  bouillon

In medium bowl combine stuffing mix, dried fruit, celery, onion, cranberry sauce, sage, thyme and turkey broth. Coat 2-quart ovenproof dish with nonstick vegetable cooking spray. Spoon dressing into dish and bake, uncovered, for 40 to 45 minutes in preheated 325 degree oven.

Makes 8 servings.

Per Serving (approx):
Calories 260
Carbohydrate 60 gm

Protein 4 gm
Sodium 420 mg

Fat 2 gm
Cholesterol 0 mg

Rye-Apple Stuffing

1 green apple, chopped
1 onion, chopped
1 celery stalk, chopped
6 tablespoons butter
5 slices dark rye bread, torn
  into small pieces

1 cup turkey or chicken broth
1 cup chopped cranberries
1 egg, lightly beaten
Salt and pepper to taste
1/4 cup apple brandy

In medium skillet sauté apple, onion and celery in 4 tablespoons of the butter for 3 minutes. Mix with bread crumbs. Add broth, cranberries, egg, salt and pepper. Mound in greased casserole.

Baste with remaining butter and apple brandy and bake at 350 degrees for 50 minutes.

Makes 6 servings.

Per Serving (approx):
Calories 285
Carbohydrate 30 gm

Protein 5 gm
Sodium 717 mg

Fat 13 gm
Cholesterol 67 mg

Mediterranean Medley

3 tablespoons olive oil
1/2 cup finely chopped onion
3 cloves garlic, minced
2 green onions, thinly sliced
   (white part plus 2 inches of
   green)
2 medium carrots,
   very finely chopped

2 medium zucchini,
   unpeeled very finely chopped
1 1/2 teaspoons lemon juice
1/2 teaspoon grated lemon zest
3 sun-dried tomatoes (oil
   packed), very finely chopped
2 tablespoons chopped fresh
   basil or 1 teaspoon dried
Salt to taste

In olive oil sauté onion and garlic over low heat until they begin to soften. Add green onions, carrots and zucchini. Cook slowly until tender. Stir in lemon juice, lemon zest and sun-dried tomatoes. Cook briefly, stirring to blend flavors. Add basil at last minute. Add salt if necessary.

                      Makes 2 cups, 8 servings.

Turkeys in their wild state generally mated in pairs and during the breeding season it was a case of the "survival of the fittest." The survivor had his choice of the flock and proudly walked away with his mate. Cases have been recorded where a large, wild tom would fight and kill another tom and take unto him the new mate, while his first mate was sitting. It is owing to this rule that we have such a fine bird today. When man tries to confine and in-breed this great bird of the forest, nature steps in and says, "no."

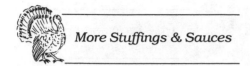

Mushroom Cream Sauce with Tarragon

From our friends at the Kendall-Jackson Winery, here is a wonderful sauce to accompany your favorite turkey dish.

1 pound button mushrooms, thinly sliced

1 stick plus 1 tablespoon unsalted butter

1 cup homemade chicken stock (unsalted or reduced-sodium)

2/3 cup whipping cream

2 tablespoons finely chopped parsley

2 tablespoons finely chopped fresh tarragon or 1 teaspoon dried

1/3 cup pine nuts

Sauté mushrooms in 1 stick butter over medium heat, stirring frequently, until tender. Add chicken stock and continue cooking, stirring occasionally, until liquid is reduced by half. Add cream and continue cooking and stirring until liquid is again reduced by half. Add parsley and tarragon and cook briefly, stirring to blend flavors. Sauté pine nuts in remaining 1 tablespoon butter over medium heat until golden brown on both sides. Sprinkle over sauce.   Makes 2 cups, 8 servings.

Curried Pineapple Glaze

Just enough curry powder is used in this glaze to give it an elusive flavor and fragrance.

2 teaspoons cornstarch
1 teaspoon curry powder
1/4 teaspoon minced instant onion
1/8 teaspoon garlic salt
2 tablespoons cold water

2 tablespoons brown sugar
1 can (8 1/4 ounces) crushed
  pineapple
1 tablespoon butter or margarine
Salt and pepper to taste

Mix cornstarch, curry powder, onion and garlic salt; stir in cold water. Heat pineapple with brown sugar. Add cornstarch mixture and stir over low heat until smooth and clear. Stir in butter, salt and pepper.

Makes about 1 cup, enough to glaze a medium turkey breast or half breast.

Sherried Cranberry Glaze

1 can (8 ounces) jellied
  cranberry sauce

1/3 cup sherry

In small saucepan combine cranberry sauce and sherry. Cook slowly, stirring, until mixture is only slighly runny.

Makes about 1 cup, enough to glaze a medium turkey breast or half breast.

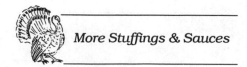

Caribbean Salsa

An interesting, spicy salsa that is good with hot or cold turkey.

2 cups mango peeled and cut
    into 1/4-inch cubes
1/2 cup cucumber peeled,
    seeded and cut into
    1/4-inch cubes
1/4 cup chopped cilantro
2 tablespoons finely chopped
    green onion

1/2 jalapeño pepper, seeded
    and finely chopped
3 tablespoons fresh lime juice
1 1/2 teaspoons brown sugar
1 teaspoon minced fresh ginger
Dash of black pepper

In medium bowl combine mango, cucumber, cilantro, green onion, jalapeño, lime juice, brown sugar, ginger and black pepper. Cover and refrigerate at least 1 hour to allow flavors to blend.

Makes 8 servings.

Today's market turkey is a "mammoth" bird, weighing about three and one-half times as much as the wild turkeys the Pilgrims ate. Moreover, the "new" turkey consumes 30 percent less feed and requires more than one month less growing time to reach market age than turkeys of 20 years ago. As an added plus, today's turkeys have about 25 percent more meat than turkeys of the 1950s.

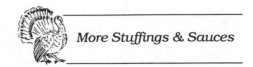

Wine and Garlic Marinade

2 cups dry white wine
1/2 cup olive oil
10 to 12 cloves garlic, crushed
6 slices lemon
2 teaspoons dried thyme
  (optional)

2 teaspoons dried basil
  (optional)
2 teaspoons salt
2 bay leaves (optional)
1 teaspoon black pepper

In wide, shallow bowl, combine all ingredients; reserve half. Add 3 to 4 pounds turkey to remaining marinade; cover and refrigerate for 1 hour or longer, turning occasionally.

To grill, drain turkey and discard used marinade. Grill turkey until cooked through, basting with reserved marinade.

Makes about 2 1/2 cups marinade.

Beer Marinade

3 tablespoons spicy brown
  mustard
3 tablespoons brown sugar
3 tablespoons oil
1 tablespoon Worcestershire
  sauce

1 teaspoon hot pepper sauce
1 teaspoon salt
1/2 teaspoon black pepper
1 can (12 ounces) beer
1 extralarge onion, sliced
  into rings

In medium bowl combine first mustard, brown sugar, oil, Worcestershire sauce, hot pepper sauce, salt and pepper. Stir in beer and onion. Use as marinade for 4 to 6 pounds turkey. Cover and refrigerate for 1 hour or longer, turning occasionally.

Onion rings may be grilled for 2 to 3 minutes on each side and served with turkey.   Makes about 2 cups marinade.

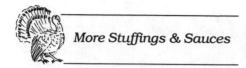

Traditional Barbecue Sauce

1 cup chili sauce
1/2 cup firmly packed
  brown sugar
1/4 cup oil
2 tablespoons cider vinegar
2 tablespoons soy sauce

1 tablespoon spicy brown
  mustard
1 1/2 teaspoons chopped fresh
  oregano (optional)
1 to 1 1/2 teaspoons liquid
  smoke (optional)

In small bowl combine all ingredients. Use as basting sauce for grilling 4 to 5 pounds turkey during last 10 to 15 minutes of cooking. Turn turkey often to avoid scorching.   Makes 1 1/2 cups barbecue sauce.

Chutney Barbecue Sauce

Prepared chutney is a shortcut to creating a delicious basting sauce. It results in deeply browned turkey.

1 jar (8 1/2 ounces) mango
  chutney
1/3 cup wine vinegar

1 tablespoon spicy brown
  mustard
1 tablespoon brown sugar
1/4 teaspoon cayenne pepper

In small bowl combine all ingredients. Use as basting sauce for grilling 4 to 5 pounds turkey during last 10 to 15 minutes of cooking. Lightly oil turkey before cooking, and turn often to avoid burning.

      Makes about 1 1/2 cups basting sauce.

Index

Additional copies of this book *The Great Turkey Cookbook: 385 Turkey Recipes for Every Day and Holidays,* are available at book, gift and gourmet food stores.

Or, you may order directly from the publisher by phone, fax or mail.

Each copy is $19.95, which includes shipping and handling.

By phone, call (800) 777-1048 with your Visa or Mastercard.

By fax, call 408-722-2749 with your Visa or Mastercard.

By mail, send your personal check, money order, or credit card information to: The Crossing Press, P.O. Box 1048, Freedom, CA 95019.

If you would like to receive our cookbook catalog, call toll-free (800) 777-1048, or write to us at the address above.